W9-AQY-686

Functional Approaches to Writing
Research Perspectives

Writing Research

Multidisciplinary Inquiries into the Nature of Writing

edited by Marcia Farr, University of Illinois at Chicago

Arthur Applebee, CONTEXTS FOR LEARNING TO WRITE: STUDIES OF SECONDARY SCHOOL INSTRUCTION

Marcia Farr (ed.), ADVANCES IN WRITING RESEARCH VOLUME ONE: CHILDREN'S EARLY WRITING AND DEVELOPMENT

Lester Faigley, Roger Cherry, David Joliffe, and Anna Skinner, ASSESSING WRITER'S KNOWLEDGE AND PROCESSES OF COMPOSING

Sarah W. Freedman (ed.), THE ACQUISITION OF WRITTEN LANGUAGE: REVISION AND RESPONSE

In preparation

Carole Edelsky, WRITING IN A BILINGUAL PROGRAM: HABIA UNA VEZ

Judith Langer, CHILDREN READING AND WRITING: STRUCTURES AND STRATEGIES

Ann Matsuhashi (ed.), WRITING IN REAL TIME: MODELLING PRODUCTION PROCESSES

Leo Ruth and Sandra Murphy, DESIGNING WRITING TASKS FOR THE ASSESSMENT OF WRITING

Jana Staton, Roger Shuy, Joy Kreeft, and Leslie Reed, INTERACTIVE WRITING IN DIALOGUE JOURNALS

Elizabeth Sulzby, EMERGENT READING AND WRITING IN 5–6 YEAR OLDS: A LONGITUDINAL STUDY

William H. Teale and Elizabeth Sulzby (eds), EMERGENT LITERACY: READING AND WRITING

Functional Approaches to Writing Research Perspectives

Barbara Couture
Wayne State University

Ablex Publishing Corporation
Norwood, New Jersey 07648

Printed in Great Britain

Library of Congress Cataloging in Publication Data

Couture, Barbara.
Functional Approaches To Writing.
(Writing Research)
Bibliography: p.
Includes index.
1. Written communication. I. Title. II. Series:
Writing Research (Norwood, N.J.)
P211.C68 1986 001.54′3 86-7865
ISBN 0-89391-375-8

Ablex Publishing Corporation
355 Chestnut Street
Norwood, New Jersey 07648

Contents

Preface

'The value of a theory,' writes M. A. K. Halliday, 'lies in the use that can be made of it, and I have always considered a theory of language to be essentially consumer-oriented' (1985: 7). This consumer-orientation is particularly apparent in *Functional Approaches to Writing: Research Perspectives*. All of the authors who have contributed to it share Halliday's assumption about the attributes that give value to a linguistic theory, and most of them interpret and elaborate hypotheses he and his co-workers have developed against the behavior of writers and readers in real-world settings. But the chapters collected here are by no means restricted to mere studies in applied linguistics (valuable as such studies often are), for the interchange is everywhere in evidence between the theory and the data the theory is designed to explain. Thus this volume will appeal to two groups who have not always seen the similarities in their interests: theoreticians concerned with the development of descriptive tools and the refinement of analytical statements, and practitioners interested in gaining deeper insights into the functions of language in the circumstances where texts are produced and consumed.

One of the distinctive traits of the Firth–Halliday tradition, now generally known as SYSTEMIC LINGUISTICS, is attention to the CONTEXT OF SITUATION, a concept that the coiner of that term said 'must burst the bonds of mere linguistics and be carried over into the analysis of the general conditions under which a language is spoken' (Malinowski [1923] 1949: 306). These contexts may be text internal (as illustrated by studies of cohesion and elaboration in writing). They may be text external (as in inquiries into the behavior of hearers and readers responding to texts). Or they may be directed to the dialectic between internal and external contexts that shows how language users process texts (as in investigations of relations between text and ethos). What is significant in this array of perspectives is that the authors do not regard themselves as belonging to distinct and separate traditions of inquiry (e.g. linguistics, sociology, psychology, or pedagogy). Instead they see themselves as working on a common problem, that posed by writers and speakers mediating meaning with readers and listeners in particular situations. This compatability is a consequence of another characteristic of the Firth–Halliday tradition, the notion that language behavior is 'poly-systemic,' that is, shaped by a set of distinct but interconnected patterns of choice. Hence, scholars working on quite different aspects of language behavior are presumed to be working on the same task; their allegiance is to the clarification of the mystery of how meaning potential acquires form, expression, and value rather than to the canons of their sectarian fields.

Such an approach to linguistic structure and to the transfer of meaning naturally invites speculations about the ideology of language use and about the differing values the community places on acts of speaking and writing (an idea particularly investigated by Barbara Couture in this volume). The connection between text and evaluation invites a series of questions of great practical interest: why are some student essays particularly admired (or the reverse)? why are some children praised for their narratives (and others merely acknowledged)? why are some business or professional communications significantly rewarded (and some barely tolerated)? what makes the difference between texts admired for their transparency and texts shunned (or perhaps revered) for their opacity? The answers to these questions do not lie exclusively in the texts themselves (and thus cannot be measured solely against linguistic standards of unity, coherence, emphasis, and grace). The answers are to be found in the interplay of language and context, the proprieties of articulation and admiration, and the opportunities a culture offers for the expression of meaning potential.

A preface is not the place to expatiate upon the special virtues of each chapter; that task is executed in the editor's introduction that follows. But it is possible in this brief space to suggest the position of *Functional Approaches to Writing: Research Perspectives* in its own context. This book brings together the findings of scholars working in four geographically distant nations: Britain, Canada, the United States, and Australia. They have never conferred as a group, but they have in common an overlapping set of values, similar perspectives on the role of their research in influencing people who write in social contexts (and the people who teach them), and close attention bestowed by an unusually meticulous editor who has worked with each author to ensure the highest standards of accuracy and clarity. Thus these scholars are united by their prior reading and writing and by this present volume into a 'society of explorers,' a group dedicated to the notion that 'discoveries are made by pursuing possibilities suggested by existing knowledge' and by a conviction that 'the surmises of a working scientist are BORN OF THE IMAGINATION SEEKING DISCOVERY' (Polanyi 1966 [1967]: 67, 79). Those who read this book will become members of that same society and will, I hope, be influenced in their own reflections and practice as members of our linguistic community.

Richard W. Bailey
The University of Michigan

BIBLIOGRAPHY

Halliday, M. A. K., 'Systemic Background,' in Benson, J. D. and Greaves, W. S. (eds) (1985: 1–15), *Systemic Perspectives on Discourse: Selected Theoretical Papers from the 9th International Systemic Workshop*, Advances in Discourse Processes 15, Norwood, N.J., Ablex.

Malinowski, B., 'The Problem of Meaning in Primitive Languages,' supplement to Ogden, C. K. and Richards, I. A. ([1923] 1949, 10th edn: 296–336), *The Meaning of Meaning: A Study of the Influence of Language upon Thought and of the Science of Symbolism*, New York, Harcourt Brace: London, Routledge and Kegan Paul.
Polanyi, M. (1966 [1967]), *The Tacit Dimension*, Garden City, N.Y., Anchor Books.

Introduction

1 Bridging epistemologies and methodologies: research in written language function

Barbara Couture
Wayne State University

This book is about written language functions and about written language research. The essays here are united in their investigation of language as social action—an approach to textual study that crosses traditional boundaries of discipline and method to uncover what written language is, how it works, how it affects readers, and what it demands of authors.

The functional approaches to written text presented here are most closely related to the work of scholars from the so-called London School of Linguistics as reinterpreted in the systemic linguistics of Michael Halliday and his followers. The London School challenged investigations of language in isolation, claiming that our understanding of meaning in text is dependent on the 'context of situation,' a concept promulgated by Malinowski ([1923] 1949) and meaning the immediate textual and extra-textual context in which an utterance is performed. This concept was later expanded by both Malinowski (1935) and Firth ([1935] 1957) to refer to the entire cultural environment encompassing a communication event.

Both Firth and Malinowski believed that meaning in language arises primarily out of speakers' and listeners' recognition of conventional social situations which are associated with linguistic choice. Halliday agrees with this central premise but also asserts that language itself is as central to meaning as the social activity it reflects. It allows us to achieve a wide variety of meaning potential within a given context: 'Language not only serves to facilitate and support other modes of social action that constitute its environment, but also actively creates an environment of its own, so making possible all the imaginative modes of meaning, from backyard gossip to narrative fiction and epic poetry.' In short, while language is configured in part by the social action it supports, it can also create a social context within which it means: 'As we learn how to mean, we learn to predict each [language and context] from the other' (Halliday 1978: 3). Halliday conflates textual and contextual meaning, defining language as SOCIAL SEMIOTIC.

This view of language as social semiotic has dramatic consequences for scholarly investigation of written discourse. If we accept it, then we must break down barriers within traditional investigatory fields that limit our examination of language.

First, we must reconsider what territory should be covered in an adequate language theory; a scholar who explains language as lexical and syntactic components reduced to a formal linguistic system, yet ignores SEMIOTIC systems of meaning that exist outside the text, has presented a deficient perspective; the fact that the nature of contextual meaning has been the purview of psychologists, sociologists, anthropologists, and literary aestheticians (who have adopted perspectives from the social sciences) does not justify a narrow view. An explanation of textual function must account for the semiotic systems that language creates and the extratextual meanings referenced by language.

Second, we must insist upon PRAGMATIC evidence for theoretical claims about language, that is, upon text at work in actual communication situations rather than text composed specifically to illustrate a theoretical point. A theory that explains texts produced in isolation, but does not account for texts produced in real-world contexts, denies that language and context together contribute to meaning potential (see Jordan in this volume).

Finally, we must seek HEURISTIC universals in explaining textual function (see Couture, Chapter 4 in this volume). If language is social semiotic, then interpersonal activity is the enabling force empowering the interface between language and context. Structural descriptions that describe textual function, but have no heuristic value—that is, no potential to show how language users generate and interpret texts in varying social situations—repudiate that interface. An adequate functional theory of language must unite speakers, listeners, and situations, and seek the sources of sociosemantic congruence.

Given the methodological imperatives suggested by an exploration of language as social action, it is not surprising that scholarship in the functions of written language has traversed what heretofore have been separate domains in the study of language: the fields of literature, linguistics, and composition.[1] The epistemological and methodological boundaries often assumed for each field, schematically represented in Table A, have not provided sufficient

Table A Epistemological and methodological aims of studies in literature, linguistics, and composition

Disciplinary area	Investigative thrust	Method	Epistemological domain	Questions to be answered
Literature	Theory	Explanation	Semiotics	What is this phenomenon? How does it work?
Linguistics	Research	Proof	Pragmatics	What does it do?
Composition	Pedagogy	Application	Heuristics	What does it require?

explanation in investigations of written language function. I say 'often assumed' because publishers and academic departments continue to categorize textual studies as representing one or another of these fields; unfortunately, such pigeon-holing disguises the multifunctional aims of this research to unite semiotic, pragmatic, and heuristic approaches to textual analysis.

The 'hybrid' scholarship in written language function, of course, does not as a body reflect only the work of Halliday. Nor does it necessarily make overt reference to language as social semiotic or reflect entirely a shift in the bases of knowledge regarded as central to each field of language study.

The aims of literary study have shifted from an elitist interest in aesthetic appreciation of poetic text to an egalitarian emphasis on the importance of reading communities to the assessment of textual value in both literary and ordinary language (see Miller 1979). But, interestingly, this scholarly shift parallels a similar change in the educational interests of college and university students: more and more students are coming to post-secondary education eager to learn 'practical' skills that they can apply immediately in the workplace. Reader-response approaches to textual analysis have practical value in higher education. A literary theory that is also a discourse theory, validated in the interpretation of actual texts in a variety of contexts, has heuristic potential for the production and interpretation of future texts: it becomes a tool with real-world application.

The criticism of Michel Foucault fits this new paradigm. Consider, for example, his exploration of authorship that explains the significance of authorial presence for textual interpretation. Foucault claims that a text's author-function can 'reveal the manner in which discourse is articulated on the bases of social relationships' (1977: 137). Authorship, in effect, is what distinguishes a text's influence upon the knowledge base of a field: 'A study of Galileo's works could alter our knowledge of the history, but not the science, of mechanics; whereas, a reexamination of the books of Freud or Marx can transform our understanding of psychoanalysis or Marxism' (1977: 135–6). Not only does Foucault assert the contextual contribution of authorship to textual meaning; he also asserts the need for this theory to be tested in texts and contexts other than those he cites:

> Unfortunately, there is a decided absence of positive propositions in this essay, as it applies to analytic procedures or directions for future research, but I ought at least to give the reasons why I attach such importance to a continuation of this work. Developing a similar analysis could provide the bases for a typology of discourse. . . . [1977: 136–7]

He further predicts his theory's heuristic potential to explain textual function and defines new criteria for critical theory, criteria which demand that theory both explain what text expresses and account for how it is produced, valued, and transmitted:

> This form of investigation might also permit the introduction of an historical analysis of discourse. Perhaps the time has come to study not only the expressive value and formal transformations of discourse, but its mode of existence: the modifications and variations, within any culture of modes of circulation, valorization, attribution, and appropriation. [1977: 137]

His own attempt to explain the author-function is as expansive as the above criteria suggest: Foucault moves from a consideration of authorial presence in literary language, to the interpretive language of psychoanalysis, to the referential language of science, to the appropriated language of business—clearly, the critical domain is no longer solely language as art.

In linguistics, scholars' renewed efforts to describe the functions of actual language have been promoted by economic benefit as well as academic interest. To be sure, a sincere attempt to recover from the narrow emphases on formal structure reflected in Chomsky's transformational grammar governs systemic linguists' exploration of actual language use (see Jordan in this volume). But funding lies in another direction now as well. Teaching English as a Second Language (TESL) has become big business, a practical problem with considerable economic consequences. The focus of TESL instruction must be upon the functions of language within a context rather than upon a study of language structure in isolation. TESL scholarship has led both to development of sociosemantic theories of language function and to tests of that theory as it explains differences in textual meaning potential and heuristic utility for language teaching (see, for example, the research reported in Selinker *et al*. 1981).

A focus on semiotic theory, pragmatic research, and heuristics for language teaching is evident in the work of several linguists. For example, Fawcett (1980) has developed a complex theory of language as it reflects both the social and psychological semiotic; Jakobson (1960) has shown the potential of a functional analysis of language to reveal the pragmatic differences between poetic and ordinary language; and Pike (1964) has shown the heuristic value of tagmemic theory to help students generate effective expository composition. But the merger of these three approaches to analysis of text function is most fully met in the work of Michael Halliday.

Halliday's proposed grammar of English satisfies his own stringent requirement for representing meaning potential both within language and outside the text. The roots of his functional grammar are not in the formal components of lexis and syntax but rather in semantics. Halliday identifies three kinds of meaning generated in any language event: ideational meaning that reflects reportorial logic and representation of experience; interpersonal meaning that reflects social relationships between discourse participants; and textual meaning that allows discourse participants to recognize a stretch of language as meaningful text (see Bernhardt and Brandt in this volume). Halliday systematically relates his semantic scheme to meaning systems within language and to the larger social context. His functional grammar explains how multifunctional meanings are generated in a communication event; it shows how those meanings are realized in the formal syntactic and lexical components of language's grammatical system; and it explains how linguistic features reflect choices from a 'higher-level semiotic,' systems of meaning above language, such as those designating textual genre (1977: 193). Naturally, his grammar is complex (see Halliday 1985), as it must be to explain the complexity of actual communication, but it also stands up to empirical test.

Halliday has applied his theory of language function to the analysis of literary style, illustrating, for instance, how an analytic review of clausal structure in terms of 'its process, participants, and circumstances' can reveal systematic features that correlate with our interpretation of how a literary passage represents real-world experience. Certain features in a literary work are 'brought into relief' through 'the whole of the writer's creative use of "meaning potential"; . . . the nature of language is such that [authors] can convey, in a line of print, a complex of simultaneous themes, reflecting the variety of functions that language is required to serve' (1971: 352, 360).[2] In short, he has identified the sources of textual ambiguity and explained them as purposeful and systematic.

Halliday has also extended his work in the functions of language to the practical problems of language teaching. While convinced of the virtues of studying language for its own sake, he has 'no objection' to the view that 'an academic subject should be judged by its results.' The relationship between theory and application is complementary, each having the potential to advance the other: 'Application . . . contributes to theory; but if the range of application is not to remain static the "pure" research must go on' (Halliday *et al*. 1964: 7). Beyond citing the creative interplay of linguistic theory and application, Halliday sees the application of theory as a responsible outcome of the language scholar's interest in educational processes:

> My interest in linguistic questions is ultimately an 'applied' one, a concern with language in relation to the process and experience of education. . . . The sociolinguistic patterns of the community, the language of family, neighbourhood and school, and the personal experience of language from earliest infancy are among the most fundamental elements in a child's environment for learning. [1978: 5]

Throughout his work in theory, research, and teaching, Halliday has responded to the full semiotic complexity of textual communication, meeting the challenge of explaining actual language and asserting the contribution of linguistic theory to everyday social concourse.

Finally, researchers in English composition, with their practical focus upon improving writing instruction, have made new discoveries about the nature of the composing process that delineate the relationships between the contexts for writing and the effectiveness of texts. Research here has paralleled literary critics' interest in interpretive communities as well as systemic linguists' interests in the functions of textual features. Recently, fruitful research in the contexts for writing has been conducted in the workplace, a response to societal demand for skilled writers who can produce documents that will function in organizational contexts (see, for instance, Couture and Goldstein 1985; and Brown and Herndl in this volume).

The effort to move compositional studies from narrow work in the teaching of expository writing to expansive research in written language and discourse theory received its greatest impetus in 1977 with the publication of Mina Shaughnessy's *Errors and Expectations*. In this exceptional book, Shaughnessy validates the classroom as a place for serious research into the functions of written language. Through the meticulous study of error in student writing, she derived a systematic method for teaching that addresses dysfunction in expository composition and explains the linguistic causes of that dysfunction. Shaughnessy reveals how problematic linguistic choice is influenced by contexts for writing, that is, by the experience of the student writer in educational settings. At the same time, she proposes systematic solutions for problems in student writing. For example, she describes the problems student writers have with syntax as symptomatic both of their inexperience with the written mode and of their rational, though inept, response to conflicting demands: in writing, they are expected to express thought with fluency, as in speech, and also to consolidate ideas with the formal markers of hierarchical relations anticipated by readers. It is not surprising, given these opposite constraints, that student writing often becomes 'derailed,' as Shaughnessy puts it; that is, it takes off in an unexpected direction as the writer attacks simultaneously the task of pushing prose forward and relating its parts. Writing instructors who must address this problem will be more successful, Shaughnessy asserts, if they help students 'develop the verbal responsiveness to [their] own thoughts and to the demands of [their readers] that produces genuinely mature syntax' (1977: 89). Shaughnessy, like Halliday, viewed the study of language behavior as a social and personal responsibility—her humane concern is reflected in the conclusions she derived from her own work: Basic Writing 'students write the way they do, not because they are slow or non-verbal, indifferent to or incapable of academic excellence, but because they are beginners and must, like all beginners, learn by making mistakes' (1977: 5). We can hope to solve writing problems in school, in business, and in government through the studied observation of communication in actual contexts if we design research with the aim of resolving the communication dilemmas of those whom language serves.

Shaughnessy's work has inspired an attitude toward composition that is reflected in the best composition research today: writing research should view the communication problems of writers as research questions whose answers lie in the processes and products of writing and hold promise of explaining the varied ways we can mean in written discourse. This legacy of research and theory emerging from practice has continued in studies of writing and writers throughout the English-speaking world, not only in academic contexts but in business, industry, and government settings as well. Research like Odell, Goswami, and Herrington's investigations of context and style in business documents (see, for example, 1983), Faigley and Witte's studies of revision and textual cohesion (see, for example, Faigley and Witte 1981; and Witte and Faigley 1981) and Christie's and Martin and Rothery's patient analyses of the functions of children's writing (see, for example, Christie *et al*. 1984; and Christie and Martin and Rothery in this volume) emerges from the pressing need to solve the problems of communicating in today's world. It is rooted in a theory of language as it has meaning in context and is validated in the description of actual language use.

The trend toward merging the disciplinary foci of literature, linguistics, and composition will encourage a more comprehensive and powerful approach to textual analyses—one that explains language and how it works, shows evidence of what it does, and applies to the compositional and interpretive tasks that it requires of writers and readers.

The essays in this book represent this forward direction in written language investigation. They are loosely arranged as they address each of the formal questions that have characterized the studies in linguistic semiotics, pragmatics, and heuristics displayed in Table A. As readers will see, each essay is actually multifunctional in its approach, treating simultaneously issues of theory, research, and practice.

The essays in Part I offer functional descriptions of specific linguistic features in different varieties of written text. Each also proposes a method of textual analysis that may lead to a more comprehensive theory of written language function. In an ethnographic study of the composing behavior of writers in corporate settings, Robert L. Brown, Jr. and Carl G. Herndl attempt to explain two 'puzzling' linguistic features in business communications: writers' persistent use of 'superfluous nominalizations' and of 'narrative structure,' despite their supervisors' advice to do otherwise. Their research not only reveals the source of these linguistic anomalies, but also asserts the importance of a phenomenological approach to the study of linguistic behavior in corporate and classroom settings. In a meticulous investigation of the use of the phrase *do so* in written and spoken language, Michael P. Jordan tests a theoretical claim (about environments in which *do so* is used) against a large corpus of examples from written and spoken texts. He also explains criteria for comprehensive investigations of language use, discussing the relevance of such study to the development of functional language theory. Part I closes with Mary Ann Eiler's careful analysis of thematic structure as it reveals written text genre. Evaluating the work on thematic structure by Halliday and several other linguists, Eiler assimilates this scholarship in an analysis of a scientific text, demonstrating how thematic structure is a heuristic feature enabling genre identification.

The essays in Part II explore how language systems function in text to convey meaning. Each explains how written texts reveal situational conditions leading to their composition and constrain readers' possible interpretations. In my own essay, I propose a systematic analysis of ideation in text that reveals linguistic correlates of ideational value. The proposed model represents both textual and extratextual meaning systems that come into play in the construction and interpretation of written text. Deborah Brandt analyzes the structure of three texts composed by the same student writer, showing how these texts' exophoric references, cohesive devices, and thematic structure reveal the social contexts in which each of them were produced. Edward L.Smith, Jr. compares linguistic choices that develop author–reader relationships in the writing of experienced and inexperienced writers to demonstrate how interpersonal functioning is systematically developed in effective writing. In the final essay here, Michael Hoey and Eugene Winter show how clause relational analysis, an examination of lexical and grammatical features that direct a reader's cognitive process of relating ideas in discourse, explains the underlying interaction between writer's intention and reader's interpretation.

The essays in Part III concentrate in part on the question of how written language works but more directly on the question of what it does to readers. These studies test possible correlations between teacher-ratings of quality in student writing and the presence of linguistic features associated with specific communicative functions. Each essay also provides an explanation of experimental methodology and evaluates results as they suggest future research. Carolyn G. Hartnett extends other scholars' investigations of the relationship between textual cohesion and writing quality; she identifies two global categories of cohesive devices influencing topic maintenance and development and tests whether the presence of one, the other, or both influences readers' perceptions of quality. Christine A. Hult examines how linguistic markers of overall structure or rhetorical frame affect readers' evaluation of communicative effectiveness. Pamela Peters, applying an adaptation of Halliday's semantic system, determines through experiment whether linguistic features that assert a dominant semantic function have an impact on a teacher's grades in academic writing.

Part IV concludes the volume with four essays that directly apply functional language theory to teaching composition. Stephen A. Bernhardt offers an insightful explanation of functional language theory as it is relevant to teaching writing (an essay particularly useful to instructors who are not familiar with systemic theory). Martin Davies explores an often ignored aspect of written text—its reference to intonational meaning—illustrating through a 'reading aloud' experiment how intonational meaning reveals sources of difficulty for readers in written text. The final two essays, Frances Christie's and James R. Martin and Joan Rothery's, examine children's writing as it expresses genre, drawing two different though equally compelling conclusions about the importance of teaching both teachers and students the linguistic components of generic structure in school writing.

All the essays here are bold in their scope, imaginative in their approach, and responsive to a pressing need for teachers, students, readers, and writers to acquire a systematic understanding of the functions of written communication. The task they approach is as difficult and complex as language itself; thus, it is not surprising that the contributors to this volume often challenge the reader with more questions than their scholarship answers. My hope, and I trust the hope of every author here, is that our readers will join with us to meet that very challenge in continuing to examine written language in ways that join the epistemic aims of theory, research, and practice.

In closing, I wish to thank Robin P. Fawcett and Frances Pinter for endorsing this project and Wayne State University for providing me with support for preparing the manuscript. My deepest thanks go to Joyce R. Buchanan, who entered manuscripts and corrections on the wordprocessor, and to Richard W. Bailey who advised me in my selection and review of manuscripts submitted for this collection. Lastly, I thank my husband, Paul, and my parents, Angela and Chester Zawacki, for their loving support.

Barbara Couture
Ann Arbor, Summer 1985

NOTES

1. 'Composition' here includes studies in rhetoric and in the teaching of speech and writing.
2. I must note that this is the very point that Fish fails to understand in his criticism of Halliday's stylistics. He mistakes Halliday's analysis of the transitivity patterns in Golding's *The Inheritors* as a narrow effort to prove a Darwinian interpretation of the novel. It is true that Halliday offers this perspective as a context for interpretation, but his major conclusion from the transitivity analysis is simply to show that Golding's novel presents human experience in a way that differs strikingly from the ordinary ways in which speakers of English relate experience and thus highlights the relation of experience in itself as something the reader should interpret in a special way. Halliday concludes that a 'theme that is strongly foregrounded' by a special use of language 'is especially likely to be interpreted at more than one level' (1971: 360), a point that Fish himself suggests in asserting that Halliday's grammatical analysis in the end suggests 'that the explanation for . . . meaning is not the capacity of a syntax to express it, but the ability of a reader to confer it' (Fish 1973: 129).

BIBLIOGRAPHY

Christie, F. *et al.* (ed.) (1984), *Children Writing: Study Guide*, ECT418 Language Studies, Geelong, Vic., Deakin University Press.

Couture, B. and Goldstein, J. R. (1985), *Cases for Technical and Professional Writing*, Boston, Little, Brown.

Faigley, L. and Witte, S. (1981), 'Analyzing Revision,' *College Composition and Communication*, **32** , 400–22.

Fawcett, R. P. (1980), *Cognitive Linguistics and Social Interaction: Towards an Integrated Model of a Systemic Functional Grammar and the Other Components of a Communicating Mind*, Heidelberg, Julius Groos.

Firth, J. R., 'The Technique of Semantics [1935],' in Firth, J. R. (1957: 7–33), *Papers in Linguistics, 1934–51*, London, Oxford University Press.

Fish, S. E., 'What Is Stylistics and Why Are They Saying Such Terrible Things About It?,' in Chatman, S. (ed.) (1973: 109–52), *Approaches to Poetics: Selected Papers from the English Institute*, New York, Columbia University Press.

Foucault, M., 'What Is an Author?,' in Bouchard, D. F. (ed.) (1977: 113–38), *Language, Counter-Memory, Practice: Selected Essays and Interviews by Michel Foucault*, Bouchard, D. F. and Simon, S. (trans.), Ithaca, N.Y., Cornell University Press.

Halliday, M. A. K., 'Linguistic Function and Literary Style: An Inquiry into the Language of William Golding's *The Inheritors*,' in Chatman, S. (ed.) (1971: 330–65), *Literary Style: A Symposium*, London, Oxford University Press.

Halliday, M. A. K., 'Text as Semantic Choice in Social Contexts,' in van Dijk, T. A. and Petöfi, J. S. (eds) (1977: 176–225), *Grammars and Descriptions: Studies in Text Theory and Text Analysis*, Research in Text Theory 1, Berlin, Walter de Gruyter.

Halliday, M. A. K. (1978), *Language as Social Semiotic: The Social Interpretation of Language and Meaning*, London, Edward Arnold: Baltimore, University Park Press.

Halliday, M. A. K. (1985), *An Introduction to Functional Grammar*, London, Edward Arnold.

Halliday, M. A. K., McIntosh, A., and Strevens, P. (1964), *The Linguistic Sciences and Language Teaching*, London, Longmans.

Jakobson, R., 'Closing Statement: Linguistics and Poetics,' in Sebeok, T. A. (ed.) (1960: 350–77), *Style in Language*, Cambridge, Mass., The MIT Press.

Malinowski, B., 'The Problem of Meaning in Primitive Languages,' supplement to Ogden, C. K. and Richards, I. A. ([1923] 1949, 10th edn: 296–336), *The Meaning of Meaning: A Study of the Influence of Language upon Thought and of the Science of Symbolism*, New York, Harcourt Brace: London, Routledge and Kegan Paul.

Malinowski, B. (1935), *Coral Gardens and Their Magic: A Study of the Methods of Tilling the Soil and of Agricultural Rites in the Trobriand Islands*, 2 vols, New York, American Book Company.

Miller, J. H. (1979), 'The Function of Rhetorical Study at the Present Time,' *ADE* [Association of Departments of English] *Bulletin*, **62**, 10–18.

Odell, L., Goswami, D., and Herrington, A., 'The Discourse-Based Interview: A Procedure for Exploring the Tacit Knowledge of Writers in Nonacademic Settings,' in Mosenthal, P., Tamor, L., and Walmsley, S. A. (eds) (1983: 220–36), *Research on Writing: Principles and Methods*, New York, Longman.

Pike, K. L. (1964), 'A Linguistic Contribution to Composition: A Hypothesis,' *College Composition and Communication*, **15**, 82–8.

Selinker, L., Tarone, E., and Hanzeli, V. (eds) (1981), *English for Academic and Technical Purposes: Studies in Honor of Louis Trimble*, Rowley, Mass., Newbury House.

Shaughnessy, M. P. (1977), *Errors and Expectations: A Guide for the Teacher of Basic Writing*, New York, Oxford University Press.

Witte, S. P. and Faigley, L. (1981), 'Coherence, Cohesion, and Writing Quality,' *College Composition and Communication*, **32**, 189–204.

Part I
Describing the functions of written language

1 An ethnographic study of corporate writing: job status as reflected in written text

Robert L. Brown, Jr. and Carl G. Herndl
University of Minnesota

1.1 TWO PROBLEMS IN BUSINESS WRITING

Scholars and practitioners of business communication are well aware of the varieties of discourse practiced in business settings, ranging from simple memos and letters to complex proposals, procedural manuals, and reports. And, of course, they also know that a number of conventional writing strategies are accepted as more effective than others in most business writing situations, strategies such as organizing information from general to specific and using strong verbs and few nominalizations.

Though many accept conventions for effective on-the-job writing intuitively, researchers of technical communication have begun to confirm these intuitions empirically; these conventions do help readers process written prose (for a summary of recent research that links style with readability, see Selzer 1983). Further, corporate managers, responsible in many ways for the quality of writing in an organization, have responded both to the research and to the advice offered in technical and business writing textbooks in urging their staff to follow the recommended strategies—as our own investigations in fifteen Minnesota corporations confirm.[1]

Given that the effectiveness of certain conventions in technical style seems accepted by both scholars and professionals in the workplace, we present in this chapter what we initially encountered as a puzzle and offer some possible solutions. In our preliminary interviews with training-and-development managers and technical managers in fifteen corporations, we learned that bright, able professionals were often quite resistant to adopt some style conventions believed to characterize effective professional writing. Four corporate training-and-development managers and three technical managers we interviewed cited two common writing behaviors reflecting this resistance:

- After being told that their writing is 'verbose' and 'muddy' and after learning in seminars how to recognize and eliminate SUPERFLUOUS NOMINALIZATIONS in their writing, corporate writers continue to fill their prose with such structures.

- After being told by their supervisors that NARRATIVE STRUCTURES are unacceptable in executive reports, recommendations, and proposals, corporate writers stubbornly continue to narrate the entire project.

Psycholinguistic, text-processing research has concluded that nominalized prose is more difficult for readers to process (see Coleman 1964 and 1965). And common sense (guided by pragmatics) tells us that it is harder to infer a course of action from a long narrative text than from a set of summarizing assertions or recommendations. Our informant-managers emphasized their faith in these assumptions and in their writers' general intelligence and ability. Why, then, did their writers seem to act against their own best interests in refusing to adopt these conventions?

This seemingly irrational behavior intrigued us. Our informants told us of their employees' consistent success with time-management seminars, with oral-presentation courses, and even with aspects of writing and communication other than those we cited as troublesome. To a writing teacher or linguist, it appears quite straightforward to define the inappropriate linguistic structures—excessive nominalizations or narrative structures, say—and then to suggest change. Why did writers resist this change so strongly when they seemed receptive to other instruction?

We guessed that we were missing the center of the issue. Since the *formal* case was so straightforward, we inferred that stylistic and discourse features preferred by these writers must have complex cultural sign FUNCTIONS; the choice to use such features was not simply guided by the wish to achieve clarity or ease of reading. We set out to define what political and psychological forces motivated the language behavior, believing that an ethnographic study of the corporate environment might reveal the information we needed.

An ethnographic study explains a phenomenon in terms of a culture. We assumed that the corporate environment is a culture unto itself, an assumption well-supported by Deal and Kennedy (1982), Bormann (1983), and Hymes (1984). Beyond this basic assumption, we allowed no others to shape our activity. We did NOT, for instance, begin with fixed hypotheses. Rather, following Kantor's construction of ethnographic research as an hypothesis-generating activity, we allowed our interviews and textual analyses to 'shape, alter, and refine' our investigation (Kantor 1984: 74).

To ensure our sensitivity to bias, we began with two warnings to ourselves. First, we considered that the political/psychological function of discourse differs from culture to culture and that our cultural biases blind us to other cultures' constructions of linguistic reality. Because we are members of an ACADEMIC culture, necessarily influenced by our culture's view of things linguistic, we could not assume that corporate writers and technical professionals saw things our way (see Goffman 1971). Second, we considered that our models and metaphors for linguistic description can blind us to the phenomena we study. For instance, our models for linguistic empirical research suggest that we should define a formal structure, isolate it from its cultural context, and then reify its independent existence (see Shuy 1981). Such a study of superfluous nominalizations or inappropriate discourse structures would undoubtedly confirm them to be merely unhappy formal choices from an inventory of forms in free variation.

Our preliminary interviews with the corporate managers suggested the guiding foci we needed. Our informants clearly identified their skilled writers and used their work to illustrate points about writing and communication. Our informants also clearly cited power relations—and the anxiety they produce—as problematic. Hence, we began our work predisposed to examine how language establishes and supports such relations in the corporate culture, reflecting and perhaps determining writers' roles in their workplaces. And we decided to trust our informants' intuitions. When they identified a writer as skilled, we listened. When they showed us what they considered good writing, we accepted their word; they should know, they are responsible for effective communication in their units.

Our preliminary interviews suggested two aspects of the CULTURAL CONTEXT which strongly related to writing behavior:

- the writer's STATUS in the work group as a central peer or admired worker as opposed to just one of the 'other guys' in the shop, and
- the writer's ANXIETY, variously caused and frequently related to job security.

We aimed to investigate how these aspects of the corporate culture might affect writers' use of superfluous nominalization and inappropriate narrative structures. Our emergent conclusion, simply stated, was that these language features had acquired such powerful and favorable significance as signs of group affiliation that writers lost sight of their effects on readability.

What follows is a trace of our investigation—our theoretical speculation, our interviewing, our text analyses—and an argument for the culture-centered ethnography of writing which emerges. We remind the reader that our work suggests theory, not the conclusions of empirical research. Working in the traditions of Gricean pragmatics (see Grice 1975), sociolinguistics, and ethnography, we suggest motivations for language behavior generally and for professional writing in particular. Also, our work is speculative, not conclusive. We report what we consider significant tendencies in writers' behavior and their intuitions about why they behave as they do.

1.2 DEFINITION OF ANALYZED FEATURES

The text features of superflous nominalization and inappropriate narrative text structure are nearly perfect candidates for sociolinguistic investigation. As we will explain, these features can be monitored easily and show clear political/psychological significance.

1.2.1 Superflous nominalization

In technical and professional communication, writers are often advised to use strong verbs rather than create superflous nominalizations, that is, nominalized forms of a verb with dummy verbs inserted to preserve their verbal function in the sentence. Here are some examples of verbs converted to superflous nominalizations:

observe → make an observance,
examine → undertake an examination, and
announce → provide an announcement.

Superfluous nominalizations contain the usual morphological markers (e.g. *-ence, -ion, -ment, -aint*, or Ø) and always occur in 'verb-direct object' syntax. Unlike other features associated with muddy writing, such as strings of prepositional phrases, strings of relative clauses, passivization, and technical vocabulary, superfluous nominalization is seldom justified by rhetorical strategy or discourse structure. Further, constraints of grammar and syntax do not require writers to nominalize. Nominalization also makes text-processing slower by adding additional transformation complexity and bulk. If our training and development managers' reports are right, their writers KNOW that they should avoid nominalization but nominalize anyway. We can only conclude that their behavior must be otherwise motivated.

1.2.2 Narrative structures

Narrative structures are texts organized by time sequence. Clearly, narrative structure is appropriate in response to rhetorical situations that require recounting events over time, such as documenting a procedure. We studied documents where narrative structure was not required and yet the writer adhered to it, even when asked—often ordered—to do otherwise.

1.3 THE NOMINALIZATION STUDY

1.3.1 Method and results

We conducted our ethnographic study of nominalization in two *Fortune 500* corporations with very different management styles and products. One—a computer and business-service company—is widely diversified. Here, largely autonomous divisions compete sharply for business both within and outside the corporation. The other—an agricultural, commodities, and consumer goods company—is far more informally organized. Reporting relationships evolve from the current business demands and differ from group to group. Here, personal style is informal—first names are used at all levels; one manager described the atmosphere as 'like a small-town.'

We interviewed in three steps. First, we contacted twelve upper managers in line or support services: three credit managers, two management information service managers, two consumer product line managers, three sales or customer representative managers, and two grain-merchandising managers. Each supervised fifteen to twenty-five middle managers or other professionals. We questioned these people casually, seeking general information about the workplace and the roles communication played in it. We then asked them if they could identify the best writers/communicators in their group. They could, in every case.

Second, we spoke with eight reputedly good writers (as identified by our twelve managers) in twenty-minute conversational interviews, openly exploring their views of writing in the workplace and their own writing processes. Though the interviews were casual, we explored one core issue with all the writers: their sense of job security. We asked them to tell us whether and how their reporting/supervisory roles had changed in the last six months, whether they anticipated change in the immediate future, what caused the change, how they felt about it, as well as how they felt about their job security generally. Moving from workplace relationships to texts, we collected samples of the writers' recent work, asked them to identify at least two 'interesting' pieces, and conducted short discourse-based interviews about these pieces (see Odell and Goswami 1982). By 'interesting,' we meant writing that requires conscious thought and planning, not 'boilerplate.' Our subjects typically regarded their interesting documents as 'hard' writing that had consequences. We allowed our writers to identify sections of text especially 'interesting' to them for the initial parts of the interview and concluded by asking them to explain their selection of one or two nominal structures.

Third, we conducted an additional set of interviews with several of the good writers' peers, using this same procedure. We also asked this group to identify the 'good' writers in each of their units. These workers never contradicted the managers' evaluations of who were the 'good' writers. Four of them suggested additional 'good writers,' but every one named the initial eight the upper managers had identified.

Hence, two clear groups of workers emerged from our analyses of writers supervised by our management informants in each workplace:

- The CENTRAL PEERS—the respected 'good communicators' (who often turned out to be the best product managers or grain traders as well). These were the eight good communicators initially identified by management.
- The OTHER GUYS—good-to-adequate workers, all comfortable with the idea that the central peers in their group were better with words—and maybe with other business skills as well. We studied twenty-six other guys.

For each of these thirty-four subjects, we read and analyzed at least four pages of their writing (a thousand words), typically more. We asked them for writing

Table 1.1 Distribution of superfluous nominalizations in writing samples

Subject group	Average superfluous nominalizations per 1,000 words	Range
Central peers	6	5–8
Other guys	12	10–18

samples produced within the last six weeks which they considered 'representative' and which demanded original planning and drafting—no 'boilerplate,' no texts organized by the table of data being summarized, and so forth. In this material, superfluous nominalizations surfaced in distinctive distributions.

Table 1.1 shows the range of average superfluous nominalizations for the central peers to be relatively narrow, ± 3, with the feature distributed across different writers' samples more or less normally. The other guys vary far more, the averages ranging by ± 8, with the most extreme cases displaying three times the average of the central peers. Even within these ranges, the most nominal writer in the central peer group does not quite reach the frequency of the least nominal other guy.

It is difficult to draw absolute conclusions from these data, primarily because we have no established norm for nominalization, superfluous or otherwise. Since any deep predicate can be realized in many surface forms, we cannot set a formal standard. And the relevant empirical norm does not exist. Few stylistic analyses of large corpuses have been broken down by genre, much less by workplace, register, or job family. Representative linguistic data bases like the Brown corpus have grouped texts by type, making only gross divisions by medium (e.g. daily vs. weekly newspapers) or by broad genre (e.g. editorial vs. reporting copy in newspapers; religion vs. skills and hobbies, genres defined by subject matter; see Kučera and Francis, 1967; and Francis and Kučera, 1982). Cultural linguistic analyses of the sort we are proposing are so new that the relevant baselines have not yet been set. We can, however, comment on a few trends, quickly observed:

- A recent issue of *People* magazine that we analyzed contained no superfluous nominalizations in a 2,000-word random sample from the text proper: two showed up in the copy of two computer advertisements (*People*, 28 May 1984).
- An article in the *American Economic Review* for December 1983 revealed fifteen superfluous nominalizations in every thousand words of text and far more 'legitimate' nominalizations (E. G. West and M. McKee, 'De gustibus *est* disputandum: the phenomenon of "merit wants revisited",' pp. 1110–21).
- A recent issue of *PMLA* ([1984], No. 3 [99]) showed superfluous nominalization at the rate of 0 to 12 incidences per every thousand words for three samples from three articles, reflecting a wide variety of styles within the genre of American literary criticism. (Though most academic composition texts recommend the verbal style, academic writers in professional publications respond variously to their own and their colleagues' advice.)

Applying these standards, we can say simply that our thirty-four subjects nominalize far more frequently than some groups and less frequently than others: our writers use superfluous, morphologically-marked nominal forms about nine times in every thousand words of text. Yet our samples drawn from strikingly different publications suggest that nominalization varies from language culture to language culture. We think its distribution is significant in our population of corporate writers.

As we said earlier, we believed the superfluous nominalization feature to be politically/psychologically motivated by the corporate environment. To test this assumption, we examined our writers' interview data more closely to determine if attitudes toward the work environment might distinguish another way to group our population and to re-examine the distribution of the nominalization feature. Writers' responses to questions about their positions in the workplace revealed two new groups: those SECURE in their jobs and those whose jobs were VOLATILE OR VULNERABLE. The volatile/vulnerable workers had changed or thought they might change their positions in the workplace. They had been promoted or demoted. Their reporting relationships had changed. They had a new manager. Their division or department had undergone reorganization, or else they expected it soon. Change—imminent or recent, real or imagined, dreaded or eagerly anticipated—made the difference.

In grouping our sample by this new variable, we found that central peers in secure jobs nominalize at about the same rate as their colleagues in volatile/vulnerable jobs; we found no significant or even suggestive differences. Not so for the other guys. Those in vulnerable positions fell at the top of the range for the group (see Table 1.2). The distinction between the 'secure other guys' and the 'volatile/vulnerable other guys' is statistically significant ($p < .05$).[1]

Some other equally interesting observations about psychological/political motivators influencing nominalizations in corporate writing bear anecdotal reporting:

- Writing for the eyes of upper management or for powerful people outside of the corporation was more heavily nominal—consistently. Whether the powerful audience was addressed directly or 'copied' made no difference. When writing up the corporate hierarchy, nominalization goes up. When writing down, nominalization goes down.
- Our most insistent nominalizer was a black male manager reporting to a white female. His most nominal texts were those sent or copied to her. When writing to peers or subordinates, his tendency toward superfluous

Table 1.2 Distributions of nominalizations for central peers and other guys as influenced by job security

Subject group	Average superfluous nominalizations per 1,000 words	Range
Central peers		
Secure N = 3	6.0	5–8
Volatile N = 5	6.2	5–8
Other guys		
Secure N = 8	10.6	10–11
Volatile N = 18	15.6	12–18

nominalization decreased. In an interview with one of us, his speech was formal and hypercorrect—at the start. Over the course of an hour's conversation, he became comfortably informal and lucid, perhaps realizing that he was not meeting his old English teacher and that his ability as a market analyst and manager was recognized.

- Heavy nominalization characterized the writing of subjects from one of our two corporations, a firm in a state of continuous internal reorganization. (One of the managers we interviewed from this firm had worked in three different reporting relationships in the last fiscal year.) Writers in this organization may also have felt pressure to compete; divisions of the corporation were in open economic competition with each other for limited business, internally and externally.

1.3.2 Superfluous nominalization: an explanation

'The frequency of superfluous nominalization correlates with the degree of anxiety or uncertainty.' That is how one of us first expressed our major conclusion about nominalization in drafting this chapter—with two to five nominalizations (depending on whether you see '*anxiety*,' '*uncertainty*,' and '*frequency*' as deep predicates occurring as predicate adjectives at an intermediate stage of the derivation). Our group's way of talking is powerfully compelling, affecting even our own way of writing. Our problem, of course, is to explain why. We have posited the motivations for such behavior: lesser professional stature (being one of the other guys) and job insecurity (experiencing considerable change in a job situation). We can suggest two other possible causes.

1.3.2.1 *Dysfluency: stress and mediocre competence affect linguistic fluency*

Speakers and writers under stress are less fluent. Stroke victims' linguistic error rate (qualitatively dependent upon the area of damage) rises when they are tired or upset. Second-language speakers' fluency drops under stress. Basic writers' use of a range of syntactic structures drops under examination pressure; in fact, students do better, in general, on take-home exams than under the pressure of time in class. All of this suggests an easy explanation for superfluous nominalization in corporate writing; the other guys, whose writing skills are less developed to begin with, lose what control they do have over their writing processes when they are under pressure. They are not central among their peers because they do not express themselves well, and vice versa. And maybe they are not as good at what they do in other areas either. Maybe skill with language corresponds to competence generally. This all has a certain appeal and probably some truth. And it fits well with the current and popular mythology of meritocracy. But we are not convinced that dysfluency caused by mediocre competence or stress entirely explains our writers' behavior.

1.3.2.2 *Hypercorrection: superfluous nominalization is overvalued as a prestige feature*

Those intensely nominalizing other guys have grasped a valid sociolinguistic principle: nominalization, superfluous and otherwise, characterizes the language of their culture and also that of the academic social-scientific culture which educated many of its members. Nominalization is, in fact, a favored means for achieving semantic density, a sign of syntactic maturity, a formal trace of literate cognition, and a feature of published writing and spoken language in academic cultures (see Hunt 1965; Daiker, Kerrek, and Morenberg 1978; and Danielewicz 1984). The other guys simply overvalue the feature; they use it more often and in more environments—linguistic and rhetorical—than the initiated central peers. In short, they hypercorrect their prose, producing forms which, while not ungrammatical, are either too frequent or inappropriate.

If hypercorrection were the only motivator, it should be a simple matter to explain the linguistic facts to weak writers and to tell them to back off a little. It is not that simple. The hypercorrection explanation ignores the power superfluous nominalization has as a political/psychological sign, even though it may accurately explain its distribution; the dysfluency explanation ignores this factor as well. We will elaborate our explanation of superfluous nominalization as 'sign' later, after we have considered the related discourse-level phenomenon, narrative text structure.

1.4 THE NARRATIVE STRUCTURES STUDY

1.4.1 Method and results

We selected our informants from technically-oriented work environments isolated in a year's ethnographic research in fifteen companies. We assumed that writing bears the marks of its production, and its cultural traces are highlighted when it crosses from one language community to another. We were particularly interested in technical writing submitted to managers or to the editorial staffs—writing which moves from a highly specialized technical community to groups with other concerns, customer-relations professionals or corporate management, say. So we identified strategic positions in corporate structures at the intersections of 'critical paths' for communication.

In initial interviews with corporate vice-presidents, often those responsible for corporate communications, we studied organization charts and located strategic positions. We found these critical path intersections filled by EDITORS in publications or communications departments or by senior MANAGERS in technical divisions. These editor/managers were our major informants. All were technically knowledgeable professionals in management positions; all had more than five years' experience. For their writing—and often for their technical work as well—young technical professionals reported directly to these experienced editor/managers who assigned the writing tasks, evaluated them on their writing performance, and exercised final quality control over the written product.

We interviewed these editor/managers in an informal way, guiding the conversation with prepared questions, but allowing them to talk on issues they thought critical. Whenever possible, we also interviewed one of the technical professionals they supervised, comparing their views. We taped all interviews and compiled notes from the tapes. We conducted follow-up interviews to clarify and elaborate interesting issues. We sent our interview notes to our informants for their comments and corrections. In a few cases, we sent our preliminary findings to especially astute informants and were gratified to find they agreed with our accounts.

Our interview data revealed that our informants were troubled about the tendency of writers in their groups to use narrative discourse structure when other discourse modes would have been more appropriate. The most articulate editor/manager we encountered—an executive vice-president in a technical consulting firm—described the problem this way:

> [People with technical backgrounds] attempt to deal with the question by recapping a time sequence: 'The first level of analysis on this project involved gathering external data on organization, and considering demand . . .'; 'Next we followed that . . ., and after that . . .' They take it in some kind of chronological recitation of what they did, as opposed to selecting from it those key things that will influence a decision-maker to accept their recommendation.

This informant would prefer to get 'key things that will influence decision makers.' The engineers gave him instead narrative logs of their engineering projects. His final comment about the problem is telling and synoptic:

> We see a level of quasi-scientific neutrality with the apparent hope that the facts will speak for themselves. . . . We are in the business of being consultants, . . . of making recommendations. To leave that [the recommendations] to the interpretation of the reader, in our business, is a fatal error.

Pressed for more information, this manager confirmed that inappropriate narration was disproportionately frequent in his technically-trained peoples' writing. The head of the economics analysis division of a large public utility also attested to the ubiquity of narrative structure in his economists' writing and added, without prompting, that the problem was greater among his engineers. These editor/managers recognized their young professionals' frequent insecurity in their new roles. Pressure, cost overruns, delays, bugs in the software, and hassles from the customer pushed them into defensive postures, and the defensiveness manifested itself in overwriting—particularly in the form of narrative structures.

Our sense from all of the interviews was that the editor/managers and the young technical professionals they supervised had quite different interests. This case was particularly apparent in the observations of a software engineer:

> My manager just wants the data that fits the deal she's trying to cut. I don't think that way. In [my last year's work], pieces of what she calls 'extra information' have turned out to be the start of new architectures. I just can't leave out stuff that way.

A simple observation: the editor/managers' product is often the DOCUMENT—the project report or proposal or software-with-documentation; the young professionals' product is typically the TECHNICAL PROCESS. The perceived function of the writing depends upon where one stands in the production cycle.

1.4.2 Narrative structures: an explanation

From speakers' or writers' choices of structures, we can infer their model of the audience and the relationship they construct with it (see Brown and Beach, forthcoming). To understand inappropriate narrative structures in corporate writing, we need to understand the corporate speakers' or writers' cultural roles. All language structure 'signifies' (see Barthes [1953] 1977). And all linguistic signs, in the language of psychodynamic psychologies, are multiply determined (see Wälder 1936). An author's choice to narrate when a reader (in this case his or her supervisor) advises differently is a good example of a sign so determined. Combining dysfluency and hypercorrection explanations with some common-sense cultural analysis, we offer three multiple determinants for the choice to narrate.

1.4.2.1 *Narration is easy, automatic*

The narrative is the first structure for extending texts that children acquire and the only one that many basic writers handle with ease. It probably has its source in visual memory: remember the sequence of events and verbalize them as you do it. Corporate writers favor it when they dictate or write under pressure: eidetic memory organizes the text.

1.4.2.2 *Narratives preserve distance; they do not direct people's behavior*

The narrative, like other speech acts, is distinguished by its effect on the discourse participants in a context (for examples of discourse distinctions, in pragmatic theory, see Searle 1975; Labov and Fanshel 1977; and Brown and Levinson 1978). The pragmatic thrust of narrative discourse reflects specific contextual motivators in the corporate environment and hence supports particular communicative roles. As our vice-presidential informant told us, managers are in the business of directing others' behavior. Making recommendations asserts their expertise, their ability to assume a directive role. Young technical professionals are in the business of careful technical analysis. Narrative structures assert their care and competence by recapitulating the technical process they conducted while allowing them to remain passive in transactions with customers and clients.

1.4.2.3 *Narratives mirror the structure of the scientific method*

Narratives relate a problem-posing and problem-solving process, a process of data gathering and integration from accounts of normal science in textbooks and from the modeling of these processes in lab courses. As such, they reflect a logical process for which technical professionals bear some unconscious affection. As Foucault, Derrida, and some of the ego psychologists might put it, these persons' professional SELVES derive from and determine this discourse (see Erikson 1968; Foucault 1972; Derrida 1976; and Brooke 1984).

1.5 TOWARD THEORY AND APPLICATION

1.5.1 The major theoretical claims

As we have claimed and as our research confirms, no single explanation can account for language in social context; discourse bears multiple meanings, and its aspects are multiply determined. We suggest four variables which taken together account for why our writers act as they do in their workplaces. Though we detail these variables as relevant to our work, we believe they deserve attention in sociolinguistic analysis generally.

1.5.1.1 *Writers often tend toward dysfluency*

Speakers and writers often err—from carelessness, from ignorance, and from many other things. Though textbooks and pedagogy, both corporate and academic, often focus on writers' purported ignorance, the actual behavior of writers does not support dysfluency as the most likely cause of some behavior. Although all writers make mistakes (our subjects included), our observations suggest that what linguists may easily interpret as mistakes or ignorance can be very deliberate behavior. As the reader will recall, our subjects were not only told not to nominalize and not to narrate, but they had also taken writing seminars training them how to do otherwise. Nevertheless, they still persisted with these writing styles.

1.5.1.2 *Linguistic structure and function influences writers' choices*

The seemingly eccentric or irrational examples of language behavior we have observed exhibit logical grammatical choices—considering their syntactic, semantic, pragmatic, and phonological function. These forms are not 'chosen' at random.

Nominalization removes or obscures the case relations surrounding the deep predicate; for instance, agency and instrumentality vanish when the verbal form becomes a noun. In the case of superfluous nominalization, the dummy verb replaces the dangerous predicate with an innocent or positive action—rather than 'recommending,' the writer ends up simply 'making' or 'offering' a recommendation. It is interesting and not accidental that passive structures occur so frequently with nominalization; together they allow writers to remove themselves totally from their reported actions.

Narrative discourse represents the world of events, leaving the agent or doer of those events—often the writer—out of the picture. It gives—as one of our engineering managers put it—'just the facts, ma'am,' leaving the reader to act on the basis of those facts. It asks nothing, demands nothing. It implies neutrality on the writers' part and faith in the reader's ability to evaluate and decide.

1.5.1.3 *Cultural initiation affects linguistic usage*

It is one thing to note that weak corporate or technical writing contains too many nominalizations, and quite another thing to note that all writing in that culture is heavily nominal—by some cultures' standards—and that superfluous nominalization systematically relates to the way initiates behave in the culture to which they aspire.

The descriptive indices of sociolinguistic analysis, such as variability, style-shifting, and hypercorrection, usefully describe speakers' and writers' language behavior as they gradually become members of a new cultural group. Hypercorrections are not simple errors; they may be evidence that novices in the culture have overgeneralized the rules. Such sociolinguistic description supports ethnographic analysis of writing: it shows the formal relationships between an individual's language features and group practices. But it does not fully explain people's motivation for hypercorrecting.

1.5.1.4 *The power of language as sign dominates*

Sociolinguists typically assume that any linguistic choice is significant, communicating information about speakers and their attitudes toward hearers, topics, contexts, and so on. Our observations in the corporate environment confirm such an assumption. Our informants always responded to the effects of their words on their places in the organization—some acutely self-aware, others influenced by significations beyond their control.

Using superfluous nominalization and inappropriate narrative structure is only irrational behavior if we assume that writing should be economical and transparent. Often it should. But these features do more than influence the ways we process prose; they are SIGNS as well. And it is their sign function that is sometimes in direct conflict with their communicative/transactional function.

Nominalization marks academic and corporate language. It is significant in absence and presence, allowing members of groups to use the form to mark and define themselves. The Anglo-American literary tradition disfavors nominalization—a significant absence. This stylistic signification informs the composition textbooks which it produced. But much European literary theory and most British and American social-science writing is heavily nominal—as is business writing. These stylistic tendencies mark writers in social-science and business 'groups.' As our informants told us and showed us, their need to communicate 'group' solidarity was often primary, especially when their roles in the organization seemed in jeopardy.

Narrative structure mirrors both the process/methodology and the DISCOURS of science and technology. Its pragmatic function allows writers to take roles which match their sense of themselves and their favored functions in the corporate environment: task-centered, impartial, orderly, non-directive. To write scientific narratives is to recapitulate and reinforce one's sense of this social place.

In our view of things, ostensible core conventions of 'good writing' go the way of standard dialects in sociolinguistics: the conventions shift and change, to be replaced by other conventions, all dictated by contextual criteria. What is 'good' is what meets the complex needs of the language culture. This view troubles those of us who teach writing, of course. In the case of superfluous nominalization, it leaves us approving or at least accepting language which we may find hard to read. But it helps us—raising consciousness—to recognize that we teachers privilege readability, transparency, and a myth of apolitical neutrality because we, too, are members of a language culture. When we recommend a way of writing, we reinforce our own group affiliations.

1.5.2 Ethnography and pedagogy

Asked what corporations should do about changing the writing behavior that we studied, we might answer: 'lower the level of insecurity in your organization.' What keeps this from being a mere flippant remark is its core of truth. Several of our organizations already recognized and responded to it with innovative management solutions to poor writing—quality circles for major writing projects, for example. The core insight for teachers is that all language has a cultural basis. If we do not recognize and accommodate it, our teaching fights the culture—and always loses. Ethnographic research reveals language/culture relationships, and it can thus inform our teaching objectives and methods. Four findings that are relevant to teaching practice emerge from our work.

1.5.2.1 *Form/structure based teaching obscures the social basis of writing in particular language cultures*

At best, purely formal-structural emphases miss the more interesting rhetorical dimensions of language choice. At worst, the formal structures that teachers didactically recommend and disrecommend not only mark their favored cultural affiliation but also imply an adversarial attitude toward the cultural affiliation of the student audience.

1.5.2.2 *Errors do not always represent the writer's ignorance*

Errors may be evidence of a writer's growth-in-progress—if they are hypercorrections of legitimate forms, for instance. These formal excesses signal speakers' and writers' growing control of their culture's discourse. The 'hypercorrection' explanation also suggests how teachers should respond to these culturally significant features in students' texts: clearly not with an attack. The aim should be not to eliminate the hypercorrect feature, but rather to help the writer manage it, to conform his or her practice to the norms of the culture.

The roots of hypercorrection are aspiration and uncertainty; the pedagogical solution may be mastery of the cultural discourse—and a sense of place in the organization, whether it be a classroom, a business office, or wherever. When writers feel competent about their skills and secure in their workplaces, their need to hypercorrect may vanish.

1.5.2.3 *Writers need to learn to write for the audience who is observing the transaction*

When we first heard writers in corporations discuss the consequences of the 'copy list,' we thought we had found something unusual. They were not reflecting the commonplace observation that professional writing has 'multiple audiences.' Instead, they were describing a 'layered' speech event in which the writer addresses an audience (or audiences), and the entire transaction is observed AS A TRANSACTION by a known or imagined overlooking 'other.'

In perceiving written discourse as an observed transaction, teachers' sense of the structure of their own culture's written speech events changes. They concede that every journal article, every textbook is observed, and that writers select language for the observers as well as for the audience to which they direct the text. As we ourselves are writing this somewhat self-reflexive text, we sense overlooking editors, publishers, and personnel committee members, as well as our audience of interested language scholars.

Our professional writing students—in corporations and in the academy—find great comfort and insight in recognizing and accepting that professional writing is often display behavior in a very public place. Once this is clear, it is easier to move on to issues of good written business practice or good technical reporting.

1.5.2.4 *Writing instruction can motivate certain writing practices through linking them with group affiliation*

Writing style marks groups. Desire for affiliation and support always motivates writers; it motivates those who respond to their writing as well. A young engineer offering as narrative report of a software-development project is presenting, in a sense, a life's work—in both structure and content. A manager—or a technical writing teacher—who rejects the report on formal grounds is likely to make several other negative gestures toward the report writer unintentionally:

- reject the writer's work and with it the writer's source of professional competence and self esteem;
- make the writer more insecure by communicating that his or her words—and the work they mirror—are not appropriate in the teacher/manager's culture; and
- undercut his or her supervisory authority through polarizing the exchange: a language teacher's or manager's criteria are not engineering criteria; the writer thus has license to ignore it.

The training managers we met in our preliminary interviews reported employees' sense that writing instruction was irrelevant to their jobs: they were reporting a bad cultural fit between teacher-language and professional writer-language. One cannot, for example, reject nominalization—superfluous or not. To do so is to reject a sign of group affiliation and thereby the group. In doing so, teachers are simply wrong; they have no culture-free basis for their preference, and they are recommending an unhappy linguistic/political course.

Nominalized writing does work on the job. Like it or not, much social-science and business writing gets along just fine with heavily nominal style. Teachers can, of course, tell students about the psycholinguistic and political consequences of stylistic choices, yet they must balance the preference for clarity with political grace (see Hake and Williams 1981; and Williams 1981).

1.6 EPILOGUE

We end with two strikingly different but significant texts—both treating the way language lets us build ourselves from roles available in society. The author of the first—theoretically distanced and self-aware—talks about the reciprocal relationship of self and culture. The author of the second—eloquently naïve—illustrates it:

> We deal with a process 'located' in the core of the individual and yet also in the core of his communal culture, a process which establishes, in fact, the identify of those two identities. [Erikson 1968: 22]

* * *

We're in with the in crowd; we go where the in crowd goes
We're in with the in crowd; we know what the in crowd knows
We've got our own way of walking, yeah
We've got our own way of talking
[Dobie Gray (1965), 'The In Crowd,' B. Page (lyricist), BMI, Elvis Presley Music, Hill and Range Songs]

Both common sense and theory recognize the tight bond of language, culture, and self. All that good ethnographic language analysis has to do is figure out—richly and clearly—what each 'in crowd' knows. Then we will know about their own ways of talking.

NOTES

1. We wish to thank the Bush Foundation of St. Paul and the Graduate School of the University of Minnesota for support of our research. We are particularly grateful to the employees of fifteen Minnesota corporations, anonymous by request. They gave their time generously, and it is often their insights we report.

2. The observed statistic was $p = 0.028$ for the Mann–Whitney test.

BIBLIOGRAPHY

Barthes, R. ([1953] 1977), *Writing Degree Zero*, Lavers, A. and Smith, C. (trans.), New York, Hill and Wang.

Bormann, E., 'Symbolic Convergence: Organizational Communication and Culture,' in Putnam, L. and Pacanowsky, M. (eds) (1983: 99–122), *Communication and Organizations: An Interpretive Approach*, Beverly Hills, Calif., Sage.

Brooke, R. E. (1984), *Writing and Commitment: Some Psychosocial Functions of College Writing*, Ph.D. dissertation, University of Minnesota (see *Dissertation Abstracts International*, sec. A, 1984, **45**, 2507–A).

Brown, R. L., Jr. and Beach, R., 'Discourse Conventions and Literary Inference: Toward a Theoretical Model,' in Tierney, R. (ed.) (forthcoming), *Understanding Readers' Understanding*, Hillsdale, N.J., Lawrence Erlbaum.

Brown, P. and Levinson, S., 'Universals in Language Usage: Politeness

Phenomena,' in Goody, E. N. (ed.) (1978: 56–324), *Questions and Politeness: Strategies in Social Interaction*, Cambridge Papers in Social Anthropology 8, Cambridge, Cambridge University Press.

Coleman, H. B. (1964), 'The Comprehensibility of Several Grammatical Transformations,' *Journal of Applied Psychology*, **48**, 186–90.

Coleman, H. B. (1965), 'Learning of Prose Written in Four Grammatical Transformations,' *Journal of Applied Psychology*, **49**, 332–41.

Daiker, D., Kerek, A., and Morenberg, M. (1978), 'Sentence Combining and Syntactic Maturity in Freshmen English,' *College Composition and Communication*, **29**, 36–41.

Danielewicz, J., 'The Interaction Between Text and Context: A Study of How Adults and Children Use Spoken and Written Language in Four contexts,' in Pellegrini, A. D. and Yawkey, T. D. (eds) (1984: 243–60), *The Development of Oral and Written Language in Social Contexts*, Advances in Discourse Processes 13, Norwood, N.J., Ablex.

Deal, T. and Kennedy, B. (1982), *Corporate Cultures*, Reading, Mass., Addison-Wesley.

Derrida, J. (1976), *Of Grammatology*, Spivak, G. (trans.), Baltimore, Johns Hopkins University Press.

Erikson, E. (1968), *Identity, Youth, and Crisis*, New York, Norton.

Foucault, M. (1972), *The Archeology of Knowledge*, Smith, A. M. S. (trans.), New York, Pantheon Books.

Francis, W. N. and Kučera, H. (1982), *Frequency Analysis of English Usage: Lexicon and Grammar*, Boston, Houghton Mifflin.

Goffman, E. (1971), *Relations in Public: Microstudies of the Public Order*, New York, Basic Books.

Grice, H. P., 'Logic and Conservation,' in Cole, P. and Morgan, J. L. (eds) (1975: 41–58), *Speech Acts*, Syntax and Semantics 3, New York, Academic Press.

Hake, R. and Williams, J. (1981), 'Style and Its Consequences: Do as I Do, Not as I Say,' *College English*, **43**, 433–51.

Hunt, K. W. (1965), *Grammatical Structures Written at Three Grade Levels*, NCTE Research Report 3, Champaign, Ill., NCTE (National Council of Teachers of English).

Hymes, D., 'Linguistic Problems in Defining the Concept of "Tribe," ' in Baugh, J. and Sherzer, J. (eds) (1984: 7–27), *Language in Use: Readings in Sociolinguistics*, Englewood Cliffs, N.J., Prentice-Hall.

Kantor, K. J., 'Classroom Contexts and the Development of Writing Intuitions: An Ethnographic Case Study,' in Beach, R. and Bridwell, L. (eds) (1984: 72–94), *New Directions in Composition Research*, New York, Guilford Press.

Kučera, H. and Francis, W. N. (1967), *Computational Analysis of Present-Day American English*, Providence, R.I., Brown University Press.

Labov, W. and Fanshel, D. (1977), *Therapeutic Discourse: Psychotherapy as Conversation*, New York, Academic Press.

Odell, L. and Goswami, D. (1982), 'Writing in a Non-Academic Setting,' *Research in the Teaching of English*, **16**, 201–23.

Searle, J., 'A Taxonomy of Illocutionary Acts,' in Gunderson, K. (ed.) (1975: 344–69), *Language, Mind, and Knowledge*, Minnesota Studies in the Philosophy of Science 7, Minneapolis, Minn., University of Minnesota Press.

Selzer, J., 'What Constitutes a "Readable" Technical Style?,' in Anderson, P. V., Brockmann, R. J., and Miller, C. R. (eds) (1983: 71–89), *New Essays in Technical and Scientiftic Communication: Research, Theory, Practice*, Baywood's Technical Communications Series 2, Farmingdale, N.Y., Baywood.

Shuy, R. (1981), 'A Holistic View of Language,' *Research in the Teaching of English*, **15**, 101–11.

Wälder, R. (1936), 'The Principle of Multiple Function: Observations on Over-Determination,' *Psychoanalytic Quarterly*, **5**, 45–62.

Williams, J. M. (1981), *Style: Ten Lessons in Clarity and Grace*, Glenview, Ill., Scott, Foresman.

2 Close cohesion with *do so*: a linguistic experiment in language function using a multi-example corpus

Michael P. Jordan
Queen's University—Kingston

2.1 AN ARGUMENT FOR ANALYSIS OF ACTUAL LANGUAGE USE

Not too long ago, investigations of oral and written language in use were all but abandoned by scholars of linguistics in the wake of Noam Chomsky's *Syntactic Structures* (1957). Chomsky (1957 and 1965) and others questioned the scholastic value of such analysis and started the search for intuitively derived 'kernel sentences' and 'deep structures' of language from which, they claimed, users generate actual use through a detailed set of 'transformations.' These researchers argued that the study of instances of actual use (or 'performance') is a trivial activity in view of the intellectual need for investigation into the innate ability (or 'competence') of native users of the language.

Today, Chomsky's influence continues to be strongly felt; however, many linguists have returned to the study of actual language use on the premise that language can best be understood through such an analysis rather than by studying isolated made-up instances of language devoid of any context or communicative social function. Those who counter Chomsky's approach argue first that linguists can study only instances of linguistic performance (they cannot study or even determine what is in the brain), and second, that a systematic study of examples of language as it is used to communicate (and not just to prove a point of theory) is a well-established, scientifically defensible technique for describing language. This practical and largely empirical approach to language research is represented by work in language theory of the French and Prague school structuralists and is echoed today in the SYSTEMIC LINGUISTICS of Michael Halliday and the TAGMEMIC LINGUISTICS of Kenneth Pike.

Many linguists after Chomsky assert that language analysis should be within some theoretical framework, explicit or implicit, which governs the choice of research projects in working toward an integrated theory of language. In their view, a truly atheoretical approach would be little more valuable than presenting raw data, as it would fail to contribute to an overall explanation of an area of language. Any attempt to correlate sets of empirically derived results within a wider theoretical framework is, of course, a laudable aim as long as verified conclusions determine the model and not the reverse. The understandable need to extend and/or justify a model, however, must not blind the researcher to data or conclusions that might lead to alteration or improvement of the underlying assumptions of the model.

This chapter argues for the scholarly value of a descriptive analysis of language that reflects actual use rather than purely intuitive knowledge about language systems. It presents an analysis of a selected area of language free from what could be regarded as undue restrictions imposed by the assumption of one or another established theoretical basis for analysis and description. This approach at the same time builds upon and contributes to work which is slowly developing an explanation of the syntactic, semantic, and cohesive elements of texts in educated English use (see, for instance, Hoey and Winter in this volume [ed.]).

The study of actual language use involves collection of examples, painstaking study and classification, and very sophisticated description, using some of the examples collected to illustrate the systems discovered. To study even a very small aspect of language use (such as close cohesion with *do so* as in this chapter) and to relate it to known scholarship, the linguist needs to study hundreds or thousands of examples of a particular occurrence and to compare these examples with related occurrences of similar language functions. (*Do so* cannot be studied meaningfully in isolation from *do this*, *do that*, and *do it*, for example.) This work, coupled with the need for sound knowledge of related scholarship in the area of investigation, makes the task a formidable one indeed.

The work here demonstrates such a linguistic 'experiment' in the scientific tradition for independent verification (or otherwise) of a claim made by eminent linguists regarding a particular usage of English. The principle to be tested is the claim by Halliday and Hasan that *do so* is 'less frequent in all cases where the presupposing clause is structurally related to the presupposed one' (1976: 116). Hundreds of examples of *do so*, its variants, and related constructions have been collected to form a corpus as a basis for the experiment. These primary data have been filed on cards, and selections from these are used as illustrations throughout this text.

The task of verifying the usage of *do so* has been chosen for this experiment as it can be constrained within reasonable limits while demonstrating the validity of corpus-based language analyses. Other discussions of the use of corpus-based analysis can be found in Huddleston *et al.* 1968; Winter 1974; and Jordan 1978. The goal of describing usage in 'educated English' through examining primary data was first articulated by the Communications Research Centre (CRC) established at University College, London, England in 1953. Its many projects included a twelve man-year analysis of scientific and technical writing (Huddleston *et al.* 1968), the creation of the Survey of English Usage with its related grammar (Quirk *et al.* 1972), and work on paralinguistic features and elicitation experiments. The *do so* corpus presented here includes a few examples collected for the

Survey of English Usage referenced by the coding system under which they are on file at the CRC.

Analysis of textual cohesion, such as this chapter's analysis of *do so*, is ideally suited to the investigative approach described here; however, analysis of other aspects of language, such as grammatical structures within the clause and sentence, for example, require different techniques. For these, generalizations about structure are motivated by the investigator's desire to design systematic, explanatory frameworks. Yet, even the theoretical conclusions of linguists about syntactic systems should stand the test of close scrutiny based upon observation of language in use as well as be integrated with systems describing semantics in context and discourse structure and signaling.[1]

This chapter begins the discussion of *do so* with a brief summary of some parameters that govern corpus-based text analysis. Following this is an outline of theoretical assumptions about the functions of *do so* in oral and written use that my own experiment seeks to validate, a description of *do so* within four broad categories of cohesion, and finally, criteria for use of *do so* versus counterpart forms that are based upon the data collected.

2.2 GUIDELINES FOR CORPUS-BASED TEXT ANALYSIS

2.2.1 The use of technical terms

In analyzing primary language data without referring to a particular school of thought, a researcher must explain observations with technical terms that are not exclusive to one or another language theory. This stricture is in fact a great advantage since the use of widely accepted terms not only helps non-linguists follow the discussion, but also allows linguists desiring to place original work within their own analytical preferences to do so without undue efforts in 'translating' terms.

A great difficulty for young linguists today is that they must be familiar with several branches of theoretical work in order to understand even minimally the findings offered. For instance, works relevant to our *do so* experiment by Lees (1960) and Crymes (1968) are presented within TRANSFORMATIONAL-GENERATIVE (TG) and tagmemic frameworks respectively. Terms such as 'pro-cluster substitution correlations' and 'suffusive predicatids' make Crymes's work difficult to follow unless the reader has some background in tagmemics (especially in Allen's [1966] variation). The same difficulty attends work by Huddleston in Huddleston *et al.* 1968, as later rewritten within the TG framework (Huddleston 1971) and thus made more obscure to anyone not familiar with TG analysis. (The rewritten version, in relying on the theoretical TG model, is also more open to question.) In contrast, the original version, loosely within a systemic framework, is far easier for non-linguists to follow.

Studies that build models slowly and define new terms and rules sensibly and only when necessary are more accessible to scholars at large and more easily adaptable to teaching purposes. Thus every effort is made here to describe the findings in accessible terms, not exclusive to any theoretical framework of analysis. Where I have found it necessary to include discussion of related scholarship, I have used widely accepted terms (as in Quirk *et al.* 1972) and have avoided the use of specialist terms found only in one branch of theoretical study.

2.2.2 The study of actual use

If we accept Lyons's definition of linguistics as 'the scientific study of language' (1968: 1), then we must be concerned with demonstrable fact rather than opinion—a point well made by Roberts:

> We are told [by grammarians] . . . that pronominal *this* is used by so-and-so and . . . by so-and-so, all reputable writers and God-fearing men. Very well! But how shall we know that these are not merely aberrations, occasional freedoms taken by experienced writers? . . .
>
> . . . The major lesson we learn from reading the works of [grammarians] . . . is that in language one should beware *ipse dixits*. . . .
>
> [The fact that] someone queried 625 competent judges and that 419 of them gave it as their opinion that it is all right to use pronominal *this* with vague reference . . . is interesting. But we are still in the fog of opinion. We want to know what the facts are, not what various people, however competent, think the facts may be. Is there no way to get at the facts? [1958: 269–70]

Roberts demonstrates how 'to get at the facts' in his own study of discourse referents where he selects a single large text for his corpus, classifies the types of referent, and then determines the number of each type in his text (see Jordan 1978).

My work is philosophically close to the approach taken by Roberts but differs in that it is a study of short passages of text representing many genres and including speech and writing. In essence, my work records actual utterances or written statements of educated users of English as evidence for the general acceptability of these uses. Aberrations and elicitation experiments (asking people what they think is correct) are also mentioned briefly in passing, as these are points raised by Roberts in his discussion of 'factual' research which deserve some response.

2.3 PRELIMINARIES ABOUT THE USE OF *DO SO*

The task before us is clarified by Halliday and Hasan's example and related discussion of the use of *do so* in *Cohesion in English*:

> In fact the form [of do] with 'so' is less frequent in all cases where the presupposing clause is structurally related to the presupposed one; so
>
> (3:65) I want to read this document. You can sign it after I've done so.

is likely to mean 'after I've read it' (with the tonic on 'done') rather than 'after I've signed it' with the tonic on 'I've'; the latter meaning would probably be expressed as 'after I have done.' [1976: 116–17]

Although Halliday and Hasan are comparing here *done so* with the verbal substitution *done* (as in *I don't believe you have* DONE), they make the assertion that *do so* is first less frequent and then unacceptable when its referent (or 'antecedent') is structurally related to the occurrence of *do so*. Their discussion of the second sentence of 3:65 asserts that *done so* cannot occur in a subordinate clause when its reference is in the main clause of the same sentence, and this assertion is the main point to be tested.

We should first note that many linguistic examples used by Halliday and Hasan to demonstrate their conclusions about the substitute *do* and variants could be regarded as strange forms of English (especially by native speakers in North America) and perhaps not the best basis for general conclusions:

3:58a Does Granny look after you every day?—She can't do at weekends, because she has to go to her own house. [p. 114]

3:61a John is smoking more now than Mary is doing. [p. 115]

3:64a Shall I make an announcement? You can do now.[2] [p. 116]

Although forms such as these are substitutes for *do so* in some dialects of British English, they will probably be regarded as totally unacceptable to American and Canadian readers who would find a form of *do so* more suitable in each case. It is interesting to note here that Crymes cites the following as unacceptable: 'Jean can arrange the flowers better than her mother can *do*' (1968: 70). Where researchers fail to agree on what forms are acceptable, as in this instance, we must seriously question the conclusions.

Furthermore, the research of Halliday and Hasan omits comment on some restrictions on *do so* imposed by the use of an auxiliary. My own investigations of language use suggest that the auxiliary plus a form of *do* (e.g. *have done*) rarely share the same environment as a form of *do* plus *so* (e.g. *have done so*). The following example of *have done* does not have a form suitable for *do so*:

(2:1) It is unfortunate that conditions make such an article necessary—but since that is so, let's recognize the situation—as you have *done*./[3] [*Ontario Engineering Digest*, January 1976: 5]

Halliday and Hasan also do not consider the use of *I have done* in the sense of *I have finished* as in:

(2:2) When are you going to be *done* with that program? [*Ladies' Home Journal*, January 1982: 14]

If interpreted in this sense, *I've done* in Halliday and Hasan's example 3:65 could mean something quite remote in the text, perhaps meaning after *I've done everything I'm doing*. A further complication in comparing *have done* with *have done so* is the use of an auxiliary without the form of *do*. For example, in Halliday's example 3:65, the phrase *after I have* instead of *after I've done so* would clearly refer to the signing and not the reading. As we shall see later, the use of the auxiliary without *do* is quite close to forms of *do so*. In fact, note how Halliday and Hasan's strange examples cited earlier become more acceptable for some native speakers of English when auxiliaries appear without the verb *do* added: *She can't at weekends*; *John is smoking more now than Mary is*; and *You can now*. All these instances suggest that it is unwise to try to compare the closeness of referents for *do* with *do so* using theoretical examples or simply those at hand as Halliday and Hasan appear to have done.

2.4 AN ANALYSIS OF *DO SO*

Although Halliday and Hasan chose to compare *I've done so* with *I've done*, other writers (Harris 1952; Crymes 1968; Winter 1974; and Jordan 1978) have compared *do so* with *do this*, *do that*, and *do it* as these three other forms often share similar environments and have other features in common. This study, therefore, compares *do so* to the three other forms and investigates the nuance of meaning suggested by the selection of one over another (see Karlsen 1965, on differences between *that* and *this*; see Jordan 1978, on differences between *do that* and *do this*).

The main focus of this study, however, is upon determining the extent of close cohesion for *do so*, and this necessarily involves concentrating on examples in which the use of *do so* alone may be suitable. Some of the examples could include as substitutes one or another of the three counterparts *do this*, *do it*, and *do that* or the primary form *he can*, but not the secondary form *he can do*. To avoid giving the impression at this stage that the counterparts and the primary form *do so* are not interchangeable in some contexts, I offer the following example:

(2:3) I kept telling myself I'd have to talk to Avril soon about Lawrence but somehow, when I decided to *do it*, I always lost my courage. [*True Story*, October 1975: 70]

Here *do so*, *do this*, *do that*, as well as *when I decide to* are all acceptable substitutes for *do it*, but *to do* is not.

In the following analysis, I refer to four principal varieties of close cohesion as the basis for description:

- cohesion between subject and verb;
- cohesion within a nominal group (noun phrase);
- cohesion between subordinate clause and main clause; and
- cohesion by clause coordination.

I examine each of these instances of close cohesion with the use of *do so* and conclude with a brief analysis of counterpart forms. This discussion represents only part of a much larger possible analysis of clausal substitution in English and perhaps points the way to further work in this area.

2.4.1 Subject–verb cohesion

Although subject–verb cohesion is not the closest form of cohesion in which *do so* is found, it yields perhaps the most highly characteristic use of *do so* that is rarely shared by other substitute forms. My attention was drawn to the use of *do so* in close cohesion, in fact, by these notices written by three writers for similar purposes:

(2:4) Drivers using this car park *do so* at their own risk. [Notice at car park, Southend Aircraft Museum, Essex, England, June 1976]

(2:5) Children using this playground *do so* at their parent's risk. [Notice on play area, Knebworth Fête, Herts, England, June 1976]

(2:6) Notice to parents and children. This is an ADVENTURE playground. It is not supervised. Those who use it *do so* at their own risk. [Notice at Knebworth House, Herts, England, June 1976]

Now, either these are acceptable instances of close cohesion with *do so* or else the writers are in a conspiracy to disprove established linguistic findings. The possibility that these occurrences are aberrations (a danger Roberts mentions) is remote indeed, but further examples are needed to make sure, as in these from speech:

(2:7) 'But, uh, industries that want to go metric can and have *done so* but I don't see why that should affect the pounds and pints and yards and inches and so on in the shops.' [Hatfield Polytechnic, A1–1117]

(2:8) 'The alternative for Smith now is to accept majority rule, to say so, and get on with it, or to let others get on with it who will *do so*.' [Reported direct speech, *Daily Telegraph*, 23 March 1976: 12]

Example 2:8 is a little more difficult to follow as its more usual form would be *or let others who will do so get on with it*. In the usual form, the referent for *do so* comes after *do so* (cataphoric reference) rather than before it (anaphoric reference).

Examples 2:7 and 2:8 provide further evidence for the acceptability of subject–verb close cohesion for *do so*. But is this a phenomenon found only in England or typical of colloquial use unacceptable in printed form? More examples suggest the answer:

(2:9) I have always considered that many of the people who use profanity *do so* because they lack the ability to communicate freely. [*Ontario Engineering Digest*, January 1978: 6]

(2:10) Couples who sit watching television instead of talking *do so*, he says, because they are afraid of admitting they can't stand each other! [*Here's Health*, April 1976: 69]

Clearly, *do so* in subject–verb close cohesion is acceptable in various contexts. Nevertheless, we might further test the acceptability of *do so* in subject-verb close cohesion by investigating whether *do so* functions this way in more complex sentences than we have shown—for example, those with an introductory *that* clause. The answer again becomes clear with examples:

(2:11) They all knew *that* many women don't have the choice—*that* many women who work outside the home *do so* because they have to. . . . [*Redbook*, February 1978: 92]

(2:12) It must insist *that* tenants who can afford to pay an economic rent for their houses should *do so* instead of sitting pretty on subsidies. [Survey of English Usage, W.15.1.49–1]

(2:13) It is easy and expedient to assume *that* a truck working well will continue to *do so*. [*Sunday Telegraph*, 15 February 1976: 59]

As indicated by Examples 2:12, examples can also help us determine the acceptable use of *do so* with modals preceding the substitute form.

A final example demonstrates that subject–verb cohesion with *do so* can occur where cohesive relationships are complex:

(2:14) Of the 317 ballot papers, 314 had been claimed by the time the ballot closed at noon. This indicated that, though the total who voted was one greater than *did so* in the second ballot, one MP who drew a ballot paper had omitted to use it. [*Daily Telegraph*, 6 April 1976: 1]

In Example 2:14, the subject–verb cohesion occurs within the subordinate clause *though . . . ballot* between the verb *voted* in the relative clause defining the subject and the subject of the comparative clause of the complement! It seems that *do so* is quite suitable for such instances of complex close cohesion, casting further doubt on Halliday and Hasan's claim against the use of *do so* in such instances.

My use of many examples to demonstrate small points is intended to demonstrate the method researchers must follow in investigating language use. As researchers usually report only major conclusions of language analyses and not all the data and research, they have a serious obligation to ensure that their findings are representative of their primary data and thus truly reflect actual English use. A further guideline imposed on researchers is that they cannot simply ignore or discard a proven occurrence, just because it is very difficult to explain or does not conveniently 'fit' into a developing or established model. As an example, the instances of subject–verb cohesion cited here do not fit readily into my own past descriptions of substitution (see Jordan 1982 and 1985b); this, however, has made their discovery doubly important as they became the stimulus for my development of the following explanation within an expanding theoretical framework explained in Winter 1977 and 1982; Hoey 1983; and Jordan 1984a, 1984b, and 1985a.

2.4.1.1 *Structure of subject–verb cohesion*

Example 2:10 is selected as the basis for my structural analysis of subject–verb cohesion as it contains a clearly signaled relation of logic and has no partition of the subject (with *many* or *most*, for example). In the discussion that follows, I have omitted reference to the source clause *he says* as this does not affect the

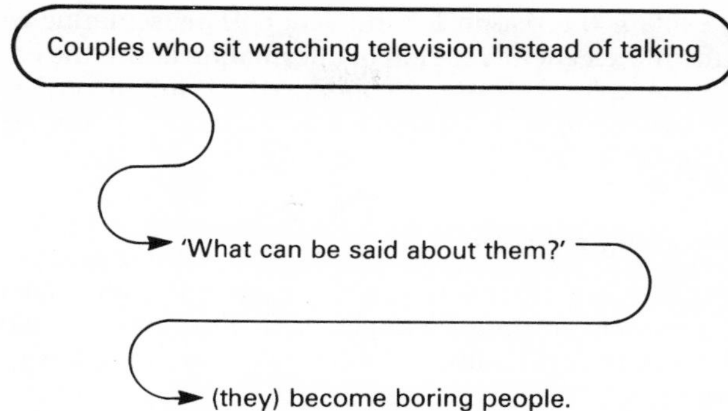

Figure 2.1 Diagram of Connective relationships in 'Couples who sit . . . become boring people.'

structure. Principles illustrated in the description of the basic structure of this relatively simple example can be applied to more complex ones.

The subject of Example 2:10, *Couples who sit watching television instead of talking*, consists of the noun *couples* and a defining relative clause which restricts the subject to certain types of couples. If the sentence had been *Couples who sit watching television instead of talking become boring people*, the relationship between the entire subject and the predicate could be described by the question 'What can be said about them?' mediating between them (see Figure 2.1).

However, to explain subject–predicate relationships in Example 2:10, we need to split the subject into its two parts to show the structure of the sentence. Now two questions are required to describe connective relationships, one about the entire subject and one about the action defining the specific subset of couples (see Figure 2.2).

In Example 2:10, *do so* re-enters the actions of the relative clause into the

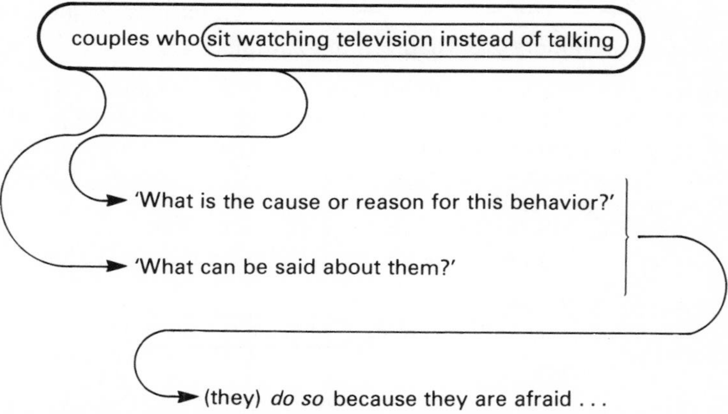

Figure 2.2 Diagram of Connective relationship in example 2:10

predicate to explain the reason for the action. This semantic relation is IN ADDITION to the more general relation of information about the entire subject, and thus the example expresses a condensed 'simultaneous' relation (the simultaneous answering of two questions about separate inputs)—a concept discussed in Jordan 1978.

2.4.2 Nominal group cohesion

Do so and variants are often very closely connected with their referents in coordinated nominal groups. Example 2:15 illustrates cohesion between coordinated subjects and Example 2:16 between coordinated prepositional complements:

(2:15) To meet the requirements of variety and style within the economic framework of substantially shorter production runs, and to *do so* while retaining economic viability, is therefore the nub of the body-builder's problem. [*New Scientist*, 9 October 1975: 87]

(2:16) But many of them are sympathetic towards what we are doing and about our reasons for *doing so*. [*North Hertfordshire Gazette*, 4 March 1976: 20]

The subject of Example 2:15 is quite complex. A to-infinitive nominal *to meet . . . runs* coordinates with the substitute form which includes the first part in the form of the substitute but is modified by the clause of circumstance 'while retaining economic viability.' An illustration clarifies this (see Figure 2.3).

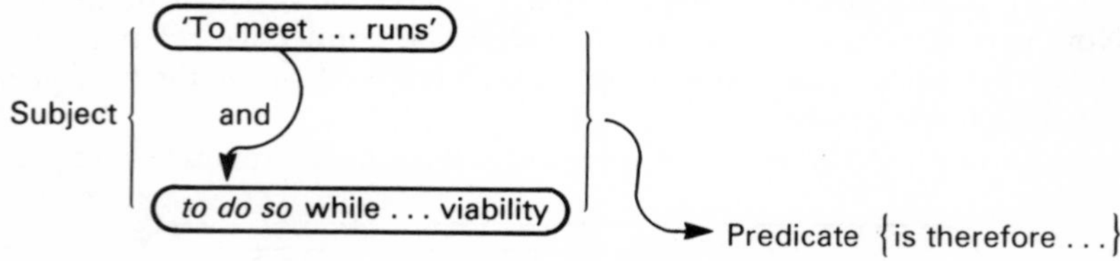

Figure 2.3 Diagram of example 2:15

Example 2:16 is similarly complex, but this time the complication occurs after the main verb. The grammar of the adjective *sympathetic* as predicate of the verb *to be* demands explicit or implicit complementation with prepositions, and in this example, the prepositions *towards* and *about* are used in coordination (see Figure 2.4).

The nominal *our reasons for* DOING SO is an ASSOCIATED NOMINAL with the nominal *what we are doing* as its TRIGGER and with the overt signal *reasons*

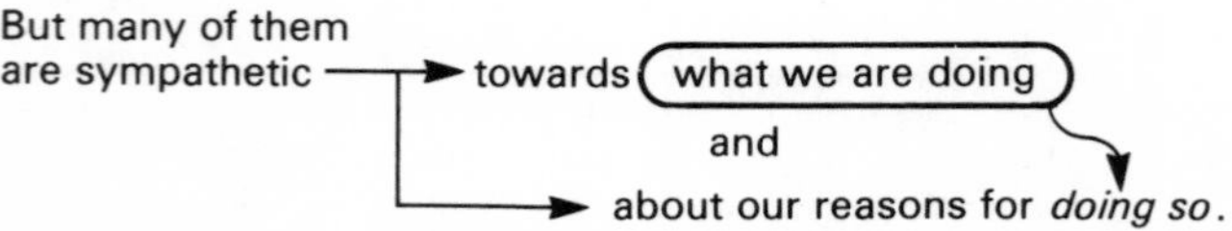

Figure 2.4 Diagram of example 2:16

indicating the relation between the two nominals (as discussed in Winter 1977; and Jordan 1985a). (Associative semantics in texts is further discussed in Hawkins 1978; and Jordan 1981 and 1982; with additional developments in Jordan 1983a, 1983b, 1984a, 1984c, and 1985b.)

2.4.3 Subordinate clause cohesion

Halliday and Hasan's discussion of Example 3:65 claiming that *do so* cannot occur in a subordinate clause when its reference is in the preceding main clause is difficult to reconcile with Example 2:17, remarkably similar to their 3:65:

(2:17) I append the names of two referees to whom I am personally known, and will send you the third as soon as I am authorized to *do so*. [Survey of English Usage, W.7.8.11]

There can be no question here that *do so* in the clause dominated by the subordinator *as soon as* refers to *send you the third* in the preceding main clause—not to anything in the first main clause. Here is another example with three clauses in one sentence, again with the referent for *do so* occurring in the closer of the two preceding clauses:

(2:18) If you have appointed a proxy to vote in person for you, you may nevertheless vote at this election if you *do so* before your proxy has voted on your behalf. [Herts County Council circular 1976]

The referent for *do so* in Example 2:18 is *vote at this election* in the main clause and not *appointed a proxy* in the initial subordinate clause. We know this because 'if you have appointed a proxy before your proxy has voted on your behalf' makes no sense at all. Thus, as with the previous example, we see how real examples enable us to be quite sure about what kinds of reference are acceptable—and again we show Halliday and Hasan's conclusion to be invalid.

Further examples show that even when *do so* is cataphoric, the referent can still be located in the main clause immediately following the subordinate clause:

(2:19) When this statement was prepared your account was not up to date. If you have not already *done so* please remit minimum payment due as indicated below. [Bank of Nova Scotia Chargex 1978]

(2:20) 'If I was allowed to *do so*, I could make the yard into an extremely viable commercial concern taking in business from civilian companies, but obviously military work is our principal task.' [*Daily Telegraph*, 2 June 1976: 8]

In discussing similar examples, Karlsen points out that 'with *do* the general connectors very often refer to the action of a verb in the independent clause: *so* always does' (1959: 169). This view of close cohesion, of course, supports my own observations.

2.4.4 Cohesion by clause coordination

Do so also provides additional cohesion between coordinated clauses. When *do so* occurs in a clause coordinated to another, its referent occurs in the closest clause preceding it and not in one farther away:

(2:21) Some people object to this type of 'cold' analysis, and argue that decisions on safety are usually and necessarily emotional. To compare emotions is impossible, and any attempt to *do so* can lead to argument and even war. [*New Scientist*, 30 October 1975: 275]

(2:22) '[Question]'

'Yes I think the holidaymaker can look after himself but has he the machinery to *do so?*' [Hatfield Polytechnic, A1–094]

In Examples 2:21 and 2:22, the referent is re-entered by *do so* bound within the grammar of the nominals *any attempt to do so* and *the machinery to do so*, which form the subject and object respectively of the coordinated clauses. This observation is explained further in Jordan 1985a, where clauses or whole sentences are shown to be the triggers for associated nominals containing embedded substitute forms.

Example 2:23, an instance of subordinated elliptical coordination with the referent in the first of the two coordinated clauses, illustrates how closely *do so* and its referent can be structured. It also demonstrates how the referent for *do so* can be interpreted clearly as being in the immediately-preceding clause:

(2:23) We hope you will enjoy the meal which has been selected for you based on Canada's Food Guide. This was necessary because we did not receive your menu for today. If you wish to make your own menu but have not yet *done so*, please check with the Nursing Staff. [Kingston General Hospital, Ontario, 1983]

2.5 GENERAL CRITERIA FOR *DO SO* AND COUNTERPARTS

Now that the use of *do so* and variants has been established for several types of close cohesion, we should be tempted to investigate further. Many of the examples of *do so* cited in the previous pages are only suitable for *do so* and not the counterparts *do it*, *do this*, or *do that*. Hence, *do so* must have certain language environments involved with close cohesion that are exclusively reserved for its use, and it should be possible to develop criteria for the use of *do so* as opposed to its counterparts. This chapter does not attempt the rigorous analysis necessary, but instead establishes broad tendencies as a possible basis for further work.

The distinction between *do this* and *do that* has already been discussed in detail in Jordan 1978. The main conclusion is that *do this* is used more for reasoned discussion and when the substitute clause is used purely to re-enter a clause into a new clause without answering a question about the re-entered clause. In contrast, *do that* is used more often in assertive or dogmatic statements and especially when the clause containing it has a relationship to the referent clause (i.e. answers a question about it), for example:

(2:24) The price of getting my son out of jail was recognizing this court and turning my back on the Republican movement. *That* I will not *do*. [*Daily Telegraph*, 26 February 1976: 2]

Unlike *do this*, *do that*, and *do it*, the substitute predicate *do so* is very rarely used in marked forms such as *This I did*; *That is what they are doing*; and *It can be done* (an exception being *So I did*). This should lead us to suggest that *do so* is a polite, reasoning, formal form of use compared with *do that* and, to some extent, *do it*.

The differences among these four main substitute predicates reflect subtle shades of meaning. We can describe these differences from observing the frequencies of occurrence of each type in genres such as advertising, informal speech, or formal documents, but the author's selection of one form or the other in each specific case may be a matter of personal choice or stylistic preference and not a mark of genre. Bolinger acknowledged this kind of limitation in interpreting research results as follows:

> That many of the examples I have given are not sharply delineated is not an argument against them. In the sphere of word choice everything depends on appropriateness to context, and appropriateness comes in degrees. [1972: 71]

While clear cases of choice associated with genre or some other contextual factor can be cited, there will inevitably be instances where the distinctions are blurred and the choice becomes a matter of personal style or preference. Labov (1975) argues for the use of 'clear case' examples to describe the extreme polarities of meaning associated with different word choice, and I have followed this suggestion for the remainder of this chapter in which I demonstrate close cohesion as a criterion for *do so*.

2.5.1 Close cohesion as a criterion for *do so*

2.5.1.1 *Testing the criterion against examples*

We have established *do so* to be suitable in many forms of close cohesion and now seek to demonstrate a more important generalization: that selection of *do so* rather than one of its counterparts provides a nuance of meaning associated with close cohesion. In other words, if in a given context *do this* or another form has a certain referent, the use of *do so* instead will force the interpretation of a closer referent to the substitute clause itself. Let us examine this claim by again testing it against actual use, starting with a highly intriguing example:

(2:25) They cut a slice of cake or make a sandwich before going to watch television, they prepare a snack at mid-morning, they finish up what is in the serving dishes without really being aware of *doing so*. [*Slim and Beauty*, June 1976: 11]

The referent for *doing so* in Example 2:25 is unclear. Our understanding of *do so* with subordinate clauses would initially make us think that the referent is only the preceding clause. Note, however, that the writer chose not to include an *and* immediately before this clause, and this unusual deletion could be interpreted as an attempt—and a not altogether successful one—to widen the referent of *do so* to include all three main clauses in the sentence. Use of the embracing *all* as in —*all without really being aware* would have worked, but a clearer way to include the wider referent would be: *They cut a slice of cake or make a sandwich before going to watch television, they prepare a snack at mid-morning, and they finish up what is in the serving dishes. And they* DO THIS *without really being aware of it*. The orthographic sentence break and the use of *do this* clarifies the reference. But would *do so* have worked in this context?

Even when *do so* is not in close syntactic association with its referent, it forces a potentially tighter control over the referent than does *do this* in similar contexts. An attempt to substitute *done this* for *done so* in Example 2:26 illustrates this point:

(2:26) However, two teaspoons of honey next evening produced five hours of oblivion and, finally, on the following night, after 'chewing' two spoonfuls and gulping down a third (it seems feasible that one dose 'swallowed whole' would be digested more slowly and with lasting effect), I slept for nine, dreamless, untroubled hours. And with two exceptions, have *done so* every subsequent night. [*Here's Health*, April 1976: 48–9]

In Example 2:26, inter-sentential coordination with *and*, ellipsis of *I*, and use of *done so* all make the referent the last clause only. Use of *with two exceptions I have* DONE THIS *every subsequent night* would have led the reader more clearly to refer to all of the non-parenthetical text starting with *finally*.

The potentially wide referential power of *this* as sole nominal head is demonstrated with scores of examples in Jordan 1978. I present two examples here to illustrate the wide reference of *do this* compared to *do so*. The first example:

(2:27) I regularly go to a gym and do weight training, paying special attention to my waist and hips. After training I take some vitamin pills (Vitamins A, B, C, D, E) and Casilan added to two pints of milk. I have been *doing this* for nearly two months. . . . [*Here's Health*, May 1976: 97]

Example 2:27 shows that the clause *doing this* can refer to two previous sentences; the form *and have been doing so* in the same sentence would have referred to the closest one only. It would do so because of the inherently close cohesive nature of *do so*. Another example:

(2:28) My spirits improved when I got on the motorway, however. Here I was on the open road to freedom, excitement, life! I turned on the car radio and hummed along with the music. I passed a big lorry. The driver waved at me. I smiled back, feeling young and free and attractive. I should have *done this* years ago. [*True Story* (UK), October 1975: 50]

The referent in Example 2:28 is the whole situation of the narrator running from her husband and children which is detailed in several paragraphs besides this. One of the features of *this* is its ability to refer to such general concepts and whole situations. In Example 2:28, *this* obviously does not refer only to the incident with the truck driver. The converse would be true for *I smiled back, feeling young and free and attractive as I did so* where the referent would be *smiled back*. Further, it would not be possible to use *done so* and achieve the wider reference of *done this*; *did this* in the rewritten version would sound rather strange in comparison with *did so*.

A more definitive treatment of the cohesive differences between *do so* and *do this* would have to include ELICITATION EXPERIMENTS—investigations where native users of the language are asked to provide assessments of examples given to them (see Section 2.5.1.2). However, our previous analyses seem to justify an initial claim of connection between *do so* and close cohesion that cannot be made for *do this*.

Let us now examine *do so* as it compares with *do it*. Unlike *do this*, *do it* can create very close cohesion

(2:29) You learn acting by *doing it*. [*Romance*, February 1976: 7]

or can have quite a remote referent

(2:30) Please write and tell me your 'funnies', even if it was one of those 'asides' made by the woman sitting next to you. Postage will be refunded on request and please—only the name of your federation—not the speaker or Institute. Come on, don't think about it. *Do it* now—and if we can get it published we can all enjoy a jolly good giggle. [*Home and Country*, April 1976: 125]

The referent in Example 2:30 is separated from its re-entry *do it* by two whole sentences. Where the referent is close, *do so* and *do it* will compete, and *do so* will be interpreted as more formal than *do it*:

(2:31) Also, if you have a few key trustworthy friends or associates you can ask about the company, you should *do so*. [*Ontario Engineering Digest*, February 1978: 16]

(2:32) We return the draft transfer which we approve, as amended in red, and you will note that we propose to ask the directors of the company to execute the document in the usual way. The directors have already verbally agreed to *do so*. [Survey of English Usage, W.7.11.62]

Do it is used more informally than *do so*, especially when the referent is exophoric (not included in the text):

(2:33) 'Why don't you send me your hints on how to *do it* for yourself' [CKWS Television, Canada, 24 October 1983]

(2:34) '*Doing It* in Style' [title of an article, *Stimulus*, Newsletter of the Society for Technical Communication, Eastern Ontario, October 1983: 2]

The examples I have cited in comparing uses of *do so* with *do this* and *do it* seem to suggest that many environments of close cohesion are quite specifically suitable for *do so*. However, this approach has its limitations. We can PROVE to a high degree of certainty that *do so* occurs in many different environments of close cohesion, but the degree of certainty is less when we try to establish the tendency for *do so* to take on a closer referent or the relative referential power of *do so* compared with *do this* or the levels of formality of a specific use.

The reason for the lower degree of certainty with these latter claims is that different people use the language in slightly different ways (known as their IDIOLECTS), and we must expect to find 'contradictory' examples where idiolectic differences are possible. A linguist's idiolect, of course, must not be allowed to affect the judgment of the language use and this is a further argument against using made-up examples as a basis for research: the linguist is apt to make up examples in his or her own idiolect and remain blissfully unaware of 'real use' examples which run contrary to the conclusions reached.

To conduct research into the idiolectic preferences of a language, the linguist can conduct an elicitation experiment. Quite simply this means asking native users of the language what the referent is or which is more formal or which they would prefer in a given example. Of course, accurate judgments can only be made if the respondents are given adequate contexts, including the purpose and readership of the text, but determining syntactic acceptability by elicitation may not require this. Describing the principles of elicitation research is beyond the scope of this chapter, and the method is thoroughly discussed in Greenbaum and Quirk 1970. An elicitation experiment with *do so* has been documented, however, and a brief discussion of this is relevant here.

2.5.1.2 *Testing the criterion with an elicitation experiment*

As I have indicated before, the aim of my experimental analysis of *do so* is to demonstrate that theories about language structure should be based upon observations of actual language use, and not made-up examples of probable usage. Parameters for conducting experimental research to investigate language use likewise should be derived empirically. For instance, in conducting an elicitation experiment to test the use of *do so* as opposed to other variant forms, it seems logical that one would collect samples of actual language use with *do so*, substitute the variant forms, and ask native speakers which usage they prefer and what the referent for the substitute forms appears to be in each case. In short, the elicitation experiment as an examination of actual language use should begin with a hypothesis gleaned from actual observation. Unfortunately, the only elicitation experiment conducted thus far to investigate uses of *do so* has not been constructed in this recommended way.

Michiels (1977) asked twenty-two informants for their judgment of the referents for eighteen made-up examples of comparing *do so* with variant forms presented orally using a prepared script with standard stress and intonation patterns (see Crystal and Quirk 1964). Most of the responses produced clear (but rarely unanimous) judgments that suggested reasonably clear conclusions.

The aim of this experiment was to compare *do so* with *do so too*. In an attempt to verify the work, I sought real examples of *do so too* in the extremely large corpus of the Survey of English Usage—the scholarly project of which this small experiment was a part. I failed to find a single example in the survey and in years of subsequent unstructured searching. However, there are many examples of *so did* in the survey; I shall record one here:

(2:35) After Mass, the 66-year-old Pontiff spoke to the convicts. Wardens and prisoners wept during his speech. *So did* the Pope. [Survey of English Usage, 8fa.2.27]

Presumably a possible variant of Example 2:35 is: *The pope did so too*. But this is probably a rare marked (emphatic) form. The occurrence of *did so too* in a special structure (as highlighted in Michiels's study) must be many more times unlikely.

Elicitation experiments can be valuable tools for verifying linguistic hypotheses; however, a useful elicitation experiment testing the usage of a linguistic feature such as *do so* must reflect hypotheses suggested by samples from a set of real data.

2.6 CONCLUSION

Clearly much more work remains before we can fully understand the use of substitute clauses in English and the re-entry of clauses and sentences with overt signaling or implicit connection. Efforts to understand these uses in combination with efforts to describe all systems of lexical cohesion between clauses and sentences are central to our understanding of cohesion in English.

This study has examined but one small aspect of language use that reveals how language features support cohesion. My examples collected from actual language use in speech and writing show that, contrary to Halliday and Hasan's theoretical claim, *do so* occurs freely in many forms of close cohesion within a sentence. Some 'clear case' examples in my corpus also indicate that *do so* functions differently than its counterparts *do this*, *do that*, and *do it* in that it provides a nuance of meaning associated with close cohesion.

The emphasis in my analysis has been predominantly on *do so* with close cohesion within the sentence. This might give the impression that *do so* only occurs in such environments. In fact, *do so* occurs frequently with its referent in the preceding sentence, and further study is needed to explain its referential affinities both within and between sentences. Works by Crymes (1968) and Quirk *et al.* (1972) identify certain groups or types of verbs for which *do so* can and cannot substitute. Their scholarship must be validated by further study based on many examples of actual use. As with my study, analyses of verbal criteria for *do so* must be compared with overlapping criteria for *do it*, *do this*, and *do that*.

My linguistic 'experiment' with *do so* not only attempted to verify (or in this case reject) a previous finding but also to demonstrate an experimental technique. My analysis shows how language can be treated like any natural phenomenon and how the claim that linguistics is a 'science' can be taken quite literally in many respects, despite the fact that some aspects of language vary depending on the personal preference of speakers and writers, on subtle shades of meaning, on levels of formality, and other factors. A great deal of information about language use is definitively determinable through structural analysis of actual samples. Elicitation experiments are one way of obtaining reliable data on matters of preference, particularly if they are designed around a corpus of real examples.

Linguistics is the scientific investigation of a human phenomenon. While theory of language use will naturally go beyond what we can empirically test, I believe that any theory that cannot stand up to empirical validation is of little use to our efforts as 'human scientists' to better understand language.

I will close with the following analogy: when Galileo used the primary data of telescopic observations to show the moons of Jupiter, followers of Aristotle refused even to look through the instrument, claiming that Galileo's conclusions had to be wrong because they were inconsistent with Aristotle's treatise on the subject. Galileo countered by saying that any general theory has to be consistent with demonstrable conclusions based on primary data, not the other way around. I believe that scholars investigating the functions of language should do so with that same caveat firmly in place.

NOTES

1. Yngve (1982) is uncomprising on this point, noting that 'any attempted compromise' a researcher might suggest when a theory about language does not support actual observation of what people do with language 'is doomed to incoherence.'
2. Symbols indicating intonation in the original have been omitted.
3. Italics are added to *do so* and substitute forms in quoted examples to assist the reader. Indentation indicates a paragraph start and a solidus (/) indicates a paragraph end in the originals.

BIBLIOGRAPHY

Allen, R. L. (1966), *The Verb System of Present-Day American English*, Janua Linguarum, Series Practica 24, The Hague, Mouton.

Bolinger, D. (1972), *That's That*, Janua Linguarum, Series Minor 155, The Hague, Mouton.

Chomsky, N. (1957), *Syntactic Structures*, Janua Linguarum, Series Minor 4, 's- Gravenhage, Mouton.

Chomsky, N. (1965), *Aspects of the Theory of Syntax*, Cambridge, Mass., MIT Press.

Crymes, R. (1968), *Some Systems of Substitution Correlations in Modern American English*, Janua Linguarum, Series Minor 39, The Hague, Mouton.

Crystal, D. and Quirk, R. (1964), *Systems of Prosodic and Paralinguistic Features in English*, The Hague, Mouton.

Greenbaum, S. and Quirk, R. (1970), *Elicitation Experiments in English: Linguistic Studies in Use and Attitude*, London, Longmans.

Halliday, M. A. K. and Hasan, R. (1976), *Cohesion in English*, London, Longman.

Harris, Z. S. (1952), 'Discourse Analysis,' *Language*, **28**, 1–30.

Hawkins, J. A. (1978), *Definiteness and Indefiniteness: A Study in Reference and Grammaticality Predication*, London, Croom Helm: Atlantic Highlands, N.J., Humanities Press.

Hoey, M. (1983), *On the Surface of Discourse*, London, Boston, Allen and Unwin.

Huddleston, R. D. (1971), *The Sentence in Written English: A Syntactic Study Based on an Analysis of Written Texts*, Cambridge, at the University Press.

Huddleston, R. D., Hudson, R. A., Winter, E. O., and Henrici, A. (1968), *Sentence and Clause in Scientific English*, London, Communication Research Centre, University College.

Jordan, M. P. (1978), *The Principal Semantics of the Nominals 'This' and 'That' in Contemporary English Writing*, Ph.D. dissertation, London, Hatfield Polytechnic (see *Dissertation Abstracts International*, sec. C, Summer 1978, **38**, 533).

Jordan, M. P. (1981), 'Some Associated Nominals in Technical Writing,' *Journal of Technical Writing and Communication*, **11**, 251–64.

Jordan, M. P. (1982), 'The Thread of Continuity in Functional Writing,' *The Journal of Business Communication*, No. 4 (**19**), 5–22.

Jordan, M. P. (1983a), 'Co-associative Cohesion in English Texts,' *Technostyle*, No. 2 (**2**), 5–12.

Jordan, M. P., 'Complex Lexical Cohesion in the English Clause and Sentence,' in Manning, A., Martin, P., and McCalla, K. (eds) (1983b: 224–34), *The Tenth LACUS Forum*, Columbia, S.C., Hornbeam Press.

Jordan, M. P. (1984a), *Fundamentals of Technical Description*, Malabar, Fla., R. E. Krieger.

Jordan, M. P. (1984b), *Rhetoric of Everyday English Texts*, London, Boston, Allen and Unwin.

Jordan, M. P. (1984c), 'Structure, Style and Word Choice in Everyday English Texts,' *TESL Talk*, Nos. 1 and 2 (**15**), 60–7.

Jordan, M. P. (1985a), *Fundamentals of Technical Prose*, Malabar, Fla., R. E. Krieger.

Jordan, M. P., 'Non-Thematic Re-Entry: An Introduction to and Extension of the System of Nominal Group Reference/Substitution in Everyday English Use,' in Benson, J. D. and Greaves, W. S. (eds) (1985b: 322–32), *Systemic Perspectives on Discourse 1: Selected Theoretical Papers from the 9th International Systemic Workshop*, Advances in Discourse Processes 15, Norwood, N.J., Ablex.

Karlsen, R. (1959), *Studies in the Connection of Clauses in Current English: Zero, Ellipsis, and Explicit Form*, Skrifter fra Norges Handelshøyskole i rekken spratlige avhandlinger 8, Bergen, J. W. Eides.

Karlsen, R. (1965), *On 'Identifying,' 'Classifying' and 'Specifying' Clauses in Current English*, Årbok for Universitetet i Bergen, Humanistisk Serie, 1964, 4, Bergen, Norwegian Universities Press.

Labov, W. (1975), *What is a Linguistic Fact?*, Peter de Ridder Press Publications in Linguistic Theory 1, Lisse, The Netherlands, Peter de Ridder.

Lees, R. B. (1960), *The Grammar of English Nominalizations*, Research Center in Anthropology, Folklore and Linguistics 12, Bloomington, Ind., Indiana University Press.

Lyons, J. (1968), *Introduction to Theoretical Linguistics*, Cambridge, at the University Press.

Michiels, A. (1977), 'More on *Do so* and Verb Phrase Substitution,' *Études Anglaises*, **30**, 57–8.

Quirk, R., Greenbaum, S., Leech, G., and Svartvik, J. (1972), *A Grammar of Contemporary English*, London, Longman.

Roberts, P., 'Pronominal *This*—A Quantitative Analysis,' in Allen, H. B. (ed.) (1958: 267–75), *Readings in Applied English Linguistics*, New York, Appleton, Century, Crofts.

Winter, E. O. (1974), *Replacement as a Function of Repetition: A Study of Some of its Principal Features in the Clause Relations of Contemporary English*, Ph.D. dissertation, London, University of London (see *Dissertation Abstracts International*, sec. C, Autumn 1977, **38**, 4).

Winter, E. O. (1977), 'A Clause-Relational Approach to English Texts: A Study of Some Predictive Lexical Items in Written Discourse,' *Instructional Science* (special issue), **6**, 1–92.

Winter, E. O. (1982), *Towards a Contextual Grammar of English: The Clause and Its Place in the Definition of Sentence*, London, Boston, Allen and Unwin.

Yngve, V. H., 'Bloomfield's Fundamental Assumption of Linguistics,' in Morreall, J. (ed.) (1982: 137–45), *The Ninth LACUS Forum*, Columbia, S.C., Hornbeam Press.

3 Thematic distribution as a heuristic for written discourse function

Mary Ann Eiler
American Medical Association

3.1 THEME AND DISCOURSE GENRE

Writers and readers depend upon many linguistic signals to convey and redeem meaning in texts—signals that work systematically because language itself is a text-generating system that provides for semantic, syntactic, and rhetorical choice. Writers select from these options, given the genre constraints of their work, and readers interpret them in the light of conventional uses. We all know this intuitively or abstractly, but how can we capture as much analytically and empirically? How can we make heuristic generalizations regarding text design that in fact reflect actual writers' choices?

One approach is to make case studies of texts, observing writers' products as specific incidents of linguistic choice and correlating such choice with use and function. For this study, I have examined a particular variety of text—a lecture-chapter on physics—in order to demonstrate that its discourse functions can be identified by patterns of linguistic choice. My analysis shows that genre is realized within the linguistic system that governs text formation itself—language's textual component. In fact, an analysis of THEMATIC CHOICE and DISTRIBUTION—one aspect of the textual component as realized in the features of a specific text—can reveal heuristic structures defining a genre. To demonstrate this claim, I will explain how thematic choice and distribution express genre through a discussion of the characteristics of a particular text that I will examine in detail. At the same time, I will outline some procedures that should govern a researcher's approach to a study of this kind.

3.2 SELECTION OF A TEXT FOR THEMATIC ANALYSIS

The text I selected for analysis is a lecture-chapter from *The Feynman Lectures on Physics: Mainly Mechanics, Radiation, and Heat*. Professor Feynman, together with several collaborators, wrote this book, the first of a three-volume set, for first- and second-year students at the California Institute of Technology. The genesis of the text included: preparation and delivery of lectures by Professor

Feynman, a tape recording and transcription, and a final editing to make the lecture suitable for a textbook. In the 'Foreword,' we learn that what was initially considered a 'minor' undertaking became a major task: 'It was, in fact, a major editorial operation to transform the verbatim transcript into readable form, even without the reorganization or revision of the subject matter that was sometimes required.' The selection discussed here, 'Chapter 37. Quantum Behavior,' displays a most interesting variety of spoken and written registers in conveying scientific information. My analysis sought to capture primarily the inter-register dimensions of 'language in action' versus 'formalized written event.' The editors of the Feynman lectures themselves appeared sensitive to these dimensions remarking, 'We have no illusions as to the completeness, smoothness, or logical organization of the material . . .,' and observing that although the task of writing up the spoken material was originally assigned to part-time graduate students, 'it was not a job for a technical editor or for a graduate student, but one that required the close attention of a professional physicist for from ten to twenty hours per lecture!' (Feynman *et al.* 1963: 7, 8).

My study shows that this written translation of a spoken lecture is DEFINED as a text of this type through the linguistic realization of thematic choice.

3.3 DISTINCTIONS IN THEMATIC CHOICE

Central to both a working and a theoretical definition of THEME is a view of the clause as a domain of both syntactic choice and the components of message that comprise the possibility of choice. Theme, in this general and largest sense, as Halliday explains, is concerned not only with 'what is being said' but with 'what has gone before in the discourse' (1967: 199).

Some confusion regarding the definition of 'theme' derives from a need to distinguish between two separate but related understandings of the term, not only within Halliday's systemic grammar, but also in rival linguistic theories. In systemic grammar, 'theme' is both the general name for an array of syntactic functions or roles and the more specific name for the information focus of the clause. 'Thematization,' on the other hand, refers to the sequence of elements in the clause. Theme plays a role in thematization because it occupies the first position of a clause, thus influencing information distribution. The theme 'is what is being talked about, the point of departure for the clause as a message; and the speaker has within certain limits the option of selecting any element in the clause as thematic' (Halliday 1967: 212).

A second source for potential confusion in defining theme stems from two rival linguistic approaches to it. Fries (1983) identifies these approaches as the 'combining approach' and the 'separating approach.' In the combining approach, derived largely from Mathesius (1939), the theme of a sentence identifies both known or given information and the 'information from which the speaker proceeds.' In the separating approach, however, 'given' information and 'the information from which the speaker proceeds in discourse' are viewed as separate entities. Further, the combining approach asserts that theme can occur in various places in the clause (or a clause may not have theme) while the separating approach asserts that 'the theme of the clause is realized by the initial clause level constituent of that clause' (Fries 1983: 116–17).

Advocates of the separating approach admit that while theme can be associated with the 'given,' the two are essentially separate options. Rather than conflate or equate these constituents, Halliday, for instance, approaches a spoken English text as 'structured simultaneously on the two dimensions of given–new and theme–rheme, the former determining its organization into discourse units and . . . the latter starting from its organization in sentence structure and framing each clause into the form of a message about one of its constituents. . . .' (1967: 223).

Analysis of theme in this study treats theme in its distinct role 'as information from which the speaker proceeds.' Theme, in this sense, is essentially the element that is realized by first position in the clause and that serves 'as the communicative point of departure for the rest of the clause' (Quirk *et al*. 1972: 945). In analyzing the lecture-chapter, I considered three dimensions of theme as the 'communicative point of departure for the rest of the clause': MARKED and UNMARKED THEME, CLINED versus FIXED THEME, and COMPLEX THEME ENVIRONMENTS.

3.3.1 Marked and unmarked theme

Marked theme is realized in the foregrounding or fronting of clause elements such as initial complements or adjuncts that would normally not occur in the first position: MY DOLL *I'd hug anytime* (versus my cat); BEFORE GOING TO BED, *she hugged her doll*. The degree of markedness, however, raises questions regarding the scope of thematic position and has motivated theoretical disputes within systemic linguistics.

Unmarked theme status, conversely, signifies the expected or 'natural occurrence' of theme as predicated on the mood of a clause. In a declarative clause, for example, the subject constitutes unmarked theme: *The little girl hugged her doll*. In an interrogative clause like *Did the little girl hug her doll*? the fronted auxiliary *do* expresses unmarked theme. Similarly, the WH- element expresses unmarked theme in WH- questions: *What did the little girl hug*?

Though the differences between marked and unmarked theme appear clear conceptually, scholars disagree as to whether marked theme should include all fronted features other than those defined above as unmarked. Quirk *et al*. viewed the inclusion of fronted adverbials, for instance, as incompatible with what they called 'a unitary concept of theme.' Their argument is that adverbials, primarily disjuncts and conjuncts, usually appear in the first position and hence should be considered unmarked. This, however, 'would mean overruling the unmarked status of other elements (e.g., initial subject in statements) or alternatively acknowledging the possibility of two co-existing thematic elements in the same clause.' In a sentence like *Often in the summer we would go boating*, they argue, the occurrence of more than one adverbial in the fronted position further demonstrates 'that regarding initial adverbials as thematic is incompatible with a unitary concept of theme.' They concede that certain adjuncts, like place adjuncts, are so closely bound to post-verbal position that in thematic fronting they 'behave . . . more like complements or objects than like disjuncts or conjuncts.' They cite the following:

(i) *Into the thick of the smoke* we plunged [italics in original]
(ii) *Into the thick of the smoke* plunged the intrepid cavalry [italics in original]

and explain that 'the "complementary" status of these adjuncts is shown by their association with subject–verb inversion when the subject is a noun phrase heavier than a pronoun.' While conceding that 'certain adjuncts, especially those which would otherwise immediately follow an intransitive or intensive verb, may be treated as "marked theme" when placed initially,' Quirk *et al*. conclude that initial adverbials in general should not qualify for thematic status in the clause (1972: 947–8).

In this study, I examine all features occupying the first position; I coded MARKEDNESS, but considered it in my analysis only when it distinguished the genre. The latter consideration led me to reject the position of Quirk *et al*. that initial adverbials should not qualify for marked thematic status.

3.3.2 Clined versus fixed theme

Another concern in analyzing theme is determining which elements should be included as occupying the first or thematic position in a sentence. Again, scholars differ on this issue.

Muir claims that 'binding adjuncts' like *if* and *because* and 'linkers' like *and* and *or* are 'fixed in position and . . . not relevant to the theme system' since their position does not result from choice (1972: 97). Halliday (1973), conversely, maximizes thematic choice through his notion of gradience or CLINE from what must come first to what most or least probably comes first. In all cases, theme remains a meaningful choice. The theme of an *if* clause is its CONDITIONALITY just as the theme of clauses beginning with relating elements or conjunctions like *and*, *but*, *or*, and *nor* indicate ADDITION, CONTRAST, SELECTION, and EXCLUSION, respectively.

Fries also focuses on first position, but expands possibilities for thematic status: 'For something to carry meaning . . . it must be the result of choice . . . [;] if a word or phrase is required to appear first in its clause it will be considered to be thematic . . .,' but it will not exhaust the theme of that clause (1983: 119). He agrees with Halliday that the theme–rheme distinction can apply to various grammatical levels.

To view theme as relevant at different grammatical levels allows one to examine theme distribution in connected discourse—the direction that my study takes. Like Fries, I have investigated how theme at sentence level 'forms part of a larger pattern which governs the flow of information in any English discourse' (1983: 144). Also following Fries's approach, I have examined how theme is extended to segments other than those in fixed first position, depending upon the element of choice in placing a feature first. Fries notes that some connectors are only weakly thematic; consider, for instance, *but* as an initial element compared to *however*:

> . . . if a clause begins with the word *but*, the thematic status of *but* in that clause will be weak, since it can only occur initially in its clause. *But* will be considered thematic within its clause, however, since the idea expressed by *but* could be expressed by other words which are not required to occur initially within the clause (e.g., *however*). [1983: 119]

The following two sentences discovered in my own research on classroom writing about literature demonstrate invariant and variant positions and also support the extended theme position:

(i) Montresor knew of Fortunato's pride, so he kept comparing him to his competitor, Luchesi.
(ii) Montresor knew of Fortunato's pride; therefore, he kept comparing him to his competitor, Luchesi.

So, in the first sentence, is weakly thematic because of its fixed position, thus extending the thematic position to *he*. *Therefore* in the second sentence is strongly thematic because of its variant position (see Eiler 1979).

3.3.3 Complex theme environments

Thus far we have considered issues of thematic position and grammatical categories as they affect an analysis of theme; we must also consider semantic function. If thematic position can be occupied by more than one element, it can also control multiple functions. Such possibilities have led some scholars to distinguish SIMPLE and COMPLEX themes. Halliday observes that thematic position may be occupied by 'more than one adjunct' and gives examples where thematic function may be interpreted as consisting of single clause elements (simple theme), or conversely, extending to two or more elements (complex theme). A thematic element like *yesterday before dinner* constitutes simple theme while *in Sheffield the other day* demonstrates complex theme (Halliday 1967: 219).

We can make further distinctions between simple and complex themes. The following sentence has a complex theme: *For three years with every ounce of his strength he struggled against the disease*. In this sentence, two functions correlate with thematic position. *For three years* designates TIME. *With every ounce of his strength*, however, indicates MANNER. Neither time nor manner alone exhausts the semantic field of theme here. Yet in this next example, elements in thematic position signal only one discourse function, namely that of time: *Next Wednesday before two o'clock . . .* Such expansion within one function constitutes simple rather than complex theme.

Thematic functional diversity may spread between and among clause elements. Consider the following: *Later, however, in the beginning of the 19th century, poetry again reflected a classical interest*. Although *later* and *in the beginning of the 19th century* have the same function of time, *however* functions as a concessive conjunct here. Thus, *Later, however, in the beginning of the 19th century* comprises a complex theme environment.

The analysis of thematic distribution remains a complicated undertaking despite the above distinctions. For example, thematic inter-relationships and variations can exist within a function and, when so occurring, demonstrate considerable linguistic delicacy (see Bernhardt in this volume for a discussion of delicacy in systemic grammar [ed.]). In the sentence *Often in summer we would go boating*, we find an example of this delicacy in that *often* conveys temporal duration while *in summer* connotes time as well as seasonal location. For this study, however, I did not make such delicate distinctions within a function; that is to say, I considered fronted groups like *often in summer* to comprise simple theme.

3.4 METHOD OF ANALYSIS

In my study of the lecture-chapter, I explored the functions that the themes in this discourse expressed, the relationship between particular types of function and thematic patterns of distribution, and the tendency of certain types of theme to cluster in given components of a text. In selecting a methodology to analyze theme in the lecture-chapter, my intention was not to establish an exhaustive linguistic conceptualization of theme. Rather I sought to distinguish just three things: which elements are in the initial position at the sentence level as a result of choice; how choice of elements serves as the communicative point of departure for the rest of the sentence; and how the distribution and semantic function of thematic elements in this text suggest a heuristic for its discourse genre. To these ends, I incorporated the more 'elastic' interpretations of theme advanced by Halliday and Fries in the following analytic procedures:

- All sentence level themes were analyzed and coded.
- Independent clauses were treated as separate sentences:
  - (a) Fixed conjunctions like *and*, *but*, *or*, *nor*, *yet* were coded as weakly thematic, as were fixed conjuncts like *so*.
  - (b) Elements following fixed conjunctions or other positionally fixed elements were included as more strongly thematic.
- Fronted dependent clauses were treated holistically as thematic units for the larger sentence.
- Fronted non-finite clauses (e.g. infinitive), groups (e.g. prepositional), and word level elements were also coded regardless of their rank level since rank is not a determinant of function. (Rank in systemic grammar refers to positioning grammatical units on a rank scale according to their size. A typical rank scale from largest to smallest in English is: sentence, clause, group , word, morpheme [Berry 1976: 7].)
- Nominalizations as theme and sentences having existential subjects, anticipatory *it*, and other special features were included.
- Complex theme environments were identified according to the functions represented. (Parentheticals occurring in intra-clause environments were not interpreted as constituting complex theme and thus were excluded

from analysis. An example from the sample text is *for instance* in the following: *If we find, for instance, that an electron . . .*)

- Marked and unmarked themes were coded but commented upon in the analysis only if they seemingly contributed to a discovery or understanding of genre.
- Incomplete sentences or fragments were treated in a variety of ways. If the incompletion involved ellipsis of only one element (e.g. subject or verb), the incompletion was treated as a separate sentence. If the incompletion could not be supplied readily through expression of the elliptical item, the incompletion was combined with the appropriate preceding or following sentence. If the expression represented a 'false start' or an aborted sentence, it was excluded.
- Eight occurrences of exclamations, quasi-exclamatory comments, and interjections like *so much for water waves, so much for bullets, now for our summary, but no!, aha!, yes!*, and *so!* were not conducive to thematic coding and excluded from analysis. Eight interrogatives were also excluded from analysis.[1]

Table 3.1 Thematic distribution in chapter on quantum behavior

Thematic element	Total	Percent of thematic distribution
Nominal and pronominal subjects (excluding first- and second-person pronouns)	142	26.4
First- and second-person pronouns*	122	22.7
Nominalizations	8	1.5
Fixed elements		
—coordinators and conjuncts	81	15.1
—Initiators	4	0.7
Variable conjuncts	20	3.7
Disjuncts	22	4.1
Adjuncts		
—*When* clause	18	3.3
—Other time adjuncts	17	3.2
—Adjuncts excl. time	56	10.4
—Conditional clause	29	5.4
Anticipatory *It*	11	2.0
Existential subject	8	1.5
All categories	538	100.0

* Includes imperatives.

Table 3.1 presents the distribution of thematic elements by type in absolute counts and percent distributions for the chapter. Although distribution can indicate the relevance of a feature in determining the genre, only when coupled with an analysis of the discourse function and content can we draw conclusions about heuristic value.

The following sections present a detailed analysis of each thematic type in Table 3.1 along with my interpretations regarding each category's heuristic value in determining the genre of the lecture-chapter. In addition, I draw conclusions about directions for future research on thematic distribution as an indicator of genre.

3.5 MAJOR FINDINGS

3.5.1 Nominal and pronominal subject as theme (excluding first and second pronouns)

Over a quarter (26.4 percent) of all thematic positions in the lecture-chapter are held by nominal and pronominal subjects (excluding first and second pronouns). Nouns and pronouns account for the majority (79.4 percent) of the 142 items in this category. Included in this latter group are general nouns or pronouns (e.g. *things, no one, anything, all, some*), content-specific nouns (e.g. *quantum behavior, quantum mechanics, Newton*), anaphoric, cataphoric, and deictic pronouns (e.g. *they, it, this, that*), and noun headwords with modifiers (e.g. *a bullet which happens to hit one of the holes, every electron, the intensity of the new wave*). If we include headwords after weakly thematic fixed positions, such as *things* after *but* in *but things on a small scale just do not act that way*, we find an additional twenty-nine items for the total of 142 nominal or pronominal subjects as theme.

Our first category for analysis is predictably the least interesting in establishing a textual heuristic for the lecture-chapter: subject headwords have unmarked thematic status and 'natural' occurrence in declarative English syntax. If, however, the thematic occurrence of these features were to be studied more delicately for lexical semantic relations and cohesive patterns, patterns which distinguish text genre might emerge. This analysis remains for future study.

3.5.2 First- and second-person pronouns as theme

First- and second-person pronouns as theme account for just under a quarter (22.7 percent) of the items in our thematic distribution. Pronominal *we*, including instances after fixed elements, occupies eighty-nine of the 122 thematic positions for 16.5 percent of the total thematic distribution. If we consider reader (audience) or speaker (author) involvement as displayed in the use of the imperative, we find twelve thematic instances, ten involving the pronoun *us* (e.g. *Let us*) and two implying *you* (e.g. *Notice!*), bringing the count of first- and second-person pronouns occupying thematic positions to

111. Eight occurrences of thematic *you* and three instances of imperatives after weakly thematic coordinators complete the total of 122 first- and second-person pronoun thematic positions.

The frequency of first and second pronouns is a prominent determinant for the genre the lecture-chapter represents. *We* occurs both in the sense of an editorial *we* and as a bonding of author and reader in a joint enterprise, which, in the case of the lecture-chapter, is the learning experience or the transmittal of information.

In *A Grammar of Contemporary English*, Quirk *et al*. elaborate on the special uses of pronominal *we*. The editorial *we* may be used by a single individual, such as a lecturer, as in *As we showed a moment ago* instead of *As I showed a moment ago*. In such cases, the *we* is preferred in an effort to avoid *I*, 'which is felt to be a little egotistic.' In still another use of *we* (e.g. *as we saw in Chapter 3*), the first-person pronoun is a replacement of *you*, which, the authors explain, 'is felt to be too authoritative.' In such cases, *we* seeks to identify the writer and the reader as involved in a joint enterprise. As examples, the authors suggest *We now turn to a different problem* as compared with *Let's turn to a different problem* which suggests the absent subject *you* (i.e. *you let us turn* . . .) (Quirk *et al*. 1972: 208). Examples of the latter type do occur in the lecture-chapter but not with the frequency of the non-imperatives.

3.5.3 Nominalizations as theme

Only eight nominalizations occur in the lecture-chapter and this is hardly an argument that nominalization in itself be included as a heuristic feature for texts of this type. However, of the eight instances, seven are identification clauses, that is, clauses 'organized into . . ."cleft sentence[s]" with equative form' (Halliday 1967: 223). And if we examine these seven nominalizations further, we note that, in six cases, the participant is expressed through the first-person plural pronoun *we*. Section 3.5.2 above explains how pronominal *we* contributes to the interpersonal role relations of instructor/student in the lecture-chapter.

In his observations on identification clauses, Halliday suggests that they are characteristic of spoken texts:

> This is a highly favored clause type in modern English, not least in informal conversation. Where the non-identifying clause specifies a process and its participants, the identifying clause adds the further information that one of the participants is definable by participation in the process: in *what John saw was the play*, 'the play (and nothing else)' is the exclusive goal of John's perception, as far as the communication situation is concerned. [1967: 224]

In the sentences from the lecture-chapter containing fronted identification classes, nominalizations and GOALS include the following:[2]

(3:1) *What we have dealt with* is called the 'classical theory' of electric waves. . . .

Table 3.2 Distribution of fixed coordinators and conjuncts

Thematic element	Number	Percent
And	39	48.1
But	22	27.2
So	17	21.0
Or	2	2.5
Yet	1	1.2
Total	81	100.0

(3:2) *What we will call 'an event'* is, in general, just a specific set of initial and final conditions.

(3:3) *What we measure with our detector* is the probability of arrival of a lump.

These sentences containing fronted identification clauses with pronominal *we* underscore both the oral and instructional dimensions of the lecture-chapter. Hence, we could conclude that features of this type are in fact heuristic for this text variety.

3.5.4 Fixed elements as theme

3.5.4.1 *Coordinators and conjuncts*

Fixed coordinators and fixed conjuncts occupy eighty-one weakly thematic positions in the chapter, or 15.1 percent of the total thematic distribution. Table 3.2 shows distributions of specific items in this category.

The most significant distributions in terms of an attempt to establish a heuristic for text classification are those of the coordinators *and, but*, and the result conjunct *so*.

The extensive presence of *and* reinforces the oral nature of the lecture-chapter. *And* can express multiple semantic relationships between clauses (Quirk *et al*. 1972: 560–1). Some of the semantic connections expressed by *and* between clauses from the lecture-chapter include RESULT REFLECTING CHRONOLOGICAL SEQUENCE, as in

(3:4) Because atomic behavior is so unlike ordinary experience, it is very difficult to get used to *and* it appears peculiar and mysterious to everyone . . . [;]

CHRONOLOGICAL SEQUENCE WITHOUT RESULT, as in

(3:5) [speaking of electrons going through holes 1 and 2] Well, perhaps some of them go through 1, *and* then they go around through 2, and then around a few more times or by some other complicated path . . . [;]

CONTRAST, as in

(3:6) Historically, the electron . . . was thought to behave like a particle, *and* then it was found that in many respects it behaved like a wave . . . [;]

and COMMENT, as in

(3:7) Even the experts do not understand it [i.e. atomic behavior] in the way they would like to, *and* it is perfectly reasonable that they should not. . . .

Examples 3:4–3:7 show that *and* as a fixed coordinator is weakly thematic but functionally diverse in this text. The speaker's dependency on *and* to fulfill a variety of functions is typical, of course, of oral discourse.

The distribution of *but* can be interpreted as functionally related both to the progress of the lecture (i.e. what we will study or focus upon and why) and the process of scientific inquiry as a process that tests expectations. Instances of *but* that contribute to the progress of the lecture include:

(3:8) We could, of course, continuously skirt away from the atomic effects, *but* we shall instead interpose here a short excursion. . . .
(3:9) '. . . then by closing hole 2, we changed the chance that an electron that started *out* [italics in original] through hole 1 would finally get to the backstop . . .' *But* notice!
(3:10) So we will give now the *introduction* [italics in original] to the subject of quantum mechanics, *but* will not be able actually to get into the subject until much later.

The contrastive function of *but* denotes an 'unexpectedness,' as Quirk *et al.* explain, that 'depends on our presuppositions and our knowledge of the world' (1972:565). This function of contrasting expectations with observations serves well to illustrate the method of scientific inquiry, as we see in the following examples from the chapter:

(3:11) Newton thought that light was made up of particles, *but* then it was discovered . . . that it behaves like a wave.
(3:12) We know how large objects will act, *but* things on a small scale just do not act that way.
(3:13) What we are observing is that light *also* [italics in original] acts like electrons . . . we *knew* [italics in original] that it was 'wavy,' *but* now we find that it is also 'lumpy.'

Each of these examples contains a verb phrase expressing a perception or observation followed by *but*, introducing a contrasting perception or observation.

The coordinator *so* reinforces the oral nature of the lecture-chapter in its function as an informal expression of seeming result. Examples of *so* in the corpus either indicate a partly continuative and partly summative semantic connection between clauses or indicate the meaning *it follows from what we have said* (see Quirk *et al.* 1972: 669). The following illustrate both these meanings:

(3:14) We could, of course, continuously skirt away from the atomic effects, but we shall instead interpose here a short excursion in which we will describe the basic ideas of the quantum properties of matter. . . . *So* we will give now the *introduction* [italics in original] to the subject of quantum mechanics. . . .

(3:15) If we count the clicks which arrive in a sufficiently long time—say for many minutes—and then count again for another equal period, we find that the two numbers are very nearly the same. *So* we can speak of the *average rate* [italics in original] at which the clicks are heard. . . .

In Example 3:14, the meaning is continuative and summative and may be paraphrased, following Quirk *et al.*, as *so you see that's the situation we're in*. The semantic function of *so* in Example 3:15 is resultative: *it follows from what we have said*.

3.5.4.2 *Initiators*

The four occurrences of the initiator *well* represent less than 1 percent of all thematic positions. Their presence, nevertheless, is worth noting. Quirk *et al.* observe that initiators like *well, oh*, and *ah* are distinctive 'because of their high frequency in spoken English.' These initiators 'can serve both as response utterances and as indicators of conversations' (1972: 274). Instances in the lecture-chapter like *'Well,' you say, 'What about Proposition* A?' and *Well, that is not too surprising* attest to the 'oral lecture' origins of the chapter and reinforce the interpersonal relations expressed in the text, particularly those between the instructor and student.

3.5.4.3 *Variable conjuncts*

Combined variable conjuncts such as *still, that is, then, however*, and *now* occur in twenty instances, accounting for 3.7 percent of the thematic distribution. *Now* as a conjunct of transition occurs in seven instances and is discussed in Section 3.5.5.2 below. Thirteen variable conjuncts remain, including four occurrences of *then* in a complex theme environment following *if* conditional clauses. The variable conjuncts as a group do not appear to constitute a heuristic for the lecture-chapter; rather they serve as cohesive markers common to a variety of written genres, as in Example 3:16:

(3:16) *That is*, the jolt given to the electron . . . is such as to change the electron's motion. . . .

The variable conjunct *still*, however, functions like *but* in advancing the structure of the lecture as in Example 3:17:

(3:17) In discussing these, we will find that the 'classical' . . . theory fails. . . . *Still*, we will deal only with the classical part. . . .

3.5.4.4 *Disjuncts*

Disjuncts occur in thematic position in the lecture-chapter twenty-two times, or as 4.1 percent of all themes. Of these twenty-two instances, seven are in complex thematic environments or after weakly thematic elements, for example:

(3:18) Well, *perhaps*, some of them go through 1, and then they go around through 2. . . .

Disjuncts throughout the chapter tend to express attitudes such as DOUBT, EXPECTATION, SURPRISE, CERTITUDE, QUALIFICATION, and CONCESSION. This is not surprising given the focus of the lecture-chapter on the 'personal' testing of scientific hypotheses.

3.5.5 Adjuncts as theme

3.5.5.1 When *clauses*

Temporal *when* clauses occur in eighteen thematic positions, representing 3.3 percent of thematic positions.[3] Like the fronted conditionals, discussed later, *when* clauses occur in descriptions of various experiments and after weakly thematic fixed elements as well as in complex theme environments. Similar to the fronted conditionals, they frequently reflect the logical procedures involved in testing and, in this sense, represent a combination of the functions of conditional, circumstantial, and temporal clauses. Unlike sentences containing *when*, meaning *at the time(s) at which* (Quirk *et al*. 1972: 272), *when* fronted clauses in the lecture-chapter can often be rewritten with the subordinator *if*. Consider, for example, the following *when* examples from the lecture-chapter with the *if* substitution in brackets:

(3:19) When [if] hole 2 is covered, bullets can only pass through hole 1. . . .
(3:20) When [if] hole 1 is closed, we get the symmetric curve P_2 drawn in the figure.
(3:21) When [if] there is more motion at the source, there is more intensity. . . .

In addition to the above, an *if* rewrite with the inferential conjunct *then* is semantically acceptable in nearly all fronted occurrences of *when* (or *and when*) clauses in the lecture-chapter. In those cases where substitution is semantically permitted, a deep structure causality underlies the clause, either in a statement of procedures to handle the data (e.g. *When we work up our data*, that is, *cause our data to be worked up*) or in a description of experimental process (e.g. *When there is more motion at the source*, that is, *more motion is caused at the source*). This causality does not underlie cases where substitution will not work.

The distribution pattern of the *when* clause suggests another study to determine the heuristic value of temporal features in determining a genre. One could analyze a text and compare whether a given feature occurs in thematic positions more frequently or even exclusively in those parts of a text that delineate procedures (such as the discussion of experiments) or if the given type occurs in the discursive portions of text.

3.5.5.2 *Other time adjuncts*

The analysis of time adjuncts in the lecture-chapter is somewhat problematic since time sequence is relevant to descriptions of experimental procedure as well as to the logical progression of the text itself. This problem led me to consider the conjunct *now* as a time adjunct. In seven of the nine occurrences, however, I interpreted *now* as a conjunct of transition. Such a distinction is weak, as Greenbaum explains: 'We interpret *now* as a conjunct because that is the more plausible interpretation in the context and not because there are formal criteria of position or punctuation to distinguish the conjunct from the adjunct' (1969: 56). The seven instances where *now* functions as a conjunct in the lecture-chapter include the first sentence after a section title introducing a new topic (e.g. *An Experiment with Electrons*); contexts where *now* means *following from what I say* or *let me see* or is used in an admonitory sense; and illative contexts where *now* means *since that is so* (Greenbaum 1969: 56, 73).

The use of the conjunct *now* often advances the instructional purpose of the lecture-chapter, suggesting progression in thought and conclusions. The mutual involvement of the instructor and the student in the experiments is conveyed, for example, in the following RUMINATIVE use of *now*:

(3:22) *Now*, let us measure the wave intensity for various values of *X*. . . .

In Example 3:22, *now* reinforces the collaborative function of *we*. *Now* in its illative *since that is so* function is evident in the Example 3:23:

(3:23) You remember that when we discussed the microscope, we pointed out that due to the *wave nature* [italics in original] of the light, there is a limitation on how close two spots can be and still be seen as two separate spots. . . . So *now* [or since that is so] when we make the wavelength longer than the distance between our holes, we see a *big* [italics in original] fuzzy flash when the light is scattered by the electrons.

The illative use of *now* typifies the inferential force of inquiry that predictably would characterize scientific or philosophical tracts. In Example 3:24, time is implied by *historically* and reinforced by *now*:

(3:24) *Historically*, the electron, for example, was thought to behave like a particle, and then it was found that in many respects it behaved like a wave. So it really behaves like neither. *Now* we have given up.

Now in its various functions reveals the complexity of the chapter: the oral delivery and signaling of an argument presented in a collaborative learning structure, concerned with scientific inquiry.

Time adjuncts, other than *now*, occur in an additional fifteen positions: *then* occurs four times either initially or after fixed coordinators; *first* or *at first* in four instances; and various other time adjuncts in seven instances for a total of seventeen (including the two instances of *now*), or 3.2 percent of the thematic positions in the text. In this chapter, such adjuncts advance both the sequence of the lecture

(3.25) *First*, you should realize that we should talk about probability because we cannot say definitely where any particular bullet will go. . . .

as well as its content

(3:26) *Later* . . . it was found that light did indeed sometimes behave like a particle. . . .

Like *now*, the other time adjuncts perform a signaling function, pointing to the progress of the experiments discussed.

As suggested in the discussion of the *when* clause, further analyses of larger texts might isolate specific instances of occurrence of time adjuncts and pose questions like 'To what extent is the temporal sequence expressed that of an experiment and to what extent that of the larger more comprehensive text?' The answers to such questions could confirm the heuristic value of time adjuncts in determining genre.

3.5.5.3 *Adjuncts other than time*

Adjuncts other than time account for fifty-six items in our analysis, or 10.4 percent of all thematic positions in the lecture-chapter. They include adjuncts in strict initial position, in thematic position after weakly thematic fixed coordinators and conjuncts, and in complex theme environments. Table 3.3 illustrates the distribution of adjuncts other than time.

Adjuncts of source and location acount for over a third of the adjuncts other than time. Examples of source and location adjuncts at various rank levels include *in the last few chapters in front of the beach*, *at those places where, from this observation*, and *from the number recorded in column 1*.

Some of the adjuncts other than time from the lecture-chapter are of the variety Huddleston calls 'marked attribute theme' where the subject follows the verb in all cases. Huddleston observes that 'The effect is to put the subject in the position where, other things being equal, it will carry the nuclear stress of the tone group, this making it the focus of new information '(1971: 316, 319).

Table 3.3 Thematic distribution of adjuncts other than time

Type of adjunct	Total	Percent of thematic distribution
Source and location	20	35.7
Focus	11	19.6
Process/means	10	17.9
Combined others	15	26.8
Total	56	100.0

In the chapter on quantum behavior, adjuncts expressing 'marked attribute theme' include:

(3:27) Beyond the wall is a backstop . . . which will 'absorb' the bullets when they hit it.
(3:28) To the right of the source we have again a wall with two holes, and *beyond that* is a second wall. . . .
(3:29) Beyond the wall is another plate which will serve as a 'backstop.'

Although the sentences with initial locative adjuncts in Examples 3:27–3:29 reflect central tendencies in the language (Quirk *et al*. 1972: 477–8), they also underscore the 'anatomy' of the experiment and advance the DIRECTION of the lesson. Hence, they represent, by their very selection, the meaning potential of language deployed in a particular context and thus suggest a heuristic for determining the type of genre to which a specific text belongs.

Adjuncts of focus and process (or means) are the next most frequent adjuncts other than time in thematic positions in the lecture-chapter, each representing about one-fifth of this group of features. Focusing adjuncts in the chapter gives precise focus to the events of the experiment:

(3:30) *In this* case we would observe that the original wave is diffracted at the holes. . . .
(3:31) *In terms of the intensities*, we could write

$$I_{12} = I_1 + I_2 + 2\sqrt{I_1 I_2}\cos\delta \ldots.$$

Adjuncts of process or means delineate the procedures used to conduct the experiment or specify the discussion of the experimental event:

(3:32) *In telling you how it works* we will have told you about the basic peculiarities of all quantum mechanics.
(3:33) Surely, *by making the light dimmer and dimmer*, eventually the wave will be weak enough that it will have a negligible effect.

The remaining fifteen adjuncts (just over a quarter of all adjuncts other than time) cumulatively express a variety of functions such as INSTRUMENT (*with this apparatus* . . .), VIEWPOINT (*historically* . . .), CAUSE/REASON (*because atomic behavior is* . . .), CONCESSION (*even* . . .), PURPOSE (*to try to understand* . . .),[4] and TARGET (*to our electron apparatus* . . .). Since no one of these dominates significantly, their function as a heuristic for variety of genre remains uncertain. Additional studies of scientific texts are needed to determine both their frequency and use. Hypothetically, adjuncts expressing INSTRUMENT will occur in discussions of procedure, VIEWPOINT in the more epistemological aspects of text, CAUSE/REASON in methodology, and so forth.

3.5.5.4 *Conditional clauses*

Conditional clauses total twenty-nine or 5.4 percent of all thematic positions in the chapter. Fronted conditional *if* clauses occur in twenty-four initial thematic positions; *if* conditional clauses in thematic positions after coordinators and the fixed conjunct *so* occupy an additional five positions. (The total includes three *if* conditional clauses in complex theme environments.)

If conditional clauses form an interesting distribution in those text segments that reinforce the scientific content of the discourse. Twenty-one of the twenty-four fronted *if* clauses in strict initial positions are in the descriptions of experiments on water waves, electrons, the watching of electrons, and the dimming of lights. They also occur in the treatment of experiment modification or conclusions and in counter-arguments to experimental procedures. In two instances, they appear in the explication of a scientific maxim—Heisenberg's uncertainty principle. The first instance of the fronted *if* clause occurs in the author's conjecture of 'a somewhat idealized experiment in which the bullets are not real bullets, but are indestructible bullets':

(3:34) *If the rate at which the machine gun fires is made very low*, we find that at any given moment either nothing arrives or one and only one . . . bullet arrives at the backstop.

Frequent occurrence of *if* clauses followed by the inferential *then* is a predictable feature of scientific treatises, for such clauses express conditionality, often indicating hypothetical procedures or the dependency relationships among circumstances. Where the inferential *then* is not stated in conditional clauses from the corpus, it is implied.

As noted above, three conditional clauses from the corpus appear in complex theme environments. All three occur with attitudinal disjuncts that reinforce the scientific tenor of the discourse:

(3:35) If we use 'gentler' light perhaps we can avoid disturbing the electrons so much.
(3:36) If one looks at the holes or, more accurately, if one has a piece of apparatus which is capable of determining whether the electrons go through hole 1 or hole 2, then one *can* [italics in original] say that it goes either through hole 1 or hole 2.
(3:37) Except that once in a while, if there were two clicks very close together in time, our ear might not sense the separation.

In Example 3:35, the disjunct *perhaps* expresses a degree of doubt as to the effectiveness of the procedure described in the *if* clause. In Example 3:36, the disjunct *accurately* emphasizes the requirement of precision or exactitude when performing the task described in the *if* clause. In Example 3:37, the phrase *except that once in a while* reflects both doubt and the desire for precision. All three further demonstrate that multiple function in complex theme environments can reveal the genre of a given discourse.

The occurrence of fronted *if* clauses does have special significance as a determinant of genre in the lecture-chapter despite the fact that conditional clauses 'tend to occur in initial position in the superordinate clause' in any kind of discourse (Quirk *et al*. 1972: 746). In this corpus, such clauses cluster in those segments that most clearly delineate scientific experiments and thus appear to be a distinctive feature of descriptions of logical processes or operations. This specific function of *if* clauses in the lecture-chapter is reinforced by elements occurring immediately after the *if* fronted clause (excluding the implied or stated inferential then). Of the twenty-four instances where *if* conditional clauses assume thematic positions, nearly one-third (seven instances) are followed by clauses with EXPERIMENT oriented subjects like *probability, the plate, the rate*, and *electrons* or anaphoric references to such subjects through *it*. Half of the twenty-four clauses following *if* clauses express author–reader collaboration; eleven contain *we* in subject position; and one refers to a collaborative first person through the possessive (i.e. *our ear* . . .).

The context of the hypothetical experiment is clearly the major influence on the distribution of *if* fronted clauses in the lecture-chapter. In addition, nearly a third of these clauses (30 percent) occur in front of clauses whose subjects are either experiment-specific and half (50 percent) express author–reader collaboration through *we*. Thus the *if* clause followed by a clause with a subject focusing on the discourse topic or author–reader collaboration appears to be a heuristic structure for this type of discourse.

3.5.6 Anticipatory *it* and existential subject

It occurs in the subject position in eleven instances and *there* in eight, for percentage distributions of 2.0 and 1.5 percent respectively. Although I have no text-specific interpretation for these occurrences, I can say that predication of this type does relate to choice of theme. As Halliday explains of the sentence *It was John who broke the window*:

> Structurally predication maps the function of identifier on to that of theme, giving explicit prominence to the theme by exclusion: 'John and nobody else' is under consideration, [1967: 236]

The difference between *it* and *there* is one of specificity: 'With *it* the theme is defined (uniquely specified), with *there* it is described (non-uniquely specified) . . .' (Halliday 1967: 238).

Quirk *et al*. treat existential *there* as EMPTY THEME, explaining that the 'point of this device becomes clearer when it is recalled that the initial element or theme of a clause typically contains given information, and is the point of departure for the introduction of new information later in the clause' (1972: 958).

The eleven instances of postponed subject through the anticipatory *it* construction and the eight instances of existential *there* occur at various points in the chapter. Here are a few examples:

(3:38) There is one lucky break, however—electrons behave just like light.
(3:39) There did not happen to be a photon around at the time the electron went through.
(3:40) It is as though closing one hole *decreased* [italics in original] the number of electrons. . . .

To argue that these instances constitute a heuristic in the lecture-chapter is premature. They did not appear to denote any specific values associated with scientific inquiry or delivery of instruction in the text examined.

3.6 SUMMARY

This study began with the premise that text is predicated on choice and that form of language choice varies depending on use and function. A study of thematic distribution in text not only advances this position but also clarifies how data are presented and findings communicated. Further, it demonstrates how text is a form of social interaction—in the case of the lecture-chapter analyzed here, the interaction between student audience and instructor. Thematic analysis also invites the question: 'How does a text mean what it means?' It reveals how text-forming or rhetorical strategies relate to the way particular types of information are conveyed and interpreted.

In the course of this analysis, I have demonstrated that several features of the lecture-chapter are indeed heuristic for its genre. Dominant use of first and second pronouns advances the interpersonal aspect of the chapter as lecture through a bonding of author and reader in a joint learning enterprise. Thematic coordinators like *and, but*, and *so* are not only functionally diverse, but also correlate at times with text content, delivery, and topic. *And* and *so* reinforce oral delivery, while *but* contributes to the progress of the lecture. Thematic disjuncts, primarily attitudinal, correlate with the experiment content of the chapter and the uncertainty involved in the testing of hypotheses. Similarly, *when* temporal clauses express the functions of condition, circumstance, and time passage in thematic positions and thus promote the 'sense of scientific procedures.' *Now* suggests progression in thought and conclusions and advances the instructional purpose of the chapter. Adjuncts other than time structure the anatomy of the experiment and are often responsible for the sense of direction in the lesson. Finally, *if* conditional clauses express hypotheses, conditions, and dependencies that characterize scientific treatises.

Additional research should focus not only upon analysis of thematic varieties but also include, as we have here, the total distribution of any one element or clause in a given text. To do so is to address critically the issue of central tendencies both as they reflect the linguistic system and as they define specific genres. Such research can establish more extensively the relationships of verbal and non-verbal environments to text design and discourse function.

NOTES

1. Although it is clear that the interrogatives in the lecture-chapter evoke a response and promote the 'collaborative learning' function of the lecture-chapter, from the point of view of linguistic classification, the examples I found were in strictly fixed thematic positions (e.g. *What is the probability that a bullet which passes through the holes in the wall will arrive at the backstop at the distance* x *from the center?* Unlike the fixed coordinators, they exhibit no functional diversity. Furthermore, the eight instances of interrogatives in this corpus did not occur in complex theme

environments that would allow for extension of theme (see Section 3.3.3). The criterion of theme-as-choice only applies to whether the question itself should be asked.

2. Italics are added in numbered examples unless otherwise noted.
3. The following sentence is included in this count as equivalent to a *when* clause: *Everytime we hear a 'click' from our electron detector (at the backstop), we also see a flash of light either near hole 1 or near hole 2.*
4. In systemic grammar the infinitive is ranked and interpreted as a clause. Here its function is adverbial and adjunctive.

BIBLIOGRAPHY

Berry, M. (1976), *An Introduction to Systemic Linguistics: 2 Levels and Links*, New York, St. Martin's Press.

Eiler, M. A. (1979), *Meaning and Choice in Writing about Literature: A Study of Cohesion in the Expository Texts of Ninth Graders*, Ph.D. dissertation, Chicago, Illinois Institute of Technology (see *Dissertation Abstracts International*, sec. A., 1980, **40**, 4571–A).

Feynman, R. P., Leighton, R. B., and Sands, M. (1963), *The Feynman Lectures on Physics: Mainly Mechanics, Radiation, and Heat*, Reading, Mass., Addison-Wesley.

Fries, P. H., 'On the Status of Theme in English: Arguments from Discourse,' in Petöfi, J. S. and Sözer, E. (eds) (1983: 116–52), *Micro and Macro Connexity of Texts*, Papers in Textlinguistics 45, Hamburg, Helmut Buske.

Greenbaum, S. (1969), *Studies in English Adverbial Usage*, Miami Linguistics Series 5, Coral Gables, Fla., University of Miami Press.

Halliday, M. A. K. (1967), 'Notes on Transitivity and Theme in English, Part 2,' *Journal of Linguistics*, **3**, 199–244.

Halliday, M. A. K. (1973), Transcript of Lectures, Chicago, University of Illinois at Chicago Circle.

Huddleston, R. D. (1971), *The Sentence in Written English: A Syntactic Study Based on an Analysis of Scientific Texts*, Cambridge, at the University Press.

Mathesius, V. (1939), 'Otak zvaném aktauálním členění věty' [The So-Called Information-Bearing Structure of the Sentence], *Slovo a Slovesnost*, **5**, 171–4.

Muir, J. (1972), *A Modern Approach to English Grammar: An Introduction to Systemic Grammar*, London, B.T. Batsford.

Quirk, R., Greenbaum, S., Leech, G., and Svartvik, J. (1972), *A Grammar of Contemporary English*, London, Longman.

Part II
Exploring the processes of written language production and interpretation

4 Effective ideation in written text: a functional approach to clarity and exigence

Barbara Couture
Wayne State University

4.1 TOWARD AN ANALYSIS OF EFFECTIVE TEXTUAL IDEATION

As scholars and writers, we no doubt have more than once uttered 'I tried to write that piece today, but I didn't have any good ideas.' And oddly enough that lament often follows tireless sessions when we have generated lots and lots of ideas on paper, but none we regard as 'good.' Though the problem of distinguishing a 'good' idea in writing has plagued generations of writers and many more readers, scholars have not yet produced a FUNCTIONAL DESCRIPTION of the written communication of a valued idea.

In my view, a functional description of effective ideation in written text should balance expectations for completeness and utility. A COMPLETE description would reflect all the kinds of semantic choice realized in any kind of actual written discourse that conveys ideas effectively in any kind of situation. (We are a long way from a 'complete' description of this kind; nevertheless, scholars of written discourse in a variety of settings have identified several features that support and clarify the communication of ideas.) A USEFUL description would have heuristic value for writers, aiding their efforts to generate ideas that communicate effectively for themselves and to their readers. They can appeal to many handbooks advising how to organize literary and expository texts and ensure audience appeal, but none that I have seen provide a comprehensive, manageable heuristic for effective ideation.

In this chapter, I define effective textual ideation and propose a functional scale of linguistic features that promote it. My scale describes effective ideation as a function of linguistic choice, ranging from more elliptical to more explicit expression. In developing this scale, I begin from the premise that an effective idea in text conveys a message about a topic with clarity and exigence for both the writer and reader in a given context. Textual scholarship in several disciplines suggests that clarity and exigence are addressed through two kinds of meaning systems: TEXTUAL LOGIC and SEMIOTIC CONVENTION. These two systems are realized in written text through a range of grammatical and lexical features that make more or less explicit reference to their underlying structures. Experimental modeling suggests that we can explain effective textual ideation by analyzing on an 'explicitness' scale those linguistic choices that convey conceptual logic and contextualize the discourse. As my analysis of a sample written text shows, a network describing effective ideation must account for both kinds of semantic systems in order to accurately explain ideation in written text and to have heuristic utility for writers.

4.1.1 A definition of effective ideation

The definition of 'effective ideation' adopted here is derived from descriptions of valued textual communication in both rhetoric and literature. Valued written communication, whether poetic or transactional, is pointed and purposeful and displays qualities of conceptual clarity and contextual exigence. In short, a valued poem as well as a valued essay conveys a discernable message that has some kind of felt relevance to the writer or reader in a given context. This definition of valued written communication, though static, has behind it a sense of the process of writing and reading both as a discovery of new ways of thinking and as an assimilation of these concepts in the thought processes of writer and reader.

The rhetorical objectives of 'logical message' and 'situational relevance' are substantiated by current research and teaching practice. In their highly regarded text *Rhetoric: Discovery and Change*, Young, Becker, and Pike, for example, claim that the 'ethical goal' of prose writers is to 'be discoverers of new truths as well as preservers and transmitters of the old.' In constructing a message for rhetorical discourse, writers must discover 'an ordering principle, or hypothesis' that governs the hierarchical arrangement of information that will be presented in the discourse. In constructing the shape of the discourse, the writer looks for 'shared experiences, shared knowledge, shared beliefs, values, and attitudes, shared language' (1970: 9, 120, 172).

Similar objectives guide effective literary writing, though the way in which these objectives are instantiated are quite different. In citing a similarity of objectives in literary and transactional communication, we are, of course, positing a view of literature which assumes an appeal to a reader. Holland elaborates this view in a psychoanalytic approach to reading, claiming that the literary audience reads with the aim of perceiving and creating the thematic focus of a text, its message. The individual in constructing this message while reading, recreates his or her own identity, reconfirms experiences shared with others, and makes a 'creative push to achieve new satisfaction,' to make new discoveries and insights (1975: 125). Holland concludes that the goal of literary criticism is to explore the individual and communal messages of texts as interpreted and made new by readers:

> . . . the true focus of criticism has to be the relation between oneself and the text, and the sensible thing for literary people to do is to acknowledge that focus and write and talk accordingly, sharing our samenesses and differences in interpretation so as to create an evergrowing resource of responses we can share. [1975: 248]

Holland distinguishes the processes of individual and group text appreciation as processes of discovering one's own identity and one's relationship to a group through interacting with a text, processes that appear to parallel Young, Becker, and Pike's description of effective composition: one must both make an individual discovery and locate its shared features with the outside context.

In sum, a text's literary or rhetorical value is bound up with its potential both to promote logical CONCEPTUALIZATION (that is, reconstruction of a message) and semiotic CONTEXTUALIZATION (that is, incorporation of extra-textual meaning systems that give the text message situational relevance). This view suggests that we can evaluate textual meaning-potential by ranking a text's features as they contribute to the reader's conceptualization and contextualization of its content.

I suggest that a scale that ranks EXPLICITNESS OF EXPRESSION holds promise as a tool for correlating text features with ideational effectiveness. At one end of the scale are text features that express messages in a highly elliptical, perhaps even cryptic form. To comprehend the meaning of these messages, the reader must go beyond the text to make the logical connections necessary to understand the message intended. A well-known example of elliptical text is the prose of Joyce's *Finnegans Wake*. An ordinary reading of the logical relations implied by the grammar and lexis of that text does little to uncover its sense; a meaningful interpretation of the novel requires extensive reference to contextual meaning systems—some invented by Joyce, others extant in multi-national myth and culture. Readers who do not have access to the contextual meaning that enhances Joyce's work are not likely to interpret it in the same way as those who do, if they can make much sense of it at all. Further, it is doubtful that any reader would interpret the work as Joyce might have done. At the other end of the explicitness scale are features that make meaning clear with the least possibility of conflicting interpretation. Equally competent speakers and readers of the same language would interpret the message of a highly explicit text similarly. An example of such explicit discourse is a technical writer's description for a general audience of a piece of equipment, such as a thermometer or a pressure gauge. Generally, the technical writer's aim is to have the reader understand the text message in the same way that he or she does. Language in this kind of discourse makes clear reference to concepts, objects, and persons in the experience of large numbers of people.

Ranking the features of a text on a scale of explicitness of expression, I believe, can tell us why some texts fail to convey messages effectively in certain contexts and others succeed in doing so. Ranking on an explicitness scale requires a clear description of what is meant by explicit textual ideation. This description, in turn, requires an explicit understanding of the underlying structure of semantic systems evoked through textual ideation.

4.1.2 Logical and semiotic meaning

The structure of written discourse reflects two kinds of meaning systems: LOGICAL meaning which is realized in a discourse's propositional content and SEMIOTIC meaning which is realized in the discourse's reference to meaning systems above language and outside the text. The combinatory potential of these two kinds of meaning enables a text to convey ideas to its readers. Theorists and empiricists have described this simultaneous functioning of logical and semiotic meaning in various ways.

In a philosophical approach to text analysis, Ricoeur explains the communicative function of both literary and non-literary text in terms of interactive 'propositional' and 'dialogic' meaning. Discourse conveys 'propositional content' through the fundamental opposition of the linguistic properties of 'identification' (or subject meaning) and 'predication in one and the same sentence'; discourse creates contextual relevance through social 'dialogical' constraint which puts the propositional content in a context that can be mutually shared by speaker/author and listener/reader. Propositional content pushes ideas forward while 'the dialogue reduces the field of misunderstanding concerning the propositional content and partially succeeds in overcoming the non-communicability of the experience' (Ricoeur 1976: 10, 11, 17).

Through conducting extensive analyses of both text and reader response, van Dijk and Kintsch have demonstrated empirically the simultaneous working of logical and semiotic systems in written discourse production and interpretation. Their theory directly focuses on the text as it traces logical and contextual meaning at both the micro- (sentence) and macro- (discourse) level. They describe the logical structure of discourse as a composition of semantic units that identify 'propositions' and 'superordinate propositions' (1983: 45–7). The contextual structure of discourse, in their view, is achieved through its reference to conventional knowledge frameworks, or schemas, which can be elaborated by a number of textual variables. A schema functions much as the abstract 'dialogic' property that Ricoeur attributes to textual communication; it 'provides the reader with a basis for interpreting the text,' helping the reader to fill in 'gaps' in his or her construction of its propositional content:

> Missing information can be assigned default values if it appears insignificant, or it can be actively looked for in the text. Deviations from the schema either may be accepted and registered, or, if they appear to be major ones, may become the bases for a problem-solving effort trying to account for them. [1983: 48]

Van Dijk and Kintsch mention several empirical studies of their own and other scholars that validate readers' reference both to propositional structure and conventional schemas as critical input for the interpretation of unfamiliar texts. Like Ricoeur, they explain the dynamics of textual interpretation as a process of simultaneously constructing logical sense and rooting information in an extra-textual semiotic, creating situational relevance.

4.1.3 Implications of logical and semiotic semantics for ideational description

The interplay of logical and semiotic meaning in textual interpretation suggests that we must explain effective ideation in two ways; we must evaluate textual features as they promote the understanding of a text's logical content (conceptualization) and the relating of textual content to extratextual systems (contextualization). This criterion does not imply that we speculate about how individuals think, accounting for the dynamics of perception and reasoning, nor about how they interact, explaining how social concourse creates semiotic meaning systems. Rather, it requires that we describe reader conceptualization and contextualization as these processes are triggered by linguistic choice.

Although the two ideational systems we seek to explain are highly complex, their underlying structures are fairly transparent. We can cite remarkable similarity in scholars' current research into logical and semiotic ideation in text—similarity despite major disagreements as to whether textual meaning is a function of conceptualization or of contextualization or both.

4.2 LOGICAL CONCEPTUALIZATION AS A FUNCTION OF TEXT

4.2.1 The logical semantic system

Scholars' descriptions of logical conceptualization of textual meaning generally refer to three kinds of components, realized by a variety of means in single sentences and in entire discourses: topics, comments about topics, and logical connections between the two.

At the sentence level, topics correspond to sentence subjects, comments to the statements made about the topics (which often contain other topics that stand in some logical relation to the sentence subject), and logical connections to connectives explicit in specific vocabulary items (e.g. a relationship of contrast as expressed by the verb *differ*) or in grammatical connections (e.g. a relationship of contrast made by the coordinator *rather*). At the discourse level, topics correspond to theme sentences or introductory paragraphs, comments to support arguments, and logical connections to transitions.

Scholars' identification of these three elements as central to logical conceptualization of discourse meaning is fairly consistent. Van Dijk, for example, describes a three-component structure when he identifies propositions as the 'semantic structures defining texts, action, and cognition, both at the micro- and macrolevel.' A proposition contains a predicate and one or more arguments; the predicate expresses 'a relation between individual objects,' that is, between the arguments, which in turn are ordered and have different functions such as 'Agents, Patients, Instruments, Sources, [and] Goals' (1980: 16, 17). These functions stand in logical relation to one another as the object talked about (topic) and as the objects (comments) in dependent relation (connection) to those talked about.

This 'topic-comment-connection' structure is not exclusive to expository discourse. In developing his theory of SUBJECTIVE CRITICISM, Bleich claims:

'Even the most complex acts of language may be viewed as necessary logical variants of predicative acts. Predication is not simply a linguistic structure; it is the elemental form of conceptual thought.' He goes on to describe predication or the creation of ideas in language as the 'linkage of topic and comment,' an internal subjective 'act of symbol formation consisting of two parts, each dependent on the other, confined strictly to words . . .' (1978: 50, 51).

In a series of essays on an individual's relationship to language, Percy refers to an irreducible system of three components that enables ideational communication. He describes Helen Keller's remarkable discovery of the logical connection between *water*, the physical liquid, and WATER, the word, as an emblematic instance of a triadic logical relation he calls the 'delta factor.' Extending the delta metaphor to ideas as realized in a sentence, Percy explains that a 'sentence utterance is a triadic event involving a coupler and the two elements of the uttered sentence,' the two elements being the subject and predicate (or topic and comment) (1975: 167).

But Percy makes an important distinction in the semantic triad underlying ideation: the two elements connected in a sentence may be two symbols (subject and predicate) or a symbol and the object it symobolizes (the distinction of the 'signifier' and the 'signified'). He notes further that the coupling, though represented sententially, is actually done 'by the utterer' and by the 'receiver of a sentence,' each of whose 'couplings' of word with object or word with word or topic with comment will differ. Given this eventuality, Percy contends that a model of communication must account for the separate coupling of two components by the utterer and receiver. He further defines 'successful' communications as 'those transactions in which the same elements are coupled by both utterer and receiver and in the same mode of coupling' (1975: 167).

If we join these congruent perspectives, we can easily derive from them a diagram of the writer and reader's processes of logical conceptualization as they both interact with a text. Figure 4.1 shows an idealized successful

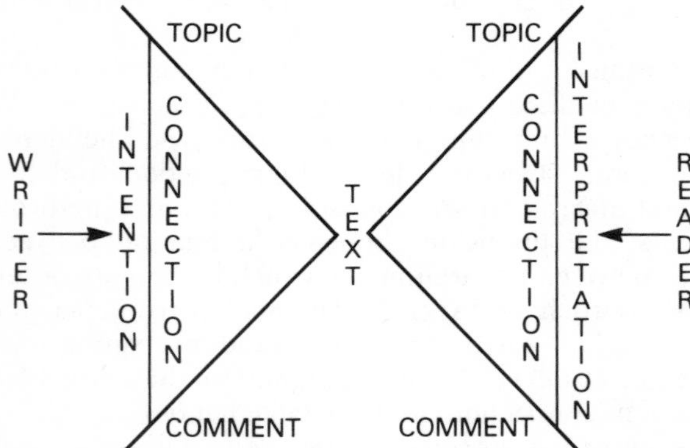

Figure 4.1 Idealized view of logical conceptualization

communication event where the processes of writer and reader conceptualization are parallel—that is, the writer's intention matches the reader's interpretation. If we accept van Dijk's notion of the proposition as the basic unit of conceptual meaning in text at the micro- and macrolevel, the diagram serves as a representation of the communication of the overall message of unified discourse and of each of the many separate messages conveyed at the sentence level and below. If we adopt Percy's view of effective communication, we assume the processes of intention and interpretation to have the same result.

Some readers, of course, would find problematic the definition of valued ideation as that where meaningful connections are made in 'the same' way by utterer and receiver. On the one hand, it ignores the filtering of the text through the separate psychological states (which can never be totally synchronous) of author and audience. On the other hand, it fails to account for texts that are engaging and satisfying precisely because their logical structure 'deconstructs' probable conceptualizations of the writer/reader by presenting opposing messages in the syntactic and rhetorical structure.[1] But, for the moment, let us accept this model and go on to explain how it is realized in written text.

4.2.2 The logical system as realized in text

Many scholars have classed textual features that contribute to building the topics, comments, and connections that promote logical conceptualization both at the sentence and discourse level.

We can cite first the work on sentence-level theme as it serves to point to the conceptual topic of a sentence (in Halliday's view, THEME is the initial element in a clause [see 1967: 212; see also Fries 1983; and Eiler in this volume]). Theme, along with the grammatical systems of transitivity and mood, operates to give ideational coherence to discourse. Though thematic structure 'is the text-forming structure in the clause,' it has a role in creating or eliminating semantic ambiguity (Halliday and Hasan 1976: 311). A comparison of two sentences that respectively show harmonious and disharmonious interplay of the linguistic systems of transitivity, mood, and theme demonstrates this process:

(i) Susan stroked the cat gently.
(ii) These ponies the children were given by their grandparents.

In sentence (i), the grammatical subject, informational theme, and situational actor occupy the same initial slot and are realized by the same formal item, *Susan*, leaving no ambiguity about the topic of the discourse. In sentence (ii), however, three topical foci are suggested. *The children* is the grammatical subject; however, *these ponies* names the informational focus of the sentence (its theme). The situational actor, *their grandparents*, appears neither as subject nor theme. Because it ambiguously cites three topical foci, the sentence creates functional disharmony and ambiguity about its central message (sentence (ii) and analysis are taken from Halliday and

Hasan 1976: 311). Analyses of the systems of transitivity, mood, and theme as they operate through grammar can explain how sentence structure supports or undermines conceptual logic as readers interpret it.

For descriptions of how topics are maintained within sentences and developed over longer stretches of text, we can cite the growing body of research on logical relations expressed both within and between sentences. In this domain, Hoey has made great strides in describing the textual source of two categories of basic meaning-relations, LOGICAL SEQUENCE and MATCHING:

> Logical Sequence relations are relations between successive events or ideas, whether actual or potential. . . .
>
> Matching relations are relations where statements are 'matched' against each other in terms of degrees of identicality of description. [1983: 19–20]

In addition to identifying semantic categories of clause relations, Hoey classifies linguistic features as they signal clause relations and identifies grammatical connections (formed by subordinators and conjuncts), lexical connectives, and repetition as signals of clause relations (1983: 17–30; for additional descriptions of features that express clause relations, see Hartnett, Hoey and Winter, and Jordan in this volume).

In a similar effort to build a model of ideational relationships developed in discourse, Meyer posits five categories of logical relationships that operate in discourse: 'collection,' 'causation,' 'response,' 'comparison,' and 'description.' In effective discourse, the rhetorical relationships referenced and established in its top-level structure 'can serve to organize the text as a whole.' Meyer distinguishes the relationships between top-level and sentence-level structure by applying case grammar analysis (which names agents, actions, goals, and other participants in sentence-level propositions) to show how overall organizing principles are realized at the sentence level. Because the relationships in her model 'closely follow those suggested by the text,' Meyer claims that her system is well 'suited to examining logical relationships and comprehension of these relationships explicitly or implicitly stated in text' (1985: 17, 20, 33).

Clearly, analyses of actual discourse are available that show how semantic systems promoting logical conceptualization are realized in linguistic features at every level, from a particular formal item to a combination of features that signal overall discourse structure. I have discussed above only analyses of logical structure in expository prose; such descriptions of poetic language have also been attempted with success (see, for example, Jakobson 1960; and Halliday 1971). These multiple resources relating text structure to propositional logic can help account, though only partially, for effective textual ideation.

4.2.3 The logical system as heuristic for ideational value

If the object of written communication is to convey concepts clearly to a distant reader, we might conclude that the more explicitly a text points to topics, comments, and the connections between them, the more effectively it will communicate ideas. To rank ideational effectiveness, we could simply categorize features at sentence and discourse level as they fall on a scale ranging from more elliptical to more explicit and conclude that the more features that contribute to explicit expression, the better. Such ranking would assume, of course, that 'clarity' is the essential determinant of effective textual ideation.

This ranking has some utility for explaining the failure of the student text in Figure 4.2 to articulate ideas effectively. This text, the first paragraph of an essay written as an assignment for a remedial class in college composition, neither develops topics nor makes logical connections between them. Further, it assaults the reader with macro-structuring devices that impose a logical structure at the discourse level that is not supported at the sentence level.

The sample text begins by naming a topic, *marriage*, and defining it with a dictionary definition. This gloss is followed by the question—*Why are marriages not surviving?*—which is meant, the reader assumes, to convey the comment about the topic that will be expanded later. Yet no language intervenes between the dictionary definition of marriage and the rhetorical question that follows to suggest how these will be connected. We have no view of *marriage* that suggests that *survival* is an issue that relates to it conceptually, and certainly no inkling of that relationship is revealed in the definition offered. Despite this omission, the author goes on to name *reasons* why marriages are not surviving, creating further difficulty. She names broad, abstract topics, not specific reasons for the dissolution of *marriages*. The terms *economics*, *different opinions*, and *interest in other people* call up a host of associations, largely irrelevant to the essay's message about why marriages do not last. These terms are not collocated in any way; they are not lexical items chosen because they have a coherent relationship to the break-up of a social compact. In fact, each of these terms represents a *topic, comment*, and *connection* in itself that is not made explicit to the reader. For instance, *economics* could mean 'Marriages are not surviving because more and more couples are not prepared to share the responsibility for handling joint income,' and *interest in other people* could mean 'Young couples do not know how to keep relationships with the opposite sex from conflicting with those with their mates at home.'

An instructor in a basic composition course could do much to help a student make ideas more explicit in rhetorical discourse through analyzing the features that promote logical conception. If I were to rank on our explicitness scale the textual features discussed here, I would register them

What is a marriage? Webster's dictionary states it as being 'a journey in close association' or the 'joining of a man and woman in holy matrimony.' Now after marriage has been defined, Why are marriages not surviving? Perhaps Economics, Different opinions, or even a interest in other people, and of course there are other reasons, but these are just some reasons why, I want to point out.

Figure 4.2 First paragraph of student expository text (verbatim)

as highly elliptical. The student's elliptical style represents the kind of prose one might expect in the planning stages of expository writing. *Economics* and *different opinions* are much like the 'rich bit[s]' described by Flower and Hayes (see 1977: 456), key words the writer might come up with in planning a discourse to stand for complex ideas not yet fully elaborated. Although identifying this elliptical style helps us describe why this paragraph lacks clarity and hence is ineffective, it does not tell the whole story about its ineffective message development.

The EXPLICITNESS ranking tells us nothing about the writer's and reader's need for more explicit expression in order to conceptualize the message of the discourse. And that need will vary with internal and external constraints: first, with the internal constraint imposed by the writer/reader's personal assimilation of the text with his or her accumulated understanding of other things relative to it; and second, with the external constraint imposed by cultural expectations for a text in a particular communication context. We might define these constraints as reference to an INTERNAL and an EXTERNAL SEMIOTIC. However we designate them, we must account for them in our structural model of textual ideation.[2]

Internal semiotic constraints will dictate one range of explicit expression for the writer and one for the reader, both of them dependent on their individual, psychological needs for explicitness in order to comprehend the discourse in a given situation. External semiotic constraints will dictate another range for explicitness based on the text's relationship to conventional communication situations in the shared cultures of writer and reader.

I can easily demonstrate the relationship between one's internal semiotic and the need for explicit expression in writing by referring to a common form of transactional discourse: a shopping list. When I write a shopping list for myself, it is highly elliptical, with idiosyncratic abbreviations for products I purchase regularly. Were I to send someone else to the store with this list, I would find it necessary to 'fill in the blanks,' and to write out some abbreviations in full (my idiosyncratic ones), perhaps providing additional information about brand names of products I always choose but never cite on my list. My elliptical shopping list and the more explicit one for my helpful surrogate shopper are equally functional, but mine reflects my internal semiotic, my routine shopping ritual. Thus, it need not elaborate details of this routine because I know these perfectly well; they are stored in my internal semiotic.

But elliptical communication is not only meaningful to individuals, as my example suggests. Scholars have noted that elliptical text, whether transactional or literary, can be interpreted quite easily by large numbers of listeners and readers when it refers to an external semiotic shared by the discourse participants. For example, Hasan notes that, in ordinary conversation, elliptical expression can be perfectly clear when it evokes contextual meaning that is not explicit in the text. She remarks that elliptical texts that rely on outside contexts are characteristic of the 'implicit' (rather than 'explicit') verbal style:

> The difference between explicit and implicit styles can be stated most conveniently in terms of what a normal person needs in order to interpret an utterance as it is intended by the speaker. Where explicit style is concerned, the correct interpretation of a message requires no more than a listener who has the average working knowledge of the language in question. When, however, the message is in the implicit style, its intended more precise meanings become available only if certain additional conditions are met. . . . [1984: 109]

Hasan's definition of 'implicit' and 'explicit' style does not place a value judgment on either style; rather it distinguishes a different set of requirements for the communicative success of each style.

In a similar discussion of ellipsis in poetic language, Barthes observes that ellipsis is not disturbing, perhaps not even noticed, when it operates in a known field of reference:

> [The structures of ellipses] are altogether artificial, entirely learned; I am no longer any more astonished by La Fontaine's ellipses (yet, how many unformulated relays between the grasshopper's song and her destitution) than by the physical ellipsis which unites in a simple piece of equipment both electric current and cold, because these shortcuts are placed in a purely operative field: that of academic apprenticeship and of the kitchen. . . . [1977: 80]

Both Hasan and Barthes assume systems of meaning outside the text whose extralinguistic reality is confirmed by the communicative success of implicit and elliptical expression. But one's comfort with that reference is relative both to one's knowledge of the external meaning system that supplies logical connections and to one's willingness to accept potential ambiguity.

We cannot, then, solely develop a scale of ideational value on the basis of the more or less explicit expression of topics, comments, and the relationships between them at the sentence or discourse level. Explicitness of expression must be balanced against the psychological requirements of the reader and writer for message clarity and the range of 'explicitness' required or desired in certain communication situations—in short, against the text's relationship to internal and external semiotic systems.

We can, in fact, describe several conventional patterns of assimilated concepts shared in our culture that have linguistic correlates. Further, we have methods of assessing what external patterns of assimilation an individual is likely to evoke when approaching a text in certain kinds of contexts.

4.3 SEMIOTIC CONTEXTUALIZATION AS A FUNCTION OF TEXT

4.3.1 The semiotic semantic systems

Like logical conceptualization, the processes of semiotic contextualization realized in texts have generic components, though they are more numerous and form several varieties of semantic systems. Scholars have recently made great progress in describing conventional schemes common in written discourse. At the micro-level, these systems of choice form lingistic REGISTERS and at the macro-level, DISCOURSE GENRES. Perhaps the most explicit descriptions of meanings evoked by registers and genres have been developed by systemic linguists (see, for example, Hasan 1977; Gregory and Carroll 1978; and Martin 1984).

Linguistic registers define conventional instances of 'language-in-action' (Gregory and Carroll 1978: 64). They are collections of certain lexical choices and conventional syntactic arrangements that express consistent simultaneous reference to a specific field, tenor, and mode associated with conventional discourse situations. The kind of language used by preachers in sermons forms a register, as does the kind of language used by sports reporters in giving the play-by-play description of a football game, and the language of scientists reporting experimental research results.

Linguistic genres define conventional instances of organized text. As defined here, 'genres' include conventional literary discourse forms, such as the short story, the novel, and the sonnet, and conventional varieties of non-literary text, such as the informational report, the proposal, and the technical manual.[3] Although some linguistic registers are associated regularly with certain genres (for example, the language of scientific reporting is associated with the experimental research report), the choice of register is independent of the choice of genre (see Couture 1985).

4.3.2 The semiotic systems realized in texts

The selection of a register and of a genre imposes certain 'explicitness' constraints on a speaker/writer's expression of message and on a listener/reader's process of interpretation. Registers and genres communicate ideas in themselves that can either support or subvert the ideas a reader or writer might interpret as a function of a text's logical structure. We can illustrate these points by examining just a few aspects of some functional descriptions of registers and genres proposed recently for literary and expository discourse.

Registers are conventionally adopted ways of speaking or writing that often specify the attitude the reader is to take toward conceptualizing the ideas in the discourse. For instance, they determine the listener/reader's expectations that the discourse will develop hierarchically ordered logical relationships, that it will contain facts to be built upon in succeeding communications, and that it will require reference to some systems of meaning outside the text. These expectations are cued by conventional linguistic features that comprise a given register.

The language of newspaper reporting, as Crystal and Davy note, is structured to engage the reader in a reported 'story.' It often contains short clauses, initial adverbials, and short paragraphs, and it makes extensive use of coordination, giving readers a sense of immediacy and urgency and bringing them to the event as participants (see Crystal and Davy 1969: 180–5). This register, admittedly, is very broadly defined, overlapping many 'other varieties of English (such as scientific language)' and absorbing 'a great deal of idiosyncracy on the part of . . . individual journalist[s].' Nevertheless, the reportorial aims of clarity and objectivity show in this style's general avoidance of complex sentence structures that might possibly 'produce obscurity and unintelligibility' (Crystal and Davy 1969: 184, 190). Because the language of newspaper reporting (as opposed to editorializing) avoids explicit judgment, we expect it to contain fewer subordinators and embeddings indicating 'generalizations and support' or 'causes and consequences' or 'similarities and differences' than a more persuasive register might. The language of newspaper reporting invites the reader to assimilate the facts and events recorded and to offer his or her own interpretation; it expects its audiences to involve themselves in the act of making logical sense of its content.

Another written register, 'traditional bureaucratic language,' has the opposite function of disengaging the reader from the act of logical conceptualization while distancing the speaker/writer from the listener/reader. According to Redish, this style, which appears in bureaucratic memos, reports, and guidelines, is 'nominal, full of jargon, and legalistic.' It overtly denies the responsibility of the writer to make something clear to a reader, and through this distancing, it promotes the image of 'a strong, impersonal, and therefore impartial, institution' (1983: 152, 153, 162).

Several factors promote the continued use of this 'complexified style' in government offices—a style that 'is not just ordinary English with hard words and long sentences' but also negates the language's purpose to communicate. Among them are the government's tradition of using legalistic language, the image of the government as the 'impersonal guardian of the public welfare,' and writers' wish to associate themselves with the prestigious work of the government (Redish 1983: 161, 162). The writers of 'traditional bureaucratic language' either consciously or unconsciously choose to let the meaning of this register assert the institutional values of distance, prestige, and power and thus dominate the lexical and syntactic content of their discourses. For them, explicitness requirements are far less than for those who come to the discourse to absorb its content, not its assertion of social values.

Some registers do more than assert general attitudes toward the text. These varieties, often persistently referenced in ritualistic forums, evoke an entire set of ideas outside the text. This evocation can be so great that the particular content of a text in these registers does not add to the body of ideas referenced by the register itself.

Two examples of this ritualistic language, as we might call it, are 'religious' and 'Marxist' language. As Crystal and Davy note of the language of religion, the 'kind of language a speech community uses for the expression of its religious beliefs on public occasions is usually one of the most distinctive varieties it possesses' (1969: 147). The distinctiveness of religious language, they claim, is due to its cultural base in primary texts (the Bible and common prayers), traditional formulations of belief (linguistic variety is shunned as it risks 'inconsistency' and possible 'heresy'), and the 'revered ancestry' of 'familiar words and phrases' (1969: 149). The vocabulary of religious language is emblematic of historical precedences and postulates.

Barthes makes this same point about the ritualized, ideological register of Marxist language:

> Marxist writing is presented as the language of knowledge. . . . It is the lexical identity of writing [in this language] which allows it to impose stability on its explanations and a permanence in its method. . . . Each word is no longer anything but a narrow reference to the set of principles which tacitly underlie it. . . . [It] is like an algebraical sign representing a whole bracketed set of previous postulates. [(1953) 1977: 23]

Marxist language interrupts the reader's efforts to create logical conceptualizations of the text content, asking the reader to rely on a set of ideas DEVELOPED OUTSIDE the text for a text's interpretation.

When a ritualistic register dominates a text, the reader's judgment of the text's ideational effect may have little to do with whether or not its lexical content and syntax suggest a new message; ideational value may instead be a function of the register's power to call up an old message intact, through symbolic reference to specific networks of meaning in an ideological semiotic.

While registers impose explicitness constraints at the level of vocabulary and syntax, genres impose additional explicitness constraints at the discourse level. They define conventional patterns of linguistic structure for a complete discourse, and they are intertextual—that is, they are defined by their capacity to evoke other texts. As Scholes explains: 'The genre is a network of codes that can be inferred from a set of related texts. A genre is as real as a language and exerts similar pressures through its network of codes, meeting similar instances of stolid conformity and playful challenge' (1985: 2). Both literary critics and rhetoricians traditionally associate genre with a complete, unified textual structure. Unlike register, genre can only be realized in completed texts or texts that can be projected as complete, for a genre does more than specify kinds of codes extant in a group of related texts; it specifies conditions for beginning, continuing, and ending a text.

The body of scholarship describing literary and transactional genres is immense, ranging from theoretical, philosophical discussions of discourse aims to pragmatic, prescriptive discussions of textual format. Both theoretical and empirical research suggests that readers and writers have overall expectations for how discourse in a conventional genre presents ideas in terms of referentiality and inference, and those expectations are reflected in a text's more or less explicit development of a message. In general, the writer's choice to write in an expository genre is a contract with the reader to communicate an explicit message, while the choice to write in a poetic genre is a promise to suggest implicit meaning.

Readers expect generic structure of expository discourse to complement and support the explicit development of a text message. In his *Conceptual Theory of Rhetoric*, D'Angelo asserts that all expository discourse represents a set of conventional 'logical and psychological patterns which listeners and readers of our language understand, and indeed anticipate' (1975: 18). These psychological 'patterns' are analogous to what linguists call generic structure, psychologists call schemas, and rhetoricians call rhetorical modes.

D'Angelo regards them as more than cultural conventions for conveying ideas: 'These patterns are symbol systems which are objectively distinct from thinking, yet which refer directly to it' (1975: 18).

The idea that expository genres reflect thinking patterns is a subject of debate as is the exact contribution of generic structure to readers' perception of ideational content. Mayer asserts that readers have to locate an overall structure at the macro-level to 'learn' new ideas from prose. For instance, readers should anticipate the subsequent schematic design when searching for 'idea units' in a scientific explanatory text: a 'rule' statement or 'the most general statement of the observed relationship among variables'; explanations of the rule that give 'the underlying components, show[ing] how they relate to one another, and how they account for the rule'; and a 'causal chain' relating these components (1985: 73–5).

While looking for a schema may be helpful to a reader in processing expository prose, a clearly developed schema may not be the key to effective ideation in all referential discourse. Kieras asserts that the explicit development of logical relationships at the sentence level is more relevant to a reader's understanding of the ideas of a technical passage than the articulation of an overall design or schema: 'The schema notion seems to have very little applicability to the comprehension of technical prose. A more appropriate theoretical approach would be one emphasizing those aspects of comprehension that work at the level of processing individual content facts' (1985: 94). In general, however, analyses of expository or referential prose design suggest that effective expository writing follows conventional generic patterns that emphasize logical relations, such as CAUSE AND EFFECT, GENERALIZATION AND SUPPORT, and QUESTION AND ANSWER. Of course, research on reader-response to ideas in expository prose has for the most part concentrated upon comprehension, not upon the overall effectiveness of idea presentation. Not surprisingly, such research tends to demonstrate that more comprehensible discourse has a macro- and micro-structure that makes topics and comments and logical relations explicit. Whether the ideational thrust of ALL expository texts puts a premium on comprehension is open to question. An internal memo written in 'traditional bureaucratic language' may thwart the outside reader's efforts to perceive logical structure, yet effectively communicate institutional values and be regarded internally as successful. Nevertheless, the fact that so much research has been devoted to logical comprehension in itself suggests that it is highly valued in referential genres.

By contrast, emotional satisfaction appears to be most valued when readers search for ideas in literary discourse. Explorations of reader-response to literary works have distinguished two kinds of satisfaction that readers get from ideas presented in literary text: the satisfaction of pattern construction that comes from reading literature regarded as art and the satisfaction of pattern recognition that comes from reading popular literature.

In drawing up a taxonomy of discourse types, Applebee claims that literature we value highly in our culture provokes 'conflict within the paradigms of each succeeding generation, pushing towards a new and broader perspective' (1977: 94). When popular literature draws upon our sense of pleasure at being presented with a pattern, we can enjoy and explore it thoroughly, as in 'play':

> The pleasure that [popular literature offers] . . . is a pleasure of mastery, and just as a child becomes bored when he has fully mastered a skill, dropping some of its elements from his play and taking up new problems, so too we can expect the reader to become bored when he has mastered the principles underlying the stories he is reading. [1977: 87]

Although Applebee does not say as much, I believe the pleasure of popular literature is also the pleasure of the familiar. Like confiding in a trusted friend, reading a popular novel (or watching a TV serial) is a 'safe' activity that places us in a world where answers are always found and expectations are always met. Readers of business writing experience a similar pleasure from discourse that follows the standard format for a lab report, a bid proposal, or a policy statement.

The tension between familiarity and discovery not only distinguishes literary discourse types, but also creates a polar distinction between poetic and prosaic registers within literary genres. Barthes makes an elegant statement of this polar distinction in describing the linguistic aims of classical and modern poetry:

> Images [in classical poetry] are recognizable in a body; they do not exist in isolation; they are due to long custom, not to individual creation. . . . Classical conceits involve relations, not words: they belong to an act of expression, not of invention. . . .
>
> . . . Modern poetry, since it must be distinguished from classical poetry and from any type of prose, destroys the spontaneously functional nature of language, and leaves standing only its lexical basis. . . . Connections are not properly speaking abolished, they are merely reserved areas, a parody of themselves, and this void is necessary for the density of the Word to rise out of a magic vacuum, like a sound and a sign devoid of background, like 'fury and mystery'. [(1953) 1977: 45–7]

Barthes' contrasting descriptions of classical and modern poetry distinguish 'prosaic' and 'poetic' discourse styles; a distinction that can be made in texts called either 'poetry' or 'prose.' Poetic language proposes new relations between concepts, relations that contrast with those conventionally drawn in prosaic or ordinary language. Whether a text's language is perceived as poetic or prosaic is dependent on the relative novelty of its logical structure. The conventions of classical poetry, now regarded as prosaic, in their beginnings must have appeared inventive. Now these conceits form a register, and the overall design of classical poems has become generic.

The register of poetic language, at the elliptical end of our explicitness scale, contrasts with conventional language use; the genre of modern poetry, an innovative structural framework for completed text, contrasts with traditional literary genres: modern poetry is generic in its potential to define a complete discourse, yet unique in its historical relationship to structures of previous text.

Unlike register, genre identifies a discourse as text; like register, it establishes a semantic space in which discourse makes a certain range of sense. When an author writes a report or a poem, the reader has certain expectations for the kinds of logical relations to be presented in either, the former to be more explicit and conventional and the latter to be more implicit and unique. Genre, like register, can also be invoked by an author to present a message in itself—conveyed in a complete conventional structure. In fact, generic structure in what Smith calls 'prefabricated discourse' IS the text's message: 'Though the statement [of greeting card verse] is personal, it is not the statement of the person who composed it. . . . In fact, no one is saying it, and it is not a message. . . . [It] is designed to *be* a message under appropriate circumstances' (1978: 58). Smith cites 'greeting card' verse as a typical prefabricated discourse; we might add 'self-help' essays as well. When prefabricated utterances such as these are expressed on the 'right' occasions, the reader calls up cued sentiments and feelings and does not attempt to decode a message from the lexical content and syntactic structure of the text.

In sum, registers and genres control the reader's interpretation of textual messages in two ways:

- They designate whether or not the reader should rely on a text's lexical and syntactic content to uncover a message—that is, whether the reader should expect the text's logical development to be explicit or implicit.
- They express meanings in themselves that may support or deny messages derived from a text's propositional content.

Both these message functions have implications for effective textual ideation.

4.3.3 The semiotic systems as heuristics for ideational value

In section 4.2.3, I asserted that explicitness of expression had a functional correlate in 'clarity,' but that clarity is not all that determines the effectiveness of textual ideation. The textual expression must also have EXIGENCE—that is, it must be relevant to the assimilated knowledge systems of the writer and reader in the shared context the text invokes. In choosing the word *exigence* to describe effective contextual meaning, I have called upon the dual process of conceptualization and contextualization to enhance a complex concept.

In my view, a text's exigence is its ability to become an integral part of a situation requiring a joining of minds, perceptions, and values. In Bitzer's view, exigence is a component of the text's rhetorical situation:

> Exigence is the necessary condition of a rhetorical situation. If there were no exigence, there would be nothing to require or invite change in the audience or in the world—hence, there would be nothing to require or invite the creation and presentation of pragmatic messages. When perceived, the exigence provides the motive. [1980: 26]

Bitzer separates the exigence of a situation from the exigence of the text whose development 'commences with the critical relation between persons and environment and the process of interaction leading to harmonious adjustment' (1980: 25). I believe that a text that is situationally relevant is an exigence in itself; it provides a meeting place for ideas and persons that will coalesce to generate new situational exigences. The text's appropriate relationship to registers and genres, and to the semiotic systems that establish situational relevance, enables its emergence as an exigence.

To achieve an 'appropriate relationship' to systems of genre and register, a text must contain lexical and syntactic choices that:

- consistently represent registers and genres accessed;
- harmoniously combine selections from conventional registers and genres; and
- effectively balance the message functions implied by genre and register with the messages implied by its propositional content.

The first criterion has obvious utility: if a reader cannot discern the text's reference to a register or genre because the text's features do not clearly point to particular systems, the text's capacity to attain situational relevance is diminished or misdirected.

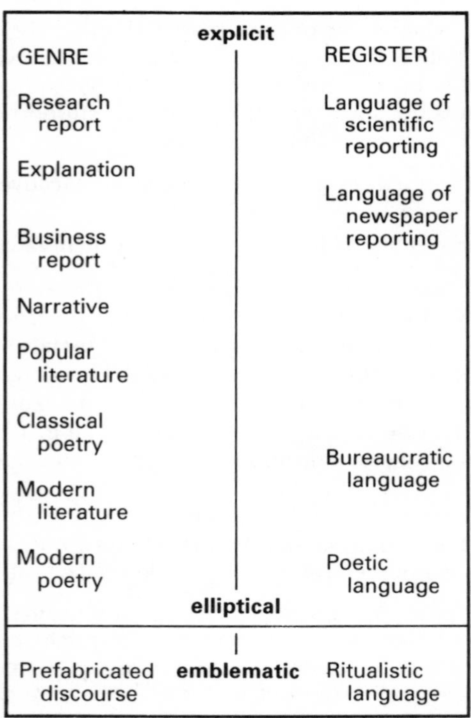

Figure 4.3 Ranking of registers and genres on scale for explicitness of expression

As the scholarship mentioned in section 4.2.2 suggests, we can rank both genres and registers as they impose a demand for logical explicitness in a given text. As the ranking in Figure 4.3 displays, the selection of the RESEARCH REPORT genre coupled with the selection of the LANGUAGE OF SCIENTIFIC REPORTING carries with it stringent expectations for logical explicitness, whereas selection of the NARRATIVE REPORT along with its complementary register, THE LANGUAGE OF NEWSPAPER REPORTING carries with it a lesser demand for explicitness of logical relationships. The choice to communicate in an emblematic register or genre, such as ritualistic language and prefabricated discourse, is a choice to avoid or defer all personal responsibility for the explicit expression of an idea. In fact, the concept of explicit expression is irrelevant in these systems (hence, they are placed outside the proposed scale). Here the writer chooses simply to reference whole systems of ideas called up from somewhere outside the text. The effectiveness of discourse in this register and genre is dependent upon the adequacy of the speaker/writer's articulation of the features of these systems.

Since the two sides of the scale are independent, a writer could select a genre that implies a high degree of explicitness (like a business report) and at the same time select a register that demands less explicitness (such as bureaucratic language). In doing so, the writer must decide which criteria for explicitness he or she wishes to dictate linguistic choice (clear hierarchical development of message and support demanded by the REPORT genre or implicit expression of the cultural values of impartiality, power, and prestige associated with BUREAUCRATIC style). Ranking of registers and genres on an explicitness scale may help explain why writers have difficulty addressing some contexts successfully: when a situation makes contradictory demands, the writer may choose a register and genre with disparate explicitness requirements, rather than couple selections from harmonious systems. The ranking can also reveal ways that writers fail to balance effectively the message potential of these semiotic systems against the lexical and syntactic content of their texts. An application of the scale to the student text in Figure 4.2 provides an illustration of this point.

The generic form of the sample text is EXPLANATORY ESSAY , and the student writer, in part, has executed its features adequately. She begins by naming and defining her topic; then she names the aspect of the topic she intends to explain (*why marriages are not surviving*) and gives reasons that provide the explanation. The overall structure resembles the pattern for 'scientific explanation' described by Mayer (1985). However, the register she has chosen to execute her explanation is not appropriate for this genre; her language is poetic, requiring the reader to make connections based on the syntactic placement of concepts and their relationship to conventional, cultural views of marriage.

We can highlight this poetic use of terminology by reorganizing a portion of the student text to take the form of a poem, as shown in Figure 4.4. When structured as such, elliptical reference to *economics* and *different opinions* seems somewhat more acceptable to the reader because the genre itself contextualizes the discourse in a situation where explicit reference is not

Why are marriages not surviving?

Perhaps

Economics

Different opinions, or
even an
interest in other people

and, of course there are
other reasons, but

these are just some reasons
why (I want to point out)

Figure 4.4 Student text structured as a poem

demanded and ambiguous reference is valued. The fact that the words *Economics* and *Different* are capitalized here (as they were in the original) suggests that the author is imbuing these words with a special sense, a sense not suggested by their dictionary meanings. The parenthetical reference to the narrator's view highlights the poem's dual function as an artifact and personal expression, giving the message meaning in both a universal and personal sense.

Of course, the text in Figure 4.4 is not a very good poem, but I would be willing to say that it is a better poem than it is an expository composition! In so saying, I have identified another source of the original text's failure to achieve effective ideation—it fails to meet the reader's expectation for communication in the genre it ostensibly represents. In referencing an explanatory genre in its overall structure, the author obligates herself to provide explicit logical development. The text fails because she selects a register with explicitness constraints that do not allow her to fulfill that promise.

4.4 SUMMARY AND IMPLICATIONS

In this chapter, I have demonstrated that effective ideation is a function of two kinds of meaning systems realized through text: conceptual logic and contextual semiotic. Through systematic lexical and syntactic choices that express logical relationships between topics and comments at the discourse and sentence level, the text promotes the reader's conceptualization of its overall message. Through linguistic choices that comprise registers (conventional ways of saying things in certain contexts) and genres (conventional forms of overall discourse structure), texts present a relevant context for ideational interpretation.

When a text expresses conceptual messages with a level of explicitness appropriate to its articulation of register and genre, it is more likely to be ideationally effective. I say more likely, because although all the linguistic selections suggested by logic and the cultural semiotic may be consistent and well coordinated to develop a unified message, the value of the message is still subject to the individual judgment of writer and reader. The reader will evaluate whether the choices of register and genre are situationally apt and whether the text maintains a proper balance between its reference to these systems and its propositional content.

Even given this important limitation, it seems worthwhile to explore the capacity of a dual perspective on textual meaning to describe linguistic choice as it influences readers' interpretation. This latter objective has many challenging consequences; here I will elaborate just four of them.

First, examining discourse as it expresses logical and semiotic meaning systems may explain why texts receive mixed reviews from their readers. One source of possible difficulties may be the selection of a register and genre which have conflicting explicitness requirements for logical development (like the student text examined here). Another might be selection of features from several different registers or several different genres in the same text, giving conflicting messages about the appropriate contextualization of the text message (see Couture 1985). Studies of texts that display purposeful, controlled selection of features from a variety of genres versus texts that mix genres unsuccessfully may reveal text heuristics for combining genres for special purposes.

Second, a dual semantic analysis may result in a more informed approach to teaching style and form. Execution of appropriate style and format for a given situation requires the careful integration of linguistic choices from several systems of meaning. Actual texts present a mix of styles and forms that make them exigent in their response to a particular situation. Writers not only need to know what features distinguish register and genre, but also how they are melded in some communications to meet needs not satisfied by the particular articulation of a single system of conventions.

Third, attention to texts' capacities to express logic and to relate to a context may reveal the historic source of linguistic idiosyncracy in communications that address particular contexts—idiosyncracies that may work against the ideational effectiveness of these communications. Some investigations in this vein have been made for military communications, particularly personnel reports used to evaluate officers for promotions. Haering (1980) suggests that the conflicting aims of evaluating an officer and making an argument for promotion in the same discourse have resulted in Navy personnel developing a strictly codified language that in effect means something quite different from what might be inferred from a propositional analysis of its content. Because high performance ratings are necessary for promotion, officers making evaluations have adopted a personnel rating scale and evaluative descriptors that consist almost entirely of superlatives. A comparison of the propositional content of this specialized communication with the contextual meaning attributed to it could uncover sources of communicative dysfunction and provide an analytic impetus for change.

Finally, a dual perspective on the meaning systems referenced in written communications can help writers to address larger concerns about how their communications contribute to current epistemologies. To assert that effective ideation represents a balance between conceptual clarity and contextual exigence is to confirm that neither intellectual logic nor appeal to situational variables alone presumes communicative success—a position that poses difficulties for those who through their writing would seek universal truths, ideas devoid of bias toward a particular way of seeing or doing things. Yet even if writers consciously choose to strip their prose of contextual bias in an effort to be maximally inventive, their efforts will not be entirely successful.

The power of contextual constructs to bias inventive thinking is more insidious than many of us may wish to believe. For instance, Miller (1978) suggests that Western culture as a whole is limited in its efforts to seek new knowledge because of its reliance upon technological semiosis to seek answers to human problems. Inhabitants of a technologized culture seek answers to questions, rather than new questions to answer; technologized cultures have substituted 'closed-system [deductive] logic for open-system reason.' Closed-system logic shapes modern science and 'has become a self-justifying necessity' (Miller: 233, 234). The consequences are awesome:

> If we believe that our relationship with the world is objective, that the external world determines our knowledge of it, then the concept of ethos evaporates—there can be no character to our knowledge or action, other than the idiosyncratic or the mistaken. That loss is the most rhetorically powerful consequence of technology. [1978: 236]

In short, if we believe that only certain ways of seeking knowledge of the world are 'truthful,' we prejudice ourselves against genuine discovery and ultimately against change.

In this chapter I have proposed an analytic system of ideational value in written discourse, outlined the components of that system, suggested its heuristic value, and assessed its explanatory power. But in doing so, I have only begun to do what we must in order to describe how any kind of text functions—that is, explore how language unites our worlds and ourselves.

NOTES

1. DeMan observes with some awe this tendency in both literature and criticism, claiming that it makes these kinds of texts the 'most rigorous' and the 'most unreliable language in terms of which man names and modifies himself,' a paradox central to their interpretive value (1979: 140).
2. Schmidt supports this imperative in a thoughtful examination of criteria for a comprehensive communicative text theory. He claims that two semantic analyses are possible for any textual communication event: one 'intensional' interpretation and the other 'extensional' interpretation:

> One might postulate a process of linear *intensional* interpretation where a recipient decides (during the linear reading of the textformula) which cognitive structure stored in his memory he assigns to syntactically analyzed structures[;] . . . in

addition one might postulate a process of *extensional* interpretation where the recipient has to decide whether the intensionally interpreted structures/elements of structures can be referentially related to a real or fictive world. [1977: 57–8]

3. Systemicists have defined genre more broadly, including conversational varieties of text (see Hasan 1977, for example).

BIBLIOGRAPHY

D'Angelo, F. J. (1975), *A Conceptual Theory of Rhetoric*, Cambridge, Mass., Winthrop.

Applebee, A., 'The Elaborative Choice,' in Nystrand, M. (ed.) (1977: 82–94), *Language as a Way of Knowing: A Book of Readings*, Symposium Series 8, Toronto, Ontario Institute for Studies in Education.

Barthes, R. ([1953] 1977), *Writing Degree Zero*, Lavers, A. and Smith, C. (trans.), New York, Hill and Wang.

Barthes, R. (1977), *Roland Barthes*, Howard, R. (trans.), New York, Hill and Wang.

Bitzer, L. F., 'Functional Communication: A Situational Perspective' in White, E. E. (ed.) (1980: 21–38), *Rhetoric in Transition: Studies in the Nature and Uses of Rhetoric*, University Park, Penn., Pennsylvania State University Press.

Bleich, D. (1978), *Subjective Criticism*, Baltimore, Johns Hopkins University Press.

Couture, B., A 'Systemic Analysis of Writing Quality,' in Benson, J. D. and Greaves, W. S. (eds) (1985: 67–87), *Systemic Perspectives on Discourse 2: Selected Applied Papers from the 9th International Systemic Workshop*, Advances in Discourse Processes 16, Norwood, N.J., Ablex.

Crystal, D. and Davy, D. (1969), *Investigating English Style*, London, Longman.

van Dijk, T. A. (1980), *Macrostructures: An Interdisciplinary Study of Global Structures in Discourse, Interaction, and Cognition*, Hillsdale, N.J., Lawrence Erlbaum.

van Dijk, T. A. and Kintsch, W. (1983), *Strategies of Discourse Comprehension*, New York, Academic Press.

Flower, L. S. and Hayes, J. R. (1977), 'Problem-Solving Strategies and the Writing Process,' *College English*, **39**, 449–61.

Fries, P. H., 'On the Status of Theme in English: Arguments from Discourse,' in Petöfi, J. S., and Sözer, E. (eds) (1983: 116–52), *Micro and Macro Connexity of Texts*, Papers in Textlinguistics 45, Hamburg, Helmut Buske.

Gregory, M. and Carroll, S. (1978), *Language and Situation: Language Varieties and their Social Contexts*, London, Routledge and Kegan Paul.

Haering, G. (1980), 'Fitness Report Finesse,' *United States Naval Institute Proceedings*, No. 1 (**106**), 34–8.

Halliday, M. A. K. (1967), 'Notes on Transitivity and Theme in English, Part 2,' *Journal of Linguistics*, **3**, 199–244.

Halliday, M. A. K., 'Linguistic Function and Literary Style: An Inquiry into the Language of William Golding's *The Inheritors*,' in Chatman, S. (ed.) (1971: 330–65), *Literary Style: A Symposium*, London, Oxford University Press.

Halliday, M. A. K. and Hasan, R. (1976), *Cohesion in English*, London, Longman.

Hasan, R., 'Text in the Systemic-Functional Model,' in Dressler, W. U. (ed.) (1977: 228–46), *Current Trends in Textlinguistics*, Research in Text Theory 2, Berlin, Walter de Gruyter.

Hasan, R., 'Ways of Saying: Ways of Meaning,' in Fawcett, R. P., Halliday, M. A. K., Lamb, S. M., and Makkai, A. (eds) (1984: 105–62), *The Semiotics of Culture and Language: 1 Language as Social Semiotic*, London, Frances Pinter.

Hoey, M. (1983), *On the Surface of Discourse*, London, Allen and Unwin.

Holland, N. N. (1975), *5 Readers Reading*, New Haven, Yale University Press.

Jakobson, R., 'Closing Statement: Linguistics and Poetics,' in Sebeok, T. A. (ed.) (1960: 350–77), *Style in Language*, New York, Wiley.

Kieras, D. E., 'Thematic Processes in the Comprehension of Technical Prose,' in Britton, B. K. and Black, J. B. (eds) (1985: 89–107), *Understanding Expository Text: A Theoretical and Practical Handbook for Analyzing Explanatory Text*, Hillsdale, N.J., Lawrence Erlbaum.

de Man, P., 'Semiology and Rhetoric,' in Harari, J. V. (ed.) (1979: 121–40), *Textual Strategies: Perspectives in Post-Structuralist Criticism*, Ithaca, N.Y., Cornell University Press.

Martin, J. R., 'Language, Register, and Genre,' in Christie, F. *et al*. (eds) (1984: 21–30), *Children Writing: Reader*, ECT 418 Language Studies, Geelong, Vic., Deakin University Press.

Mayer, R. E., 'Structural Analysis of Science Prose: Can We Increase Problem-Solving Performance?,' in Britton, B. K. and Black, J. B. (eds) (1985: 65–87), *Understanding Expository Text: A Theoretical and Practical Handbook for Analyzing Explanatory Text*, Hillsdale, N.J., Lawrence Erlbaum.

Meyer, B. J. F., 'Prose Analysis: Purposes, Procedures, and Problems,' in Britton, B. K. and Black, J. B. (eds) (1985: 11–64), *Understanding Expository Text: A Theoretical and Practical Handbook for Analyzing Explanatory Text*, Hillsdale, N.J., Lawrence Erlbaum.

Miller, C. R. (1978), 'Technology as a Form of Consciousness: A Study of Contemporary Ethos,' *Central States Speech Journal*, **29** , 228–36.

Percy, W. (1975), *The Message in the Bottle: How Queer Man Is, How Queer Language Is, and What One Has to Do with the Other*, New York, Farrar, Straus and Giroux.

Redish, J. C., 'The Language of the Bureaucracy,' in Bailey, R. W. and Fosheim, R. M. (eds) (1983: 151–74), *Literacy for Life: The Demand for Reading and Writing*, New York, Modern Language Association of America.

Ricoeur, P. (1976), *Interpretation Theory: Discourse and the Surplus of Meaning*, Fort Worth, Tex., Texas Christian University Press.

Schmidt, S. J., 'Some Problems of Communicative Text Theories,' in Dressler, W. U. (ed.) (1977: 47–60), *Current Trends in Textlinguistics*, Research in Text Theory 2, Berlin, Walter de Gruyter.

Scholes, R. (1985), *Textual Power: Literary Theory and the Teaching of English*, New Haven, Yale University Press.

Smith, B. H. (1978), *On the Margins of Discourse: The Relation of Literature to Language*, Chicago, University of Chicago Press.

Young, R. E., Becker, A. L., and Pike, K. L. (1970), *Rhetoric: Discovery and Change*, New York, Harcourt, Brace and World.

5 Text and context: how writers come to mean

Deborah Brandt
University of Wisconsin–Madison

5.1 TOWARD UNCOVERING CONDITIONS FOR TEXTUAL MEANING

Most teachers and scholars of written composition would agree that the act of composing involves many processes whose traces are not evident in written texts. Identifying the mode of a text or enumerating its T-unit lengths or the density and range of its cohesive devices may lend insight into the structures of written texts (see, for example, Hunt 1965; and Witte and Faigley 1981); however, it can describe only one or another static outcome of the writer's dynamic and complex effort to make meaning. (Indeed, a recognition of the gap between text analysis and the actual experience of bringing forth texts gave rise to the PROCESS MOVEMENT in composition studies.)

Yet the finished text need not be abandoned in our pursuit to understand the composing act—not, that is, if we shift our focus from the formal features of an isolated text toward the whole text as an instance of language functioning in a context of human activity. From this view, the text appears as an instrument of social interaction, conveying multiple messages about the social world in which it has been developed. From this view, the text becomes, as Beaugrande and Dressler observe, 'a document of decision, selection, and combination' (1981: 35), a record of a writer's response to the exigencies of the communicative setting in which the text is composed. From this perspective, we can choose to question not only what mode a text adopts, but also what 'sociosemantic' conditions, to borrow a term from Halliday (1978 and elsewhere), have given rise to that mode; not only the length of T-units or the number and kinds of cohesive devices a passage carries, but also in what way those devices become viable strategies for meaning-making within a given context.

Text analysis from a sociosemantic perspective can uncover the links between the structure and processes of a text and the structure and processes of the larger social system in which that text participates. I hope to demonstrate here how patterns of text features directly relate to the conditions for meaning with which a writer has worked during the composing of a text. Approaching written composition from this perspective, I believe, can give both writers and teachers new insights on the composing process—insights discovered when that process is perceived in its relationship to a finished text. Since Halliday's theory of language as social semiotic has provided the backdrop for my own analysis of written text, I shall briefly review his theoretical stance and follow with my interpretation of its relevance to an analysis of written composing processes as revealed in student writing.

5.2 A THEORY OF 'LANGUAGE AS SOCIAL SEMIOTIC' APPLIED TO WRITTEN TEXT

Language, says Halliday, looks and behaves the way it does because of the work it does for us. Its functions are not external uses to which it is put so much as they are fundamental properties of the language itself (1973, 1974, 1975, and 1978). Halliday elucidates the systematic link between language and the social environment in his now well-known tripartite explanation of the semantic functions of language. Through the IDEATIONAL, INTERPERSONAL, and TEXTUAL functions of language, a text embodies the social situation in which it participates (see Bernhardt and Smith in this volume for an explanation of these semantic functions [ed.]). Halliday's theory of semantic function establishes a way of viewing any text, whether spoken or written, as an outgrowth of a context of human activity. A text arises from a situation and in turn manifests that situation in its lexical and linguistic structures. Of course, whenever we refer to text structures, it must be understood that those structures are actually choices a writer or speaker has made for representing or substantiating a situation.

The relationship between context and oral speech is readily apparent to us because spoken language encounters frequently take shape around the understanding that participants share through their mutual access to an extralinguistic setting. For instance, a dialogue between two people changing a flat tire will derive its sense and coherence from the unfolding activity at hand. The connection between context and written speech, however, is less clear. Indeed, because written texts are so much more explicit than oral texts, they are sometimes described as context-free, as carrying within themselves the means to be understood without an appeal to external context. Olson, for instance, has characterized written texts as 'autonomous' and divorced from contexts of situation (1977: 272). Malinowski ([1923] 1949) first made the distinction between the context-dependency of spoken utterances and the context-independence of written utterances. Interestingly, he later renounced the distinction, maintaining that the meaning of even the most abstract discourse is grounded in contexts of experience (see Malinowski 1935; for a discussion of Malinowski's changed position, see Langendoen 1968: 15–35).

As Malinowski's insights suggest, the greatest differences between writing and speaking do not lie so much in their relative reliance on context, but rather in the radical differences in the functional contexts in which the two normally occur. In short, the activities that we conduct or supplement with speech differ from those we conduct or supplement with writing. However, the process of using context to constitute language and language to constitute context and of relying on the interplay of both to constitute meaning is much the same when we turn from speaking and listening to writing and reading.

Today, scholars along with Halliday are beginning to acknowledge writers' and readers' mutual reliance on social context in writing and interpreting text. Their studies in speech act theory, textlinguistics, and reading processes point out that underlying any text are networks of 'pragmatic presuppositions,' the 'conditions necessary for a sentence to be appropriate in the context in which it is used' (Bates 1976: 22). Research demonstrates that writers rely on readers to bring to bear stores of prior knowledge and expectations in order to make sense of what they read (see the wealth of scholarship in reader-response criticism, for example, Suleiman and Crosman 1980). Scholars now generally agree that successful texts are not context-free, but rather guide readers to construct appropriate, mutually significant aspects of context by which meaning can be shared. Likewise, successful writers plan their texts around unwritten conditions for meaning that direct lexical and syntactic choices having mutual significance for their readers.

In the following discussion, I concentrate (somewhat arbitrarily, I admit) on three types of text structures that reveal text and context relationships and can serve as at least partial indices to the 'conditions for meaning' with which a writer has worked during the composing of a text. These elements are: EXOPHORIC REFERENTS (references to a world outside the text), COHESIVE DEVICES (the means by which a writer makes a text 'stick' to itself), and THEMATIC STRUCTURE (choices a writer makes for sequencing information across a clause and throughout a text).

5.3 SOME INDICATORS OF SOCIAL CONTEXT IN WRITTEN TEXT

5.3.1 Exophoric referents

Exophoric referents point to entities outside a text; they direct a reader to retrieve information not from somewhere else in a text but from some 'extratextual' context to which the reader presumably has access. If I write 'In response to your memo, we will ship the merchandise within the next two weeks,' I assume my reader can identify which *memo*, which *merchandise*, and, in the absence of a date and letterhead, which *we* and which *two weeks* I am writing about. This sentence is very much bound to some real world that writer and reader share in common and to which both appeal for sense of the text.

Exophoric text features are common in spoken discourse (e.g. *This is wet, Put it here*), but often appear in written discourse to point to some 'real' context present to both writer and reader (e.g. *your memo, the moon*) or to elements that can be inferred to be present IN THE TEXT WORLD in which writer and reader participate. Thus, in the following passage, the phrase *the seeds* appears inferentially as part of the situation that the passage evokes: *Onions can be planted toward the end of March. Prior to planting, the seeds should be soaked overnight.*

Exophoric referents are especially pertinent to text and context relationships because they are an index to the given reality that a text participates in: both the 'real world' domains that underlie a text and the 'text world' a writer assumes a reader shares by virtue of reading a text. Through real world references, we see the world which in a sense preexists a text, the domain of prior experience to which a writer has chosen to link a text and the domain of shared existence through which the text is understood. Exophoric referents can both designate a shared or shareable world and embody roles within that world. And obviously the nature of this shareable world, as well as the nature of the role a writer is able to adopt in that world, bear directly on the writer's capacity and options for making meaning. These referents are clues to a writer's assumptions about the reality that a text itself is establishing for a reader, the reality to which both writer and reader are entitled to appeal for sense. Hence an analysis of exophoric referents can uncover in part the world with which a writer has worked during the composing of a text—a world that constitutes a major CONDITION FOR MEANING during the act of composition.

5.3.2 Cohesive devices

Cohesive devices signal conditions opposite from the ones indicated by exophoric references. While exophora gestures outward to a world, cohesion is endophoric, pointing inward to other parts of a text. Where exophora speaks of an EXTRA-LINGUISTIC context beyond a text, cohesion speaks of the need to create context through text itself. Where high levels of exophora may be evidence of high levels of shared understanding preexisting between writer and reader, high levels of cohesion are more often evidence of efforts to establish such shared understanding explicitly.

Though exophora and cohesion point in opposite directions, cohesive devices are no less a part of a writer's response to contextual conditions and to the options available for representing meaning under those conditions. In composing, a writer makes constant decisions about how to reference and to relate lexical items in a text: should a word be repeated? should a synonym be used? can a pronoun be used in place of an earlier item or an entire passage? how should relationships among parts of a text be represented? These decisions are often based on the same criteria used in choosing exophoric references, criteria having to do with the extent of shared writer–reader knowledge and with the writer's powers, given a set of contextual conditions, to develop understanding through text patterns. Thus, while cohesion is sometimes described as a text-based phenomenon, its origins and ultimate meaning are actually contextual.

Halliday and Hasan's *Cohesion in English* (1976) presents an exhaustive taxonomy of five major categories and nearly twenty-five sub-categories of cohesive devices and applies this taxonomy in the analysis of various texts.

For the purposes of this study, I would like to concentrate on two major categories: REFERENCE and REITERATION.

Cohesive or endophoric reference is similar to exophoric reference in that it points away from itself; it embodies 'an instruction to retrieve from elsewhere the information necessary for interpreting the passage in question' (Halliday and Hasan 1976: 33). But unlike exophoric reference, by which the retrieval must take place in some world beyond the text, endophoric reference points to a feature in the text itself. Both exophora and endophora establish definiteness, yet only endophora secures and stabilizes text-specific reference.

Endophoric reference establishes a semantic tie between a referent and another part of a text by indicating the 'identity of the particular thing or class of things that is being referred to' (Halliday and Hasan 1976: 31). Personal pronouns, demonstrative pronouns, and comparatives can all create cohesive reference. For instance, *he, there*, and *another* all create cohesive reference in the following passage: *John planned to meet only three board members in the school room to discuss the tax. To his surprise, he found another there when he arrived*.

Endophoric reiteration achieves cohesion through repeated naming or labeling of a text referent. Lexical reiteration includes repetition of the same term, the use of a synonym for that term, or the use of a word that represents a more general category of the original item (e.g. *flowers* for *roses*). Repetition, of course, is a device for assigning importance or weight in a discourse. Things that get mentioned repeatedly in a text are usually what the text is 'about'; they are the referents the writer and (usually) the reader find pertinent to a situation at hand.

Reiteration, when viewed as a meaningful structure—as a strategy for meaning-making, can also be a clue to 'selections of orientation' on a speaker's or writer's part (see Halliday and Hasan 1976: 292n.). When writers use the same term throughout a text (rather than a series of synonyms), they limit the interpretation of that term; when writers use synonyms, they may encourage a more open and inclusive interpretation by the readers. Using patterns of synonyms can also establish for a reader a frame of reference for a term, a 'territory' of meaning that elaborates and enriches understanding.

5.3.3 Thematic structure

The THEME of a clause—its first syntactic unit—announces 'what the discourse is about right now.' Theme generally coincides with the sentence subject. The writer's choice to place a feature in the theme or first position as opposed to in the RHEME or remainder of the clause both affects information distribution in the clause and its message. When writers choose not to place the subject first in a clause, for instance, they may be indicating to the reader a new focal point in the discourse.

Theme represents one of the options that writers have beyond the constraints of grammar for emphasizing one element over others. Halliday calls theme the 'point of departure' for a writer's message (1967: 212). Theme is a manifestation of COMMUNICATIVE STRUCTURE; it is writer-and-reader-based, a sign of a writer's conception of 'the world as we, writer and reader, both at this moment share it.' Thus a look at a writer's handling of theme across a discourse is of interest here as yet another index of the relationship of social context and textual option (see Halliday 1967, for a discussion of MARKED and UNMARKED THEME [also see Davies and Eiler in this volume (ed.)]).

Patterns of theme and rheme can, of course, be traced intratextually as a rheme from one part of a text becomes the theme in another. Such a chain is demonstrated in Example (i), where *Cyrena Dutt* and *graduation requirements* shift from rheme to theme positions:

(i) The Board of Education this morning named Cyrena Dutt as new superintendent of schools. Dutt, a native of Philadelphia, is a vigorous advocate of longer school days and tougher graduation requirements. Graduation requirements will top the agenda of the next board meeting.

The origins of sentential themes are not limited to previous text, however. Themes, like exophoric references, may be derived from elements in an extratextual context which the writer chooses to bring into thematic focus. In Example (ii), *congress* functions this way:

(ii) Guerrilla resistance continues to mount in El Salvador following national elections. Congress began debate on a new aid package for the troubled region.

When themes do not correspond with the grammatical subject, they may provide a reader with an interpretive framework for the rest of the sentence. The semantic focus of Example (iii) follows from an initial emphasis on contrast:

(iii) Unlike other families in their neighborhood, the Scamaliones prefer to stay home during their vacations.

And the initial element *fortunately for us* in Example (iv) casts an evaluative focus on the information in the rest of the sentence:

(iv) Fortunately for us our income tax return was not audited.

No matter what their origins, sentential themes are a sensitive gauge of a writer's decisions about the focus of the discourse, the here-and-now from which a written utterance can and should depart. Of course, thematic emphasis at the sentence level does relate to larger discourse topics or macrothemes; some researchers have shown how local sentences relate to a more abstract 'aboutness' in a discourse (see van Dijk and Kintsch 1983; and Witte 1983). But theme is also grounded locally in the progressive development of a text and the evolving understanding that a writer assumes to share with a reader. In its relevance to the moment-to-moment focus of a discourse, theme is especially pertinent to relating written texts to the contexts in which they were produced.

5.4 AN ANALYSIS OF STUDENT COMPOSITION: REVEALING THE WRITER'S CONDITIONS FOR MEANING

To illustrate how text reveals the context for composing, I will turn now to an analysis of three passages written by the same student writer under different sets of circumstances. The exophoric referents, cohesive devices, and thematic patterns in these passages show how the texts reveal a shared writer–reader context and reveal the semantic constraints and opportunities that marked the contexts of each composition. My analysis demonstrates not only the capacity of written language to reflect conditions beyond itself, but also explains some of the social conditions which give rise to textual characteristics, the conditions which bear on a writer's capacity to mean during the composing of a text.

The findings reported here are part of a larger study of forty-eight texts written by twelve students enrolled in an introductory composition course that I taught at Indiana University (see Brandt 1983). The texts shown here are representative of the larger sample of texts in their use of exophora, cohesion, and thematic structure. My comments about them are for the most part pertinent to other essays written for the same assignments.

Figure 5.1 displays the opening paragraph of a typical academic essay, a student response to a set of questions I prepared for my composition course. I had begun the course by asking students to consider the question 'Why do we write?' I asked students to compile 'inventories' of all the writing they undertook or received during a week-long period. After classifying items in their inventories according to the functions that they served, the students compared their inventories—each student comparing his or hers with those of three other classmates. Finally, each student wrote a preliminary, informal report of his or her findings addressed to the rest of the class. To assist students in writing that report, I distributed a set of questions (see Figure 5.2).

The text in Figure 5.1 gestures outward to *three inventories* and to *categories* within those inventories which are under analysis. The existence of the inventories and their contents are presuppositions upon which this writing is based. The exophoric references indicate that these inventories are in the context of situation to which writer and reader presumably have mutual access, the circumscribed world of a particular classroom activity. In fact, all exophoric references in the entire text from which Figure 5.1 is taken are either to the inventories, to the language in the teacher's questions (Figure 5.2), or to the authorial 'I,' the person whose name appeared at the top of the paper. None of the exophoric references are to a world beyond the

> Each of the three inventories I've examined lists items of writing under specific headings. Noticeably, each inventory divorces personal writing from 'external' forms. There is a sense throughout that self-motivated writing is a thing apart. The categories of each list are chosen to cover, in a general sense, the same areas of writing.

Figure 5.1 Opening paragraph of homework essay

Study the inventories of three classmates as well as your own. What patterns can you find among the inventories? What are the striking similarities? Any striking differences? If someone were to do a study of 'written literacy among typical college students' on the basis of the information you have collected, what kind of conclusions might he or she draw? Why? Would these conclusions be accurate or fair? Why or why not?

Figure 5.2 Text of teacher's questions for homework assignment

classroom. The localized exophoric references reflect the high level of shared writer (student) to reader (teacher) knowledge characteristic of school-sponsored writing. And the specialized and circumscribed nature of the exophora demonstrates that the meanings this student could reach and express in these circumstances were largely constrained to the domain set by the teacher's assignment. Only through this literally 'given' world could the student come to mean.

The constraints of the classroom assignment are also reflected in the student's use of cohesion. The major cohesive device employed in the text of Figure 5.1 is lexical reiteration, such as in the repetition of *inventory(ies)*, *writing*, and *list(s)*. Endophoric reference is nearly absent; the writer directs his text outward to a situation he attempts to explain, rather than inward in an effort to develop text-specific explanations. This strategy reflects the situational constraint of responding to a set of questions posed by the teacher (Figure 5.2). The terms which recur in the passage can be traced to the lexicon of the teacher's questions and to the topic of inquiry that the class had been involved in overall (i.e. the role of writing in students' lives). The writer's orientation is toward the teacher's discourse; his writing not only takes place on the teacher's terms but IN the teacher's terms. Reiteration in this paragraph seems to signal compliance with the assignment, an effort to synchronize 'my' meaning with 'the teacher's' meaning. The lack of elaboration also attests to the high degree of prior understanding that the student-writer assumes to share with the teacher-reader by virtue of their mutual participation in the 'extra-textual' context of the class itself.

The themes in this opening paragraph serve as yet another device for the student to synchronize his text with the situation embodied in the teacher's questions. The student's semantic focus is indicated thematically by *each of the three inventories I've examined* and *the categories of each list*; he thematically signals that he has complied with the assignment to reach some analytic conclusion about the inventories with *There is a sense throughout*. . . .

The uses of theme to synchronize student meaning with teacher meaning are strikingly apparent when we look at examples of the opening lines of other students' texts written in response to the same questions. Six examples appear in Figure 5.3. Obviously, the point of departure for these students' essays is to signal that the teacher's instructions have been followed and that the ensuing discussion will take place within the bounds of those instructions.

The students' language indicates the very high level of agreement about 'what's going on' in this context, and the similarity of lexis and structure of

1. Each of the three inventories I've examined lists items of writing under specific headings.
2. Upon studying the inventories of three classmates I came to some observations which can be informative in helping explain how writing plays a part in our lives.
3. After studying the inventories of my group as well as my own, I discovered that we have roughly similar stuff under different categories.
4. In my study of my inventory and other people's inventories, I found that of all the written materials that documents such as a driver's license, credit card, and other receipts were the most abundant of all the articles.
5. During my study of writing inventories involving myself and two of my classmates, I see and understand that there is a relationship which connects these inventories with each other.
6. Studying the inventories in front of me, I see that the majority are of personal and educational origin.

Figure 5.3 Opening sentences of homework essays written by different students

these openings attests to the small range of linguistic features that students found appropriate for introducing these compositions—namely those that reflect the constraints of the teachers' instructions. This is not a surprising response. In an interesting study of classroom interaction, Edwards and Furlong remark on the compelling constraints imposed by a teacher's language:

> It is the teacher, then, who normally controls what is and can be meant in the classroom. The restricted range of communicative options open to pupils is therefore inseparable from the restricted range of *semantic* options. . . . What [students] can mean is normally bounded by what the teacher considers to be relevant, appropriate, and correct. [1978: 31–2; see also Stubbs 1976; and Stubbs and Delamont 1976]

The sample texts in Figure 5.3 have in common language that is 'relevant, appropriate, and correct' relative to their teacher's assignment.

The entire opening paragraph of our representative student's essay (Figure 5.1) in all its exophoric, cohesive, and thematic structures reveals the highly specialized and semantically constrained conditions under which the student composed. The meaning of these textual choices becomes more apparent when we compare them to exophoric, cohesive, and thematic patterns in a text written by the same student under quite different contextual conditions.

Figure 5.4 displays the opening paragraph of an essay by our representative student on the so-called literacy crisis among American youths. After doing the inventory project, my class examined the issue of the cultural value of writing and reading. Students read several published articles expressing divergent views about literacy. The assigned articles included: Merrill Sheils, 'Why Johnny Can't Write,' *Newsweek*, 8 December 1975: 58–65; Neil Postman (1970), 'The Politics of Reading,' *Harvard Educational Review*, **40**: 244–52; Daniel Shanahan (1977), 'Why Johnny Can't Think,' *Change*, No. 9 (**9**): 10–11; and Timothy J. Bergen, Jr. (1976), 'Why Can't Johnny Write?,' *English Journal*, No. 8 (**65**): 36–7.

In recent times the question of a 'literacy crisis' has come to notice in the discussions of educators and parents of students graduating in this country. More and more teachers and administrators of schools seem convinced that there has been a drop in the standard of literacy of the American student. Certainly something must be happening—some change occuring in the society—to warrant this concern. However, the possible causes for the present state of alarm may be historical, sociological, and certainly deep-rooted. The solution to the problem, whatever it is, will depend on the nature of these causative factors.

Figure 5.4 Opening paragraph of an essay on the literacy crisis

After extensive discussion, students wrote essays about the literacy issue, addressing them to the audience for one of the journals in which the articles had been published. The author of the text in Figure 5.4 chose to write to what he called 'a *Newsweek* audience.' The essay opening shows that the student responds to the needs of his wider audience in several ways, especially by explicitly elaborating the situation to which his text relates. The situational context registers in the exophoric references, notably *this country* and *the society*. The writer gestures to a common, everyday world, the world as we all take it to be. These references depend on a reader's general knowledge, not on privileged knowledge assumed by the writer in his response to the 'inventory' assignment. The domain from which the 'literary crisis' essay originates seems to be the common, here-and-now world the writer shares with all other members of American society, and it is through an appeal to this shared world that the writer attempts to represent his views concerning the issue of literacy.

The 'literacy crisis' passage also contains cohesive devices which function differently from cohesive devices in the passage responding to the 'inventory' assignment. For the 'inventory' essay, the author could rely upon a high level of shared knowledge; for the 'literacy' essay, he had to employ a varied combination of reiterative and referential devices in order to develop a shared understanding by way of the text itself. Consequently, he chose synonomy rather than repetition and endophoric reference rather than exophoric reference in structuring the passage in Figure 5.4. The synonomic lexical features *drop in the standard of literacy*, *the present state of alarm*, *this concern*, and *the problem* effectively elaborate his original term, 'literacy crisis.'

The 'literacy crisis' passage is also more heavily self-referential than the 'inventory' example, containing demonstrative pronouns (e.g. THIS *concern*, THESE *causative factors*) and specificity of reference (e.g. THE *present state of alarm*, THE *solution to* THE *problem*). The shift in this writer's strategies of cohesion from lexical repetition to synonomy and endophoric reference reflects the contextual circumstances under which he composed the second assignment. The changed assumptions about shared reader–writer knowledge and the need to stake out a position on the topic prompted more explicitness, elaboration, and attention to definition of terms.

Thematic choices in the 'literacy' passage also attest to the writer's awareness of a need to orient the reader to the real-world problem he will address. He begins with the orienting introductory phrase *in recent times*. He also thematically highlights evaluative or interpretive language with *certainly* and *however*, signaling an argumentative stance toward the message of his text. Such language announces the type of discourse this will be—argument—and hence is another indication of the writer's distance from his audience and the greater textual effort needed to substantiate a situation.[1]

My final examples for analysis manifest yet another context of situation where conditions register in the kind of exophora and cohesive and thematic devices the writer has chosen. The passages in Figures 5.5 and 5.6 respond to my class assignment to interview someone in an academic discipline or other profession and find out, among other things, what role writing plays in a particular field. Students wrote about the interviews in essays addressed to the class as audience.

The opening paragraph in Figure5.5 is taken from a paper about an interview its writer had conducted with a French-American poet and professor of comparative literature. The author is the same writer who composed the other two passages analyzed above. The exophoric references in this passage, unlike the generalized references in the passage from the 'literacy essay,' tend to evoke a particular setting: *the teacher, the wall, the ungainly machine*. Instead of referring to an existing mutual world, these references activate a new world; they create a scene for the reader to participate in.

The exophoric references in the passage in Figure 5.5 (and in Figure 5.6, discussed below) are to what I call the 'text world.' They point to elements to which the reader has inferential (and imaginative) access by virtue of reading the text. Evoking a scene through exophoric references obviously relates to the role of narrator that these writers adopted as they reported their interviews to others. Exophora serves as a device to draw readers into the settings from which text meaning will arise.

The tendency for the interview accounts to recreate a specific setting to draw readers into the text world of a narrated episode is also reflected in the patterns of collocation, that is, the appearance of features that reference ideas or things that by convention are conceptually related. In fact, the dominant cohesive device in the passage in Figure 5.5 is collocation; note, for instance, *wall/door, sat/facing, pen/papers, classic Frenchman/berets/croissants*. Reiteration (*laugh/laughed* and *pictured/thought*) and pronoun reference (*he* as interview subject and *I* as interviewer) also create cohesive strands in this passage. Although *I* is ultimately exophoric, pointing out to the writer, its recurrence is endophoric, referring to the *I* who is, in a sense, a character in the narrative.

A focus on the characters of the narrative is, in fact, apparent in the sentential themes of the opening paragraph in Figure 5.5. The student

> The teacher sat with his back to the wall, facing the door as I came in. He laughed as I fumbled with pen and papers and the ungainly machine I had brought for the interview. I could only laugh myself, for he was exactly as I had pictured the classic Frenchman. I thought of berets, croissants, and accordions played by the Seine.

Figure 5.5 Opening paragraph of an interview essay

> In outward appearance he is not a big man, but rather average in size, dressed in the working blue collar dress. The car he drives is small. At home he spends time gardening and cutting the grass around a well-kept house while relaxing on the riding mower. His children usually run here and there, feeding the chickens and hoeing the garden.

Figure 5.6 Second example from an interview essay

announces that his discourse is about *the teacher* and *I*, himself, a thematic pattern that is consistent throughout the entire essay. Interestingly, the larger discourse theme of the essay, as it develops, is the tension between the poet-professor, a staunch humanist, and the student-interviewer, a budding physicist and an advocate of high technology.

Figure 5.6 displays a passage from another student's essay responding to the 'interview assignment.' The writer of this passage uses the thematic choices somewhat differently to highlight attributes of the person whom the essay is about, and these attributes frame the information we receive: *in outward appearance, the car he drives, at home, his children*. These thematic choices are deliberate as the writer goes on to tell about how he has observed this man from a distance without knowing what the man did for a living. This 'detective' approach registers in the thematic progression of the paragraph, demonstrating how writers are able to share certain understandings and perspectives with readers through the functional information structures of discourse.

My students' very different—and, as their teacher, I must say sophisticated—uses of exophora, cohesion, and theme in the interview assignment stem from the greater need they had under the 'interview' conditions to create context- and text-specific meaning through their written language. Their previous assignments originated from classroom experiences and were on assigned topics; this task, by contrast, involved an experience outside the class that was not known beforehand by their readers (including their teacher). We could expect an essay written under these circumstances to rely very little on a presupposed, extratextual setting for comprehension.

In the foregoing discussion, I suggest that textual features in finished texts can be linked to conditions originating in the contexts of their composition. How a writer chooses to refer and represent seems particularly constrained by such factors as the nature of previous discourse present in the context, the level of shared reader–writer knowledge which preexists a text, and the discourse role a writer plays or is expected to play in the text. In responding to a teacher's written questions, for instance, our representative student writer adopted reiteration and exophora as a strategy for complying with the 'terms' of the assignment and for embodying the high levels of shared prior knowledge which existed in the circumscribed world of the classroom. For the interview paper, the same writer used reiteration and collocation, in orchestration with exophora, to enact a world in which readers could participate. While a textual strategy in one circumstance can serve a quite different function (and hence take on quite different meaning) than it does in another, the CHOICE of a device is in itself always meaningful and hence provides another glimpse into the sociosemantic conditions that a writer has at hand.

5.5 IMPLICATIONS FOR RESEARCH AND TEACHING IN COMPOSITION

One of the most promising contributions that functional language studies can make to the field of composition is the development of a new and fruitful way of looking at texts. Rather than erasing any trace of their context of origin, written texts—as much as spoken texts—bear indelible marks of the social and semantic conditions from which they arise. Indeed, it is largely through the recognition of these marks that readers are able to comprehend texts.

I have attempted to show how three aspects of text—exophoric references, cohesive devices, and thematic structure—relate to conditions for meaning in a writer's context of composition. Through exophoric reference, one can glimpse the given world that a writer assumes to share with a reader, the world from which, in a sense, a writer launches a text. Cohesion, although often treated strictly as a textual element, is presented here instead as a context-sensitive STRATEGY. Through patterns of reference and reiteration, for instance, writers reflect their assessment of the need—and leeway—they have for labeling and elaborating in their texts. Choice of theme is also an indication of a writer's attention to what is and can be in reader–writer focus as a discourse unfolds.

Scholars in textlinguistics, pragmatics, and speech act theory are beginning to explore the capacities of written texts to reflect and perpetuate social processes. As understanding in these areas expands, we can expect more comprehensive and systematic approaches to text analysis. Equally promising is the concurrent interest in the nature of 'communicative competence,' the underlying knowledge and strategies by which language users understand each other and make themselves understood. These trends confirm Kjolseth's observation that the 'analysis of language, whatever its pretentions, is not a way out of society but rather leads one further into its workings' (1972: 53).

Functional text analysis can reveal how writers use the resources of written language to enact meanings in everyday discourse. A systematic analysis of the writing from various contexts—from classrooms to boardrooms—will increase awareness of HOW written language functions in those contexts and of WHAT writers and readers in those contexts know and share in common. Study of the texts of one writer composed in a variety of contexts could uncover the range of an individual's 'writing repertoire' and show how strategies developed in one context are retrieved and adapted for another. Further, an analysis of texts collected from children as they mature could elucidate writers' initiations into the ways of meaning through text.

Linguistic research on the functions of language in the classroom could go far in helping teachers understand the character of students' writing. In the past decade, several scholars have studied spoken interactions between teachers and students (see, for instance, Edwards and Furlong 1978; Mehan 1979; and Stubbs 1976). Written interactions between teachers and students, students and students, and between students and textbooks remain to be investigated. The results of my study suggest to teachers that they carefully consider writing assignments in terms of the conditions for meaning that they offer to students, including the discourse role they encourage and the state of shared writer–reader knowledge that may exist prior to composing.

Techniques of discourse analysis which relate text to context and parts of text to each other can aid composition teachers in reading students' papers more fully for the interpretative processes which underlie them. Shaughnessy's *Errors and Expectations* (1977) powerfully demonstrates the benefits of reading a student's writing not for what it says about what the student does not know but for what it says about what the student DOES know. Further examinations of the nature and functions of textuality can help writing teachers recognize how students' writing demonstrates their textual knowledge and competence and how a student's text represents deliberate and thoughtful choices made in response to the potential for meaning-making that the student found or could make available in a context for composition.

Learning to write is learning to exploit the relationship of context and text in ways that will be meaningful and satisfying to others. As Halliday has observed, 'Being appropriate to the situation is not some optional extra in language; it is an essential element in the ability to mean' (1974: 35).[2]

NOTES

1. I should thank Martin Nystrand for pointing out instances of genre markers in texts.
2. I wish to acknowledge gratefully the comments of David Bleich, Barbara Couture, Martin Nystrand, and Marilyn Sternglass on earlier versions of this chapter.

BIBLIOGRAPHY

Bates, E. (1976), *Language and Context: The Acquisition of Pragmatics*, New York, Academic Press.

Beaugrande, R. A. de and Dressler, W. U. (1981), *Introduction to Text Linguistics*, Longman Linguistics Library 26, London, New York, Longman.

Brandt, D. (1983), *Writer, Context, and Text*, Ph.D. dissertation, Bloomington, Ind., Indiana University (see *Dissertation Abstracts International*, sec. A, 1984, **44**, 3045–A).

van Dijk, T. A. and Kintsch, W. (1983), *Strategies of Discourse Comprehension*, New York, Academic Press.

Edwards, A. D. and Furlong, V. J. (1978), *The Language of Teaching: Meaning in Classroom Interaction*, London, Heinemann Educational Books.

Halliday, M. A. K. (1967), 'Notes on Transitivity and Theme, Part 2,' *Journal of Linguistics*, **3**, 199–244.

Halliday, M. A. K. (1973), *Explorations in the Functions of Language*, London, Edward Arnold.

Halliday, M. A. K. (1974), *Language and Social Man*, Schools Council Programme in Linguistics and English Teaching 2, vol. 3, London, Longman.

Halliday, M. A. K. (1975), *Learning How to Mean: Explorations in the Development of Language and Meaning*, London, Edward Arnold: Baltimore, University Park Press.

Halliday, M. A. K. (1978), *Language as Social Semiotic: The Social Interpretation of Language and Meaning*, London, Edward Arnold: Baltimore, University Park Press.

Halliday, M. A. K. and Hasan, R. (1976), *Cohesion in English*, London, Longman.

Hunt, K. W. (1965), *Grammatical Structures Written at Three Grade Levels*, NCTE Research Report 3, Champaign, Ill., NCTE [National Council of Teachers of English].

Kjolseth, R., 'Making Sense: Natural Language and Shared Knowledge in Understanding,' in Fishman, J. A. (ed.) (1972: 50–76), *Advances in the Sociology of Language 2: Selected Studies and Applications*, The Hague, Mouton.

Langendoen, D. T. (1968), *The London School of Linguistics: A Study of the Linguistic Theories of B. Malinowski and J. R. Firth*, Research Monograph 46, Cambridge, Mass., The MIT Press.

Malinowski, B., 'The Problem of Meaning in Primitive Languages,' supplement to Ogden, C. K. and Richards, I. A. ([1923] 1949, 10th edn: 296–336), *The Meaning of Meaning: A Study of the Influence of Language upon Thought and of the Science of Symbolism*, New York, Harcourt Brace: London, Routledge and Kegan Paul.

Malinowski, B. (1935), *Coral Gardens and Their Magic: A Study of the Methods of Tilling the Soil and of Agricultural Rites in the Trobriand Islands*, 2 vols., New York, American Book Company.

Mehan, H. (1979), *Learning Lessons: Social Organization in the Classroom*, Cambridge, Mass., Harvard University Press.

Olson, D. R. (1977), 'From Utterance to Text: The Bias of Language in Speech and Writing,' *Harvard Educational Review*, **47**, 257–81.

Shaughnessy, M. P. (1977), *Errors and Expectations: A Guide for the Teacher of Basic Writing*, New York, Oxford University Press.

Stubbs, M. (1976), *Language, Schools and Classrooms*, London, Methuen.

Stubbs, M. and Delamont, S. (eds) (1976), *Explorations in Classroom Observation*, London, John Wiley.

Suleiman, S. R. and Crosman, I. (eds) (1980), *The Reader in the Text: Essays on Audience and Interpretation*, Princeton, N.J., Princeton University Press.

Witte, S. P. (1983), 'Topical Structure and Revision: An Exploratory Study,' *College Composition and Communication*, **34**, 313–41.

Witte, S. P. and Faigley, L. (1981), 'Coherence, Cohesion, and Writing Quality,' *College Composition and Communication*, **32**, 189–204.

6 Achieving impact through the interpersonal component

Edward L. Smith, Jr.
University of Texas at Austin

6.1 COMPARING GUIDELINES FOR EFFECTIVE WRITING WITH ACTUAL WRITING PRACTICE

Many teachers of written composition acknowledge the importance of structuring a prose text to meet the needs of a particular audience. They have been enlightened by studies of the writing process and of written products conducted with experienced and inexperienced writers in a variety of situations (see, for instance, Britton 1975; Sommers 1980; and Odell, Goswami, and Quick 1983). Still, scholars are just beginning to do sophisticated analyses of the ways authors actually approach an audience in their writing. Composition textbooks offer new writers plenty of advice for organizing a text to make the author's relationship to audience clear, but few textbooks reflect what good writers actually do.

The disparity between textbook instruction and actual practice is evident in textbook advice on how to establish POINT OF VIEW. Many composition textbooks instruct student writers to maintain a consistent tone and point of view, that is, to maintain throughout a written text a given relationship to the reader and a given perspective on the subject matter (see, for example, *The Harper Handbook of College Composition* (Shaw 1981: 111–13, 116, 484–9); *The Little, Brown Handbook* (Fowler.1980: 205–9); and *Writing with a Purpose* (McCrimmon 1980: 197–8)). This instruction is frequently accompanied by exercises asking students to identify and to correct inconsistent grammatical choices which establish a rhetorical stance toward the reader and the subject. Textbooks often treat grammatical choices of person and mood, for instance, as a set of features selected initially and employed invariably throughout a text. For example, for a relatively formal, descriptive written text, some textbooks will advise writers to choose the third person to refer to themselves and their readers throughout and to use indicative rather than interrogative or imperative verbal constructions to maintain both an impersonal relationship to the reader and an objective perspective on the subject. In conjunction with this advice, textbooks will warn students to avoid sudden shifts in tone and point of view.

These guidelines stand in sharp contrast to the actual practice of competent writers. A quick reading of many samples of professional writing, that is, expository texts in professional journals or books, will demonstrate that writers do 'shift' grammatical features that establish tone and point of view. As Nash writes in *Designs in Prose*:

> Constant shifts in tone will occur in any text that reflects the presence of its author. . . . It is not uncommon, for example, for a long text to begin in a formal style and gradually ease into a collaborative [informal] manner from which renewed excursions into formality may be made. . . . But the changes are as a rule carefully and tactfully graded. [1980: 132–3]

Nash, however, points out that changes in tone are made 'carefully' and 'tactfully' by skilled writers: well-modulated shifts in tone are acceptable, and perhaps even desirable. Nash's observations suggest that grammatical choices representing tone do not define mono-dimensional sets, for instance, 'formal' versus 'informal' choices; rather they define a range of choices, for example FROM formal TO informal. This is the way such choices are described in systemic-functional approaches to language study.

6.2 APPLYING SYSTEMIC ANALYSIS TO INTERPERSONAL FUNCTIONING IN WRITING

Interest in the application of systemic-functional theory to composition has been sparked by studies of cohesion by Halliday and Hasan and others following them. However, textual cohesion is only one aspect of written texts which may be investigated from a systemic-functional perspective. In Halliday's view, a text is the result of multiple semantic choices made in a particular social situation (see Halliday 1977). Each element of the situation—the FIELD, or type of social action, the TENOR, or the role relationships among the participants, and the MODE, or symbolic organization of the communication—is correlated with a semantic component of the resultant text: field with the IDEATIONAL component, tenor with the INTERPERSONAL component, and mode with the TEXTUAL component. In turn, each semantic component 'specifies its own structures,' that is, has particular lexical and grammatical categories which are associated with it (Halliday 1977: 176).

Semantic components can serve as focal points to classify texts. Focusing on the ideational component allows us to classify texts according to their field of discourse (e.g. scientific, religious, or legal texts), on the interpersonal component, to classify texts according to their tone (e.g. formal or informal texts) and purpose (e.g. didactic or non-didactic texts), and on the textual component, to classify texts according to their mode of discourse (e.g. written or oral texts). Of course, any text will represent a configuration of all these semantic components and can be classified further by its particular configuration. For example, a text addressing a religious subject (field) that is formal and didactic (tenor) and delivered orally (mode) might be classified as a 'sermon.' Such a configuration of ideational, interpersonal, and textual components is known in systemic theory as a REGISTER. It is the classification of texts according to their field, tenor, mode, and register—rather than according to a single criterion like content or purpose—which represents one important advantage of the application of systemic-functional perspective to composition: its ability to characterize texts in multiple ways even WITHIN various semantic components.

The value of considering continuous semantic choices that identify a text with a field, tenor, or mode is particularly evident when we examine the interpersonal functions of texts and how they establish tenor. The tenor of an individual text may represent a range of tones and purposes, realized through particular grammatical and lexical choices. However, a single tone and a single purpose for a text can be located on scales in relation to those of other texts: in terms of tone, a text can be more formal or less formal; in terms of purpose, more didactic or less so.

6.3 EXAMINING ACCEPTABLE GRADATIONS OF TONE AND PURPOSE IN PROSE

Not all writers who express a range of tones and purposes in a single text are successful in doing so. Student writers often make abrupt shifts in person or mood, especially in papers produced for introductory composition courses. By examining the graduated expression of tone and purpose in a variety of professional texts, systemic-functional analysis can help us to describe such shifts more accurately and to explain more precisely to our students the difference between successful and unsuccessful shifts.

However, before exploring how systemic analysis is useful in this way, let's examine more thoroughly those interpersonal relations which establish tone and purpose in a text and the grammatical features associated with them.

According to Halliday, the interpersonal component of meaning consists of two types of role relationships: 'social roles of the first order . . . defined without reference to language,' and social roles of the 'second order . . . defined by the linguistic system' (Halliday 1977: 202). Social roles of the first order reflect the relative social status of the participants in a discourse which remains unchanged when the discourse is completed (e.g. communication from a higher to a lower status participant in a memorandum from a supervisor to a staff person or equal to an equal in a letter from one friend to another). Social roles of the second order, however, reflect the particular roles assumed by the initiator of a discourse and projected onto the receiver, for example, questioner to responder or informer to doubter. These roles are only temporary ones, related to the purpose of the initiator, and may change after the discourse is completed or even before it is completed.

Gregory and Carroll claim that the roles played by participants and by language in an interchange reflect two kinds of tenor: 'personal tenor' or 'degree of formality' between participants (what we see evident in tone) and 'functional tenor' or 'purpose' for using language in a particular situation

(1978: 51, 53). They defend their distinction of two types of tenor, claiming that the degree of formality and purpose in a discourse may be independent of each other. For example, they note that a university lecture, the function of which is to exhort and teach, may be delivered with widely varying degrees of formality (1978: 54).

Personal tenor can be established by choices in person and voice and by the overall 'level' of vocabulary. As Gregory and Carroll point out, writers can choose from a collocated set of words that 'appeal linguistically to . . . learned attitudes or prejudices' establishing a degree of formality (1978: 53). Halliday cites both choice of person and use of sentence adverbials, like *hopefully*, as indicators of the attitude of the writer and, we can add, of personal tenor (1977: 180).

Use of deictic references may also be an index of the degree of formality of a text. When citing the extratextual situation, formal written texts often employ absolute references (e.g. *in Washington, D.C., in 1983*) rather than deictic references (e.g. *here, now*). Informal conversational speech displays more deictic references than formal writing because it is anchored to its situation of occurrence; formal writing seeks to approach absolute intelligibility, that is, to create its own context so that it can be read in any situation (see Hawkins 1977; Olson 1977; and Tannen 1980). Hence, the occurrence of deictics in writing makes it appear closer to conversation and less formal.

Though neither Halliday nor Gregory and Carroll do so, it seems useful to arrange the various choices included within these grammatical categories along a continuum. Figure 6.1 illustrates one possible arrangement of the

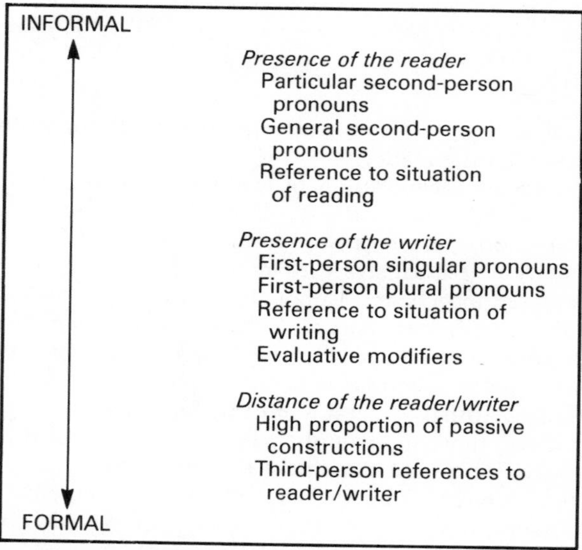

Figure 6.1 Ranking of linguistic features actualizing personal tenor

choices actualizing personal tenor, ranked from 'informal' to 'formal' values, two extremes of personal tenor identified by Gregory and Carroll (1978: 53). In the figure, features relating to the presence of the reader are ordered before features relating to the presence of the writer. The greater the informality of a text, the more the reader will be referenced through features such as pronominal address. Direct references to a reader (e.g. *you*) presume the presence of a writer. Yet, features which assert a writer's presence directly (e.g. the use of the first-person *I*) do not imply that a reader is addressed directly. Hence, texts with direct references to a reader can be considered more interpersonal. Second-person pronouns with PARTICULAR reference to the intended reader are ranked above second-person pronouns with GENERAL reference. (The latter are the informal equivalent of *one* in generalization statements.)[1] Similarly, first-person singular pronouns, referring to the writer in particular, are ranked above first-person plural pronouns when the latter refer to a single author. Finally, those features which distance the reader or writer are ranked last, as most formal; they include passive constructions which hide the agent of procedures or directives and third-person references to the writer or the reader.

Functional tenor (or purpose) is primarily actualized through grammatical choices of clause mood and modality. Clause mood expresses the writer's purpose in the text (e.g. to state, to question, to order). Modal verbs (e.g. *can, should, must*) actualize a persuasive or hortatory purpose in periphrastic imperative constructions like the following (italics added):

> Scientists *must come to terms* with the fact that they may be held accountable for the results of their work. Science *must shed* its guise of being 'for the people' when it is not directed at eliminating the causes of social problems. . . . [Science for the People, 'Biological, Social, and Political Issues in Genetic Engineering,' in Jackson, D. A. and Stich, S. P. (eds) (1979: 99–126), *The Recombinant DNA Debate*, Englewood Cliffs, N.J., Prentice-Hall : 123.]

Here the use of *must* in two consecutive sentences emphatically asserts the author's intention for the reader.

Figure 6.2 presents a continuum of features expressing functional tenor through clause mood and modality. The labels of the terminal points, *didactic* and *non-didactic*, are borrowed from Gregory and Carroll (1978: 53). They are somewhat less satisfying than the informal/formal poles of the continuum representing personal tenor. It is easier to locate personal tenor along a continuum of grammatical features than to similarly order the various functions of a discourse. However, by considering clause mood as analogous to discourse function, it becomes possible to do so. Imperative constructions most strongly exhibit a didactic function with imperatives (e.g. *now add* . . .), being more didactic than first-person plural imperatives (e.g. *Let us try* . . .). Direct questions compel the reader to respond, so they are ranked directly under direct imperatives. Periphrastic imperatives fall under first-person imperatives on the continuum (e.g. *Scientists must come to terms* . . .); some, of course, are more directive than others. Rhetorical questions are often used in a directive way to guide the reader in processing a text;

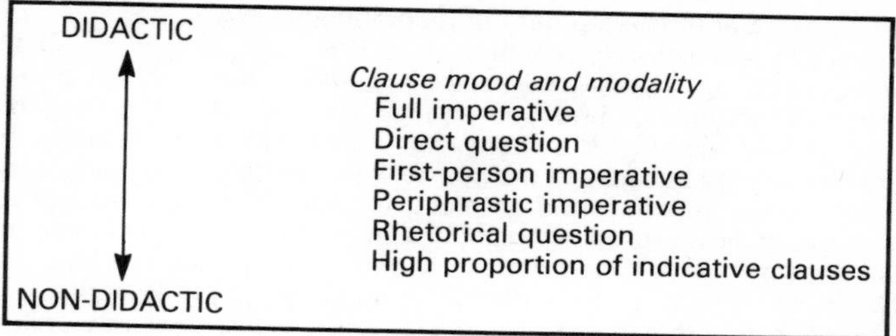

Figure 6.2 Ranking of linguistic features actualizing functional tenor

hence, they are ranked as more didactic than indicative clauses, which assert but do not direct.

Many texts have features that locate them in parallel positions on the continua in Figures 6.1 and 6.2. Although Gregory and Carroll are correct in pointing out that personal and functional tenor may be independent of one another, it is often the case that the two tenors are associated. Informal texts often contain more didactic grammatical features in the form of direct address. The following headline, subhead, and portion of text show how a popular technical magazine exploits this feature (some italics added):

> STACK 'EM UP NEATLY IN THIS STEREO TOWER
>
> *Your* components look as good as they sound—in a unit *you* make yourself.
>
> . . . *Lighting* [sic]. *Use* standard incandescent lights; fluorescent fixtures emit radio frequencies that can interfere with *your* equipment. [Carl W. Spencer (1981), 'Stack 'em up neatly in this stereo tower,' *Popular Science*, 218, 2: 138, 142.]

In the example, second-person references to the reader (*your, you, your*) are combined with a direct imperative (*use*) to produce a very informal, didactic text.

An ordering of the grammatical choices associated with personal and functional tenor on continua can help us examine whether the shifts in tone and purpose that occur in texts are well-modulated or abrupt. Text Sample A in Figure 6.3, the introduction to an exposition of potential areas of application of DNA research by an expert in the field, illustrates well-modulated shifts in tone. The progressively informal tone of the first three paragraphs is realized by a sequential movement from the more formal to the less formal grammatical choices (italicized features).

In the first paragraph of Sample A, proponents and opponents of recombinant DNA research are referred to in the third person (sentence 2); two of the superordinate clauses (sentences 1 and 3) are constructed with the passive voice. In the second paragraph, the writer identifies more explicitly with proponents of the research through the use of the first-person plural *we* in sentence 6 and increased use of evaluative modifiers; here passive voice is used only in relative clauses. The writer also makes a deictic reference to the situation of writing (*today*) in sentence 6. Finally, in the third paragraph, the writer surfaces more visibly through the use of the first-person singular *I* in

[1] The advent and development of recombinant DNA *has been portrayed* as very much a mixed blessing for mankind. [2] While *proponents* have hailed it as a source of technology that will someday solve many of the problems of environmental pollution, food and energy shortages, and human diseases, including inborn genetic disorders, its *opponents* have *bitterly* criticized research in this area because of the possibilities for accidental development and release of *highly* virulent forms of infective agents that *may* lead to epidemic diseases of unknown proportions. [3] The wisdom of developing bacterial strains capable of expressing genetic segments of eukaryotes *has also been questioned*. [4] Each view *is supported* by major groups of scientists.

[5] The *basic* problem in reconciling such *sharply divergent* viewpoints is that in most cases both the benefits and the biohazards that *have been ascribed* to the development of recombinant DNA technology are *highly speculative*. [6] *Today*, *we* are *still far* from any *demonstrated* success at producing antibodies or blood-clotting factors by fermentation, or making plants fix their own nitrogen because of insertion of bacterial nitrogen-fixation genes. [7] Conversely, however, the suggestions of E. coli harboring human cancer or cancer virus genes or developing *highly* virulent traits because of accidental introduction of uncharacterized DNA segments *appear equally far-fetched*, *speculative*, *and exaggerated*.

[8] *This article* has two purposes. [9] First, *I* should like to list and discuss some of the *major* areas where *beneficial* applications of recombinant DNA technology *are envisioned*, whether in the near or in the more distant future. [10] Second, *I* should like to note certain of those areas where both the barriers to technological success, and the potential hazards attendant upon such success, *appear* to be of *less formidable* proportions. [11] *I* believe that *we may* harvest some *tangible* benefits within a *relatively short* time, and with *little* risk, if we develop the new technology in a *meaningful* way.

[12] Apart from scientific applications toward the greater understanding of the nature and mode of regulation of eukaryotic genes, several broad areas of application of recombinant DNA technology *are recognized* in industry, agriculture, and medicine. [13] Briefly stated, these are (1) in the manufacture of drugs, chemicals, and fuels—specifically, polypeptide hormones, vaccines, enzymes, and low-cost fermentation products such as solvents, alcohol, and methane; (2) in the improvement of crop plants and crop yields, both by the extension of existing cross-breeding technologies and by the incorporation of nitrogen-fixation genes into either the crop plants themselves or their normal microbial symbionts; and (3) in the treatment of genetic disease, by deliberately introducing fragments of functional eukaryotic or prokaryotic genes into the cells of human patients. [A. M. Chakrabarty, 'Recombinant DNA: Areas of Potential Application,' in Jackson, D. A. and Stich, S. P. (eds) (1979: 56–66), *The Recombinant DNA Debate*, Englewood Cliffs, N. J., Prentice-Hall: 56–7.]

Figure 6.3 Text sample A—expert writer

sentences 9, 10, and 11, though he also retains the *we* to refer to proponents of DNA research; again, passive voice is used only in a relative clause. Another deictic reference is made to the situation of both the writer and reader in this phrase *this article* at the beginning of the paragraph.

In the fourth paragraph of Sample A, the writer returns to the formal tone established in the first paragraph. Throughout the remainder of the text (not shown here), this level of formality is generally maintained, with occasional recurrences of first-person plural pronouns. However, the first-person *I* never surfaces again.

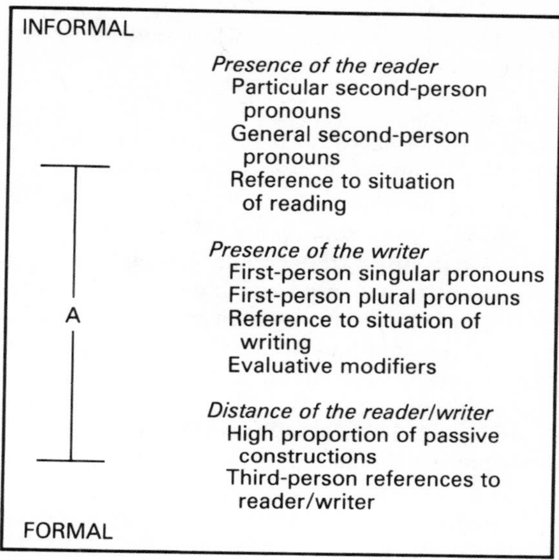

Figure 6.4 Range of variation in tone for Text Sample A

The features of Sample A shed some light on the limits within which shifts in tone may occur in a formal text written for publication in a professional book. Limits are established by the initial degree of formality in the opening sections of the text and the degree of informality achieved before the return to more formal tone. The writer may continue patterns of informal intrusion as long as the level of informality does not exceed that of the first intrusion. This pattern perfectly exemplifies that described by Nash (and cited above) in which an initially formal tone 'gradually ease[s] into a collaborative [informal] manner from which renewed excursions into formality may be made' (Nash 1980: 133).

The tone limits established in the first three paragraphs of Sample A can be thought of as representing points on a continuum of formality, defining the range of acceptable variation in tone for the text. Figure 6.4 plots the range of tone in Sample A and shows that the text displays a limited range of tone and carefully modulated shifts in personal tenor; no abrupt shifts occur from one point on the continuum to a distant point. This modulation appears more evident if we compare Text A to a text in which personal and functional tenor shift abruptly and unsuccessfully.

Text Sample B (Figure 6.5) is a student essay from an introductory composition class, written in response to an assignment on the topic 'handling stress.' The assignment asked students to read an initial quotation from an article called 'Stress Management' and then stated:

From your point of view, write an essay for fellow students on the topic of Coping with School-Related Stress. You may use material from 'Stress Management' in any way you like or ignore it altogether.

Let the goal of answering the two questions below guide you as you write:

1. What are the most significant causes of school-related stress?
2. What steps might students take in order to cope with stress?

The interpersonal stance dictated by the assignment is complicated: students had to decide from what point of view they would discuss the causes of school-related stress (the potential range would extend from a third-person omniscient to a first-person individual perspective) as well as how didactic they might wish to be in recommending steps to take in coping with stress (with a range extending from describing and recounting personal experience in declarative statements to giving advice to the reader in periphrastic and direct imperatives). Text Sample B in Figure 6.5 shows the student writer's difficulty in choosing from these possible expressions of the interpersonal component of her text (verbatim with relevant features italicized).

Perhaps most apparent in Sample B is the abrupt change in personal tenor. The writer begins in the first person, narrating the ways that she handled stress in high school. In the first paragraph, she successfully maintains a moderately informal personal tenor throughout. Then, in the middle of the second paragraph, she adopts a more informal tone using the second person pronoun *your*, followed by an abrupt jump to the generic third-person *they*, establishing a more formal tone thus far not attempted in the paper. The second person *you* and third person *they* are especially jarring because they follow one another in sentential sequence. Figure 6.6 illustrates this abrupt shift visually, plotting the range of informal/formal

[1] When *I* think about stress, the *most significant* cause in relation to school is academic pressure. [2] In *my* junior year in high school, *I* found that this was the very type of stress *I* was having to cope with everyday. [3] *My main* concerns were grades. [4]*I* had not realized, at that time, that it was not the grades so much that were *important*, but the process of learning the material being taught.

[5] Once *I* learned that being able to retain knowledge of a particular subject was *pertinent*, *I was faced* with another stress: peer pressure. [6] It is *amazing* how much influence *your* peers have on *your* academic life. [7] It seems *everybody* has fun when *they* run with the crowd.

[8] *I* had the *hardest* time coping with stress related to academic pressure. [9] *Perhaps*, the problem was *my* inability to cope with failure. [10] As someone once said to *me*, in milder terms, 'Nobody gives a care about a looser.' [11] This statement has always stuck in *my* mind. [12] This, *I* know, is not the way to think. [13] However, when analyzing this statement, *I* find it is *basically* true. [14] The way I coped with this stress was applying *myself* by doing the *best* that *I* could *possibly* put forth.

[15] As for peer pressure, *I* had few problems in combating this stress once *I* established *my* priorities. [16] There is nothing wrong with doing what the crowd does, but *remember your* responsibilities. [17] It is *easiest*, though, to remember *my* mother's favorite biblical quote: To everything there is a season.

Figure 6.5 Text Sample B—student writer

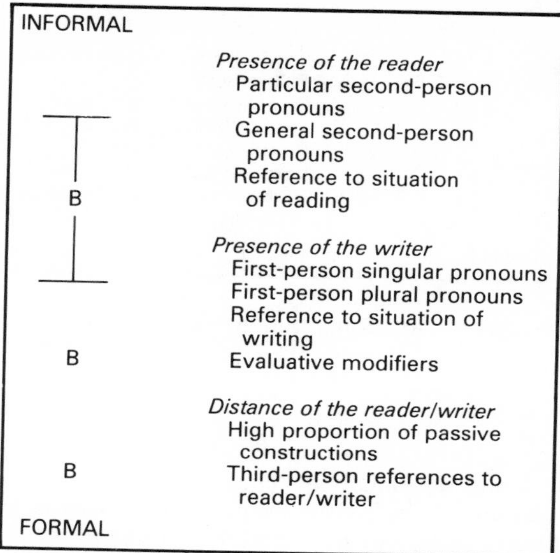

Figure 6.6 Range of variation in tone for Text Sample B

grammatical features in Text B on the continuum of features indicating personal tenor.

As Figure 6.6 shows, the initial, consistent use of first-person singular in Sample B should establish the most formal personal tenor to be employed in the essay. The writer's sudden jump to the more formal third-person generalization in her second paragraph, rather than extending the range of tenor, appears to exceed this 'most formal' limit because it is unanticipated through any increasingly formal forms.

A similar problem develops in the fourth paragraph. There the writer moves from first person (*I*) in sentence 15 to the third-person plural (*the crowd*) in sentence 16, expressing a generalization based on personal experience. She follows immediately with the second person (*your*) in the same sentence, only to return to the first person (*my mother's favorite . . . quote*) in sentence 17. These strategies seem to be at odds with each other, pointing in what ought to be mutually exclusive directions on the continuum of personal tenor. The direct imperative (*remember your responsibilities*) in sentence 16 further complicates the situation. It is not clear whether the *you* addressed by the imperative is a projection of the writer's experience onto a general-reference, second-person form or a direct address to the particular readers of the essay. If the latter is the case, this paragraph has violated the limits of functional tenor established by its first paragraphs.

The essay shifts from a descriptive account of individual experience to a more didactic, advising lecture (which may, in fact, be the underlying function the writer intended for the essay). Of course, essays which maintain

DIDACTIC	
	Clause mood and modality
B	Full imperative
	Direct question
	First-person imperative
	Periphrastic imperative
	Rhetorical question
B	High proportion of indicative clauses
NON-DIDACTIC	

Figure 6.7 Range of variation in functional tenor for Text Sample B

a relatively non-didactic functional tenor as expressed in surface features may also have an underlying persuasive purpose; no matter what the underlying tenor, though, it appears important for writers to maintain a *consistent* or well-modulated surface tenor. The violation of this principle is shown in Figure 6.7 which plots the range of didactic/non-didactic grammatical features of the essay. In all but the final paragraph of the essay, the writer has used indicative clauses, so the 'range' of acceptable variation for this essay is only a single point on the continuum. The jump to a direct imperative at the end of the essay is clearly out of place.

6.4 CONCLUSION

My analyses of Text Samples A and B illustrate that a systemic-functional description of personal tenor in written texts can reveal useful information about how good writers establish and maintain relationships to their readers—information based on empirical evidence, rather than on supposition about how *good* texts are composed. Contrary to the conventional wisdom of composition texts that dictates use of consistent tone and point of view throughout an essay, writers of professional texts do make shifts in their interpersonal stance. Systemic-functional analysis helps us to understand how those shifts can occur successfully and points to the structure of unsuccessful shifts such as those that students often make. Successful shifts are modulated on the continua of personal and functional tenor, and they occur within limits of variation established by the writer in the beginning paragraphs of a text. By focusing on the continuous nature of grammatical choices representing the interpersonal component of texts, systemic-functional theory provides a means to accurately describe such shifts. It can help researchers explain how successful texts express interpersonal tenor and guide instructors in teaching inexperienced writers ways to handle interpersonal functioning in their texts like professionals.

NOTE

1. As an illustration of this distinction, compare the specificity of reference in two interpretations of 'Can you take a train from Houston to Ft. Worth?' Native speakers of English, recognizing this *you* as a general reference, will answer 'Yes, you can.' But non-native speakers, often interpreting *you* as a particular reference, may answer 'Yes, I can.'

BIBLIOGRAPHY

Britton, J., Burgess, T., Martin, N., McLeod, A. and Rosen, H. (1975), *The Development of Writing Abilities (11–18)*, London, Macmillan Education.

Fowler, H. R. (1980), *The Little Brown Handbook*, Boston, Little, Brown.

Gregory, M. and Carroll, S. (1978), *Language and Situation: Language Varieties and their Social Contexts*, London, Routledge and Kegan Paul.

Halliday, M. A. K., 'Text as Semantic Choice in Social Contexts,' in van Dijk, T. A. and Petöfi, J. S. (eds) (1977: 176–225), *Grammars and Descriptions: Studies in Text Theory and Text Analysis*, Research in Text Theory 1, Berlin, Walter de Gruyter.

Hawkins, P. R. (1977), *Social Class, the Nominal Group and Verbal Strategies*, London, Routledge and Kegan Paul.

McCrimmon, J. M. (1980), *Writing with a Purpose: Short Edition*, based on the 7th edition, Boston, Houghton, Mifflin.

Nash, W. (1980), *Designs in Prose: A Study of Compositional Problems and Methods*, London, Longman.

Odell, L., Goswami, D., and Quick, D., 'Writing Outside the English Composition Class: Implications for Teaching and for Learning,' in Bailey, R. W. and Fosheim, R. M. (eds) (1983: 175–94), *Literacy for Life: The Demand for Reading and Writing*, New York, Modern Languages Association.

Olson, D. R. (1977), 'From Utterance to Text: The Bias of Language in Speech and Writing,' *Harvard Educational Review*, **47**, 257–81.

Shaw, H. (1981, 5th edn), *The Harper Handbook of College Composition*, New York, Harper and Row.

Sommers, N. (1980), 'Revision Strategies of Student Writers and Experienced Adult Writers,' *College Composition and Communication*, **31**, 378–88.

Tannen, D. (1980), 'Oral and Literate Strategies in Discourse,' *The Linguistic Reporter*, No. 9 (**22**), 1–3.

7 Clause relations and the writer's communicative task

Michael Hoey
University of Birmingham
Eugene Winter
The Hatfield Polytechnic

7.1 AN INTRODUCTION TO CLAUSE RELATIONS

Focusing on the ways discourses get written forces us to acknowledge something that we can sometimes overlook, namely, that every written discourse is part of an interaction. However much we choose to treat written texts as objects in our study of them, all but a small minority have their origin in the need of a writer to convey a message to one or more readers. This somewhat obvious observation suggests that text analysis that fails to recognize the interactive nature of written discourse will be inadequate in some respects. Nevertheless, linguists who have created analytic models of written text that derive their inspiration from grammatical models (see, for example, van Dijk 1972 and 1977; and Longacre 1968, 1972, 1976, and 1982) make few references to the writer or reader. Those linguists who have made proper acknowledgement of the interactiveness of written discourse have sometimes lost sight of the effects of the grammar and the lexis of the discourse in their exploration of the way readers process discourses (most notably Beaugrande 1980; and Beaugrande and Dressler 1981), or have adopted an over-simplistic conception of the relationship between discourse and interactants (see, for example, Gray 1977; and Edmondson 1981). One descriptive approach that has managed to sail successfully between the Scylla of discourse reification and the Charybdis of psychological speculation is that developed by Winter and his associates, normally referred to as CLAUSE RELATIONAL ANALYSIS. This chapter attempts to provide a brief account of this approach and to link it in with some aspects of the writer's communicative task.

We shall begin by considering what happens when we intepret words that form a nominal group. Faced with the combinations *drama school, drama teacher, drama option*, and *drama critic*, we interpret the first as a school where drama is taught, the second as a teacher of the art of drama, the third as an option in drama, and the fourth as a critic of dramatic productions. In other words, each noun-modifier nominal head pairing is treated semantically in a different way. The reader infers the semantic connection between the two words using as evidence linguistic clues where available (e.g. *-er* in teacher), the sequence of the words, the typical patterns of relationships presupposed by particular words (e.g. *critic* presupposes something to be criticized), past experience of the behavior of both words and quite probably of their combination together, and the paraphrase possibilities of the combinations. In real discourse, context also plays an important disambiguating role. The meaning of the words in combination is greater than their meaning apart and is not mechanically derivable from the grammar nor entirely separate from it. The inferential connection the reader makes is not random, of course; a writer in placing the words together expects readers to make the same link that he or she sees between them. Nor is the linguist's description of such connections entirely intuitive. Although the paraphrase possibilities of a combination may well be the least important factor in a reader's interpretation of word couplings, they are a useful way for the analyst to explore the meanings of such groups.

A special word group—prepositions—allows the linguist varying degrees of precision in the paraphrastic expression of semantic relationships. Prepositions are capable of making explicit what was already implicit in a combination of linguistic features. If the paraphrase is accepted as accurate by typical readers, the preposition does no more than spell out what a reader finds in the original coupling anyway. Of course, when authors write, it is open to them, wherever ambiguity or clumsiness may otherwise result, to spell out the relationship from the outset; so one might choose to refer to a *school of speech and drama* rather than a *speech and drama school*. Whether the information is newly introduced is also relevant. When an author first describes a *plate-like object made of steel* in a discourse, he or she is likely to call it a *plate of steel*; but once this quality becomes given information, the author is more likely to refer to the object as a *steel plate*.

These observations about the interpretation of word couplings are pertinent to the way we read and write discourses. Just as we infer a connection between coupled words, so we infer a connection between juxtaposed clauses, sentences, and indeed groups of sentences. Let us illustrate with some examples.

When we as readers encounter the following sentences in the children's book *Chirp*, we naturally interpret the second as the basis for the denied expectation in the first:

(7:1) He knew he was supposed to fly, but he couldn't. He'd never learnt how to. [Roger Hargreaves (1978), *Chirp*, London, Hodder and Stoughton: 2]

In making this interpretation, we are using similar inferential skills to those we used for interpreting word couplings (though, of course, we should not press the comparison too far). While reading, we are interpreting linguistic evidence (e.g. the ellipsis of *fly*, and the prefacing of the *to* form with *how*), and we are recognizing typical patterns of relationship; if something that is *supposed to* happen doesn't happen, we expect a reason for the occurrence of the unanticipated. Less obviously, and perhaps less importantly, we are bringing to bear our past experience of similar juxtapositions. Here is a similar example from another literary text:

(7:2) I can't swim. I wasn't allowed. [William Golding (1954 edition), *Lord of the Flies*, London, Faber and Faber: 14]

Again we have a basis for a denial, and again the connection of the two statements is signaled by an ellipsis (of *to swim*).

Paraphrases, of course, can reveal connections in both of these examples. We can paraphrase example 7:1 as:

(7:3) He knew he was supposed to fly, but he couldn't, because he'd never learnt how to;

though it is important to notice that we now have one grammatical sentence instead of two and that the subordination focuses on the 'taken-for-grantedness' of the reason. In other words, our paraphrase holds constant one aspect of the meaning only, while introducing points of difference elsewhere. Another paraphrase possibility for Example 7:1 (subject to the same constraints) is the following:

(7:4) He knew he was supposed to fly, but he'd never learnt how to, so he couldn't.

In Example 7:4, the focus is on a denial drawn as a painfully obvious conclusion from what has just been said, the conclusion being signaled by *so*. Such connectives spell out the relationship between the clauses in the same way that prepositions spell out the relationship between nouns in combination. Like the prepositions, the subordinators and conjuncts (Greenbaum's [1969] term for sentence connectors such as *so*, taken up by Quirk *et al*. [1972]) are varyingly precise and hence are used by writers to make a relationship clear. A particular function that subordinators have is to present some part of the information as inherent or 'given' or known to the situation (see Winter 1977 and 1982).

7.1.1 Clause relations defined

The inferential connections set up by writers and made by readers can be called CLAUSE RELATIONS (see Winter 1968 and following). Other labels linguists have given to these phenomena include 'propositional relations' (Beekman 1970; and Callow 1970) and 'interclausal relations' (Ballard *et al*. 1971). Quirk (1954) provided the first definition of a clause relation (in line with Sweet [1892: 146]) though Beardsley (1950) has prior claim to the concept. Quirk noted of the concessive relation that it 'may be said to exist between two parts of an utterance when one part is surprising in view of the other' (1954: 6, italics removed).

A definition of clause relations that takes into account both reader and writer is the following, compounded from Winter 1971 and elsewhere; and

Hoey 1983a: A CLAUSE RELATION IS THE COGNITIVE PROCESS, AND THE PRODUCT OF THAT PROCESS, WHEREBY THE READER INTERPRETS THE MEANING OF A CLAUSE, SENTENCE, OR GROUP OF SENTENCES IN THE CONTEXT OF ONE OR MORE PRECEDING CLAUSES, SENTENCES, OR GROUPS OF SENTENCES IN THE SAME DISCOURSE. IT IS ALSO THE COGNITIVE PROCESS AND THE PRODUCT OF THAT PROCESS WHEREBY THE CHOICES THE WRITER MAKES FROM GRAMMAR, LEXIS, AND INTONATION IN THE CREATION OF A CLAUSE, SENTENCE, OR GROUP OF SENTENCES ARE MADE IN THE CONTEXT OF THE OTHER CLAUSES, SENTENCES, OR GROUPS OF SENTENCES IN THE DISCOURSE. This admittedly cumbersome definition is making a number of points about the writing process. The first important point is that there are categorizable ways in which we process or produce sentences. These are basically of two kinds.

First, we can match pieces of information or see them as logically connected (see Winter 1974). When we match pieces of information, we are bringing them together to see how they illuminate each other. For example, in

(7:5) Fred was big. Ted was little. [P. D. Eastman (1973), *Big Dog . . . Little Dog*, London, Collins Picture Lions: 1]

the meaning of the two sentences is greater than the sum of their parts. Effectively, a third unifying proposition is the one that shows the way the two sentences illuminate each other: *Fred and Ted differ in size*. The products of the MATCHING PROCESS include CONTRAST, COMPATIBILITY, GENERALIZATION-EXAMPLE, PREVIEW-DETAIL, and, in the simplest case, TOPIC MAINTENANCE. These relations can be seen as abstractions from the questions a writer seeks to answer at particular points in his or her discourse (see Winter 1969 and 1974; and Hoey 1983a). So, for example, the question *How does* X *differ from* Y? elicits information that forms a contrast relation. Likewise, *Tell me more about* X elicits the basic topic maintenance relation (compare Jordan 1979); this could be viewed as a trivial continuity question.

Second, if we see pieces of information as logically connected, we set them up in a sequence where one is prior to the other(s). Components of the LOGICAL SEQUENCE PROCESS include CAUSE-CONSEQUENCE, CONDITION-CONSEQUENCE, EVALUATION-BASIS, INSTRUMENT-ACHIEVEMENT, and, in the simplest case, TIME SEQUENCE (see also Beekman 1970; Callow 1970; and Beekman and Callow 1974). As with the matching relations, in the sequencing process, an unstated third unifying proposition exists for any two propositions. In the case of Example 7:1, for instance, the unstated proposition might be something like *His not having learnt how to fly was the reason he couldn't fly*. Again, as with matching relations, logical sequence relations can be explained as answers to questions, such questions as *How?*, *Why?*, and *What for?* eliciting sequence relation information. The simplest question is, of course, *What happened next?*, which elicits the basic time sequence relation.

7.1.2 Clause relations illustrated

Besides suggesting that there are categorizable ways in which we process or produce sentences, our clause relations definition suggests that our lexical, grammatical, and intonational choices are in part governed by the choices we have already made as speakers/writers and those we plan to make. To illustrate this, let us engage in an imaginative re-creation of the writing act. Let us pretend to be Gore Vidal engaged in the writing of the novel *Julian*. Of course, we cannot presume to know what actually passed through Vidal's mind as he wrote; most likely he made his lexical and grammatical choices quickly and subconsciously. Nevertheless, it may be revealing to slow down and to examine some of the choices he had to make albeit intuitively. The sentences whose possible genesis we will consider are the following:

(7:6) This skirmish was not taken very seriously at Vienne. What was taken seriously, however, was the fact that Constantius had named me his fellow consul for the New Year. [Gore Vidal (1962), *Julian*, London, Heinemann: 202]

Let us start by assuming that we have decided in our role as Vidal to report three pieces of information:

(i) This skirmish [previously described] was not taken very seriously at Vienne.
(ii) Constantius had named me his fellow consul for the New Year.
(iii) This was taken seriously.

Clearly, these three pieces of information are not 'raw' material in that they already represent a series of selections and decisions, perhaps most notably the decision that the three of them should be seen as of potentially equal weight. Let us, for the purposes of further simplification, regard the presentation of the first piece of information as fixed. Our choice, therefore, is one of how to represent the two facts that follow. Of course, we are not considering all options, and we are not claiming that the options considered are true paraphrases; they are distortions of the original that serve our purpose of illustrating the differences of sequential meaning.

One option—perhaps the weakest—is to present the three sentences as we have written them sequenced in a single paragraph:

(7:7) This skirmish was not taken very seriously at Vienne. Constantius had named me his fellow consul for the New Year. This was taken seriously.[1]

But there are problems with this arrangement. The past perfect form in the second sentence encourages the reader to intepret it as the reason for the evaluation given in the first sentence (though, of course, the reader also may choose not to interpret past perfect this way). Such an interpretation would in turn encourage a reader to see the third sentence as providing a connection between the apparent 'reason' in the second sentence and what it set out to explain. If these interpretations were what we intended, however, we could set them up more clearly by using subordination and coordination:

(7:8) This skirmish was not taken very seriously at Vienne, because Constantius had named me his fellow consul for the New Year. And this was taken seriously.

The subordinator *because* and the coordinator *and* force the interpretation that people can take only one thing at a time seriously; this is sufficiently odd to make readers question our intention. In fact, we, as Vidal, do not intend our readers to connect the statements in such a way. So we have to find another way of presenting these sentences.

One new possibility is to remove the past perfect verb form and thereby remove the apparent signal of reason:

(7:9) This skirmish was not taken very seriously at Vienne. Constantius then named me his fellow consul for the New Year. This was taken seriously.

Example 7:9 is clearly unsatisfactory as prose because no clause relation is self-evident between the first and the second sentence except that of time sequence. Given that expectations of time sequence relations in narrative are endorsed more strongly when the topic is maintained, a reader would look for a cause–consequence relation between the sentences. To express this better, we could choose to write:

(7:10) This skirmish was not taken seriously at Vienne. So Constantious named me his fellow consul for the New Year, which *was* taken seriously.

As before, our decision about what relations to express affects our grammatical choices. We have inserted a conjunct and converted the third sentence into an adding-bound clause (see Sinclair 1972). Winter (1982) notes that such clauses are used to show that the information they convey can be taken for granted as true. The italicization of *was* reflects the intonational choice that we would make if the discourse were spoken. But in our role as Vidal we do not like this. We do not intend the second sentence to be seen as a consequence of the first sentence, nor do we accept the implication for the character of the narrator (*me*) inherent in Example 7:7 that it is important that something he is involved with be taken seriously.

To rule out interpretations of reason or consequence, we could nominalize the second sentence and incorporate it into the third as in Example 7:11:

(7:11) This skirmish was not taken seriously at Vienne. The fact that Constantius had named me his consul for the New Year was taken seriously.

This removes the possibility of any logical sequence connection between the first and second fact, but Example 7:11 is clumsy, though grammatically parallel in respect of the predication, and the contrast relation which the reader will infer needs reinforcing either by italicizing *was* or by the addition of a conjunct such as *however*. More importantly, readers will most probably feel thwarted by the second sentence; their expectation is likely to have been that one of the questions *Why?*, *What happened as a result?*, or *Where was it taken seriously?* would be answered after the first sentence. (This expectation has been checked informally with a number of groups of informants.) The question that is in fact intended to be answered is *What was taken seriously instead?*, a question that very few readers anticipate. Consequently, we need to smooth the readers' paths a little so that the relation, though unexpected, is clear. We can do this by fronting the question to be answered in a pseudo-cleft construction; this also has the important effect of marking the statement that corrects the readers' anticipations and of emphasizing a new subject for the clause read previously. The pseudo-cleft can be marked further as a MATCHING CONTRAST by the presence of *however* in the mid-position of its clause, which brings us back, of course, to what Gore Vidal wrote: 'This skirmish was not taken very seriously at Vienne. What was taken seriously, however, was the fact that Constantius had named me his fellow consul for the New Year.'

Clearly, such a simulation can tell us nothing about the psychological processes that produce written discourse though, as Jordan notes (personal communication), it suggests that writers fabricate continuity where the material itself does not provide it. What it does demonstrate is that lexical and grammatical choices are tied inextricably to the semantic relations between sentences. These relations not only affect the structure and sequential ordering of their clauses, but they are also signaled and rooted in the grammar of the clause. To explain the implications of these clause relations, as we have called them, for the writer's communicative task, we must first consider the reader's role in interpreting discourse.

7.2 CLAUSE RELATIONS AND INFERENTIAL AND EXPLICIT MEANING

One of the reader's tasks in interpreting written discourse is to recognize the relations between the propositions that the writer is signaling and infer those that the writer is implying. Of course, a reader has certain default expectations where no active effort is required for interpretation. For want of a better word, we shall refer to both default expectations and active interpretations as INFERENCES.

Some inferences are undoubtedly retrospective; faced with two sentences, the reader may consciously seek to find the connecting proposition that makes sense of their juxtaposition. But reading would be slow if this happened all the time. Indeed, if it did, one might question whether the reader properly understood what he or she was reading. For it seems that readers normally are able to anticipate the relations that are to come; put more naturally, they are able to guess what questions are going to be answered. We might hypothesize that given previous information, readers have a number of weighted questions that they think might be answered in the next sentence(s). Each sentence is scanned as a possible answer to these questions and the question it most nearly fits is seen as the one it is answering; this process parallels the relationship between specific questions and general clause relations that we described earlier.

Our theory of the process of reading (elaborated more fully in Hoey 1983a) accounts for the function of anticipatory signals, discussed in Winter 1977, and is compatible with an interactive view of the reading process as advocated by many other scholars (see, for example, Rumelhart 1977; Kintsch and van Dijk 1978; Widdowson 1979; and Smith 1982). Our scheme also corresponds to Beaugrande's (1984) claim that 'discourse interaction constantly draws upon the participants' expectations about what will be said or enacted—expectations based on goals, ideas, concepts, and all the levels of language processing combined' and parallels pedagogical reading schemes that urge the learner to make use of anticipatory questions in order to read more efficiently (see, for example, Aaron *et al.* 1971).

Though both theory and pedagogical practice suggest that readers actively anticipate what is to come in a written text, any such hypothesis about what readers do must be couched very cautiously. All that can be said with confidence is that if the reading process is greatly slowed down, it is possible for readers to spell out their expectations in these terms with accuracy; Bush (1983) has confirmed through experimentation that at many points in a discourse, readers have clear and accurate expectations while at other points, their expectations are less certain.

One of the factors that makes it possible for readers to make predictions or confirm that an expectation has (or has not) been met in a text is the presence of CLAUSE RELATIONAL SIGNALS of various kinds. These signals reduce the inferential role of the reader by expressing the clause relations explicitly (though the possibility of multiple relations means that the inferential role does not disappear entirely); they are the equivalent of prepositions that clarify noun couplings. It remains possible, of course, for the reader to infer connections other than those signaled linguistically, but the signaled relation is not a matter for doubt. It does not follow, of course, that if writers simply 'flagged' each sentence, all would be well; writers must consider the effects of inference in its own right.

7.2.1 Linguistic signaling of clause relations

Among the linguistic features that can signal clause relations are two varieties we have discussed already, SUBORDINATORS and CONJUNCTS. Two other kinds of features, LEXICAL SIGNALS and LEXICAL REPETITIONS, can also signal clause relations. The lexical signals that express clause relations may share the semantics of subordinators and conjuncts and yet have the grammar we associate with referential vocabulary. They were first identified by Winter (1974) who describes their unique characteristics; a representative checklist of examples is presented in Winter 1977. Hoey (1979) shows how words in the lexical signal group indicate the organization of discourses. Examples are the words *reason, difference, example, result, condition, achieve, compare, contrast*, and their variants. The reason relation in Example 7:1 could have been made explicit with a lexical signal as follows:

(7:12) He knew he was supposed to fly, but he couldn't. The reason was that he'd never learnt how to.

The use of *reason* would be highly marked in this context, however (for a definition of MARKED and UNMARKED forms, see Eiler in this volume [ed.]). Similarly, the contrast relation in Example 7:5 could have been made explicit as follows:

(7:13) Fred was big. Ted was different. He was little.

The ability of an intermediate clause to serve a mediating function in such a way is described in detail in Winter 1974 and 1979, where it is shown to be the most marked form of connection between clauses.

Lexical signals can be used by writers to anticipate the questions to be answered, as in Example 7:14:[2]

(7:14) In this paper, we shall investigate the flow behaviour of Newtonian and elastic liquids in a number of complex geometries. *Our motivation is threefold*. First, we have a general interest in the overall flow characteristics of fluids in complex geometries. Secondly, we wish to investigate how these characteristics are affected by fluid elasticity. Lastly, we are concerned with the possibility of numerically simulating the flows by using modern developments in computing mathematics. [From T. Cochrane, K. Walters, and M. F. Webster (1981), 'On Newtonian and Non-Newtonian Flow in Complex Geometries,' in *Philosophical Transactions of the Royal Society of London*, A301: 163–81]

The word *motivation* signals to readers that they should expect answers to the question *What for?*; *threefold* tells readers how many answers to expect.

More commonly, though, lexical signals appear in the middle of or after the relation in question, and their function here is to remove any doubt the reader has about what question is being answered:

(7:15) Those states which refused to submit to Malacca's suzerainty were attacked and subdued. These included Kedah, Siak, and Kampar. [Ding Eing Tan (1975), *A Portrait of Malaysia and Singapore*, Kuala Lumpur, Oxford University Press: 8]

In this instance, the word *included* signals a generalization—examples relation between the previous sentence and itself. (And the sentence we have just produced provides an example of a signal after the relation it signals in its use of the word *instance* which confirms the reader's interpretation of Example 7:15 as an example of the generalization that precedes it.)

Repetition, the final type of signal that clarifies clause relations, works in a very different way. Repetition includes not only lexical reiteration but also pronominalization and paraphrase—all the means whereby we say something again. The systematic repetition of a clause or a sentence (as opposed to the repetition of isolated words) sets up a matching relation between the clauses/sentences, though the exact nature of the relation can only be ascertained with the help of the context (Winter 1974 and 1979). A fairly extreme example of the phenomenon follows:

(7:16) Imagine driving around with a parachute clamped to your rear bumper and you'll get an idea of what aerodynamic drag feels like. Imagine driving around with 30% less parachute and you'll get an idea of what the new Audi 100cc feels like. [From an advertisement of the Audi 100cc, current in Britain in 1983; for example, see *Radio Times*, 10 February 1983]

The repetition in Example 7:16 serves as a constant that allows us to interpret what has varied—in this case, the difference between the imagined situations. Usually the effect is less marked in adjacent sentences, as in Example 7:17:

(7:17) 'That's a different thermometer. On that thermometer thirty-seven is normal. On this kind it's ninety-eight.' [Ernest Hemingway ([1944] 1977), 'A Day's Wait,' in *'For Whom the Bell Tolls' and Other Stories*, London, Heinemann/Octopus: 389]

We can show how the repetition works in this example by displaying it in tabular form as in Table 7.1. The first sentence is presented in cleft form to show up the repetition by ellipsis. The table illustrates how the naming of a kind of thermometer in the opening adverbial and of a particular temperature in the main clause serves as a constant against which the reader observes the variables: *which kind of thermometer* and *which temperature*.

Repetition is also used to relate subordinate and main clauses, signaling the replacement of clause status, as in Example 7:18:

(7:18) These considerations were the ones that led the senator, in a new bill, to propose moving the US Embassy from Tel Aviv to Jerusalem. *If they were the whole story*, there could be no good argument against the bill.

But they are not the whole story. Two other major considerations apply. ['Jerusalem distraction,' an editorial in *The Washington Post*, reprinted in *The Guardian Weekly*, 1 April 1984: 1]

Here a counterfactual conditional is repeated in its entirety, the only changes being the past/present tense shift, the addition of the negation, and, most significantly, the change of status from subordinate to independent (main) clause.

As readers make use of discourse signals in their interpretation of a text, it follows that writers may affect the readability of discourse by incorporating signals or not, assuming that writers make appropriate use of the precise contextual meanings of these signals. Linguists, let alone other readers and writers, have not yet defined all the meanings of these signals and their variations.

Table 7.1 Representation of repetition in Example 7:17

Constant	On one kind of thermometer	it's a particular temperature	that is normal
Variable	which kind	which temperature	—
Sent. 1	On that [kind of] thermometer	[it's] thirty-seven	[that] is normal
Sent. 2	On this kind [of thermometer]	it's ninety-eight	[that is normal]

We know that 'elegant variation' in signaling is likely to obscure rather than assist the interpretative process, as Fowler noted many years ago ([1926] 1965: 148–51). Likewise, we know that discourses that are under-signaled or mis-signaled may be judged rhetorically inept, if by the former we mean that the reader is not given a clear pathway through the mass of relations that make up a discourse and by the latter that the reader is led up the garden path. At the same time, we cannot assume that a writer whose work reflects a conscious knowledge of discourse signals is a better writer; the quality of the lexical selection, after all, distinguishes the master from the mediocre. Nor should we be too ready to assume that a discourse without overt signals is undersignaled. Redundancy in signaling is common, and readers vary in their reliance on signals in any case (see Woolard 1984). Moreover, in judging the aptness of signaling we must consider the degree of connection the reader will find tolerable. Beaugrande and Dressler (1981) make the point about cohesion that there is a tension for a writer between compactness and clarity; clearly, a point exists at either extreme when the reader will reject the discourse as excessively redundant or excessively compressed.

7.2.2 Clause relations and rhetorical patterns

Up to this point we have been considering the techniques writers use to communicate to readers about the clause relations that they intend between their clauses, sentences, groups of sentences, and so on. But these relations may in combination begin to form recognizable patterns.

One of the ways that writers may help their readers is to adopt a commonly used pattern; when readers recognize a pattern, their task in inferring the connections between the parts is largely done. Commonly used patterns are often language and culture specific (several essays in this volume elaborate this point; see Bernhardt, Brandt, Eiler, and Martin and Rothery [ed.]). Non-native writers must overcome an inclination to pattern their discourses in ways appropriate for readers in their own cultures when those patterns are inappropriate to the cultures/languages in which their discourses are written (see Kaplan 1966, 1972, and 1977; for a survey of relevant literature, see Houghton and Hoey 1983).

One of the culturally accepted rhetorical patterns for English expository discourses is the PROBLEM-SOLUTION pattern. This pattern has been described in detail elsewhere (see Becker 1965; Winter 1976; Hutchins 1977; Hoey 1979, 1983a, and 1983b; Ghadessy 1983; and Jordan 1980, 1982, and 1984). Its basic components are:

- SITUATION;
- ASPECT OF SITUATION REQUIRING RESPONSE (= problem for *x*);
- RESPONSE BY *y* TO PROBLEM FOR *x* (where *y* and *x* may be the same); and
- EVALUATION AND/OR RESULT OF RESPONSE (where evaluation may be by *x* or *y* or the author, or any combination of these).

We can analyze the problem-solution pattern in the same fashion as individual clauses relations and in the process assert that discourse patterns are, in fact, combinations of relations. Example 7:19 displays a discourse with the problem-solving pattern:

(7:19) *Engine supports a high speed bike*
[1]Motorbike speed freaks might take heart from a development in design pioneered by 36-year-old French engineer and racing driver Andre de Cortanze. [2]He became concerned that motorcycle speeds were often held down by the machine's centre of gravity being too high, meaning that corners have to be taken relatively slowly. [3]Backed by the petroleum company ELF, he designed the bike, shown here, [photo omitted] in which the orthodox frame has been omitted. [4]Instead the machine is held together by the 750 cc engine. [5]The result is that the centre of gravity is significantly lower than on ordinary motorbikes—for instance the fuel tank is slung beneath the engine and 17 cm lower than normal. [6]Whether or not the theory works will be shown in trials due to start by the end of the year. [7]De Cortanze plans to take the bike to the racetrack soon afterwards. ['Technology,' *New Scientist*, May 1978: 294 (sentence numbers added)]

Sentence 1 of Example 7:19 establishes the situation and anticipates the remainder of the discourse by advising the reader that a *development* will be discussed, *develop* being a typical signal of response (Hoey 1979 and 1983a). It also suggests that the response will be evaluated positively—*might take heart*—though the discourse does not fully meet this expectation.

Sentence 2 is signaled as *problem* by *too high*: *too x* is always an aspect of situation requiring a response. The problem is also indicated by *concerned, have to be*, and real world knowledge of the desirability of speed to motorbike freaks. Sentences 3 and 4 are interpreted as a response because of their position in the discourse, *designed* providing support for the interpretation. Any doubts about how to interpret this information would be resolved in any case by sentence 5, which provides a positive result (signaled by *result*) that contrasts with the problem. Table 7.2 illustrates the contrast relationship between the problem presented in sentence 2 and the result presented

Table 7.2 Contrast between problem and result in Example 7:19

Constant	the machine's centre of gravity is	at a point on the scale of height
Variable	—	where on scale
Sent. 2	the machine's centre of gravity being	too high
Sent. 5	the [machine's] centre of gravity is	significantly lower

in sentence 5 as highlighted by the repetition of the constant *the machine's centre of gravity is* followed by the variable information *a point on the scale of height*.

Further analysis reveals that the clause in sentence 2, the problem, with which sentence 5, the result, contrasts, is itself part of a cause–consequence chain. The presentation of the problem as a cause–consequence chain occurs quite commonly within the problem–solution pattern (see Hoey 1983a). The chain in sentence 2 can be represented as follows:

CAUSE — the machine's centre of gravity being too high
↕
CONSEQUENCE — corners have to be taken relatively slowly
CAUSE —
↕
CONSEQUENCE — motorcycle speeds were held down

Positive evaluation of the motorcycle cannot be given until it is possible to report a consequence to the changed cause: an evaluation is left suspended in sentence 6, *works* and *shown in trials* indicating, however, that this sentence is providing the expected evaluation element of the pattern. Sentence 7 not only answers the question *What is he going to do with the bike next, given his interest in racing?*, it also completes the evaluation by forecasting a positive application of the solution.

The problem–solution pattern is only felt to be complete if the evaluation and/or result is not negative. If negative, a further response is expected, since negative evaluation itself signals a problem, as in Example 7:20:

(7:20) . . . [1]the advent of the grain whisky process, whose product is mixed with malts to produce the standard blended Scotch, posed a problem. [2]To make grain whisky, barley is mixed with other sources of starch (normally maize flakes) to produce 'mash' which is then fermented. [3]The starch has to be converted to a sugar before fermentation can occur, and this conversion is catalysed by the enzyme diastase. [4]Scottish barley contains enough enzyme to break down its own starch in a reasonable time, but not enough to cope with the extra load of starch from the maize flakes. [5]Until now Canadian high enzyme barleys have had to be imported for the job, and at considerable expense. [6]These strains suit Canada's climate, but unfortunately do not grow well in Scotland.

[7]Now, after a ten-year programme, the Scottish Plant Breeding Station thinks it has developed its own high enzyme barley—one that will flourish on Scottish soil. . . . ['Scotch Barley Mows into Imports,' in 'Monitor,' *New Scientist*, April 1979: 187 (sentence numbers added)]

In this extract, sentence 1 provides the situation in its subject and adding-bound clause, and it anticipates the problem without specifying it. Sentences 2, 3, and the first half of 4 provide the situation necessary to understand the problem, and the second half of sentence 4 provides the aspect of the situation requiring a response, marking it by *but* and *not enough* (the opposite of *too x*). Sentence 5 provides the response, with ample clues as to its inadequacy—*had to* suggests compulsion, *until now* signals the existence of a new, alternative response to be given the reader, and *at considerable expense* negatively evaluates the response in terms of economics and introduces a new problem, *considerable expense*. The first half of sentence 6 positively evaluates a possible response to this economic problem, but the second half negatively evaluates it (*does* NOT *grow* WELL *in Scotland*). *Unfortunately* emphasizes that the problem thus remains unsolved. The negative evaluation sets up an expectation of further response; the expectation is met in the next sentence and expanded upon in the remainder of the discourse, ending with a positive evaluation of the further response.

Interestingly this PROBLEM-RESPONSE-NEGATIVE EVALUATION-RESPONSE-POSITIVE EVALUATION pattern is echoed in another fairly common pattern which might be labeled QUESTION-ANSWER-NEGATIVE EVALUATION-ANSWER-POSITIVE EVALUATION, where QUESTION is an aspect of situation requiring verbal response and ANSWER is the verbal response. This pattern appears in certain types of discursive writing and seems to be particularly typical of sermons (see Collier-Wright 1984). An example, from a theological work, is the following passage:

(7:21) [1]In what sense do the message 'The Kingdom of God is near' and the demand 'Be perfect' form a unity? [2]Indeed, are they a unity at all? [3]In more recent times this has been frequently disputed. [4]It would be possible to say simply: the fulfilling of the will of God, obedience, is the *condition* for participation in the Kingdom, for entrance into it. [5]In a certain sense this is true, yet it is not a wholly satisfactory answer. [6]For this connection could be conceived extern ally . . . [The passage goes on to consider other answers that are unacceptable and then presents, five pages further on, the author's own answer.] [Rudolf Bultmann ([1934] 1958), *Jesus and the Word*, Smith, L. P. and Lantero, E. H. (trans.), London, Fontana: 89–90 (sentence numbers added)]

In Example 7:21, sentences 1 and 2 present the question, sentence 3 presents a general answer to the second formulation, and sentence 4 provides a particular answer. Sentence 5 in part evaluates positively and in part negatively. A basis for this negative evaluation follows in sentence 6, which it also typically does in patterns of the problem–solution type. The words *satisfactory answer*, of course, are equally appropriate in either pattern.

The question–answer pattern is itself very like yet another pattern—the HYPOTHETICAL–REAL pattern, where another's view is first presented (the HYPOTHETICAL), and then either rejected or affirmed by the author (the REAL); rejection may take the form either of a DENIAL followed by a BASIS or a CORRECTION followed optionally by a basis, or some combination of these (see Winter 1974 and 1979; and Williames 1984). Discourses organized in this manner typically report a conflict between two views (one of them the author's) for the benefit of a third party and therefore are frequently attested in newspaper letter columns. Example 7:22 illustrates this type:

(7:22) [1]Dear Sir,

[2]Although perhaps not very important, may I mention a small error I have noticed in Mr Howard Linecar's article 'Historic Locomotives on Stamps' in *Stamp Monthly* March issue.

[3]Mr Linecar would seem to suggest that Sir William Stanier of the L.M.S. designed a streamlined version of his 'Pacific' type locomotive to work the 'Silver Jubilee' train of 1935.

[4]Sir William was indeed an L.M.S. man (and previously, I believe, of the Great Western Railway). [5]But the 'Silver Jubilee' was an L.N.E.R. train and the 'A4' class streamlined 'Pacifics' which hauled it were designed by Sir Nigel Gresley of the L.N.E.R.

[6]Yours very truly,
J. Maurice Clark,
Bournemouth,
Dorset. [*Gibbons Stamp Monthly*, May 1982: 60 (sentence numbers added)]

This letter begins (after the ritual address) with a signaling sentence that tells the reader in advance how the letter is to be organized, *mention* indicating that the next sentence will report something which will be corrected (*a small error*) in subsequent sentences. (Advance signaling sentences, with their appeal to the editor as arbiter of debates, are apparently common in newspaper letters [see Williames 1984].) The third sentence lives up to expectations by reporting another's claim; the fact of reportage is sufficient to indicate the hypothetical status of the information, but this is reinforced by the tentative *would seem to suggest*. Sentence 4 then affirms part of Mr Linecar's suggestion—this is the common ground between the two men—in preparation for the correction given in sentence 5, which provides the basis for an implied denial of the accuracy of the suggestion in sentence 3.

The pattern of Example 7:22 is very closely related to the question–answer

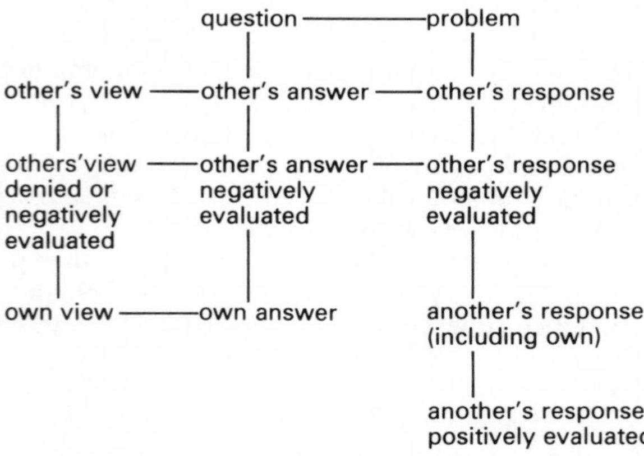

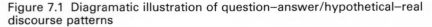

Figure 7.1 Diagramatic illustration of question–answer/hypothetical–real discourse patterns

pattern, so much so that it is possible to analyze sentence 3 onwards as a hypothetical–real pattern.

The relationship between the questions, problems, and answers in the patterns we have considered so far is indicated diagrammatically in Figure 7.1. These patterns are only a sample of the range of patterns available to a writer, space and the current state of knowledge alike preventing a fuller account. In any case, since they are patterns built out of clause relations, not quasi-grammatical structures, the number of patterns that may occur is theoretially unlimited, and all that one can hope to do is describe those most frequently used.

7.2.3 The writer's role in presenting discourse patterns through clause relations

A writer's selection of a pre-existing discourse pattern or creation of one may markedly affect the success with which he or she communicates to readers. We therefore conclude this chapter by considering a few of the ways a writer may fail in presenting a pattern.

First, a writer may undersignal. It should be quite clear that undersignaling is not the same as not signaling. Undersignaling occurs when a writer's failure to signal a relation leads to reader problems; consider, for example, the following two sentences from an article entitled 'An Eye on Drunken Drivers':

(7:23) [1]A 'breathalyser' indicates the amount of alcohol in a person's body rather than his reaction to that alcohol. [2]Dr Donald E. Sussman has developed a device which measures the unsteadiness of a drinker's eyes—just one of the neurophysiological effects of drinking. [The remainder of the discourse describes the device and preliminary tests.] [In 'Technology Review,' *New Scientist*, March 1970: 559 (sentence numbers added)][3]

The reader's difficulties with this passage begin with the first sentence. It is not clear how the second relates to it. The writer has failed to recognize that his or her lexical and/or grammatical choices need to be concomitant with the relation to be inferred. The contrast relation between part of the second sentence and the first has almost willfully been obscured. To identify it, the reader must first recognize *his reaction to that alcohol* as paraphraseable by *the effects on him of drinking alcohol* and similarly recognize *the neurophysiological effects of drinking* as paraphraseable by *the neurophysiological effects on him of drinking alcohol*. This paraphrase then tells the reader that the breathalyser and Dr Sussman's device are being contrasted because of the *rather than* in sentence 1; the reader must also accept *indicates the amount of* as paraphrasing *measures*.

The writer could have made the contrast implied in Example 7:23 clearer by writing as follows:

(7:24) [1]A 'breathalyser' *measures* the alcohol in a person's body rather than *the effects on him of drinking alcohol*. [2]Dr. Donald E. Sussman has developed a device which *measures* the unsteadiness of a drinker's eyes—just one of *the* neurophysiological *effects on him of drinking alcohol*.

Even in the rewritten version, the contrast is somewhat indirect; it is apparent that the writer of Example 7:24 has fallen prey to the vice of elegant variation and in so doing has hidden one of the intended relations between the parts.

But there is a further, more serious, difficulty with the first sentence of Example 7:23. The first sentence contains no clear signal of the problem, though the second sentence contains some signals of response in a problem–solution pattern; they are the verb *develop*, choice of the perfect aspect, and the attribution to Dr Sussman (Hoey 1979 and 1983a). Therefore, the reader cannot tell clearly whether or not to interpret what follows the first sentence as the working out of a problem–solution pattern and further has no way of assessing whether the results, which show a lack of correlation between the two devices, are good or bad. (This interpretive dilemma has been confirmed by numerous groups of students who have invariably quarreled among themselves about the 'correct' reading of the article.) If sentence 1 presents a problem, then lack of correlation is presumably to be expected; if it does not, then lack of correlation must be undesirable. A scientific discourse whose results are uninterpretable is a discourse whose existence has been rendered pointless. Yet simple addition of a single signal would have clarified the situation, as in Example 7:25:

(7:25) The problem with the breathalyser is that it measures . . .

Alternatively, a purpose clause might have been added to the second sentence, as in Example 7:26:

(7:26) A breathalyser measures the alcohol in a person's body rather than the effects on him of drinking alcohol. In order to allow measurement of the effects as well, Dr. Donald E. Sussman has developed . . .

Here, *as well* shows the two measurements to be compatible.

If undersignaling is what happens when writers fail to make clear to their readers the relations between the parts of a discourse, mis-signaling is what happens when writers mislead readers into expecting one relation or pattern when they in fact are producing another. Consider, for instance, Example 7:27, a lead article from a provincial English newspaper (paragraphing has been eliminated for convenience):

(7:27) [1]*Shock Move on Vice Roads*
[2]Kerb-crawling motorists who annoy residents in a Birmingham suburb with their search for sex are to be stopped in their tracks. [3]A scheme is being drawn up to narrow the roadways and instal bollards in an area of Balsall Heath where strong protests have been made about the kerb-crawlers and prostitution. [4]The problem has been investigated in depth by city council officials after a petition demanding action was sent last summer by householders in the Augusta Road–Park Road area. [5]Now councillors are being told that a scheme for street environment improvements is being prepared for

the housing action area at Balsall Heath which includes Park Road and Augusta Road. [6]A report to the highways sub-committee says that there is little doubt the problem can be eased by traffic management schemes, including road closures, narrowing roads at junctions and erecting bollards. [7]'A pilot scheme has been carried out in the area and has proved successful,' it adds. [Roy Smith, 'Shock Move on Vice Roads,' *Birmingham Evening Mail*, 6 April 1984: 1 (sentence numbers added)]

Example 7:27 displays problem–solution patterning and is quite unexceptionable in this regard, yet the title leads the reader to expect some other pattern. *Move* signals, quite correctly, that a response will be described in the article and *on vice roads* summarizes what will be spelt out as the problem the *move* is designed to solve. But *shock* signals that the *move* will be evaluated negatively by at least some of the readership; *shock* being broadly paraphraseable as *unpleasant surprise*. This marker then sets up an expectation of a further problem followed by negative evaluation. Nothing in the article fulfills that expectation; the only people likely to evaluate the move negatively are the prostitutes and kerb crawlers identified in sentences 2 and 3 as the problem. The writer could have avoided misleading implications by choosing the neutral word *surprise* instead of *shock*.

In talking of mis-signaling and undersignaling we have been assuming that a writer has an intention which he or she fails to realize through lack of skill. We must also take another factor into account, namely that writers may undersignal or mis-signal because they do not know what they want to say or because they have a misunderstanding of the world they report. This kind of problem appears to be reflected in Example 7:28, a school science report which records an experiment done in class to test whether a soup container conserves better than an ordinary container:

(7:28) *Making Soup*

When we got in the classroom we sat down the teacher was looking to us and the children were ansering the question then the teacher told us to get something like a bunsen burner, tripod, glass beaker containing some water, soup powder, glass rod, asbestos mat, wire gauze. Then we lit the bunsen burner trend it on the yellow flame untell the water bobed then we put the thermometer in the boiling hot water and see what it was, it was 100% hot Then we tip the soup powder in the water. We tound the bunsen burner off, and we see if the soup all right and we see the temperature of the soup if it was quit hot. We was wrighting down what it was and at the end we called try the soup and it was tomto soup, but I did not try it. it did not smell very nice but over people tryed it. we was flim by the camers there were three cammers and we had to stop in some parts when the teacher was speaking to us and we had to repeat it again. [Data collected by the Open University for P. 232 (course number), Block 6, and published as part of that course in Mary Hoffman and Janet Maybin (1979), *Supplementary Materials: Primary and Secondary Case Studies*]

We could analyze the rhetorical structure of this report noting that, although time sequence is signaled, the problem–solution pattern we perhaps perceive as readers is not. We could then go on to argue that the fact that we can make these inferences is reason for not treating the discourse as undersignaled. But such comments assume that the child in fact had seen a problem–solution pattern which she had failed or chosen not to signal. The more likely case is that the child is showing her scientific *naïveté*, not linguistic incompetence, and is reporting aptly and informally an event in her day.

Adults are inclined to interpret half-formed utterances of very small children as if they were produced as part of a well-formed exchange. Likewise, adult readers of older children's writing are inclined to infer connections that they themselves would have intended. Language teachers must take these kinds of supposition into account when evaluating the prose of their students and take care to assess the written discourse skills of young learners as they may reflect the development of corresponding intellectual skills.

7.3 CONCLUSION

In this chapter, we have argued that the clause relational approach to discourse analysis explains many aspects of the writing process. Every lexical and grammatical choice is in part affected by the choices that have already been made in the discourse and by the context in which the discourse is being produced. Furthermore, we have argued that the writer can assist the reader more directly in making the necessary inferential connections between written sentences by using one of the signaling systems inherent in a language and/or by adopting a culturally popular pattern (which itself may need some signaling).[4] If the writer chooses to take neither of these courses of action, it does not follow that the reader will not be able to select the correct inferential connections appropriate to the larger context. Yet, in some situations, ambiguity or vagueness will result if the writer does not take pains to make clear which relation or pattern is intended, and a writer who consistently fails to make clause relations explicit may create discourse that will be difficult for many to read.

Signals may mislead as well as lead. Writers sometimes abuse the signaling systems and in so doing provoke at worst incomprehension, at best irritation. Young writers who fail to make use of the signals or rhetorical patterns available may not always be demonstrating linguistic inadequacy. They may be communicating accurately their current state of understanding about their subject matter.

Clause relational analysis offers insight into interaction that underlies written discourse. Written discourse bears the same relations to the spoken exchange as the glacier does to the river: it may be tempting to talk of the glacier as a static object, but it is only properly understood when it is recognized that it flows. Written discourse 'flows,' and clause relational analysis has at least the merit of recognizing the fact.

NOTES

1. This and the subsequent versions considered are in no way to be considered paraphrases of the original; indeed, our point is that they are NOT possible paraphrases.
2. Italics here and in other numbered examples throughout the chapter are added to assist the reader, unless otherwise noted.
3. The full text of the article cited in Example 7:22 appears as an exercise in Winter 1976, and is discussed as a rhetorically inept discourse in Hoey 1983a.
4. To say this is not to imply that a complete description is available of either.

BIBLIOGRAPHY

Aaron, I. E. *et al.* (1971), Scott, Foresman Reading Systems, Glenview, Ill., Scott, Foresman.

Ballard, D. L., Conrad, R. J., and Longacre, R. E. (1971), 'The Deep and Surface Grammar of Interclausal Relations,' *Foundations of Language*, **7**, 70–118, reprinted in Brend, R. M. (ed.) (1974: 307–55), *Advances in Tagmemics*, Amsterdam, North-Holland.

Beardsley, M. C. (1950), *Practical Logic*, New York, Prentice-Hall.

Beaugrande, R. A. de (1980), *Text, Discourse, and Process: Toward a Multidisciplinary Science of Texts*, Advances in Discourse Processes 4, Norwood, N.J., Ablex.

Beaugrande, R. A. de, 'Reading Skills for Foreign Languages: A Processing Approach,' in Pugh, A. K. and Ulijn, J. M. (eds) (1984: 4–26), *Readings for Professional Purposes: Studies and Practices in Native and Foreign Languages*, London, Heinemann.

Beaugrande, R. A. de and Dressler, W. U. (1981), *An Introduction to Text Linguistics*, Longman Linguistics Library 26, London, Longman.

Becker, A. L. (1965), 'A Tagmemic Approach to Paragraph Analysis,' *College Composition and Communication*, **16**, 237–42.

Beekman, J. (1970), 'Propositions and Their Relations within a Discourse,' *Notes on Translation*, **37**, 27–31.

Beekman, J. and Callow, J. (1974), *Translating the Word of God*, Grand Rapids, Mich., Zondervan.

Bush, L. (1983), 'The Anticipatory Potential of Text Patterning in the Expository Essay,' M.A. Project, Birmingham, University of Birmingham.

Callow, K. (1970), 'More on Propositions and Their Relations within a Discourse,' *Notes on Translation*, **37**, 23–7.

Collier-Wright, C. (1984), 'Sermons: A Study of the Structure and Style of Four Anglican Sermons, with Special Reference to the Book of Common Prayer and the Authorised Version of the Bible,' M.A. Project, Birmingham, U.K., University of Birmingham.

van Dijk, T. A. (1972), *Some Aspects of Text Grammars: A Study in Theoretical Linguistics and Poetics*, Janua Linguarum, Series Major 63, The Hague, Mouton.

van Dijk, T. A. (1977), *Text and Context: Explorations in the Semantics and Pragmatics of Discourse*, London, Longman.

Edmondson, W. (1981), *Spoken Discourse: A Model for Analysis*, London, Longman.

Fowler, H. W. ([1926] 1965, 2nd edn), *A Dictionary of Modern English Usage*, revised by Gowers, E., London, New York, Oxford University Press.

Ghadessy, M. (1983), 'Information Structure in Letters to the Editor,' *IRAL* [International Review of Applied Linguistics], **21**, 46–56.

Gray, B. (1977), *The Grammatical Foundations of Rhetoric: Discourse Analysis*, The Hague, Mouton.

Greenbaum, S. (1969), *Studies in English Adverbial Usage*, Miami Linguistics Series 5, Coral Gables, Fla., University of Miami Press: London, Longman.

Hoey, M. (1979), *Signalling in Discourse*, Discourse Analysis Monographs 6, Birmingham, U.K., English Language Research, University of Birmingham.

Hoey, M. (1983a), *On the Surface of Discourse*, London, Allen and Unwin.

Hoey, M. (1983b), 'The Place of Clause Relational Analysis in Linguistic Description,' *English Language Research Journal*, **4**, 1–32.

Houghton, D. and Hoey, M., 'Contrastive Rhetoric,' in d'Anglejan, A., Cowan, J. R., Kachru, B. B., and Tucker, G. R. (eds) (1983: 2–22), *Annual Review of Applied Linguistics 1982*, Rowley, Mass., Newbury House.

Hutchins, J. (1977), 'On the Structure of Scientific Texts,' *U.E.A.* [University of East Anglia] *Papers in Linguistics*, **5**, 18–39.

Jordan, M. P. (1979), 'Clause Relations: A Linguistic Field of Study,' Paper presented at the 1979 ABC/STC Conference, Toronto.

Jordan, M. P. (1980), 'Short Texts to Explain Problem–Solution Structures—and Vice-Versa,' *Instructional Science*, **9**, 221–52.

Jordan, M. P., 'Structure, Meaning and Information Signals of Some Very Short Texts: An Introductory Analysis of Everyday English Prose,' in Gutwinski, W. and Jolly, G. (eds) (1982: 410–17), *The Eighth LACUS Forum 1981*, Columbia, S.C., Hornbeam Press.

Jordan, M. P. (1984), *Rhetoric of Everyday English Texts*, London, Boston, Allen and Unwin.

Kaplan, R. B. (1966), 'Cultural Thought Patterns in Intercultural Education,' *Language Learning*, **16**, 1–20.

Kaplan, R. B. (1972, 1st edn), *The Anatomy of Rhetoric: Prolegomena to a Functional Theory of Rhetoric*, Philadelphia, Center for Curriculum Development.

Kaplan, R. B. (1977), 'Contrastive Rhetoric: Some Hypotheses,' *ITL: Review of Applied Linguistics*, **39–40**, 61–72.

Kintsch, W. and van Dijk, T. A. (1978), 'Toward a Model of Text Comprehension and Production,' *Psychological Review*, **85**, 363–94.

Longacre, R. E. (ed.) (1968), *Discourse, Paragraph and Sentence Structure in Selected Philippine Languages*, vols. 1 and 2, Summer Institute of Linguistics, Publications in Linguistics and Related Fields 21, Dallas, Summer Institute of Linguistics and University of Texas at Arlington; reprinted, Glendale, Calif., Church Press.

Longacre, R. E. (1972), *Hierarchy and Universality of Discourse Constituents in New Guinea Languages*, Washington, D.C., Georgetown University Press.

Longacre, R. E. (1976), *An Anatomy of Speech Notions*, Peter de Ridder Publications in Tagmemics 3, Lisse, The Netherlands, Peter de Ridder.

Longacre, R. E. (1982), *A Grammar of Discourse*, New York, Plenum Press.

Quirk, R. (1954), *The Concessive Relation in Old English Poetry*, New Haven, Yale University Press.

Quirk, R., Greenbaum, S., Leech, G., and Svartvik, J. (1972), *A Grammar of Contemporary English*, London, Longman.

Rumelhart, D. E., 'Toward an Interactive Model of Reading,' in Dornic, S. (ed.) (1977: 573–603), *Attention and Performance VI*, Proceedings of the Sixth International Symposium on Attention and Performance, Hillsdale, N.J., Lawrence Erlbaum.

Sinclair, J. McH. (1972), *A Course in Spoken English: Grammar*, London, Oxford University Press.

Smith, F. (1982, 3rd edn), *Understanding Reading: A Psycholinguistic Analysis of Reading and Learning to Read*, New York, Holt, Rinehart and Winston.

Sweet, H. (1892), *A New English Grammar, Logical and Historical, Part 1*, Oxford, Clarendon Press.

Widdowson, H. G., 'The Process and Purpose of Reading,' in Widdowson, H. G. (1979: 173–81), *Explorations in Applied Linguistics*, Oxford, Oxford University Press.

Williames, J. (1984), 'An Enquiry into the Interactive Nature of Written Discourse: The Example of the Newspaper Argument Letter,' M.A. thesis, Birmingham, U.K., University of Birmingham.

Winter, E. O., 'Some Aspects of Cohesion,' in Huddleston, R. D., Hudson, R. A., Winter, E. O., and Henrici, A. (1968: 560–604), *Sentence and Clause in Scientific English*, London, Communication Research Centre, University College.

Winter, E. O. (1969), 'Grammatical Question Technique as a Way of Teaching Science Students to Write Progress Reports: The Use of the Short Text in Teaching,' Trondheim, Norway, University of Trondheim, mimeo.

Winter, E. O. (1971), 'Connection in Science Material: A Proposition about the Semantics of Clause Relations,' *CILT* [Centre for Information on Language Teaching and Research] *Papers and Reports*, **7**, 41–52.

Winter, E. O. (1974), *Replacement as a Function of Repetition: A Study of Some of its Principal Features in the Clause Relations of Contemporary English*, Ph.D. dissertation, London, University of London (see *Dissertation Abstracts International*, sec. C, Autumn 1977, **38**, 4).

Winter, E. O. (1976), 'Fundamentals of Information Structure: A Pilot Manual for Further Development According to Student Need,' London, Hatfield Polytechnic, mimeo.

Winter, E. O. (1977), 'A Clause-Relational Approach to English Texts: A Study of Some Predictive Lexical Items in Written Discourse,' *Instructional Science* (special issue), **6**, 1–92.

Winter, E. O. (1979), 'Replacement as a Fundamental Function of the Sentence in Context,' *Forum Linguisticum*, **4**, 95–133.

Winter, E. O. (1982), *Towards a Contextual Grammar of English: The Clause and Its Place in the Definition of Sentence*, London, Boston, Allen and Unwin.

Woolard, S. (1984), 'Cohesion and the Teacher: An Examination of Three Approaches to Semantic Connectivity in Text and Their Implications for Language Teaching,' M.A. thesis, Birmingham, U.K., University of Birmingham.

Part III
Determining how written language is valued

8 Static and dynamic cohesion: signals of thinking in writing

Carolyn G. Hartnett
College of the Mainland

8.1 COHESION IN WRITTEN DISCOURSE

If meaning exists in relations (see Pike 1964), words that signal relations are important resources for writers. If systems of relationships (or networks) characterize the mental processes that comprise thinking (see Lachman *et al.* 1979), it then follows that thoughtful writing will express the systematic relationships which reflect the writer's thinking. (In fact, research has shown that, in the composing process, writers create networks of working goals as they plan [see Flower and Hayes 1981]; networks characterize the process as well as the content or product of writing.) If thinking is the manipulation of an internal representation of environment (see Hunt 1983), terms which express this manipulation are also important resources for writers. Finally, if 'good writing' implies 'coherent meaning,' and if coherence is expressed partially through linguistic cohesion, it seems useful to analyze cohesion in writing as it contributes to coherence in prose. Recent scholarship demonstrates that many linguists and composition theorists have reached this conclusion. Only a few, however, have attempted to analyze systematically how cohesion contributes to coherence (see, for example, Jordan in this volume [ed.]).

A complete explanation of the cohesive devices for expressing and manipulating relations in thoughtful writing must account for how these devices contribute to comprehension, linguistic form, and rhetorical development in good prose (see Markels 1983: 450). Cohesive ties vary in the kinds of mental processes they can express; many ties simply hold a reader's attention on a topic, while others develop a topic rhetorically. These differences suggest a reorganization of the linguistic subclasses of Halliday and Hasan's (1976) taxonomy of cohesive devices in order to distinguish mental processes and to define more explicitly the effects of cohesive devices on coherence. To achieve this aim, I am proposing two subclasses of cohesive links, STATIC and DYNAMIC TIES, which work together to focus on a topic and develop it. I am further proposing that categorizing ties in this way may help explain the relationship between a writer's use of cohesive features and a reader's understanding and perception of writing quality.

Cohesion analysts have attempted to correlate writing quality with the number of cohesive devices in a given text by using Halliday and Hasan's system for tracking the cohesive devices of reference, substitution, ellipsis, conjunction, and lexical reiteration and collocation. Generally, analysts have found a positive but low correlation between writing quality and number of cohesive ties (see, for example, Witte and Faigley 1981). Quantitative measures of cohesion have not seemed much more useful as an index of the quality of adult writing than has the incidence of other quantifiable features, such as length, T-unit size, or mechanical and usage errors (see Nold and Freedman 1977; and Gebhard 1978).

Witte and Faigley (1981) conclude that a narrow pedagogical emphasis on cohesion will not improve writing significantly and that quantitative measures of cohesive ties cannot serve as simple indices of writing quality. They have suggested, however, that cohesion analysis can help distinguish stages of writing development and might provide methods of explaining concretely some of the differences between good and poor student writing. For instance, the kinds and frequencies of certain cohesive devices may reflect a student's skills of invention, the ability to discover what to say. Witte and Faigley's research shows that poorer writers use fewer 'immediate' and 'mediated ties,' fewer types of conjunctives, and fewer third-person pronouns (perhaps in an attempt to avoid pronoun reference problems). They project lexical collocation as the kind of cohesion that best reflects writing quality. Poorer writers repeat concepts and words redundantly, without adding new information; they do not use lexical collocation to extend and refine meanings as do better writers.

Pritchard (1980) has also documented the occurrence of restated but undeveloped repetitions in ineffective writing. In a study of the 'problem' sections of good and poor compositions by eleventh graders, she noted the incidence of redundant repetition as an index of writing quality. She found that problem sections in her sample essays displayed proportionately more cohesive devices of all types, and she concluded that problems arise from overuse or unsuccessful use of cohesive ties, especially ties which employ repetition, pronoun reference, and, most significantly, transitions or conjunctions. Using cohesive ties successfully is apparently not easy. Both good and poor writers may use the same kinds of cohesive ties, but they use them differently.

Other researchers have found that cohesive devices can be a source of possible ambiguity (see Mosenthal and Tierney 1984). When readers process a cohesive device, they must restructure a cohesive relationship; they must do the work of comprehending, inferring, and assuming coherence, regardless of the writer's intent. Readers expect and assume coherence whether or not a cohesive tie indicates it. Cohesive ties do not create relationships (although they can stimulate their invention); rather they express cohesive relationships that already exist in the writer's thinking. Cohesion reflects mental processes which both writers and readers perform. Although cohesive devices are visible signs of the relationships that they signal, they are at best only indicators of them. A cohesive device can mislead readers if it signals a relationship that is not intended or has multiple interpretations.

To explore the complex problem of analyzing cohesive devices and their effectiveness, let us scrutinize a student essay which exhibits various cohesive strategies—some used well and some not. The text in Figure 8.1 was written by a student in a community college basic writing class and reflects many of the typical strategies of a BASIC WRITER. In American college and university education, the term 'basic writer' has come to refer to a student who enters college without the traditional skills needed for success in the customary introductory course in English composition (see Shaughnessy 1977). Such a writer often has a mature native command of spoken language but little experience with written language and how it differs from speech.

Italicized words and phrases in Figure 8.1 highlight the basic writer's use of repetitions, demonstratives, associated terms, and parallel structures to hold attention on a topic. The concentration of these devices at the end of the paragraph indicates that this student knows principles of organization and desires a strong closing. Another indication of organization is use of the superordinate *place* before two sentences specifying *home* and *school*. These features contribute to the cohesion of the essay, yet other features that have potential for effective cohesion are misused by the writer. *Therefore* and *however* are misleading because the writer fails to add the result and contrast that these conjunctions signal. The essay could be improved by either the elimination of these two words or the substitution of *furthermore* and *specifically*, since the writer is adding another point and two examples of it.

This essay shows that even basic writers are aware of the power and importance of cohesive devices, although they fail to use them effectively. Basic writers may have trouble when they use language options with cohesive functions that they have not yet mastered. These writers often do not understand clearly where written sentences should end and where they should continue; hence, their writing commonly displays mechanical difficulties with cohesion which operates across sentence boundaries. Basic writers also may not understand the semantic relationship that a particular tie expresses, such as reference, classification, comparison, or consequence.

Part of the challenge in studying cohesive ties as they express semantic relationships, I believe, is in understanding which ties maintain relationships already drawn in the discourse and which develop new ones. Because of the difference in the *maintenance* and *developmental* functions that cohesive ties perform, it seems worthwhile to classify ties according to these major

In order to have *good* study habits, one should be aware that, in order to get *good* grades, he have *to study hard*. *To study hard* one should *set up a schedule* to study, without interfering with his work or sleep. To do *this*, one could write down his work *hours*and his class *hours*, and the *time* that he has left should be used for study. Therefore, one should *study* in a quite *place* where there is no one to distract his attention away from his work. However, I would suggest that *if one studies at home*, *he* would do so in a quite room without the T.V. going or the radio on. *If one chooses to study at school he* should avoid being around friends. *These study habits* are *good advice* to a freshman in college. Take my *advice* I know.

Figure 8.1 Essay written by basic writer (verbatim, italics added)

functions before exploring the difficulties they present for writers. We can call expressions in the maintenance group 'static ties'; these terms hold attention on a topic. Let us call expressions in the developmental group 'dynamic ties'; these develop the topic rhetorically.[1]

8.2 STATIC AND DYNAMIC TIES: TOWARD A DEFINITION

Static ties hold attention on a topic without necessarily manipulating it or changing it in any way. Many kinds of static ties are essential for achieving unity in English prose. They are pervasive, regardless of topic or mode of development. In fact, it is hard to imagine writing any extended thought without using several types of static ties.

Static ties include repetition of the same lexical item (as in the nine repetitions of *study* in the essay in Figure 8.1), demonstratives (e.g. *this, these*), third-person pronouns, definite articles (when they serve to maintain attention on a topic previously introduced), and nominal, verbal, and clausal substitution and ellipsis. Static ties are also formed by continuative conjunctions (e.g. *well*) that simply move discussion onward and by additive conjunctions (e.g. *also*) that can introduce further information, facts, or details without necessarily developing the topic. Synonyms, near-synonyms, antonyms, and collocations (terms that are expected in the environment of a given word) can also form static ties by 'association' in the mind of either the writer or the reader. Further, static ties can be formed through parallel structure. Of course, the success of parallelism depends on the selection of appropriate grammatical forms as well as semantic balance; parallel structures with tense, for instance, must contain the proper sequence of tenses to be effective.[2] Finally, choice of tense in itself contributes to static cohesion and usually accompanies other ties which more firmly maintain attention on a topic.

To express rhetorical manipulation of the topic, writers can make use of our second major group of ties, dynamic ties, which can be formed by many kinds of text features. Temporal conjuncts (e.g. *before, afterwards*) support chronological arrangement and sequence of tenses in narration. Lexical superordinates identify high-level logical relationships, as might be expressed in expository definition, for example. Hyponyms identify specific, low-level logical relationships, as might be expressed by an example illustrating a general concept. (In both inductive and deductive reasoning, superordinates and hyponyms develop the logical thrust of the discourse and point to logical coherence among major arguments.) Causal conjunctions (e.g. *therefore*) label reasoning from cause to effect. Adversative conjunctions (e.g. *but, however*) signal contrasts, and the comparative and superlative forms of adjectives and adverbs signal a discourse focus on comparison and contrast.

Dynamic ties specify how a writer manipulates an internal representation of environment. Instead of repeating an idea, they indicate how it develops, changes, or relates to something else: to a higher class or a specific example, to a cause or a consequence, or to a similar concept with some difference, such as the same item occurring at a different time. Unlike static ties, dynamic ties are both optional and sparse. Extended thought is possible without them: a contrast, for example, may be expressed by verbs like *increase, prefer*, and *surpass* (for lists of other linguistic cues to intellectual processes, see Odell 1977). Furthermore, dynamic ties can complicate prose unnecessarily. A cluster of various dynamic ties can work to contort a topic in too many different ways all at once, making writing appear dense, opaque, or even incoherent to the reader.

In sum, static ties are essential for holding attention on a topic, and a wide variety of them appear with great frequency; they reflect control of the resources for textual structure in the English language. Conversely, dynamic ties are optional but convenient devices for signaling the type of rhetorical manipulation applied to a topic; they indicate development of a topic, although development may occur without such indication. Since extending thought is a more advanced skill than maintaining attention, we can predict that student writers will use dynamic ties more rarely and find them more difficult to use than static ties.

8.3 STATIC AND DYNAMIC TIES: TOWARD ANALYZING EFFECTS

By analyzing student writing, we can test whether dynamic ties are more closely associated with the effectiveness of written discourse than are static ties. We can also test whether dynamic ties are indeed more difficult for writers. In analyzing these ties, however, the problems of student-writers become problems for analyst-readers. In particular, when writers have difficulty using dynamic ties to indicate higher level mental processes, the ties they do use may present problems to analysts who are tabulating them. Tabulators who come upon a dynamic tie that is ambiguous or poorly constructed may categorize it incorrectly or overlook it. Hence, when several tabulators analyze the same poorly constructed tie, it is possible that only a single tabulator will report it as a tie. This problem can prove to be a source of insight, however, because the tabulators' inconsistency in reporting a cohesive tie may reflect the difficulty of the tie for the writer. If the tie is difficult to construct, we can predict a high frequency of single reports of that tie when several tabulators examine the same corpus. Furthermore, if the presence of poorly constructed ties is an index of writing quality, we can expect that single reports of such ties will occur more often in essays that have been independently rated 'worst' than in those rated 'best.'

All of these considerations suggest three specific suppositions about the probable frequency of static and dynamic ties in a group of student essays collected for cohesion analysis:

- *Hypothesis 1*. A typical essay in the corpus will contain more different types of static ties than dynamic ties. This finding is expected because static ties are both essential and less difficult to write than dynamic ties.

- *Hypothesis 2*. When several readers count varieties of cohesive ties in the same corpus, they will recognize dynamic ties less easily than static ties; in particular, it is more likely that only one reader in the group will recognize a dynamic tie when he or she sees it (a single observation). This observation pattern will occur because student writers often construct ineffective dynamic ties which analyst-readers have trouble distinguishing.
- *Hypothesis 3*. When several readers count cohesive ties in papers rated holistically as best and worst, they will recognize fewer ties in the worst papers; in particular, it is more likely that only one reader in the group will recognize a tie when he or she sees it in a paper rated worst. This pattern is expected because the worst papers are likely to contain more poorly constructed ties.

8.3.1 Experimental method

To test these hypotheses, I re-examined a corpus of student writing that had been independently analyzed for quality by three readers and independently analyzed for cohesive devices by four other readers (see Hartnett 1980b). All readers were trained extensively to do these analyses.

The writing samples included 316 essays written by students in four sections of a developmental writing course at College of the Mainland, a community college in Texas City, Texas. The students were 49 percent White-Anglo, 33 percent Black, 15 percent Hispanic, and 3 percent Asian. They had all scored at least 7.5 grade-level reading scores on the Nelson-Denny reading test, and they had scored between 23 and 34 of a possible 60 on the Test of Standard Written English or had passed a lower level preparatory writing course. Their placement in this developmental writing course had been verified by a previous writing sample. The four sections of the course were taught by two instructors in two semesters.

The 'experimental' set of 316 essays included complete groups of four essays written by the same writer. Each student had written on one expository and one persuasive topic at the beginning of a semester and on another set of expository and persuasive topics at the end—four in all. Topics were switched both for times of the year and teachers. Papers were coded with numbers and given anonymously to two groups of raters who did not communicate about the project.

The volunteer readers included seven experienced high school English teachers. Using a separate 'practice' set of essays, three of these teachers were trained to perform holistic ratings and four to analyze cohesion. The three readers who performed the holistic ratings received six hours of paid training in holistic rating procedures (see Hult in this volume for an explanation of the holistic rating method [ed.]). They achieved high levels of inter-rater reliability both when reading the practice set and when reading the experimental set of essays (0.80 for the practice set; 0.96 for the experimental set). The four readers who tabulated types of cohesive devices received fifteen hours of paid training and achieved an inter-rater reliability rating of 0.80 during training; inter-rater reliability for their ratings of the experimental set of essays ranged from 0.61 to 0.92, with a mean of 0.78 weighted for a slight difference in the number of papers each read.

For this study, the cohesive tabulators referred to definitions and examples of cohesive devices derived from Halliday and Hasan's work (see Hartnett 1980a and 1980b). Their observations cover seventeen subtypes of cohesive devices: pronoun; demonstrative; comparative; same word; associated word; superordinate; general noun; substitution or omission of noun, of verb, or of clause; conjunction for addition, contrast, cause/consequence, continuity, and time; sequence of tenses; and parallel sentence structure.

The task of the tabulators was to search for one correct use of a subtype of tie as evidence that the tie was in the writer's repertoire. Tabulators recorded for each subtype the specific words in the occurrence of the tie, the number of the sentence containing it, and the referent or presupposed item and its sentence number. Tabulators were looking for the total number of different subtypes of ties used, so they did not record repetitions of a type in a paper after they had found one example of it; this limited their work and speeded it, although they still, of course, spent more time on each paper than did the holistic raters.

As I noted above, the difficulty a writer has in expressing a tie may affect the way a tabulator records it. Although the tabulators were instructed to count as cohesive ties only the ties that specifically related separate sentences and to ignore mechanical errors that did not interfere with cohesion, they still had much room for analytical error. For instance, they could be confused by fragments and run-on sentences that obscure whether or how ties operate across sentence boundaries. They could have difficulty determining whether consistent tense creates a cohesive tie; tense forms might be consistent without any obvious cohesive effect, or verb forms might be written incorrectly, making the intended tense difficult to decipher. In all, I anticipated about a dozen errors in student writing that might have led tabulators to confuse ties. Through careful discussion of these potential sources of confusion, I trained the analysts to make judgments as similarly and as accurately as possible.

8.3.2 Findings

In earlier studies, I observed a positive but low correlation between the total number of different subtypes of cohesive tie in each of the 316 essays (ranging from 0 to 8 out of 17 possible different subtypes) and the holistic quality rating (ranging from 1 to 6, the full scale); the observed statistic was $r = 0.21$ ($p < 0.001$) for the Pearson correlation test. A two-way analysis of variance showed no significant difference related to the mode of the essay being tabulated (see Hartnett 1980b).

Further analysis of the quantities of each subtype of cohesive tie for the present study revealed more specific relationships between cohesion and overall quality (the holistic rating). I analyzed the separate tallies for each of the different subtypes of cohesion as reported for 158 papers written on one

Table 8.1 Frequency of ties observed and percent observations made by a single tabulator

Type	Total N = 158		Best N = 29		Worst N = 19	
	Freq.	Percent Single	Freq.	Percent Single	Freq.	Percent Single
Static ties						
Same words	156	3	28	4	19	5
Associated words	152	14	29	7	17	24
Sequence of tenses	105	59	20	45	12	75
Demonstratives	87	51	21	48	9	33
Pronouns	76	49	14	50	12	50
Additive conj.	60	55	10	40	8	75
Continuative conj.	26	73	3	0	2	100
Parallel structure	30	83	9	78	3	67
Noun substitutes and ellipses	15	40	3	33	1	100
Verb substitutes and ellipses	3	100	2	0	0	
General nouns	3	100	1	100	0	
Clause substitutes and ellipses	2	100	1	0	0	
Subtotal	715	35	141	30	83	41
Dynamic ties						
Superordinates	96	56	23	65	11	82
Contrast conj.	27	41	5	0	4	75
Cause/conseq. conj.	22	86	3	67	1	100
Comparatives	12	92	4	100	3	100
Temporal conj.	12	92	3	100	1	100
Subtotal	169	63	38	63	20	85
Total	884	41	179	37	103	50

of two topics: 'where to eat lunch' (expository) and 'should the college have an honor code' (persuasive). Table 8.1 shows the frequency of each kind of tie as reported once per essay by the group of tabulators. Table 8.1 also indicates what percentage of these observations reflects reports by only a single observer.

For the 158 essays, tabulators reported a total of 715 instances of twelve subtypes of static ties and a total of 169 of five subtypes of dynamic ties. An essay at the mean had 4.53 different subtypes of static ties but only 1.07 different subtypes of dynamic ties, a difference predicted by my first hypothesis that a typical essay would show more subtypes of static ties than of dynamic ties. Observations made by a single tabulator accounted for

63 percent (106) of the total observations of dynamic subtypes but only 35 percent (253) of the total observations of static subtypes. The chi-square statistic of 42.231 establishes this predicted difference as extremely significant ($p < 0.001$, 1 df, Yates' continuity correction applied to chi-squared statistics). This finding supports my second hypothesis that tabulators would have more difficulty recording dynamic ties.

Papers with best and worst holistic quality ratings differed significantly in the proportion of single and multiple reports of cohesive ties ($X^2 = 4.297$, $p < 0.05$). In the twenty-nine papers with the highest holistic quality rating, only 30 percent of the 141 subtypes of static ties were reported by a single tabulator, while 63 percent of the thirty-eight dynamic subtypes were reported by a single tabulator. In contrast, for the nineteen papers with the lowest holistic rating, 41 percent of eighty-three static subtypes were reported by a single tabulator and 85 percent of the twenty dynamic subtypes were reported by a single tabulator. These figures support my first and second hypotheses about the proportions of static and dynamic ties and the ease with which tabulators would recognize each. These data also confirm my third hypothesis that worst essays would reveal that their writers had more difficulty writing ties than writers of best essays; the difference is reflected in the observers' difficulty in reporting them.

Additional findings reveal that static ties occurred in all essays, whereas dynamic ties did not, and that dynamic ties may have some bearing on writing quality yet are not essential to excellence. About three-quarters of the papers (114, or 72 percent) contained dynamic ties and these received a mean holistic rating of 4.71. The remaining papers (forty-four or 28 percent) contained no dynamic ties and had a mean holistic rating of 4.07.

As expected, some varieties of ties caused problems for tabulators. I had anticipated not only problems in interpreting ties as a whole but also in interpreting certain static ties. Tabulators had trouble recording 'sequence of tense' as it contributed to cohesion, for instance. They reported cohesive tenses in about two-thirds of all papers—in 69 percent of the best and in 63 percent of the worst. However, they did not agree consistently about whether tenses contributed significantly to cohesion; their judgments correlated for just over half (55 percent) of the observations of tense cohesion in the best papers, but for only a quarter (25 percent) of observations of tense in the worst. I believe this inconsistency in agreement reflects the student writers' difficulty with tense form and choice.

When sequence of tense is included in our analysis, the difference between best and worst essays approaches significance both for kinds of dynamic ties ($X^2 = 3.245$, $p < 0.1$) and kinds of static ties ($X^2 = 2.891$, $p < 0.1$). When sequence of tense is omitted from the analysis, experimental results are affected as follows: first, inter-rater reliability improves overall. Second, the significance of the difference between difficulty in reporting static ties and difficulty in reporting dynamic ties increases, as reflected in the ratio of single to multiple observations ($X^2 = 51.396$ instead of 42.231, $p < 0.001$ for both). Third, the difference between best and worst essays as reflected in the observations of all kinds of ties decreases

($X^2 = 2.563$, $p < 0.15$). Finally, the overall differences between single and multiple observations of static ties also decreases ($X^2 = 1.325$, $p < 0.25$).

8.4 CONCLUSION

Static and dynamic ties perform distinct functions in the textual organization of prose. Static ties connect stretches of text; dynamic ties advance the logic of the discourse. An analysis of student writing for cohesive devices reveals that students have more difficulty constructing dynamic ties than static ties and use fewer different types of dynamic ties than of static ties. The mere presence of dynamic or static ties, however, does not ensure the success of student writing. Nevertheless, the incidence of poorly constructed ties of all types does seem to relate to the overall quality of the writing. These conclusions suggest some direction for teachers and scholars of writing.

First, teachers should apply knowledge about student problems with cohesion to teach more efficiently and effectively. The relative difficulty of some kinds of cohesive ties may suggest a developmental learning sequence. Teachers should also relate rhetorical patterns to the various kinds of dynamic ties which express them. For example, lessons on the rhetorical pattern of comparison and contrast should include practice with dynamic cohesive ties that support this pattern, such as comparative adjectives and adversative conjunctions, comparative metaphors, and comparative content verbs like *resemble* and *surpass* (see Hartnett 1985).

Second, scholars should examine good writing, noting the kinds of expressions, including dynamic ties, which indicate rhetorical development. A taxonomy of such expressions could be used to measure the putative purity of rhetorical modes.

Third, researchers should reconsider the utility of trying to link overall writing quality to the quantity of cohesive devices, ignoring their functions or aptness. In *Cohesion in English*, Halliday and Hasan warn that analysis of cohesion neither interprets nor evaluates texts (1976: 328). Cohesion analysis is linguistic description which explains the techniques that cause readers to make certain inferences and presuppositions. If researchers want to use Halliday and Hasan's careful distinctions of linguistic subtypes for another purpose, they must reorganize the subtypes into categories that are relevant to the goal of their research. For example, analyses of student writing should define categories of linguistic devices by their function in compositions.

In incorporating the distinction between static and dynamic ties into a theory of how a writer produces prose, one could say that writers must use static ties to focus readers' attention, a basic mental process. Although static ties are essential for readers' comprehension and are used by good writers with great frequency and variety, their masterful use is not all that makes prose effective. While holding attention with static ties, the writer must develop a topic by adding new information and relationships to make its continuation worthwhile. Dynamic ties are useful in performing and signaling this function, but other non-cohesive devices also serve the same purpose. For these reasons, simple counts of either types or instances of all cohesive ties cannot be a completely effective index of the quality of prose.

Cohesion is a means to an end, not the end itself. Static ties are the dull but essential workhorses that pull prose together; dynamic ties are the reins, controlled by the mental processes of the driver's extended thought. The success of a writer's prose depends upon much more than successful use of any cohesive devices. Nevertheless, these features and their distinct uses can help us to describe how readers understand and writers control the textual structures that express rhetorical development in written discourse.

NOTES

1. Phelps (1985) uses the terms 'dynamics' and 'static' to describe the reader's experience and analysis of coherence. She distinguishes 'flow' from 'design' and 'transition' from 'motif,' qualities which contribute to coherence from semantic systems beyond the text. Although her distinctions are compatible with mine, we make them on different levels.
2. The strong cohesive effect of parallel structure is recognized by many analysts (see Becker 1965; D'Angelo 1975; Christensen and Christensen 1978; Pritchard 1980; and Witte and Faigley 1981). Halliday and Hasan (1976) recognize it, although it is not formally a part of their cohesion system.

BIBLIOGRAPHY

D'Angelo, F. J. (1975), *A Conceptual Theory of Rhetoric*, Cambridge, Mass., Winthrop.

Becker, A. L. (1965), 'A Tagmemic Approach to Paragraph Analysis,' *College Composition and Communication*, **16**, 237–42.

Christensen, F. and Christensen, B. (1978, 2nd edn), *Notes toward a New Rhetoric*, New York, Harper and Row.

Flower, L. and Hayes, J. R. (1981), 'A Cognitive Process Theory of Writing,' *College Composition and Communication*, **32**, 365–87.

Gebhard, A. O. (1978), 'Writing Quality and Syntax: A Transformational Analysis of Three Prose Samples,' *Research in the Teaching of English*, **12**, 211–31.

Halliday, M. A. K. and Hasan, R. (1976), *Cohesion in English*, London, Longman.

Hartnett, C. G. (1980a), 'Analyzing Cohesive Ties,' Arlington, Va., ERIC [Educational Resources Information Center] Document Reproduction Service, ED 236 654; abridged version in Fagan, W. T., Cooper, C. R., and Jensen, J. M. (eds) (1985: 175), *Measures for Research and Evaluation in the English Language Arts 2*, Urbana, Ill., ERIC Clearinghouse on Reading and Communication Skills and the National Council of Teachers of English.

Hartnett, C. G. (1980b), *Cohesion as a Teachable Measure of Writing Competence*, Ph.D. dissertation, Indiana, Penn., Indiana University of Pennsylvania (see *Dissertation Abstracts International*, sec. A, 1980, **41**, 2086–A).

Hartnett, C. G. (1985, 2nd edn), *Tying Thinking to Writing*, Texas City, Tex., College of the Mainland Press.

Hunt, E. (1983), 'On the Nature of Intelligence,' *Science*, **219**, 141–6.

Lachman, R., Lachman, J. L., and Butterfield, E. C. (1979), *Cognitive Psychology and Information Processing: An Introduction*, Hillsdale, N.J., Lawrence Erlbaum.

Markels, R. B. (1983), 'Cohesion Paradigms in Paragraphs,' *College English*, **45**, 450–64.

Mosenthal, J. H. and Tierney, R. J. (1984), 'Cohesion: Problems with Talking about Text,' *Reading Research Quarterly*, **19**, 240–4.

Nold, E. W. and Freedman, S. W. (1977), 'An Analysis of Readers' Responses to Essays,' *Research in the Teaching of English*, **11**, 164–74.

Odell, L., 'Measuring Changes in Intellectual Processes as One Dimension of Growth in Writing,' in Cooper, C. R. and Odell, L. (eds) (1977: 107–32), *Evaluating Writing: Describing, Measuring, Judging*, Urbana, Ill., National Council of Teachers of English.

Phelps, L. W. (1985), 'Dialectics of Coherence: Toward an Integrative Theory,' *College English*, **47**, 12–29.

Pike, K. L. (1964), 'A Linguistic Contribution to Composition: A Hypothesis,' *College Composition and Communication*, **15**, 82–8.

Pritchard, R. J. (1980), *A Study of the Cohesive Devices in the Good and Poor Compositions of Eleventh Graders*, Ph.D. dissertation, University of Missouri–Columbia (see *Dissertation Abstracts International*, sec. A, 1981, **42**, 688–A).

Shaughnessy, M. P. (1977), *Errors and Expectations: A Guide for the Teacher of Basic Writing*, New York, Oxford University Press.

Witte, S. P. and Faigley, L. (1981), 'Coherence, Cohesion, and Writing Quality,' *College Composition and Communication*, **32**, 189–204.

9 Global marking of rhetorical frame in text and reader evaluation

Christine A. Hult
Utah State University

9.1 ANALYZING FRAME DEVELOPMENT IN TEXTS

Experienced readers and writers share many of the same expectations in approaching expository discourse—expectations confirmed by systems of linguistic choice associated with particular uses of written language. Authors choose features from systems which define a language variety and create RHETORICAL FRAMES that readers identify with a genre or mode. Marking of the rhetorical frame is critical in many ways to an author's and reader's mutual understanding of the text.

Researchers have explored from diverse perspectives the ways in which we use frames of various kinds to organize experience. Methods of organizing experience in terms of frames, scripts, and schemata are highlighted in the work of Ableson and Shank in psychology; Minsky in artificial intelligence; Chafe and Fillmore in linguistics; Bateson and Frake in anthropology; and Goffman, Gumperz, and Hymes in sociology. As Tannen notes, the work of these scholars in different fields is unified by their 'realization that people approach the world not as naive, blank-slate receptacles . . . but rather as experienced and sophisticated veterans of perception who have stored their prior experiences as "an organized mass." ' They all 'have referred to frames and other structures of expectation' as a means of storing experience (Tannen 1979: 144). In short, researchers of language and other social phenomena seem to agree that recognizing and interpreting frames is basic to human behavior.

Framing allows us to organize our perceptions so that we can use past experience to predict and interpret new experience in varied fields and modes. In manipulating the communication mode of written language, for instance, we as readers or writers refer to rhetorical frames to produce and interpret text, frames which characterize the short story, the various forms of poetry, or the modes of narration, description, exposition, and argumentation. In fact, readers and writers, as studies have shown, RELY on rhetorical frames to discern the purpose of discourse (see Meyer 1975; and Jones 1977).

Several researchers have suggested analytic procedures to determine a text's rhetorical frame and explain its organizational pattern. Tannen (1979) has analyzed the linguistic features of narratives in an effort to discern which grammatical or linguistic cues signaled the narrative frame for the reader. Kintsch (1974) and Thorndyke (1977) have studied generalized story structures (or story frames) as they aided reader comprehension. Longacre (1976), Meyer (1975), and Thorndyke (1977) have documented the presence of hierarchical organizational patterns in narrative discourse. (Meyer, in particular, has shown the importance of the position of ideas within a text to reader comprehension.) Jones (1977) has studied the thematic and hierarchical structure of expository essays to discern the effect such structure has on readers. All of these scholars document the presence of recognizable rhetorical frames in written discourse and their positive influence on a reader's understanding of expository prose.

This chapter reports a procedure I devised for analyzing rhetorical frame and the results of my analysis of several texts to determine if frame development affects how readers' VALUE written discourse. I examined the ways in which frame development in student writing correlates with holistic grades assigned by trained readers and sought to answer two basic questions:

- How do writers signal rhetorical frame in exposition?
- How do rhetorical frames of students' essays that are highly valued or rated as 'above average' by trained readers differ from those rated as 'average'?

Applying the work of Meyer (1975), Jones (1977), Grimes (1978), and Christensen (1965), I described student texts as they communicate an ORGANIZATIONAL STRUCTURE or as they group ideas or content into larger complexes and relate them to one another (see Grimes 1978). I analyzed the organizational structure of sixty expository essays by identifying and paraphrasing sentences or groups of sentences that seemed either to convey main arguments or to provide support for arguments. After tabulating the number of words, the number of paragraphs, and the number of main arguments for each essay, I went on to statistically analyze each paper for nine additional features (see Table 9.1).

Drawing on Christensen's model of the generative rhetoric of paragraphs (1965), I classified supporting points relevant to the main argument as proceeding in either a subordinate or coordinate sequence and then subclassified these sequences further. I coded as CLARIFYING SUPPORT POINTS (c.s.) those points subordinate to the main argument and as ENUMERATIVE SUPPORT POINTS (e.s.) those points both subordinate to the main argument and coordinate to each other. (Enumerative support points provide elaboration with examples at a parallel level of specificity.) I identified as BACKGROUND POINTS those sentences including background facts or presuppositions. To assess the amount of repetition in the essays, I computed the number of REPEATED ARGUMENTS (r.a.), REPEATED CLOSING ARGUMENTS (r.c.a.) and REPEATED SUPPORT POINTS (r.s.p.) (whether clarifying or enumerative). Where paragraph boundaries did not coincide with new arguments

[1] The Federal Department of Labor estimates that one in four college graduates entering the labor market between now and 1985 will have to take jobs traditionally filled by people without college degrees. [2] Nevertheless, a good liberal arts education is the best preparation for uncertain job requirements and increased leisure time.

[3] The liberal arts education is the best preparation for professional school and for graduate studies. [4] The knowledge gained in all fields of the liberal arts curriculum are beneficial for almost all post graduate work. [5] One may ask, 'What does the humanities have to do with medicine?' [6] In reply, I might suggest that I don't know one physician who doesn't deal with other human beings and their problems. [7] Understanding people and society and what motivates them could do nothing but help the doctor relate to his patients. [8] The analytical and occupational skills gained in mathematics and the sciences would be beneficial for almost any degree and job possibilities.

[9] The liberal arts education enables the student unsure of a major or career to sample a wide range of topics within the liberal arts curriculum, while also fulfilling distribution requirements set up within the college. [10] A student may enter college with no idea of a possible major, however, while fulfilling requirements in different areas he will surely find an area of interest. [11] Moreover, the majors and job possibilities from those majors are almost endless. [12] The majors extend from anthropology to zoology, physics to economics, and so on, and career choices are almost as boundless as the majors.

[13] Not just educated in one narrow field, but with modest exposure to many, the liberal arts graduate is better prepared to deal with our ever changing world. [14] Because the liberal arts graduate has taken classes in the humanities, natural sciences, physical sciences, mathematics, etc. he is better prepared to face society and its problems. [15] Classes in the natural sciences and humanities teach the history of our world and mankind and show him how to avoid the mistakes of others while emulating their successes. [16] They give the student a look at human nature and how to deal with it. [17] The physical sciences and mathematics teach the person to organize things well and to think and write in a clear, concise logical manner. [18] In essence, the liberal arts education developes a person not just in one narrow area, but instead, developes the liberal arts graduate into a well-educated person moderately educated in many fields and facets of life.

[19] Because the job market is tight and people are faced with an ever-growing amount of leisure time, more students entering college should consider the liberal arts education. [20] The liberal arts education not only prepares you for your adult life and the job market upon graduation, it also prepares the student for further graduate work and professional schools, if that is what he desires.

Figure 9.1 Student essay # 14/B/1–1 (verbatim)

or where paragraph boundaries occurred more frequently than new arguments, I coded for UNCONVENTIONAL PARAGRAPHING (u.p.), and where the writer failed to reorient the reader to material, I coded for INEFFECTIVE REORIENTATION (i.r.). My computation of these two features along with the number of UNRELATED SUPPORT POINTS AND ARGUMENTS (u.a.) helped me assess problem areas in the organizational structure of the essays. Likewise, my computation of the number of clarifying and enumerative points at various levels in the organizational structure helped me assess the amount of content elaboration. In addition to compiling tallies of these features, I created a tree diagram for each paper to schematize the frame (see

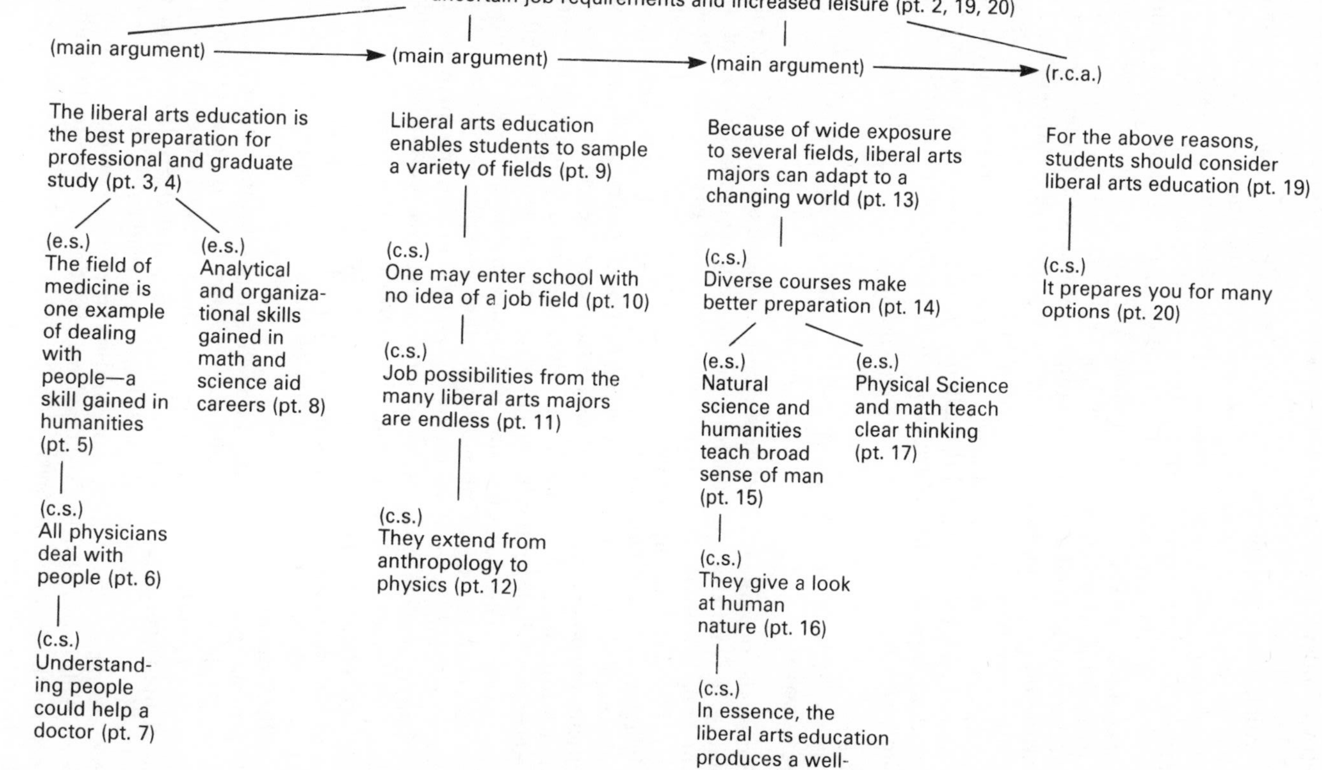

Figure 9.2 Tree diagram of student essay #14/B/1–1

Figure 9.1, Student Essay # 14/B/1–1, and Figure 9.2, Tree Diagram of Essay # 14/B/1–1).

Tree diagrams graphically illustrate hierarchical relationships and coherence in content organization. By paraphrasing the content of major and supporting points and graphing links between the paraphrased passages, a researcher can show cohesion and coherence between the various levels in the organizational hierarchy. In the diagram shown here horizontal lines show linear progression, particularly the cohesive links which tie arguments together. Vertical lines show coherence links which tie main arguments to their supporting points. Paraphrased content that does not link to other paraphrased passages is set off with a broken line. In constructing the tree diagrams, I employed my own adaptation of Christensen's model: each column linked by vertical bars represents paragraph development (see Figure 9.2). This scheme highlights hierarchical development of ideas, a prominent feature of the 'informal proof' rhetorical frame in expository writing.

9.2 COMPARING READER EVALUATION OF TEXTS WITH FRAME DEVELOPMENT

To discern the possible effect of organizational frame on readers' judgments of quality, I compared my analysis of the organizational frame of sixty student essays with readers' overall evaluations of essay quality (holistic ratings). The sixty expository essays were written as exams at the University of Michigan for placement in composition courses. Trained readers who were also experienced teachers of writing had rated the essays holistically for placement purposes. Each essay was read twice, receiving a rating of 1 through 4 from each reader ('1' indicates a high score). In a holistic rating, trained readers independently evaluate a writing sample to assign it a quality rating. The combination of lengthy training sessions (wherein criteria for evaluation and numerous writing samples are discussed) and regular re-pairing of readers seems to ensure uniformity of evaluation. When paired readers disagree about the rating of a particular sample, a third reader serves as referee. Since the individual reading of each writing sample (generally three to four handwritten pages in length) takes from three to five minutes, it is apparent that readers are making judgments based upon their internalized notions of discourse features that correlate with writing quality.

My sample group of sixty essays was chosen at random by score and topic from a complete set of holistically rated exams, each on one of two topics (see Figures 9.3 and 9.4). Of these essays, thirty (fifteen on each topic) had received high scores (a '1' from both readers), and thirty (fifteen on each topic) had received mid-scores (a '3' from both readers). Through my study of this sample group of high- and mid-score essays, I hoped to show that essays which had a clearly developed organizational structure (as indicated by my method of text analysis described above) would be valued more highly by competent readers.

Your local high school will publish a pamphlet on 'Higher Education and Some Alternatives' that will include the views of students, teachers, and alumni. Write an essay for the pamphlet that you believe would help high school seniors plan for an unpredictable job market.

Begin your essay with the following sentence (which you should copy into your bluebook):

The Federal Department of Labor estimates that one in four college graduates entering the labor market between now and 1985 will have to take jobs traditionally filled by people without college degrees.

Select *one* of the following as your second sentence and copy it into your bluebook:

A. This prediction should not discourage high school graduates from going to college, but they would be wise to major in such fields as business administration or computer science.
B. Nevertheless, a good liberal arts education is the best preparation for uncertain job requirements and increased leisure time.
C. Since it takes four years and an average of $20,000 to obtain a college degree, many high school seniors should consider alternatives to a college education.

Now complete your essay developing the argument that follows from the first two sentences. Do your best to make your argument convincing to the students who will read your advice.

Figure 9.3 Essay topic #14

To confirm my method of text analysis, two of the trained assessment readers produced tree diagrams for a set of essays which I had diagrammed previously myself. The readers followed as closely as possible the method of analysis I outlined, and they represented schematically the organizational frame they discerned in four high-score and four mid-score essays on the same topic chosen at random. I compared the readers' diagrams with those I had done earlier in the study and concluded that my method of diagramming organizational frame is reasonably reliable. For the sample of eight essays, each reader created three tree diagrams which duplicated mine; reader A drew four diagrams moderately like my own and one diagram totally unlike mine; and reader B drew five diagrams moderately like the ones I drew.

Student writing worked well for this study because it varies in quality, and the University of Michigan assessment test provided suitable samples. Though not explicitly stated in the test instrument, the test is designed to show whether or not writers can establish an organizational frame. The essay topic provides the writer with a rhetorical context and explicit instructions for development of the essay response (see Figures 9.3 and 9.4). The test instructions limit the subject, audience, and purpose of the discourse and place a special constraint on the text development by providing the beginning of the text itself. To complete the assignment successfully, the writer needs both to recognize and to produce the rhetorical frame demanded by

Your local newspaper has asked its readers to write guest editorials about citizens' groups organized to influence television programming for children. Write an editorial presenting your ideas on this subject to readers of your newspaper.

Begin your editorial with the following sentence (which you should copy into your bluebook):

Action for Children's Television (ACT) has 11,000 volunteer members who lobby for more control of program content during family viewing time.

Select *one* of the following as your second sentence and copy it into your bluebook:

A. ACT should increase its efforts because children are unable to protect themselves against questionable content or the influence of commercial advertisers.

B. ACT is dangerous in itself, as Robert Mulholland, NBC-TV president observed, 'TV must never become a medium controlled by special interests.'

C. Though ACT's concern is commendable, it must be careful not to act like groups which try to censor reading materials.

Now complete your editorial developing the argument that follows from the first two sentences. Do your best to make your argument convincing to your readers.

Figure 9.4 Essay topic #23

the task. Each essay test topic calls for an 'informal proof' where the writer is to convince or persuade the audience with specific arguments. To produce the indicated frame, the writer must plan explicitly the organizational structure and signal that structure through appropriate linguistic devices.

The raters of the essays themselves, of course, are not told to look for the 'informal proof' frame when they assign a grade. Indeed, raters do not approach the essays with any expectation other than that the essays should show the writers' competence in basic composition. Because they are experienced teachers of writing, readers of essays for placement in University of Michigan composition courses are aware, of course, of rhetorical conventions for organizing and developing expository essays. I hypothesized that readers were looking unconsciously for signs of these conventions while reading, and that they would react negatively to violations of conventions.

9.3 FINDINGS AND DISCUSSION

Through my analysis of organizational frame in student exposition, I discovered that a high quality-rating by the trained assessment readers correlated with student development of a clear frame. The high-score essay writers seemed to have a better understanding of how to apply global marking of organization to produce a more unified and coherent presentation of content and a more focused presentation of argument.

To identify the differences in the organizational frames of essays rated as average and above average by trained readers, I compared the tree diagrams of content organization for the sixty essays on two topics which had previously been rated holistically. As I have noted above, my sample included thirty essays (fifteen on each topic) which had been rated clearly as above

Table 9.1 Distribution of twelve text features in essays written on two topics by holistic score received

Text feature	Tally for essays on topic # 14 N = 30		Tally for essays on topic # 23 N = 30		Combined tally N = 60	
	High score	Mid-score	High score	Mid-score	High score	Mid-score
Average numbers of words per essay	482	463	520	387	501	425
Total number of paragraphs	63	82	69	58	132	140
Total number of main arguments	56	41	50	53	106	94
Total number of clarifying points	99	95	146	138	245	233
Total number of enumerative points	59	33	25	10	84	43
Total number of background points	22	29	36	18	58	47
Total number of repeated arguments	0	4	2	3	2	7
Total number of repeated closing arguments	7	12	5	2	12	14
Total number of repeated support points	2	44	3	28	5	72
Total number of unconventional paragraph boundaries	8	11	1	3	9	14
Total number of ineffective reorientations	2	12	2	17	4	29
Total number of unrelated arguments and support points	1	20	0	17	1	37

average (high-score) by two readers and thirty essays (fifteen on each topic) which had been rated clearly as average (mid-score) by two readers. The comparisons resulted in counts for twelve features (discussed above) which together served to indicate the organizational frame (see Table 9.1).

My statistical analysis of the organizational structure points to some interesting differences in the organizational frame development of the mid-score and high-score groups. We should note first that my feature analysis reveals a clear distinction between the essay groups simply in the average number of words per essay: the better essays are longer. This is not surprising; other researchers have confirmed that writing teachers often value length when rating essays (see Bailey *et al*. 1980). Yet, further analysis shows that mere length is not all that distinguishes the essay groups in my sample. The high- and mid-score essay groups have similar numbers of paragraphs, main arguments, clarifying support points, and background points, but differ in their distributions of several other features.

First, the high-score essays contain twice as many enumerative support points as the mid-score essays. The high-score essay writers organized the content of their essays using significantly more examples at a parallel level of specificity than did the mid-score essay writers. In other words, they provided greater elaboration. Using enumerative support points in this way persuades readers that a point is well-supported and contributes to the overall adequacy of the arguments.

Writers of high-score essays also used repetition more effectively to indicate organizational structure through emphasizing key thematic information. Essays from both student groups display about the same number of repeated closing arguments, which serve to remind the reader of the important thesis idea by concluding with a paraphrase or repetition of that idea. The two essay groups differ dramatically, however, in the number of repeated support points and differ somewhat in the number of repeated arguments. The mid-score essays contain more than ten times as many repeated support points. Excessive repetition of support points can contribute to the readers' sense that support is inadequate. Similarly, when the same arguments are repeated, the arguments themselves seem inadequate.

Both essay groups differ in the quantity of 'problem areas' in organizational structure. High-quality essays show far fewer ineffective paragraph reorientations. Mid-score essays fail to follow paragraph conventions and also display problems in reorienting the reader at paragraph boundaries (that is, in indicating the relationship between what has gone before in the essay and what is to follow in a new paragraph). The failure to reorient gives the reader the impression that arguments are not logically connected or unified. Mid-score essays also contain far more unrelated arguments and support points than the high-score essays.

All these differences between the mid-score and high-score essays point to the greater skill of high-score writers in organizing content and indicating their organizational frame for the reader. The high-score essay writers better understand how to use an organizational frame to present their arguments convincingly in a unified and coherent manner.

9.4 AN ALTERNATE ANALYSIS OF RHETORICAL FRAME

After diagramming the content organization of my sample essays, I examined the thematic structure of sentences containing main arguments in four representative essays, that is, essays which received the range of holistic scores and also had close to the average number of each of the twelve features I had analyzed for their score groups. To analyze sentences expressing main ideas in these essays, I derived a taxonomy of 'theme-highlighting devices' from Jones's analysis of theme as recognized by readers in expository texts (see Jones 1977, Chapters 2 and 6).[1] Applying Jones's study, I identified four major devices used by writers to signal theme:

- manipulating the order of sentences within paragraphs, PLACING IMPORTANT, GENERAL THEMATIC INFORMATION IN THE FIRST SENTENCE OF THE PARAGRAPH;
- manipulating the order of words within sentences, PLACING IMPORTANT THEMATIC INFORMATION IN THE SUBJECT SLOT;
- employing SPECIAL CONSTRUCTIONS to indicate important thematic information:
  (a) passives,
  (b) relative clauses,
  (c) rhetorical questions, and
  (d) topicalization; and
- employing COHESIVE DEVICES to tie thematic information into the web of discourse:
  (a) reference,
  (b) conjunction, and
  (c) lexical collocation.

In using these categories to analyze theme-highlighting devices in four representative student papers, I found that specific linguistic features in each category correlated with my analysis of the organizational content. For example, in the student essay shown in Figure 9.1, the main arguments are all located in the first sentence of each paragraph; this feature falls within my first category of devices that signal theme. In expository prose, writers conventionally use a deductive approach, proceeding from a general statement to more specific examples of support. Consequently, readers look to the lead sentence of each paragraph for main ideas and to the succeeding sentences for support, expecting paragraphs to follow the conventional organizational pattern of 'general to specific.'

Based on my experiment with the four representative essays, I hypothesized that my taxonomy of theme-highlighting devices would corroborate my analysis of organizational structure. To confirm this assumption, I asked two of the readers who had originally rated the sixty essays to identify the main arguments in these essays, and then selected sixteen essays at random by score and topic (four high- and four mid-score for each topic). (Eight of these sixteen essays were used for the tree-diagramming correlation

Table 9.2 Incidence of theme-highlighting devices in main arguments of the subsample

Device	No. of times occurring	Device	No. of times occurring
(1) Theme in first sentence in paragraph	14	(4) Cohesive ties (total)	57
(2) Important thematic information in subject slot	16	(a) reference (sentence to sentence)	10
(3) Special constructions (total)	17	(b) conjunction	12
(a) passive	2	(c) lexical collocation (repetition, paraphrase)	35
(b) relative clause	10		
(c) rhetorical question	1		
(d) topicalization	4		

described above.) For this subsample of sixteen essays, the two readers and I identified and agreed upon twenty-four sentences containing main arguments. For those twenty-four sentences, I counted the occurrence of thematic devices; the results are recorded in Table 9.2. As the table shows, all the thematic devices identified earlier seemed to be playing a role in the readers' identification of the twenty-four main arguments. Each of the twenty-four 'main arguments' sentences contains at least four of the identified theme highlighting devices, and some contain as many as eight. Yet these features occur differently in the subsample of the sixteen high- and mid-score essays. The high-score essays show the writers' skills in using all four theme-highlighting devices in their main arguments. The mid-score essays display some of the linguistic devices identified by Jones but reflect considerably less skill and consistency in the writers' use of these devices.

9.4.1 Theme in the first sentence in a paragraph

Seven of the eight high-score essays in the subsample (four on each topic) display a conventional deductive approach where arguments proceed from general thematic to specific support statements within each paragraph. (Of the thirty high-score essays in this study, twenty-eight reflected this deductive structure.) The high-score essays in the subsample show frequent use of the general-to-specific principle in ordering of sentences within paragraphs. Three-quarters of the paragraphs (73 percent or twenty-four out of thirty-three) exhibit development from general to specific. The eight mid-score essays in the subsample show less frequent use of the general-to-specific principle. Less than half of the paragraphs (41 percent or fifteen out of thirty-seven) display this pattern. Main arguments in the mid-score subsample are often buried deeply within paragraphs instead of occurring as lead sentences; further, contradictory arguments or arguments that did not fit are introduced regularly in the mid-score essays.

9.4.2 Thematic information in the subject slot

The eight high-score essays in the subsample regularly display important thematic material in the subject position in main arguments. Nearly three-quarters of the main arguments (71 percent or ten out of the fourteen) feature important topics in the subject slot; many of the remaining main arguments contain a word as the grammatical subject that simply defers the rhetorical subject (e.g. THIS *is the practical education* . . ., IT *is not merely a reaction* . . .). The eight mid-score essays may reflect some confusion about main ideas; the main ideas are hard to find and the subjects do not regularly contain important thematic material. Just over half of the main arguments (60 percent or six out of ten) feature important topics in the subject slot.

9.4.3 Special constructions

Five rhetorical questions emphasize an important idea in the eight high-score essays in the subsample. For example, in one essay, the rhetorical question 'Who is to decide what is or is not suitable viewing material for children?' highlights the student's thesis that the political group Action for Children's Television should not censor children's television viewing. In another essay, the question 'Who can predict with absolute certainty which jobs will be in greatest demand in the future?' highlights the student's thesis that a liberal arts education is best for a changing job market. Rhetorical questions do not appear at all in the eight mid-score essays. The frequency of other special constructions does not distinguish the two essay groups in the subsample.

9.4.4 Cohesive devices

For my analysis of cohesion, I counted the occurrence of REFERENCE, CONJUNCTION, and LEXICAL COLLOCATION as theme-highlighting devices in main arguments (see Table 9.2). These three cohesive devices, defined by Halliday and Hasan (1976), are categorized as potential theme-highlighting features by Jones (1977). According to Halliday and Hasan, 'reference' names the property of certain linguistic items which makes it necessary to refer to something else for the meaning of the item (e.g. words that require reference include *there, this*, and *that*); 'conjunction' indicates a semantic relationship which specifies connections between items in succession (e.g. *after* or *therefore* serve a conjunctive function); and 'lexical collocation' refers to a cohesive association between lexical items where one lexical item is systematically related to another (e.g. the appearance of *girl* and *boy* subsequent to *children* creates cohesion by collocation).

The high-score essays in the subsample display more frequent use of the cohesive ties of reference, conjunction, and lexical collocation in main argument sentences. Nearly three-quarters of these cohesive ties (72 percent, or forty out of fifty-seven) occur in the main arguments of the eight high-score essays. Though cohesive ties occur in the main arguments of mid-score essays in our subsample, they are not used where most needed (to highlight thematic information), nor are they used effectively. Often pronoun referents are unclear and conjunctions are missing or inappropriate. For instance, the pronoun *it* is an unclear reference in the following passage from a mid-score essay in the subsample:

> A typical example of a selection of courses is that of a liberal arts course. It gives one the opportunity to touch on many different topics; one of which might interest one. It gives a person the chance to communicate better with others which prepares one for uncertainties in the 'job world.'

Here, it is unclear whether *it* refers to the *selection*, *course*, or both. In this next passage from another mid-score essay, *however* is an inappropriate conjunction: 'The constitution is the supreme law of the land and should not be broken however, the people should not be caught unawares of the traps greedy people have set for them.' Here, not only is *however* punctuated incorrectly, but it also fails to clarify the logical relationship between the two clauses.

Because the thematic structure of the mid-score essays is not highlighted, the evaluators may have had a difficult time discerning which ideas are thematically prominent. If they could not accurately retrieve the organizational frame in a mid-score essay, they may have concluded that the essay really did not have much point. Analysis of the organizational structure of these representative essays further confirmed these suppositions.

As explained earlier in this chapter, the trained readers created tree diagrams for eight of the subsample of sixteen essays. These readers' diagrams agreed with mine dramatically in the assessment of coherence problems. No reader identified any coherence problems for any high-score essay among the eight, yet every mid-score essay was judged to have at least one coherence problem. For the high-score subsample group, readers determined that the theses, arguments, and support points all related logically and explicitly, just as one would expect within the 'informal proof' rhetorical frame of exposition. In short, when we correlate both thematic and organizational structure with holistic ratings, we find that writers judged to be less competent do not successfully employ either kind of structure to signal rhetorical frame.

9.5 IMPLICATIONS

When writers construct an essay according to a conventional rhetorical frame, they provide their readers with a familiar structure to help them interpret the ideas presented. The frames are learned by writers and readers through extensive experience with written language in various contexts. Although we must be cautious about drawing generalizations from descriptive analyses of limited scope, my study does suggest how writers signal rhetorical frame in exposition through the use of organizational and thematic structures. It also suggests that the rhetorical frames of above-average writers differ from those of average writers.

The research method proposed in this chapter may have useful future applications. Scholars could employ it to describe writers' executions of rhetorical frames other than the 'informal proof.' They could examine expository frames expressing causation, comparison or contrast, description, response, and chronology both as writers manipulate their organizational and thematic structures and as readers' judgments of quality correlate with frame elaboration.

In assessment programs where student writing is evaluated, explicit attention to rhetorical frame can be most useful to those planning and administering the assessment, particularly because ability to employ a frame may be linked closely to overall writing quality. Teachers can ensure that the writing test demonstrates this ability through creating test topics and contexts that require application of a particular rhetorical frame.

Teachers need to recognize and further explore the important influence rhetorical frames have on readers' judgments of quality. A writer's expression of global relationships between ideas within a rhetorical frame can be made explicit in textual organization, even in the smallest linguistic units. We have much to learn about how the explicit expression of a rhetorical frame affects readers. In the meanwhile, we can begin to teach students to recognize rhetorical frames as they read and write, helping them gain greater control over their own written language use.

NOTE

1. I should note here that I am referring to thematic structure in its rhetorical sense as structure that points to the overall theme or main idea of a prose composition, rather than in its more narrow grammatical sense as structure revealing the informational focus of a single sentence (compare Brandt, Eiler, and others in this volume [ed.]).

BIBLIOGRAPHY

Bailey, R. W., Brengle, R. T., and Smith, Jr., E. L., 'Measuring Student Writing Ability,' in Freedman, A. and Pringle, I. (eds) (1980: 137–44), *Reinventing the Rhetorical Tradition*, Ottawa, Canadian Council of Teachers of English.

Christensen, F. (1965), 'A Generative Rhetoric of the Paragraph,' *College Composition and Communication*, **16**, 144–56.

Grimes, J. E. (1978), *The Thread of Discourse*, Janua Linguarum, Series Minor 207, The Hague, Mouton.

Halliday, M. A. K. and Hasan, R. (1976), *Cohesion in English*, London, Longman.

Jones, L. K. (1977), *Theme in English Expository Discourse*, Edward Sapir Monograph Series in Language, Culture, and Cognition 2, Lake Bluff, Ill., Jupiter Press.

Kintsch, W. (1974), *The Representation of Meaning in Memory*, Hillsdale, N.J., Lawrence Erlbaum.

Longacre, R. E., 'The Discourse Structure of the Flood Narrative,' in MacRae, G. (ed.) (1976: 235–61), *Society of Biblical Literature Seminar Papers*, **10**, Missoula, Mont., Scholars Press.

Meyer, B. J. F. (1975), *The Organization of Prose and Its Effect on Memory*, North-Holland Studies in Theoretical Poetics 1, Amsterdam, North-Holland.

Tannen, D., 'What's in a Frame?: Surface Evidence for Underlying Expectations,' in Freedle, R. O. (ed.) (1979: 137–81), *New Directions in Discourse Processing*, Advances in Discourse Processes 2, Norwood, N.J., Ablex.

Thorndyke, P. W. (1977), 'Cognitive Structures in Comprehension and Memory of Narrative Discourse,' *Cognitive Psychology*, **9**, 77–110.

10 Getting the theme across: a study of dominant function in the academic writing of university students

Pamela Peters
Macquarie University

10.1 WHY A STUDY OF ACADEMIC WRITING

Writing is a curiously solitary form of communication, addressed to an absent and often unknown reader. The writer is usually much more conscious of 'what' to communicate than 'to whom.' And yet writers must engage their readers' attention and sustain it over long stretches of text, in many cases without knowing exactly what interests they may have to satisfy.

This is a particular problem for university students in large first-year lecture courses who find themselves having to write for somewhat distant faculty, but the problem of writing for a distant audience is inherent in many other forms of institutional writing as well (for example, government documents or policy statements). The difficulty of satisfying a distant reader has proved tantalizing for many celebrated writers and critics, such as T. S. Eliot and I. A. Richards, whose writing styles have recently been analyzed as a means of 'compensating' for the lack of an identifiable audience (see Donoghue [1981] 1984). Alternatively, as Ong notes, an audience may actually be created by the writer as a byproduct of his or her own prose (see Ong 1975). A profile of the audience, its interests, its orientation to and interaction in the text, is implicit in the text's wording and emerges continuously through it. The styles of established authors tend to reflect a particular audience profile. Though Ong's conclusion is based on a study of creative literature, he suggests that it is as much true of non-fiction as of fiction. If so, the task of creating an audience must be one of the demands of student composition. It undoubtedly poses a problem for inexperienced writers, who are not used to constructing a consistent audience profile and may do so erratically.

We should question the total applicability of Ong's suggestion to the student writing situation. Fiction and creative literature are highly decontextualized forms of writing (see Stubbs 1980: 109), often addressed to a broad audience with varying interests and affiliations. The writing done by undergraduates is reduced in the context of a particular institution, with certain well-defined intellectual aims, values, and practices. Through their reading, students quickly become steeped in the style of the speech community with which they must communicate (see Nystrand 1982: 1–28) and learn how to respond to an academic question. In the academic context, then, the problem of establishing an audience may not be so great.

Similar conclusions have been reached by those who have reassessed the context of academic writing against the assumptions of classical rhetoric. Scholars in rhetoric have downplayed the Aristotelian emphasis on communicating to 'persuade the audience' (see Young *et al.* 1970; and Bator 1980). Instead, they are identifying other motives that direct written expression, ones more appropriate to the academic situation, for instance, the need to think of oneself as engaging in inquiry (see Meiland 1981: 59–62) and exploring the complexities of the subject or field, rather than challenging the convictions of the unknown reader.

In the academic context, language both spoken and written typically has a constitutive rather than an ancillary role (see Hasan 1980: 17); that is, it constitutes the whole of the ongoing activity in the social situation rather than serves as an accompaniment to other activities. Both lectures and readings raise their own subjects quite independent of the physical setting for the communication, and they set their own frames of reference within the given limits of time and space. Lecturers and authors create their own contexts for discussion. The decontextualized nature of their discourse requires it to be particularly specific; there are no extra-linguistic props in the setting to help communicate ideas, as in most 'spoken-language situations' (Smith 1982: 71). In more decontextualized forms of communication, the need for specific references is reflected in higher frequencies of content words relative to words whose function 'can be described purely in terms of grammar' (Ure 1971: 445). Decontextualized speech also contains few EXOPHORIC REFERENCES, that is, words which refer to aspects of the context of situation rather than the content of the text itself (see Halliday and Hasan 1976: 18, 33).

The constitutive nature of academic discourse not only means that its language has to be more consistently ideational in its orientation, but also that it has to provide more textual features which highlight the local as well as the global structure of the text. Because academic discourse takes the form of a protracted monologue and is usually unsupported by interaction with immediate others, it must signal its own internal structure at regular intervals. Listeners and readers expect the communicator to indicate how items or points are sequenced (at least signaling where one point gives way to the next) and to show the motivation for presenting them. Apart from indications of macrostructure, readers expect from an academic text sufficient microstructural details to supply cohesion and to show the logical connections between one statement and another (see Halliday and Hasan 1976). In short, both the development of concepts and textual management assume importance as readers assess the value of academic discourse.

Furthermore, academic compositions (and expository writing in general) derive their unity and purpose from having an underlying theme or proposition. The theme serves to structure the often complex variety of information offered and to coordinate it toward a clear argumentative goal. The importance of having such a theme has always been acknowledged in our rhetorical tradition (see Couture 1985: 68), and there is little doubt that better student writers distinguish themselves by their ability to use their material in support of a proposition. So far, however, the communicator's theme or proposition has been little discussed in relation to the functional model of language; little effort has been made to distinguish a communication's theme or proposition as it relates to the field or subject matter of the discourse, the tenor or relationships established between discourse participants, or the mode or method of textual presentation. When the discourse theme has been acknowledged in relation to language function, it has been represented as one of the more delicate aspects of the discourse field (see Halliday 1977: 203; and Couture 1985: 75–9 [see also Bernhardt and Smith in this volume for a definition of 'discourse field' (ed.)]). This analysis seems appropriate because a proposition is so often a generalization formulated with regard to a specified subject area and corresponding to certain knowledge structures in that field.

An alternative might be to regard the central proposition of an extended piece of academic composition as a textual component. The proposition has a unifying value for the text, and the proposition's argumentative support dictates the structure of the text. Unfortunately, the structures of expository texts have yet to be fully articulated and the descriptions remain tentative (see Beaugrande 1980: 197–9). We might begin such analysis by assuming with van Dijk that a proposition constitutes the highest level macrostructure in an expository text and that supporting units or arguments are lower-level macrostructures. But this assumption does not settle the terms in which the 'superstructure' of an expository genre are to be described. Van Dijk suggests some possibilities, involving such thematic sequences as PREMISE–CONCLUSION, CONCLUSION–PREMISE, and PROBLEM–SOLUTION (see 1980: 107–21). Hoey argues for the prominence of the problem–solution structure in expository discourse, though he allows for others (see 1979: 60; and 1983: 31–106). But no number of suggested macrostructure sequences can account for the infinite structural diversity of academic texts.

Structural components vary with text content, and individual writers may deviate from readers' expectations in their handling of structural conventions to achieve individual purposes (see van Dijk 1977, on the interpretation of cognitive structure). For the moment then, we cannot explain the unity of an academic text in terms of an absolute set of standard structural components. Nevertheless, an effort to create broader descriptions of the academic genre or subcategorizations of it may help to resolve some of this difficulty and to show how textual macrofunctions unify academic texts.

Still, we need to ask several more questions about the academic genre besides whether thematic unity is primarily ideational or textual. For instance, we need to know whether uncertainty in the definition of the interpersonal situation affects the writer's ability to achieve overall unity in a piece or whether this is really not a problem for writers—particularly, writers in the classroom. Fortunately, the interaction of ideational, textual, and interpersonal variables in expository writing situations can be studied readily in the context of a college writing class, where numerous writers all work under the same conditions and constraints. Here, we may discover how the academic genre functions and explain the difficulties students have in producing it.

With these considerations in mind, I chose to investigate how variations in external constraints such as choice of content, audience, and overall theme affect the quality of student prose. In particular, I was interested in any correlation between the success of student writing, as judged by a teacher, and the balance among ideational, interpersonal, and textual macrofunctions in it. Assuming that all three are expressed through language, I planned to assess the relative richness or paucity of ideational, textual, and interpersonal expressions in texts written under different conditions.

10.2 THE DATA AND METHOD OF ANALYSIS

10.2.1 Overview

During their regular course work at Macquarie University, fifty students in an elective, post-freshman year writing course each wrote a series of assignments designed to test their responses to three constraints upon the expository writing situation:

- a restricted theme coupled with restricted content, audience unrestricted;
- a restricted audience coupled with restricted content, theme unrestricted; and
- a restricted audience coupled with a restricted theme, content unrestricted.

Students were of varying ages and abilities, though all had gained at least twelve credit points out of the sixty-eight needed to graduate from Macquarie University. Their chosen fields of study included geology, economics, education, politics, history, and literature. Students were not aware that their writing would ultimately be subjected to functional analysis; they simply wrote in response to the specifics of each assignment.

I analyzed each essay, assigning it an overall grade and assessing the verbal strategies which contributed to its ideational, interpersonal, and textual functioning. The essay's overall grade is an indicator of its success in achieving its primary purpose as academic discourse to articulate a theme (see criteria for grading in Section 10.2.2). My analysis of features controlling the ideational, interpersonal, and textual functioning of the discourse allowed me to determine how writers managed these macrofunctions in their efforts to articulate a theme under controlled contextual constraints.

10.2.2 Assessing the corpus

Each student paper was graded A, B, or C with + or −, or *F* as part of the regular assessment procedure for this college writing class. The grading represented an assessment of the overall effectiveness of the articulation of the major theme or proposition: did the paper communicate its theme? Was the theme well-supported or dependent on assertion or emotional appeal? Was the theme fluent, well integrated, and presented using textual conventions appropriate for the academic essay? Following the global assessment, each essay was subjected to a detailed textual analysis.

I analyzed the kinds of verbal strategies that each writer used to structure the text, to relate to the reader, and to express ideas. These strategies include:

- TEXTUAL STRATEGIES, those providing cohesion from one statement to the next or marking out the structural components of the text;
- INTERPERSONAL STRATEGIES, those representing some form of interaction with the reader; and
- EVALUATIVE STRATEGIES, those helping to interpret and classify ideational content and putting a value on it.

My categorization of verbal strategies reflects Halliday's strata of semantic functions, yet differs in one important respect. I have called verbal strategies for expressing ideas 'evaluative' rather than 'ideational' to highlight the fact that they always embody some sort of judgment, whether it is about the place of something in a taxonomy or about the nature of an action or a behavior. I categorized text features on the basis of individual usage; the same word, of course, could serve more than one function at different places in a given text. For example, the word *this* is most often used in the student essays as a textual device providing anaphoric cohesion. While serving this function, it could also function as an interpersonal device in phrases such as *in* THIS *paper I intend*. . . . When a feature appeared to serve more than one function in a single instance, I categorized it by what I perceived to be its dominant function (see Section 10.2.2.3).

After categorizing features by relevant verbal strategies, I determined which strategy or strategies seemed to be SALIENT for each writer's discussion by considering both the frequency and variety of linguistic devices used to realize each strategy. The frequency of devices used to express evaluative, interpersonal, and textual strategies can affect a reader's characterization of a text as dominated by one or another of these. Also, the variety of expressions used to realize a strategy can make it appear more or less salient for the discussion. The same expression used repeatedly to achieve a function can effectively reinforce a verbal strategy for readers in some instances and bore them in others. Therefore, I noted the frequency and the range of devices realizing each verbal strategy in every student essay and determined functional salience by weighing frequency against variety. Appendix A illustrates my method with two sample analyses of texts for salient macrofunction. The following sections describe the basis for my categorization of verbal strategies.

10.2.2.1 *Textual strategies*

Textual verbal strategies, as already noted, work both at the local and global level. Those at the latter level, which I shall refer to as MACROSTRUCTURAL DEVICES, draw the reader's attention to the structure of the overall argument and the way individual points contribute to it. An obvious macrostructural device is enumeration (e.g. *first, second*); less specific equivalents may also mark the start of a new point (e.g. *another issue, a further question*). Words such as *issue, question, argument*, and *consideration* (or paraphrases of them such as *some have argued*) assume a textual function not only at the beginnings of paragraphs but also within them. In many forms of expository discourse, underlined headings serve to mark the macrostructural units.

Textual devices of more local significance, which I have labeled MICROSTRUCTURAL DEVICES, indicate referential and logical connections between one statement and another. Some examples are *these, he, they, but, for example*, and *therefore*. These devices operate within sentences as well as across sentence boundaries. For this analysis, I counted only the grammatical devices which create cohesion (see Halliday and Hasan 1976: 6); these devices form a more or less closed set and can be compared from one writer to the next. Lexical cohesive devices were not analyzed because the specific formal items which express such cohesion can vary greatly from text to text and thus are not suitable for comparison.

Apart from their contribution to textual cohesion, the microstructural devices, particularly the logical connectors, help to mobilize the text's theme. They can even lend a spurious sense of thematic development to a discussion which lacks momentum (see, for example, Milic 1970: 253–5, on the connectives used by Jonathan Swift).

10.2.2.2 *Interpersonal strategies*

Also included in my analysis are a variety of interpersonal devices which express an awareness of audience either directly or indirectly. Devices which allow the writer to intrude in the communication directly include rhetorical questions, exclamations, imperatives, and the use of first- and second-person pronouns. Somewhat less direct intrusions are achieved by the indefinite *you* and *one*, and longer paraphrases of these: *the individual, people, the nation*. Some writers also exploit the 'here and now' notionally shared between parties in a communicative situation by using expressions such as *here, currently*, and *at the present time*. Writers can also indicate shared or common ground by providing quotations and examples which they and the reader can study together. Similarly, the use of parentheses can achieve indirect interpersonal value, at least when what is contained within them serves to anticipate a possible challenge from the reader or a possible need for clarification.

Many writers of expository discourse exploit the verb phrase to assert an indirect relationship with the reader. The English modal verbs express, as Halliday (1970) has shown, the speaker/writer's opinion or estimate of the degree of probability which ought to be attached to the statement embodying it. Thus modals such as *can, could, may, might, must, should, would*, and *will* all invite the reader to put a particular probability value on the accompanying information (e.g. NOT to regard as absolute the statement *The costs would be no greater* . . .). Modals also express the speaker/writer's assessment of the social obligations inherent in the information (e.g. *A socialist government must provide* . . .). In statements that are not clarified by surrounding context, it is not always clear whether modals express probabilities or obligations, but either way they express some form of interaction between writer and reader (see Halliday 1982: 139–40); often they are pervasive in writing with an impersonal stance.

A well-known manifestation of the desire to keep one's tenor impersonal is the use of passive forms of mental process verbs (e.g. *it is considered/admitted/recognized*). For my analysis, I chose to categorize these features as interpersonal devices, along with grammatical paraphrases of verbal modality, such as the sentence openers *it is possible that* and *it is certain that*, and the adjuncts *perhaps, possibly, of course*, and *definitely*, which can be added almost anywhere in a sentence.

10.2.2.3 *Evaluative strategies*

Evaluative strategies can be signaled by a wide range of verbal items which interpret the ideational content for the reader and express a value judgment about it. A kind of interpretation or judgment is embodied in taxonomic terms used by the writer to classify the raw material under discussion. For example, the choice of either the word *privilege* or *right* would express the writer's judgment as to whether a particular action or deed should be classed as a special favor or taken for granted. Apart from taxonomic terms, evaluative strategies are also evident in more obviously value-laden descriptors such as *enormous* or *mediocre*. These words serve to rate something on a subjective scale which often has some objective correlate. Evaluative language can serve to coordinate the writer's data with the overall argument or proposition; however, it can also become attenuated or seem tangential.

The function of evaluative language can be both ideational and interpersonal; many evaluative words can simultaneously express the writer's value judgment and influence the reader's response. When text features PRIMARILY play a part in mediating the ideational content and expressing the writer's role as observer rather than as intruder in the situation (see Halliday 1978: 117), they serve the ideational macrofunction. When categorizing such features, analysts have to judge individual instances in their contexts. In my study, I distinguished evaluative and interpersonal devices as follows: the range of perceptions and values expressed in evaluative devices is vast and open-ended; interpersonal devices, in contrast, express either largely codified tokens of interaction in the communicative situation or a limited range of judgment on the scales of probability and obligation.

10.3 THE EXPERIMENT AND RESULTS

10.3.1 Task 1: Restricting theme and content

10.3.1.1 *Method*

Each student wrote a thousand-word essay, arguing either for or against the socialization of medicine (restricted theme). All worked from a given pair of published articles on the topic (restricted content), and this material supplied ample grist for either line of argument. The students' immediate reading was limited deliberately in order to obviate the prewriting problem of assimilating material from many sources (which often adds to the difficulties of composition) and to control the content of the assignment.

Students were assigned arbitrarily the *pro* or *contra* theme according to whether their enrolment numbers were odd or even. No suggestions were made about the possible audience for this piece of writing.

10.3.1.2 *Findings*

A statistical display of student grades as they correlated with verbal strategies appears in Table 10.1. Grades register the general communicative effectiveness of the writers' arguments and show that a rather large number of students (thirty-one out of fifty or 62 percent) did not display above-average execution of the task. The exercise was written early in the course (after only two weeks) and so, for many, it probably represented their untutored writing ability relative to this course. For the purposes of this study, the exercise served as a base level of achievement against which the results of the second and third tasks could be compared.

Detailed textual analysis of the first assignment highlighted the fact that some ability to handle evaluative devices is an important component of successful academic discourse. Table 10.1 shows that the majority of writers who received *A* or *B* grades (fifteen out of the nineteen) made salient use of evaluative devices. Half of these writers (eight out of fifteen) made salient use

Table 10.1 Number of students making salient use of textual, interpersonal, or evaluative strategies by grade received for Task 1

Grade	Total students	No. using textual (T) devices exclusively	No. using inter-personal (I) devices exclusively	No. using evaluative (E) devices including E + T and E + I combinations
A−	4			4 (includes 2 E + T, 1 E + I)
B+	3			3 (includes 3 E + I)
B	4	1		3 (includes 1 E + I)
B−	8	2	1	5 (includes 3 E + I)
C+	10	3	4	3
C	13	9	2	2
C−	5	2	3	
F	3	1	2	
Total	50	18	12	20

of interpersonal strategies as well. A few students (four out of fifty, or 8 percent) achieved *B* grades without significant use of evaluative devices, and only a few students (five out of fifty, or 10 percent) received *C* grades who had used evaluative strategies. In short, the salient use of evaluative verbal strategies, often in combination with the salient use of interpersonal strategies, characterized essays receiving the better grades.[1]

Students receiving mediocre and low grades made dominant use of either interpersonal or textual verbal strategies in their essays, displaying no combinations of strategies. Those papers composed in support of the socialization of medicine frequently displayed heavy use of modals, especially *would*, often in unsubstantiated assertions about a future state of affairs. Some papers revealed that the writer was 'juggling' various available modals or paraphrases of them, perhaps to achieve stylistic variety. This capricious variation creates an unsettling effect for the reader and suggests the writer's unstable orientation to the material. Note the following example with italics added for emphasis:

> With insufficient personnel there *would* be a limit on the services that *could* be provided. The quality of service *must* suffer in some situations. The pressure on some doctors *would* be immense, and a popular doctor *could* become overburdened, and *be obliged* to lower his standards. This situation *would* possibly not be so easy to control as *could* be argued. . . .

Other papers displayed conspicuous use of the standard macrostructural cues (e.g. *another issue, a further point*), but at the same time included few evaluative strategies to clarify the thematic thrust of the information that these cues highlighted.

10.3.2 Task 2: Restricting audience and content

10.3.2.1 *Method*

Each student's second writing task was to write two four hundred-word critiques of two essays written by fellow students. The essays critiqued were those written for the first assignment with all traces of authorship removed. Each student had a different pair of essays to comment on and was asked to evaluate each independently in terms of how well it communicated, discussing features of the writing which aided or impaired the argument. Students were free to evaluate the material as they saw fit, and the judgments which they substantiated through their critiques were subject to no controls (unrestricted theme). The content of their discourse, however, was to focus on the essays at hand (restricted content). Students also knew that the essays were by their fellows and that anonymous copies of their critiques would eventually go back to the original authors. Thus students were aware of an ultimate addressee for the critiques, identifiable at least in terms of his or her membership in the class (specified, restricted audience).

10.3.2.2 *Findings*

My textual analyses of the two critiques were combined in my assessment and revealed that knowledge of the audience (the new factor) seemed to be exploited more fully by some students than others for Task 2 (see Table 10.2). Fifteen students, or 30 percent of the class, made salient use of interpersonal devices alone, just slightly more than the number using these devices alone for the first assignment. A further nine students, or 18 percent of the class, made salient use of interpersonal devices in combination with evaluative devices. Yet the salient use of interpersonal devices did not correlate with better grades.Only nine of the twenty-six students receiving *A* or *B* grades showed salient use of interpersonal strategies alone or in combination with other strategies in their papers.

Salient use of evaluative strategies, however, did correlate with better grades. The vast majority of the students receiving an *A* or *B* (twenty-three out of twenty-six) made salient use of evaluative strategies alone or in combination with other devices, with fifteen or nearly two-thirds of those with *A* or *B* grades making salient use of evaluative strategies exclusively. Fewer than half (ten out of twenty-four) of those receiving a *C* or below made salient use of evaluative strategies alone or in combination with other devices.

The averaged grades of the two critiques for Task 2 showed that thirty-two students, or 64 percent, improved their grades: a few improved dramatically (4 percent from *C* to *A*, 10 percent from *C* to*B*), and many moved up within their general grades. This improvement could be related to several factors, including the students' greater confidence in tackling the task (I held a preceding tutorial on ways to assess a piece of writing), the relative brevity of the resulting critiques (presenting fewer structural problems), and the relatively well-defined audience for the task.

Table 10.2 Number of students making salient use of textual, interpersonal, or evaluative strategies by grade received for Task 2

Grade	Total students	No. using textual (T) devices exclusively	No. using inter-personal (I) devices exclusively	No. using evaluative (E) devices including E + T and E + I combinations
A	2			2 (includes 2 E + T)
A–	4			4 (includes 1 E + I)
B+	4			4 (includes 2 E + I)
B	8		1	7 (includes 3 E + I)
B–	8		2	6
C+	6		1	5 (includes 2 E + I)
C	13	2	8	3 (includes 1 E + I)
C–	3		1	2
F	2		2	
Total	50	2	15	33

The stimulus to evaluate, of course, was built into the second assignment, and the results suggest that students responded to this stimulus: thirty-three out of fifty students made salient use of evaluative devices for Task 2 as opposed to twenty out of fifty for Task 1. Although the audience was more closely defined in Task 2 than in Task 1, nearly the same proportion of students made salient use of interpersonal devices (alone or in combination) for Task 1 as for Task 2 (twenty for Task 1, twenty-four for Task 2).

Few students seemed to make salient use of textual devices in the second assignment. The proportion declined from eighteen out of fifty (36 percent) in the first assignment to two (4 percent) here. This possibility reflects the brevity of the critiques, which did not seem to require explicit signaling of structure.

10.3.3 Task 3: Restricting audience and theme

10.3.3.1 *Method*

For the third task, each student wrote a thousand-word essay tackling the question 'A writer's subject matter always controls his or her stylistic options. Do you agree?' The essay was written under test conditions, but the topic was advertised a week in advance, and students had preparatory lectures and readings on many aspects of stylistic variation, both in fiction and in non-fiction writing. They could draw upon this background material as they pleased, so the content of the essay was of their own choosing (unrestricted content). But because the question was a sweeping statement (deliberately so), almost all pointedly disagreed with it, and thus the themes they expressed were largely controlled (restricted theme). The arguments raised in support were quite varied, however.

In order to keep the audience variable as constant as possible, students were asked to write the essay for their fellow students or, more specifically, for those who were members of the same class that semester (restricted audience).

10.3.3.2 *Findings*

As Table 10.3 shows, the majority of the *A* or *B* essays showed salient use of evaluative devices (twenty out of the twenty-six). Only a fifth of the *C* or *F* essays showed salient use of evaluative strategies (five out of twenty-four). Over half of the *C* or *F* essays (thirteen out of the twenty-four) displayed salient use of interpersonal devices alone and often a limited repertoire of them. More students made significant use of textual strategies than in the second assignment. Significant use of textual features appeared in writing at all levels on the grade scale, but did not by itself or in combination with other features correlate with better writing. As in the first two assignments, better thematic development (as reflected in the overall grade) seemed to correlate more closely with the employment of evaluative devices than with either the interpersonal or textual.

The grades earned by many students on this third task showed improvement on their earlier levels of achievement. Some seventeen members of the

Table 10.3 Number of students making salient use of textual, interpersonal, or evaluative strategies by grade received for Task 3

Grade	Total students	No. using textual (T) devices exclusively	No. using inter-personal (I) devices exclusively	No. using evaluative (E) devices including E + T and E + I combinations
A	1			1 (includes 1 E + I)
A–	1			1 (includes 1 E + T)
B+	6			6 (includes 3 E + I, 2 E + T)
B	7			7 (includes 2 E + I, 1 E + T)
B–	11	4	2	5 (includes 2 E + I, 1 E + T)
C+	8	1	5	2 (includes 1 E + I)
C	8	3	4	1
C–	7	1	4	2
F	1	1		
Total	50	10	15	25

class (34 percent) continued to show progress and improved the grades they had received on the second assignment. Thirteen others (26 percent) who had not shown progress on the second assignment did improve on the third. There were fewer *A* essays, however, perhaps because of the test situation and because the content was not as limited as for previous assignments.

10.4 DISCUSSION

The findings suggest a strong correlation between evaluative strategies and the overall effectiveness of student academic writing. In all three assignments, the use of evaluative devices was the single most important factor exploited to good effect in the most cogent writing. Quite a lot of students used evaluative vocabulary in the second assignment, and this was the most noticeable change in their writing, no doubt occasioned partly by the nature of the task. In the third assignment, a smaller percentage succeeded in making salient use of evaluative devices; here the argumentative raw material was diverse, and it was more difficult, perhaps, to select evaluative words appropriate to the material as well as the theme it had to support.

In an effort to further detail these findings, I made a study of the specific evaluative expressions used by weaker writers as opposed to better writers. I found that the evaluative language of the weaker writers often related only to the immediate subject matter they were presenting. The better writers, by contrast, found evaluative expressions which had local ideational value as well as relevance to aspects of their overall theme. For instance, the more skilled writers of the third assignments used words such as *constraints* and *demands* in reference to the conventions of particular styles, thus laying the groundwork for their general proposition about controls on style. Students using theme-specific words such as these to mark the macrostructural components of the essay gained textual advantages from them as well, for they serve as supplements to or substitutes for the conventional macro-structural cues.

Apart from their potential to link content with theme, evaluative devices may also create additional interaction with the reader. As acknowledged earlier, evaluative strategies are on the borderline between functioning ideationally and interpersonally. More extreme evaluative expressions (e.g. *atrocious, wonderful*) elicit a judgment from the reader and at the same time mediate an appraisal of something. Such words occurred frequently in some of the students' critiques (Task 2). The increased use of such expressions in these papers may reflect the writers' active responses to the specified audience.

The multifaceted potential of evaluative language seems to explain its part in the best writing examined in this study and its value for expository writing generally. Appropriately used, it serves to integrate content with theme and mediates both for the reader. Communicating with the reader in academic writing seems to depend more upon evaluation than upon deliberate gestures toward interaction.

A supplementary conclusion of this study is that student writers certainly gain by having a well-defined audience to write for—in spite of the argument that this is less important in institutional writing. General grade improvement was shown by most students on either the second or third assignment, and there are grounds for believing that this was not simply a matter of the practice effect or their enhanced understanding of written language as the course progressed. Each assignment involved a different configuration of the key variables, and while the audience was a controlled variable in the second and third assignments, other aspects of the writing context (theme/content) were different. In particular, the uncontrolled variable on the third assignment (content) demanded an ability to select and manage raw material, an ability which students had not previously had to exercise in this classroom situation. (No doubt the students had some experience in doing the latter kind of assignment for other university courses, but this experience was not part of the practice effect within the writing course itself.)

Just how writers use a knowledge of audience is difficult to determine on the strength of linguistic analysis alone. The overall proportion of students making salient use of interpersonal devices remained much the same in all three assignments, so increased writer/reader interaction was not particularly conspicuous. But my tables do not reflect the range of interpersonal devices used by the students in the second and third assignments, and these latter assignments did contain a greater variety of interpersonal strategies. The second and third assignments, addressed to fellow students, allowed the writers to use a wide range of interactive language features, not only in the form of more and varied personal pronouns, but also in more quotations, more quoted examples, and in a fuller range of modals. Though some of this diversity may be linked to other situational factors as well, greater flexibility of style seems to be occasioned by the constraint of a well-defined audience.

10.5 IMPLICATIONS FOR THEORY AND PRACTICE

My study, though limited, introduces a method for analyzing features which contribute to the macrofunctions of a communication. The study also suggests that for at least one kind of writing—academic discourse—the verbal strategies which express evaluation correlate with the overall effectiveness of the discourse, even when contextual constraints upon that discourse are varied. Others may wish to use my analytic scheme to examine the dominant strategies in other written genres.

Evaluative devices appear to be of prime importance for communicative effectiveness and thematic unity. This conclusion provides us with an answer to the theoretical question posed earlier, that is, whether thematic unity should be seen as an aspect of the ideational or textual component of discourse. It is clearly associated with the former, at least in the genre of academic discourse. In other genres where the structural units may be highly conventionalized, explicit textual cues could contribute more significantly to the perceived unity of the discourse. In academic discourse, however, the role of textual devices is auxiliary. The standard macrostructural devices can help to draw together the components of a theme, but the particular interrelationship of the components must still be expressed through evaluative devices.

The results of my study suggest some pedagogical directions. Instructors should specify the intended audience to stabilize the writing context for student writers and to help them develop the habit of thinking about their addressee. Both direct and indirect devices for interacting with the reader should be discussed in the writing class to enlarge the student-writer's repertoire of devices for engaging the reader. Students might be encouraged to think of the reader as witness to the continuous unfolding of the text; this view would naturally raise discussion about the use of standard macro-structural devices.

Above all, teachers should stress the communicative effects of using evaluative devices through close discussion of cogent expository writing. The relationship between evaluative expressions and overall theme should be analyzed in effective discourse, as should the role of evaluative features at both local and global levels. Students might be given short exercises to practice thinking of alternative evaluative (and taxonomic) vocabulary for a given theme.

I will close by remarking that any study of language function must be accompanied by a host of qualifications. We are far from defining the exact linguistic correlates of effective expression. This study has made a case, however, for the importance of evaluative language in influencing the reader's response to academic discourse—a point that writing teachers would do well to note.

NOTE

1. Analyses of results for all three experimental tasks revealed EXCLUSIVE use of salient textual (T), interpersonal (I), and evaluative (E) strategies and COMBINED use of salient evaluative and interpersonal strategies (E+I) or salient evaluative and textual strategies (E+T). No texts revealed use of salient textual and interpersonal strategies (T+I) in combination. Likewise, no texts revealed indeterminate salience or balanced use of all three strategies (T+I+E).

BIBLIOGRAPHY

Bator, P. (1980), 'Aristotelian and Rogerian Rhetoric,' *College Composition and Communication*, **31**, 427–32.

Beaugrande, R. A. de (1980), *Text, Discourse, and Process: Toward a Multidisciplinary Science of Texts*, Advances in Discourse Processes 4, Norwood, N.J., Ablex.

Couture, B., 'A Systemic Analysis of Writing Quality,' in Benson, J. D. and Greaves, W. S. (eds) (1985: 67–87), *Systemic Perspectives on Discourse 2: Selected Applied Papers from the 9th International Systemic Workshop*, Advances in Discourse Processes 16, Norwood, N.J., Ablex.

van Dijk, T. A. (1977), 'Context and Cognition: Knowledge Frames and Speech Act Comprehension,' *Journal of Pragmatics*, **1**, 211–31.

van Dijk, T. A. (1980), *Macrostructures: An Interdisciplinary Study of Global Structures in Discourse, Interaction, and Cognition*, Hillsdale, N.J., Lawrence Erlbaum.

Donoghue, D. ([1981] 1984), *Ferocious Alphabets*, New York, Columbia University Press.

Halliday, M. A. K. (1970), 'Functional Diversity in Language as Seen from a Consideration of Modality and Mood in English,' *Foundations of Language*, **6**, 322–61.

Halliday, M. A. K., 'Text as Semantic Choice in Social Contexts,' in van Dijk, T. A. and Petöfi, J. S. (eds) (1977: 176–225), *Grammars and Descriptions: Studies in Text Theory and Text Analysis*, Research in Text Theory 1, Berlin, New York, Walter de Gruyter.

Halliday, M. A. K. (1978), *Language as Social Semiotic: The Social Interpretation of Language and Meaning*, London, Edward Arnold: Baltimore, University Park Press.

Halliday, M. A. K., 'The De-automatization of Grammar: From Priestley's "An Inspector Calls,"' in Anderson, J. (ed.) (1982: 129–59), *Language Form and Linguistic Variation: Papers Dedicated to Angus McIntosh*, Amsterdam Studies in the Theory and History of Linguistic Science, Series 4: Current Issues in Linguistic Theory 15, Amsterdam, John Benjamins.

Halliday, M. A. K. and Hasan, R. (1976), *Cohesion in English*, London, Longman.

Hasan, R., 'The Structure of a Text,' in Halliday, M. A. K. and Hasan, R. (1980: 16–30), *Text and Context: Aspects of Language in a Social-Semiotic Perspective*, Sophia Linguistica 6, Tokyo, Sophia University.

Hoey, M. (1979), *Signalling in Discourse*, Discourse Analysis Monographs 6, Birmingham, U.K., English Language Research, University of Birmingham.
Hoey, M. (1983), *On the Surface of Discourse*, London, Allen and Unwin.
Meiland, J. W. (1981), *College Thinking: How to Get the Best Out of College*, New York, New American Library.
Milic, L. T., 'Connectives in Swift's Prose Style,' in Freeman, D. C. (ed.) (1970: 243–57), *Linguistics and Literary Style*, New York, Holt, Rinehart and Winston.
Nystrand, M. (1982), *What Writers Know: The Language, Process, and Structure of Written Discourse*, New York, Academic Press.
Ong, W. J. (1975), 'The Writer's Audience Is Always a Fiction,' *PMLA* [Publications of the Modern Language Association of America], **90** , 9–21.
Smith, F. (1982), *Writing and the Writer*, London, Heinemann Educational Books.
Stubbs, M. (1980), *Language and Literacy: The Sociolinguistics of Reading and Writing*, London, Routledge and Kegan Paul.
Ure, J., 'Lexical Density and Register Differentiation,' in Perren, G. E. and Trim, J. L. (eds) (1971: 443–52), *Applications of Linguistics: Selected Papers of the Second International Congress of Applied Linguistics, Cambridge 1969*, Cambridge, at the University Press.
Young, R. E., Becker, A. L., and Pike, K. L. (1970), *Rhetoric: Discovery and Change*, New York, Harcourt Brace and World.

APPENDIX A

Two Student Critiques (Task 2) and Their Analyses

Note: In Texts *A* and *B* below, brackets enclose [textual devices], parentheses enclose (interpersonal devices), and small capitals indicate EVALUATIVE DEVICES.

Text A

(Introductory paragraph) indicates which way (your) argument is proceeding but there is no summary of (your) arguments.

Paragraphs are structured WELL, i.e. introduction, body and summary of points but the FLOW of them is often INTERRUPTED BY COMPLICATED sentences. [These] sentences are HARD TO UNDERSTAND on the first reading and often (need to) be read 2 and 3 times to understand* the point (you) are making. [These] sentences (could) (perhaps) be broken up into smaller sentences instead of CRAMMING* points into one sentence.

(Your) main point is introduced in the second sentence of the essay and from there (you) set out (your) points. In discussing* [the] points, the (reader) is enlightened about the point but it isn't related back to (your) argument against socialized medicine. (Your) points [therefore] (seem) as though they are (just) set out instead of using* them in the direction of objections to socialized medicine. The argument (you) are trying to develop [therefore] LOSES its IMPACT on the (reader). . . .

Analysis of Text A

Text *A* makes salient use of interpersonal devices. The writer addresses the critique directly to the author of the essay, takes the essay for granted as their common ground, and plunges straight into comments on its *introductory paragraph*. Second-person pronouns are used repeatedly and an implicit first or second person underlies some verb forms (indicated by *) which sit awkwardly in their respective sentences. The text displays some use of textual and evaluative devices, but interpersonal ones dominate and show a highly interactive orientation to the writing task.

Text B

Essay Critique on 'The Socialization of Medicine.' An argument for the positive case.

(This paper), as the title suggests, is an argument for the introduction of socialized medicine. Many SOUND arguments in favor of the (author's) case were presented; the (reader), however, was left with little more than an UNCOMPLICATED feeling of SATISFACTION. LACK of authority for ASSERTIONS, QUESTIONABLE structure and inclusion of ERRONEOUS spelling at CRITICAL moments DETRACTED from the overall IMPACT of the paper.

[The] paper did not use, or rather choose to take advantage of any PREDICTABLE structure or essay MODEL. CAREFUL analysis reveals that apart from the initial definition of the topic which (may be) found in the first sentence, the BALANCE of the essay is (simply) a STRING OF WELL-STRUCTURED sentences. Paragraphs (appear to) have been used for no other purpose than that of ARBITRARILY dividing the text into sections. UNSUBSTANTIATED ASSERTION is often used in lieu of WELL-REASONED and WELL-SUPPORTED argument. [This] DETRACTS from the overall EFFECTIVENESS and SUCCESS of the paper. On one or two occasions EFFECTIVE use is made of the source material provided, by citing the British experience. [This] TECHNIQUE of using source material (should) be developed, as documentary or authoritative support of this kind GREATLY ENHANCES the argument being presented. . . .

Analysis of Text B

Text *B* displays salient use of evaluative devices. They are very frequent, serving both to describe aspects of the given essay and to express the writer's dissatisfaction with it. Some of the evaluative words are not so well chosen (e.g. *satisfaction* in the first paragraph, which in its ordinary use is inconsistent with the writer's overall judgment). Textual and interpersonal devices are infrequently used, and there is little interaction with the presumed reader/audience.

Part IV
Applying functional language theory to writing instruction

11 Applying a functional model of language in the writing classroom

Stephen A. Bernhardt
Southern Illinois University—Carbondale

11.1 WHAT FUNCTIONAL MODELS OF LANGUAGE DO

Functional models of language explain language by spelling out the systems of linguistic choice that are related to the varieties of meanings people want to express. In short, functional models show how people do things with language. This pragmatic orientation makes these models particularly useful for helping students learn to write. Like other uses of language, writing involves constrained choice, shaped by the social interaction to be effected in a given context. By examining the specific kinds of linguistic choice that come into play in written discourse, we can better explain to students what writers do when they write well.

Functional models assert that to understand how language works as social interaction, we need to do more than build formal systems of grammatical choice or even formal systems of semantic choice. We need to show how it is that language systems convey socio-semantics: people moving about, using language in their interactions with other people and the world. This perspective aligns functional approaches with rhetorical models that emphasize audience and situation in gauging linguistic appropriateness, from classical Aristotelian models to modern schemes—for example, those of Burke (1969) or Bitzer (1968 and 1980). Functional models of language complement particularly well both traditional and current thinking which informs our teaching of writing, from emphases on rhetorical form to concern with the contexts for writing.

The functional model of language which is presented in this chapter for use in the writing classroom owes a large debt to systemic-functional linguistics. It finds its fullest development in the writings of Halliday (see Kress 1976), with roots in work on the sociological aspects of language by Malinowski ([1923] 1949) and Firth (1957), Crystal and Davy (1969), Sinclair and Coulthard (1975), Berry (1975 and 1976), Hasan (1977), and Gregory and Carroll (1978) have all worked within the systemic-functional model, and much of their work is derived from and applicable to classroom situations.

My interest is not to detail any one model of a functional approach to language, but rather to suggest the general assumptions that functional approaches share and, in doing so, to show their relevance to the writing classroom. I refer to the FUNCTIONAL APPROACH out of convenience, without suggesting that what I say is true of all functional approaches or that all the researchers mentioned share a common position. Also, given my focus on writing, I refer to the WRITER in situations where SPEAKER/WRITER or some equally clumsy but appropriately broad term might be more precise.

In a functional model, linguistic form is seen as derived from, reflecting, or constrained by the situation surrounding the use of language. Function precedes form; the particular uses to which language is put determine the shape of any particular utterance. And, of course, multiple functions dictate even the shape of a short passage, as we can see by analyzing the text in Figure 11.1. A functional description of this text, which was removed from the cord of a hair dryer, shows us that language conveys several kinds of meaning simultaneously.

A functional analysis tells us, among other things, that language conveys SUBJECT MATTER—a text is always about something, and it refers to ideas and events. The 'hair dryer' text concerns a well-defined subject matter: the risks associated with using electrical appliances, especially around water. This very narrow content and specific activity directly determines what the writer chooses to put in the text. Most obviously, the warning is composed with predictable vocabulary. Less obviously, the cause and effect LOGIC which underlies the structure of the sentences is necessitated by the subject matter: the text is a warning about the consequences of failing to observe certain practices with the dryer.

But not only 'subject matter' and 'logical relations' shape this text. What a text is about includes more than ideational or propositional content; its CONTEXT also determines its character. What the writer chooses for both content and form assumes that, under normal circumstances, the reader would be holding the hair dryer while reading the tag. This special relationship between the text and its context precludes any need for introductory or identifying remarks saying these are warnings for the safe operation of a hairdryer. The reader does not need to be told how to interpret the text in these circumstances because the text is embedded in a very particular situation and the situation itself allows the reader to make appropriate judgments about the meaning of the text.

DANGER—TO REDUCE THE RISK OF ELECTROCUTION:

1. ALWAYS UNPLUG THIS APPLIANCE AFTER USING.
2. DO NOT USE WHILE BATHING.
3. DO NOT PLACE OR STORE APPLIANCE WHERE IT CAN DROP OR BE PULLED INTO A TUB OR SINK.
4. DO NOT PLACE IN OR DROP IN WATER OR OTHER LIQUID.
5. DO NOT REACH FOR AN APPLIANCE THAT HAS FALLEN INTO WATER. UNPLUG IMMEDIATELY.

DO NOT REMOVE THIS TAG

Figure 11.1 Hair dryer text

A text also means by virtue of its being a part of a certain kind of experience or an EXPERIENTIAL FIELD. It fits into those activities that surround it and can only be understood as it fits in with some ongoing activity. If we want to understand, predict, or prescribe the content or the logical relations of a text, we need to look toward the whole field of worldly goings-on in which the text plays its part.

Because a text links itself with wordly experiences as well as representing subject matter, it also expresses INTERPERSONAL MEANINGS. Discourse always takes place between people who relate to one another on the basis of status, authority, and intimacy. Participants in a discourse also have certain purposes, such as to teach, to delight, or to persuade. And they express attitudes toward the content of the discourse, such as firm belief, hesitancy, disgust, or whimsical aloofness. Discourse participants also play certain roles in the framework of the discourse itself—for example, questioner, respondent, or quiet listener. While such roles are more active in spoken discourse than in written, writers still need to choose roles for themselves and their readers and then to project these roles through the linguistic choices which the language affords.

The 'hair dryer' text is directly influenced by the relationship of the writer to the audience. The writer, representing a company, has the responsibility to warn customers of possible dangers, and by doing so, absolves the company from responsibility for accidents due to negligence. As in most uses of language, the purposes are complex: at one level the warnings are sound advice for the customer's benefit, while at a second level, the writer's goal is to avoid costly lawsuits against the manufacturer. The form of the text reflects this interpersonal situation: there is no need for a polite tone or for deference toward the customer's inclinations, nor is there any need for qualifications or hedging. The writer chooses linguistic options which are direct and unambiguous, issued in a series of bald imperatives intended to direct behavior. While readers may feel guilty about removing the tag or anxious about being too lazy to unplug the hair dryer between uses, they are unlikely to be offended by the imperious tone of the text.

Given the interpersonal situation, writers choose those constructions which direct behavior in the most appropriate ways. The functional approach to analyzing texts gives a central place to the assumption that such social roles play a large part in determining both the form and our interpretations of all language events. Texts do more than convey information; they also impose relationships between the participants, relationships which exert a controlling influence over many of the writer's linguistic choices.

Texts also transfer meaning through the form the writer chooses to give them. Authors must choose how and where to present subject matter to an audience. They express themselves through a certain text medium, related to other utterances of a similar type. As choices are made for the form of a written text, decisions necessarily are made about how the text fits together, about internal patterns of reference, and about patterns of reference which makes the text relevant to the situation in which it is used. One way of suggesting the richness of meaning that the form of a text assumes would be to think of every text as having an interrelated history: it is not created anew, but from other texts like it, which express similar meanings in similar situations.

The writer of the text in Figure 11.1 is working within a tradition of texts which express warnings, and this text becomes one more example of short, consumer-oriented warnings found on electrical appliances, achieving in the process some identity with other warnings about what not to do with Cuisinarts or electric hedge trimmers. We do not expect such texts to be framed in elaborate introductory or concluding remarks, nor to observe paragraphing conventions, nor even necessarily to use complete sentences. What we do expect—and what this writer gives us—is a list structure, with much of the information presented in an enumerated display, highlighted through typographic variation, headings, indentation, spacing, and so on. Discrete directives are cast in parallel grammatical series and clear, simple syntax (with the demand for clarity overriding the demand for parallel syntax in one instance). All these aspects of form—the visual design, the enumeration, the parallel syntax—make the text cohesive, showing what goes with what and how the various parts of the text constitute a coherent whole. The writer chooses linguistic options for form and presentation which make it a relatively easy task for the reader to interpret the text.

In addition to establishing these internal relations of cohesion, the writer also chooses to tie the text explicitly to the situation in which it is embedded, making the text function in a way that is highly dependent on its situation. Exophoric references to *this appliance* and *this tag* mediate between the text and its situation, providing direct links among the text, its physical manifestation, and its situation of use.

Our functional analysis of a sample text shows that writers must account for several sorts of meanings in the act of composing. By selecting what to discuss, authors establish a perspective on the content of the discourse. At the same time, they relate to their audience in specific ways by selecting options from linguistic systems that enable interpersonal meaning, notably choices of mood and modality. Finally, by selecting options from those linguistic systems that define how texts can be put together and how they show internal relationships as well as relate to their situations, the writer establishes a range of formal or textual meanings. These meanings are interwoven throughout the text in linguistic patterns of various sorts which simultaneously mean. Writers seek to blend harmoniously the several sorts of meaning that language affords into a unified text (see Hasan 1977; and Halliday 1979). Just as a musical composition is the simultaneous realization of melodic, harmonic, and rhythmic lines, none of which equals the composition when played alone, so a written composition is the simultaneous realization of several sorts of meaning, meanings which thread their way through the text and together contribute to the text's largest sense.

11.2 HOW FUNCTIONAL MODELS HAVE INFLUENCED RESEARCH IN WRITING

Much recent research has adopted a functional perspective to shed light on how writers make linguistic choices and on how their choices affect the readers of their texts. Flower, Hayes, and Swarts, for example, have studied how writers can best undertake revision of documents which cause problems for readers. They suggest a 'scenario principle,' which helps a writer envision how a particular text fits harmoniously with its context. Writers of functional documents, according to these researchers, should structure prose around a 'HUMAN AGENT performing ACTIONS in a particularized SITUATION' (1983: 42). Revising a text within these guidelines is quite a different affair from applying the non-contextual readability formulas which for years have been recommended by some business and technical writing instructors as guidelines for revision.[1] Applying a similar approach, Harweg (1980) has investigated how writers can manipulate opening strategies to create varying interpersonal functions, demonstrating how certain strategies that locate a writer in place and time are necessary when readers must be drawn into a text (when, in Harweg's terms, the text is 'obtrusive'), but are unnecessary when readers come to a text voluntarily and can be expected to read it without coaxing.

Much recent empirical research shares the presumption that to judge what is an effective text we need to consider such pragmatic questions as who will be reading the text, what purposes and reading strategies will they bring to the text, and, having read it, what they will be expected to do. These considerations have made findings of new research in writing easily adaptable to the composition classroom.

11.3 HOW A FUNCTIONAL MODEL APPLIES TO WRITING INSTRUCTION

Viewing language as multi-functional can provide a heuristic for analyzing any situation of language use. A functional model of language reminds teachers and students that more is involved in constructing a text than supplying adequate content, finding an appropriate tone or point of view, or mimicking a certain textual format, such as a five-paragraph essay. A writer must strive for a harmonious balance among functional components.

A multi-functional view of language can be a useful corrective to impulses to elevate one function of the text at the expense of others. For example, some students and teachers mistakenly assume that scientific or technical writing is somehow easier than other forms of exposition because it follows well-established formats, and writers can simply plug information into the required form. The textual function of FORMAT may, in fact, dominate some scientific/technical texts (e.g. the problem–solution format dominates some scientific journal articles), but following a standard format does not guarantee that writing such texts is a simple business.

Many scientific reports, for instance, are organized into sections which reflect the idealized process of doing research, from proposing a hypothesis within the context of related research to describing methods, stating results, and then interpreting the results in a concluding discussion. But this organization does not release the writer from deciding exactly how much information is needed in each section, what other studies to mention, whether to use the first person, how to hedge or qualify assertions, how to represent gaps or inconsistencies in the data, and how to foreground important information. In short, scientific writing is as charged with rhetorical considerations as any sort of writing; it is complex in its multiple purposes, delicate in its participant relations, and full of choices in its textual component.

All writers, whether of scientific exposition or highly subjective personal narrative, must strive for a harmonious blend of the several language functions. Functional models of language can remind us of the complexity of all language use and prevent false dichotomies from dominating our thinking, from seeing some uses of language as personal and others as impersonal or some uses as creative and others as routine.[2]

If writing teachers are to adopt a consistent, situationally bound, functional perspective, all advice they give to students must be cast in situationally relevant terms. For instance, we cannot simply offer to students the unconditional advice to begin with something interesting to the reader or to engage the reader with a strong first sentence. Along with Harweg (1980), we must abandon the notion that all texts must attempt to engage the reader initially and recognize that many texts do not function under the same constraints as those which shape our idealized classroom essays.

Furthermore, we cannot offer students 'all purpose' formulas for good writing, such as 'Begin each paper with a thesis and each paragraph with a topic sentence,' 'Vary sentence structure or word choice' (advice which is often disastrous in many sorts of technical writing), or 'Write in complete sentences and avoid fragments.' Any of these bits of advice, routinely offered without qualification in many writing classrooms, would be irrelevant for many texts, including the hair dryer text we've cited above. A functional perspective, consistently applied, pulls the rug from under all sorts of generalizations which make sense in only a limited context, such as when students write essays for grading by teachers.

In place of pat advice, a functional approach offers a framework for understanding how language works, a framework which can then be applied in particular situations. The emphasis on language use as an activity which depends heavily on context as a determinant of form gives the functional model power as a predictor of language behavior. To the extent that certain writing situations tend to occur repeatedly, with similar ideas expressed to similar audiences for similar purposes, rhetorical forms emerge which have characteristic features (see Bitzer 1980). Corporate form letters are one example; we might also think of recipes, laboratory reports, or classroom essays. Each represents a particular REGISTER: a type of text in which we expect to find characteristic vocabulary, sentence structures, organizational patterns, modes of interpersonal expression, or logical patterns of reasoning and evidence.

Functional models allow us to describe language varieties according to register and prevent us from offering all-purpose statements derived solely from our notions about what constitutes good writing. In place of unqualified generalizations, functional models offer generalizations about particular registers: what is effective for a given purpose or a given audience, within a particular context of situation. When we know a situation quite well and have experience with many texts produced within that situation, the patterns which new texts will display become predictable, subject to description and prescription. In a narrowly defined situation, we can predict not only what language functions will dominate, but also the exact language features that are likely to be present. For instance, we know from observational descriptions of classroom discourse that interaction between teachers and students is highly predictable across grade levels and subject matter. The pattern is consistent: the teacher asks a question, recognizes a student respondent (who has a relatively short time to respond with a relatively short answer), and then gives some indication of approval to the student (see Sinclair and Coulthard 1975). The situation elicits such a well-defined register, so regular in its patterning, that it amuses us to think about a student reversing the roles and saying ‘Good’ or ‘That’s right’ in response to a teacher comment.

A recognition of the predictability of some language registers serves the teacher well, especially in developing materials for special purposes, such as teaching students of English as a second language to be bank tellers or teaching engineering students to write technical report abstracts. Research offers us highly specific descriptions of well-defined written registers, from legal writing to advertising to scientific and technical writing (see Leech 1966; Crystal and Davy 1969; and Gregory and Carroll 1978). Such descriptions can help us begin to understand how language varies in predictable ways from situation to situation, an understanding which can promote informed teaching.

Instructors should make an effort to learn about written registers and how they change as the needs of reading communities change. Registers are best thought of as evolving adaptations of language to repeated human experience. Instructors should know, for instance, that some years ago, writers of scientific journal articles reported descriptions of ‘experimental method’ in an appendix. Gradually the scientific community changed its view of the relative importance of experimental methods, deeming that methods are central to the interpretation of results. Now many writers of scientific articles give the methods section a place of prominence, even putting it before the section reporting their findings (see Woodford 1968: 17–18). Similar evolutionary shifts are apparent in more familiar registers: business letter writers are adopting a more personal style, characterized by greater use of informal language, including contractions; science writers are increasingly expressing their findings in the first person and using agentive constructions rather than passive constructions. (This shift to agentive constructions is most probably motivated functionally, resulting in improved reader comprehension and speed [see Ramsey 1980].)

A functional perspective provides teachers and students with a model of variation capable of describing and explaining all language, whether written or spoken. By presenting students with diverse samples of written language and asking them to write for a variety of audiences and purposes, teachers can lead students toward increasing sensitivity to variation within a register. Teachers may, in fact, build on this sensitivity by presenting students with rhetorical cases (see Woodson 1982; and Couture and Goldstein 1985), which provide students with well-defined situations that demand a written response.

Most adults know how to vary their speech across a range of registers; they also know characteristic features of advertising or news reporting, and they are intimately familiar with the range of registers represented on network television. Not all students, however, have very highly developed intuitions about written academic registers. Hence, students often violate conventions of impersonality, of hierarchical or logical structuring, of documentation, or of substantiation of arguments. By beginning with what students do know and can command, including their facility with a range of spoken registers, teachers can help students become increasingly aware of the 'rules' for academic discourse (see Couture, Chapter 4, in this volume [ed.]).

Systemic models of language function are particularly appropriate for the writing classroom. While admitting registers, systemic models resist description which reduces language to highly predictable, patterned behavior. In such models, descriptive stress is placed not only on what are characteristic features of a given register, but also on what choices the language provides in a given situation.

Systemic grammars outline networks or systems of choice in the language that dictate syntax and reflect semantic or sociosemantic function (see Berry 1975–1976; and Halliday 1979). One network of systemic-functional grammar which has received much attention from writing teachers has been outlined by Halliday and Hasan in *Cohesion in English* (1976). The central chapters of the work, those which have most caught the attention of composition researchers, delineate in detail the options which language users have for establishing explicit ties from sentence to sentence in the creation of connected text. Looking at how language features perform cohesive functions, Halliday and Hasan have created descriptive categories which cross traditional grammatical boundaries. Members of diverse grammatical word classes, such as pronouns, conjunctions, adverbs, adjectives, and verbs, are shown to serve the same function.

The schematic approach to grouping items by functional equivalence is not new. Bain treated sentence linkage in much the same way (see Bain 1890: 94–104), and Jesperson developed both formal and functional descriptions in his discussion of 'Systemic Grammar' ([1924] 1963: 30–57). In recent work, Leech and Svartvik have organized language by function. For example, within the section of their grammar on 'Information, reality and belief,' subsections on 'Certainty,' 'Doubt or uncertainty,' and 'Belief, opinion, etc.' list, within sentences, such related expressions as *I know, I am certain/sure, It is obvious/clear/plain*, and *He has clearly/obviously/plainly*... (1975: 132). Such grouping must seem quite unusual for those accustomed to organization of linguistic categories along solely formal criteria.

Halliday and Hasan's functional approach to grammatical relations consistently presents language as networks of discrete semantic choices. The categories are defined clearly and thus easily support a teaching strategy for writing based on what options the language provides for expression of given meanings. The model respects the individuality and primacy of each instance of language use, as well as the similarities between a particular text and others of a same type.

Functional models in general allow us to work from what students know toward communicative competence in new situations (see Bernhardt 1983; Couture 1983; and Robinson 1983). We can teach students to recognize how writing involves constant choice from the options the language affords. What determines effective choice is how well a text reflects a rhetorical strategy—what the writer wants to do to whom in a given situation.

11.4 HOW A FUNCTIONAL MODEL SUCCEEDS WHERE OTHER MODELS FAIL

The emphasis on choice in a functional model of language contrasts with the error-oriented presentation of grammar in many composition textbooks. Too many composition texts fail to attend to grammar in a systematic way or to show show grammar might be motivated powerfully in the service of rhetoric; rather they overlay grammatical terms on the hodgepodge of common errors to which students are prone.

Many composition handbooks, for example, give more attention to pronouns as a likely source of grammatical error than as a resource for creating and maintaining ideational and interpersonal cohesion across a text. The popular *Harbrace College Handbook* (Hodges and Whitten 1984), for example, devotes thirty-three pages to sentence level errors involving use of pronouns. Only one page, however, is given to discussion of the function of pronouns in creating sentence linkage across a paragraph. A much more concise handbook, *The Little English Handbook* (Corbett 1980), similarly devotes twelve pages to sentence level slips of pronoun reference, but only a single page to the role of pronouns in establishing cohesion above the sentence level. Such emphasis encourages students to think that good writing can somehow be equated with an absence of grammatical error.

A better approach would stress the text-level functions of pronominals. Writers need to learn the important role of pronouns in creating cohesive text by establishing and maintaining thematic focus. In paragraphs with coordinate patterns of development, where a series of predications about the same subject is carried through successive sentences, writers can create thematic focus by beginning each sentence with the same pronoun in the subject slot. Writers can also use deictics such as *this, that, these*, and *those* to maintain focus in a subordinate series by reintroducing information from the end of a previous sentence in the initial slot of a following sentence. Personal pronouns also function to express interpersonal meanings, involving the reader in the text (e.g. references to *you*), or involving the author (e.g. *It seems to me . . .* or *I believe that . . .*).

If teachers direct students' attention to the functions of pronominals in creating cohesive texts with appropriate interpersonal roles, students may may fewer errors. Their attention will be on doing something intentionally with these features rather than avoiding problems, such as pronoun-antecedent agreement or faulty reference. Seeing pronominals as they relate to the cohesive devices of conjunction, substitution, ellipsis, and lexical patterning should give students increased control over the choices which they confront as writers. Teachers can also contextualize classroom discussion of and prescriptions for the use of other grammatical patterns, such as passives, cleft structures, parallel structures, and tense and aspect, by considering the intentions of the writer. Within the functional model, the treatment of grammar is elevated from a fragmented, sentence-level, error-oriented approach to an integrated, text-level, intentional approach, where grammar is enlisted in the service of rhetoric in the creation of meaning.[3]

Unlike traditional grammars, a functional grammar allows for increasingly fine distinctions and for accurate generalizations at a fairly high level. Consider the following pair of sentences: 'George wanted to come to some decision before leaving the meeting. Susan, *however*, felt more information was needed before she could decide anything.' In the systemic functional grammar, the italicized *however* can be described as a TIE, a textual link which presupposes information in the previous sentence, providing an explicit semantic connection which helps to show a reader that these two sentences are part of a cohesive text. More specifically, *however* can be described as an 'immediate tie' which would distinguish it from other ties which reach back over one or more sentences instead of referring to the immediately preceding sentence ('remote' vs. 'immediate'). Describing *however* as an 'endophoric' tie would further distinguish this tie as acquiring its meaning from other elements within the text rather than from reference to systems of meaning outside the text, creating an 'exophoric' link (as did *this tag* and *this appliance* in the 'hair dryer' text). More delicately still, *however* could be characterized as an 'immediate, endophoric, anaphoric, conjunctive, adversative, emphatic tie' which would further distinguish this tie as pointing back to a previous element in the text ('anaphoric' reference) as opposed to pointing forward to some anticipated element in the text ('cataphoric' reference), as a 'conjunctive' vs. 'pronominal' or some other sort of cohesive tie, as an 'adversative' rather than 'temporal' or some other sort of conjunctive tie, and so on. The limits of delicacy can be appreciated by those who have spent time with Halliday and Hasan's *Cohesion in English* (1976), an analysis which makes very fine discriminations in functional description.

Fortunately, it is neither necessary nor useful to present grammatical descriptions of extreme delicacy to students who are working to improve their writing. It is probably helpful to review the text-forming resources of the language, suggesting that pronominals, conjunctives, and lexical ties (and perhaps substitution and ellipsis, though these ties are less important to the texture of written English than to spoken) function in similar ways and signal similar semantic connections. The description of the textual system should, of course, be offered at a level of delicacy which is appropriate for the students being taught. The important thing is to offer useful generalizations without burdening students with too many terms.

Accurate descriptions at varying levels of delicacy can help keep teachers and students from becoming caught up in grammatical terminology and feeling unable to explain anything without explaining everything. Delicacy allows the description to fit the purposes of application. The emphasis on the functional roles of various grammatical systems which delicacy affords keeps the classroom use of grammar oriented toward the creation of meaning, not toward mastery of a formal system which is difficult to link to the task of writing.

11.5 SUMMARY

A functional model of language serves us well in teaching and studying writing because it is built to explain how language works. While allowing researchers to explore and describe highly specialized questions, a functional model gives teachers and students a way to describe the core of language experience at a useful level of generality. By accounting for the several sorts of meaning which function in any language act, the approach enriches our conception of language as intentional behavior and as information exchange. Like the rhetorical models with which we are familiar, a functional model moves from situation to text, articulating rhetoric and grammar in powerful ways. It provides a useful way to understand not just writing, but all language behavior, and it offers usefully broad generalizations which apply equally well to the many sorts of texts we encounter daily. A functional model is descriptive and analytic, but it also helps formulate prescriptions for effective choices in given situations. For all these reasons, it deserves attention and application in our teaching and research.

NOTES

1. Readability formulas assign a numerical value to a text that corresponds to a reading level based upon a computation of sentence length, word length, and other factors thought to influence comprehension and ease of reading. Such formulas have been under attack recently because they ignore context as a readability factor (see Huckin 1983; and Selzer 1983).
2. On the interpersonal richness of scientific discourse, see Carlisle 1978; and Halloran and Whitburn 1982.
3. Lackstrom, Selinker, and Trimble (1973) demonstrate the integration of grammar and rhetoric in their functional model of scientific registers, showing how choices of tense and aspect are determined by the attitudes of the writer toward the generalizability of the findings, rather than by notions of time or completion of research. Also, Bernhardt (1985) demonstrates that rhetorical controls govern the uses of pronominal reference in scientific research reports.

BIBLIOGRAPHY

Bain, A. (1890), *English Composition and Rhetoric: 1 Intellectual Elements of Style*, London, Longmans, Green.

Bernhardt, S. A., 'Contexts in Which Students Make Meanings,' in Stock, P. L. (ed.) (1983: 324–31), *FForum: Essays on Theory and Practice in the Teaching of Writing*, Upper Montclair, N.J., Boynton/Cook.

Bernhardt, S. A. (1985), 'The Writer, the Reader, and the Scientific Text,' *Journal of Technical Writing and Communication*, **15**, 163–74.

Berry, M. (1975–1976), *An Introduction to Systemic Linguistics*, 2 vols., New York, St. Martin's Press.

Bitzer, L. F. (1968), 'The Rhetorical Situation,' *Philosophy and Rhetoric*, **1**, 1–14.

Bitzer, L. F., 'Functional Communication: A Situational Perspective,' in White, E. E. (ed.) (1980: 21–38), *Rhetoric in Transition: Studies in the Nature and Uses of Rhetoric*, University Park, Penn., Pennsylvania State University Press.

Burke, K. (1969), *A Grammar of Motives*, Berkeley, University of California Press.

Carlisle, E. F. (1978), 'Teaching Scientific Writing Humanistically: From Theory to Action,' *The English Journal*, No. 4 (**67**): 35–9.

Corbett, E. P. J. (1980, 3rd edn), *The Little English Handbook: Choices and Conventions*, Glenview, Ill., Scott, Foresman.

Couture, B., 'Speech and Writing Research in the Composition Class,' in Stock, P. L. (ed.) (1983: 136–45), *FForum: Essays on Theory and Practice in the Teaching of Writing*, Upper Montclair, N.J., Boynton/Cook.

Couture, B. and Goldstein, J. R. (1985), *Cases for Technical and Professional Writing*, Boston, Little, Brown.

Crystal, D. and Davy, D. (1969), *Investigating English Style*, London, Longman.

Firth, J. R. (1957), *Papers in Linguistics, 1934–1951*, London, Oxford University Press.

Flower, L., Hayes, J. R., and Swarts, H., 'Revising Functional Documents: The Scenario Principle,' in Anderson, P. V., Brockmann, R. J., and Miller, C. R. (eds) (1983: 41–58), *New Essays in Technical and Scientific Communication: Research, Theory, Practice*, Farmingdale, N.Y., Baywood.

Gregory, M. and Carroll, S. (1978), *Language and Situation: Language Varieties and their Social Contexts*, London, Routledge and Kegan Paul.

Halliday, M. A. K., 'Modes of Meaning and Modes of Expression: Types of Grammatical Structure, and Their Determination by Different Semantic Functions,' in Allerton, D. J., Carney, E., and Holdcroft, D. (eds) (1979: 57–79), *Function and Context in Linguistic Analysis: A Festschrift for William Haas*, Cambridge, Cambridge University Press.

Halliday, M. A. K. and Hasan, R. (1976), *Cohesion in English*, London, Longman.

Halloran, S. M. and Whitburn, M. D., 'Ciceronian Rhetoric and the Rise of Science: The Plain Style Reconsidered,' in Murphy, J. J. (ed.) (1982: 58–72), *The Rhetorical Tradition and Modern Writing*, New York, Modern Language Association of America.

Harweg, R. (1980), 'Beginning a Text,' *Discourse Processes*, **3**, 313–26.

Hasan, R., 'Text in the Systemic-Functional Model,' in Dressler, W. U. (ed.) (1977: 228–46), *Current Trends in Text Linguistics*, Research in Text Theory 2, Berlin, Walter de Gruyter.

Hodges, J. C. and Whitten, M. E. (1984, 9th edn), *Harbrace College Handbook*, San Diego, Harcourt Brace Jovanovich.

Huckin, T. N., 'A Cognitive Approach to Readability,' in Anderson, P. V., Brockmann, R. J., and Miller, C. R. (eds) (1983: 90–108), *New Essays in Technical and Scientific Communication: Research, Theory, Practice*, Farmingdale, N.Y., Baywood.

Jesperson, O. ([1924] 1963), *The Philosophy of Grammar*, London, Allen and Unwin.

Kress, G. R. (ed.) (1976), *Halliday: System and Function in Language*, London, Oxford University Press.

Lackstrom, J., Selinker, L., and Trimble, L. (1973), 'Technical Rhetorical Principles and Grammatical Choice,' *TESOL* [Teachers of English to Speakers of Other Languages] *Quarterly*, **7**, 127–36.

Leech, G. N. (1966), *English in Advertising: A Linguistic Study of Advertising in Great Britain*, London, Longman.

Leech, G. and Svartvik, J. (1975), *A Communicative Grammar of English*, London, Longman.

Malinowski, B., 'The Problem of Meaning in Primitive Languages,' supplement to Ogden, C. K. and Richards, I. A. ([1923] 1949, 10th edn: 296–336), *The Meaning of Meaning: A Study of the Influence of Language upon Thought and of the Science of Symbolism*, New York, Harcourt, Brace: London, Routledge and Kegan Paul.

Ramsey, R. D. (1980), 'Grammatical Voice and Person in Technical Writing: Results of a Survey,' *Journal of Technical Writing and Communication*, **10**, 109–13.

Robinson, J. L., 'A Rhetorical Conception of Writing,' in Stock, P. L. (ed.) (1983: 293–5), *FForum: Essays on Theory and Practice in the Teaching of Writing*, Upper Montclair, N.J., Boynton/Cook.

Selzer, J., 'What Constitutes a "Readable" Technical Style?,' in Anderson, P. V., Brockmann, R. J., and Miller, C. R. (eds) (1983: 71–89), *New Essays in Technical Writing and Scientific Communication: Research, Theory, Practice*, Farmingdale, N.Y., Baywood.

Sinclair, J. McH. and Coulthard, R. M. (1975), *Towards an Analysis of Discourse: The English Used by Teachers and Pupils*, London, Oxford University Press.

Woodford, P. (ed.) (1968), *Scientific Writing for Graduate Students: A Manual on the Teaching of Scientific Writing*, Council of Biology Editors, Committee on Graduate Training in Scientific Writing, New York, The Rockefeller University Press.

Woodson, L. (1982), *From Cases to Composition*, Glenview, Ill., Scott, Foresman.

12 Literacy and intonation

Martin Davies
University of Stirling

12.1 INTRODUCTION

All native speakers of English have—from about the age of four—sufficient practical knowledge of the spoken language to be able to use the intonation system efficiently. For most of us this is not usually knowledge of which we are conscious, that is, knowledge we formulate or knowledge we might call 'descriptive.' Most of us usually do not acquire and do not need to acquire a descriptive knowledge of intonation. Moreover, as small children we do not have lessons about the practical knowledge we are learning. Rather, by paying careful attention to the way intonation is used meaningfully by those around us, we work out how to use it ourselves in order to express our meanings. But no one teaches us how to do this: we master it for ourselves—as we must because we cannot manage without it. In fact, we would lose tremendous potential for meaning in English if we had to chant our utterances in a monotone or had to let our voices rise and fall at random in the way unfortunate people who are deaf have to do.

However, in developing our mastery of the written language, we are not left entirely to our own devices, but rather we are taught—in addition to learning some things for ourselves. Either at home or at school, someone takes the trouble to teach us how to read and write. In order to teach us, our teachers often have to make some overt statements about the written language. They will say things like: 'You should not put a comma between the subject and the verb, unless there is something in brackets between them' or 'We put down the sounds one at a time, sometimes with a letter for each sound, sometimes with more than one letter, and sometimes with one letter for more than one sound.' Statements like these have some validity, so far as they go, and many children exposed to them have learned how to read and write without any great difficulty. In such statements, however, the notion of a sound that is connected with the written word is rather restricted. The claim that 'we put down sounds one at a time,' for instance, seems to refer to those aspects of the sounds of utterances which are represented by the spelling of them. When discussing writing, teachers rarely, if ever, make statements that show any awareness of the nature of intonation patterns across stretches of discourse, and when they do, they are unlikely to specify such awareness in any very detailed way.

Some teachers may argue that it is just as well that we do not teach anything about intonation in writing. They may say that intonation expresses attitudes, and though such expression is important, it can be accomplished through vocabulary, grammar, and punctuation, as well as through intonation. In short, why worry about intonation, since it is never represented in writing?

Ideas such as these reflect what we can call 'folk linguistics,' that is, intuitive knowledge we all have about how language works, based upon everyday experience of it. Like many such intuitive beliefs about language, the idea that intonation expresses attitudes has some truth in it, but it is not the whole story. Numerous studies of intonation have been conducted for several centuries now, and since the invention of the tape-recorder, such studies in a variety of languages have become a major research activity. Little of the research on English intonation, however, has as yet found its way into the thinking of teachers or of authors who write textbooks on reading and writing; in fact, it has been almost entirely ignored—despite the fact that intonation is a major resource for the expression of our meanings in English.

Pitch movement in English, for example, helps listeners distinguish questions from statements. If a speaker were to say the sentence *That's a wall* with a rising tone on *wall*, the listener would interpret the sentence as a question. Pronouncing the same sentence with a falling tone on *wall* would make it a statement. Few textbooks say more about such distinctions than to remark that, in writing, the first statement requires a question mark and the other a full stop; and even then, if this is said, it is not related to intonation necessarily, and it is certainly not related to it systematically. In any case, the fact that intonation does much more than discriminate between such simple pairs as these is largely ignored.

Teachers probably ignore intonation because they are not convinced that children's understanding of it will help them to become literate. But teachers' explicit understanding of it is another matter, and it can help them understand more fully the true nature of the task that children face in learning written language, which in turn can enable them to devise appropriate strategies to help them learn.

To that end, I provide here a very selective summary of some features of intonation which will enable me to present and to discuss the results of a small experiment relating intonation to the comprehension of written language. This experiment in turn shows, I believe, that teachers should take intonation more seriously in trying to understand learners' problems with writing. Finally, I suggest new approaches to literacy and intonation that should be taken into account in preparing teachers of reading and writing, not only in elementary and high schools, but also in adult education—anywhere, in fact, where the quality of reading and writing is important.

12.2 INTONATION SYSTEMS AND WRITTEN ENGLISH[1]

The general term for the range of meanings expressed by means of intonation in English is INFORMATION STRUCTURE. The information structure of a spoken text reflects three processes at work under the speaker's control. First, the speaker (apart from creating many other patterns simultaneously) groups a text (while speaking) into sections or melodic phrases known as TONE GROUPS; then, within each section, the speaker makes a particular element the focus of special attention through bearing a tonal and rhythmic stress called a TONIC; finally, the speaker assigns a particular melody to the section which is largely determined by the direction of the PITCH MOVEMENT on the tonic. These three processes in the creation of intonational meanings in text are called TONALITY, TONICITY, and TONE respectively, and they serve to express three very different functions.

The following is a brief explanation of tonality and tonicity in speech. These two aspects of intonation, in particular, have clear implications for written English, as my subsequent experiment has been designed to show.

12.2.1 Tonality

Tonality groups textual elements together independently of the groupings created by sentence and clause structure and suggests that, whatever the particular local interpretation required, a group should be interpreted in some sense as a 'unity.' Tonality or the distinction of tone groups (melodic units of sound) can be perceived in written language through observing the pauses and stresses a reader makes when reading aloud.

Of the three processes that determine information structure, tonality is the one most closely related to punctuation, although punctuation is actually, at best, a very ambivalent guide to tonality. Contenting ourselves with a representation of tonality by means of punctuation for the time being, however, we can easily sense a difference in meaning between the following two versions of the same sentence:

(i) The authority, to whom the Minister delegated the issue in a moment of fair-mindedness, decided in favor of the private operators.
(ii) The authority, to whom the Minister delegated the issue, in a moment of fair-mindedness decided in favor of the private operators.

In the first, it is the Minister who had been fair-minded; in the second, the authority. The semantic contrast between version (i) and (ii) is a matter of substantive meaning, not attitude. As teachers, we need to be able to 'handle' the ambiguity in such cases; we should be able to show that mere punctuation will not always eliminate the ambiguity, as it does here.

A simple, direct relationship does not exist between the placing of pauses in speech and the beginnings and ends of information units, nor between the placing of pauses in speech and the placing of punctuation marks in writing; nor is there any direct relationship between the beginnings and ends of information units in speech and the placing of punctuation marks in writing. These are different, independent (though related) matters: sometimes two or even all three boundaries may exist and coincide; sometimes none. This is inconvenient, especially for teachers of writing, but it is true, so we have to live with it.

While teachers must admit to students that punctuation is only a partial guide to the information structure of a written text, they can also show them that it does not have to work on its own. Thematic structure is also relevant. The THEME of a clause is the point where it starts as a message. We can show how theme relates to information structure by comparing two alternative expressions:

(i) In the morning, we must get some stamps.
(ii) We must get some stamps in the morning.

In version (i), *we* is the subject, but it is not the first element in the clause and therefore not 'theme.' When the subject is not the first element in a clause (version (i)), the choice of theme is said to be MARKED; this contrasts with UNMARKED THEME, where the subject is the first element (version (ii)). When the theme is marked, the reader will probably assign it an information unit to itself, whereas when the theme is unmarked, the reader will interpret the subject as belonging to the same information unit as the rest of its clause (unless the subject is very long). (For a more detailed explanation of marked and unmarked theme, see Eiler in this volume [ed.].) Hence, when a writer wishes to ensure that a reader interprets an element in a clause as an information unit unto itself, one of the possibilities is to make it marked theme—this will encourage the reader to assign it a separate tone group and express MARKED TONALITY as well.

The choices of marked theme and marked tonality are independent, but often marked theme will be accompanied by marked tonality. While theme is unmarked when the subject coincides with the first element of a clause, tonality is unmarked when a tone group is exactly the same length as the clause.

Tone groups may both be longer and shorter than a clause. Only one unmarked tonal stress for a given clause is possible, but several marked tonalities are possible. Speakers will choose unmarked tonality unless there is good reason to do otherwise—for instance, to achieve foregrounding or emphasis. The length of a clause can be 'good reason' to choose marked tonality and so can marked theme. A writer may emphasize a marked theme by putting a comma at its end to suggest more strongly that marked tonality is intended, but again this is a choice. When reading the text aloud, a reader may or may not take any notice of the comma, ending an information unit there or not, supplying a pause or not—an interpretative choice. All that punctuation can do in many instances is to suggest possibilities.

In summary, tonality specifies how the text is structured as a sequence of information units or 'blocks' of meanings by segmenting the text into a sequence of tone groups. All discourse is patterned into 'lengths' of information, as it were, explicitly recognizable by sound in speech, but only suggested in writing. Punctuation in writing can be a rough guide to tonality (the 'real work' is done by the underlying grammar). Further, thematic structure can suggest tonality, but this also is not a necessary condition.

12.2.2 Tonicity

Tonicity superimposes detail, within each tone group, on the pattern of tone groups which express tonality in a discourse through a combination of RHYTHM and MELODY. Since neither of these is represented explicitly in writing, discussion on the printed page requires the use of notation. For this, rhythm has to be distinguished from pitch. If we take pitch away from speech, as when speaking or chanting in a monotone, rhythm remains as the pattern of SALIENT and NON-SALIENT syllables in an utterance.

To indicate rhythm notationally, we can place an oblique line before each salient or stressed syllable, for example:

An o/blique /line will be /placed before /each /salient /syllable.

As the example sentence with notation shows, a word may or may not begin with a salient syllable. The notation carries no implication of 'right' or 'wrong': it merely records the rhythmical pattern of saliences used or intended.

To indicate a movement in pitch, we can underline the syllables within a tone group where major pitch movement combines with salience. A tone group may have more than one salient syllable in it, but only one salient syllable in the group will carry a major pitch movement. By underlining the syllable where pitch movement occurs, we can indicate three different ways of uttering the tone group *Angus has sunk the boat*; they are:

(i) /Angus has /sunk the /boat,
(ii) /Angus has /sunk the /boat, and
(iii) /Angus has /sunk the /boat.

If we say these aloud to native speakers of English, they will readily agree that each has a different meaning; tonicity accounts for the difference.

Tonicity is the choice a speaker makes about where to put the tonic, the particular combination of rhythmic salience with major pitch movement in a particular tone group. In our previous examples, we gave three possible choices for the tonic, governed by the three salient syllables in the group. Since only a salient syllable can be tonic, this is the full range of choices of tonicity possible for that rhythm. However, there are other possibilities if we assume a different rhythm. For instance, we can make *has* salient (in addition to the three syllables that are salient already) and put the tonic on *has*: /Angus /has/sunk the /boat.

Variations like these are meaningful. When we use a particular variant, we do not do so at random. It would be highly unlikely that if someone asked us '/Who has /sunk the /boat?,' we would reply (if we used only these words) '/Angus /has /sunk the /boat.' And it is also unlikely that we would say '/Angus has /sunk the /boat.' We would probably say '/Angus has /sunk the /boat.' This third alternative is the appropriate reply because it means what it 'should' mean in this context, that is, it appropriately emphasizes *Angus* as the reply to the question *who*. As these examples show, changes in placing of pitch movement DO AFFECT meaning.

Additional kinds of meaning can be expressed through MARKED and UNMARKED TONICITY. Several marked tonicities (one for each syllable that can be salient) are possible for each tone group of any length, just as several marked tonalities are possible for one clause.

We can illustrate how tonicity works to emphasize new information within a tone group by arranging the examples already shown as answers to five questions (see Table 12.1). The speaker's choice of tonic emphasizes the new information that answers each question.

Table 12.1 Different tonicities in *Angus has sunk the boat* as answers to five questions

Question	Answer
1. Who has sunk the boat?	/Angus has /sunk the /boat
2. What has Angus done to the boat?	/Angus has /sunk the /boat
3. What did Angus sink?	/Angus has /sunk the /boat
4. What has Angus done?	/Angus has /sunk the /boat
5. What has happened?	/Angus has /sunk the /boat

We can show the relationship between placement of the tonic and new information more emphatically by comparing elliptical answers to these questions to the choice of tonic in full answers (see Table 12.2). In each case, the elliptical answers, however brief, always retain the element in the clause which receives the tonic in the equivalent full answer, however much the elliptical answer leaves out. This shows that the speaker can emphasize new items in an utterance by making them tonic, that is, both rhythmically and melodically salient, and can let items already known to a listener recede into the background by making them non-tonic.

Table 12.2 Relation between elliptical answers and tonicity in full answers

Question	Elliptical answer	Tonic in full answer
1. Who has sunk the boat?	Angus.	Ang-
2. What has Angus done to the boat?	Sunk (it).	sunk
3. What did Angus sink?	The boat.	boat
4. What has Angus done?	Sunk the boat.	boat
5. What has happened?	Angus has sunk the boat. (i.e. no elliptical answer is possible here)	boat

The speaker answering the questions determines given information from the questions themselves. The first question indicates that the questioner knows that someone 'has sunk the boat'; the only information lacking is the identity of the sinker. The second one makes it plain that someone has 'done' something 'to the boat'; the only information lacking is exactly what has been done to the boat. The third question is similarly revealing. The tonicity of the answers to the first three questions is different for each, appropriately marked in each case to emphasize new information. In contrast, the tonicity for the answers to the third, fourth, and fifth questions is the same, unmarked for each, but the meanings of these answers are different. *Boat* is tonic in all three answers, but the extent of the information thus signaled as new varies according to the context of each question. In the third example, the context provided by the question narrowly restricts new information to *the boat*; and in the fourth example, new information is still restricted, although not so narrowly. The last response reflects the non-selective question prompting it; the question reveals only that the questioner knows something undefined has happened. The answer therefore is likely to contain information that is entirely unknown to the questioner; unmarked tonicity here identifies the information COMPREHENSIVELY as new.

Tonicity, then, adds a different kind of meaning to text than theme; whereas theme distinguishes what information is the starting point of the message, tonicity distinguishes what information is 'new' or not previously revealed to the reader from what is 'given' or known from the prior text. Table 12.3 displays the given–new information patterns as reflected through tonicity in the full answers to the five questions we have seen. As these examples reveal, tonicity is a key component in information exchange between a speaker and listener in both its marked and unmarked status. Marked tonicity informs the listener of what the speaker specifically regards as new information in a tone group; unmarked tonicity may signal either that all information in a tone group is regarded as new information or that the last item together with some or all of what precedes it is new.

Table 12.3 Tonicity and given–new information in *Angus has sunk the boat*

Question	Answer				
1. Who has sunk the boat?	New –	←———————————			Given
	/Angus	has	/sunk	the	/boat
2. What has Angus done to the boat?	Given ——→		–New–	←———	Given
	/Angus	has	/sunk	the	/boat
3. What has Angus sunk?	Given ———————→			– ←———	New
	/Angus	has	/sunk	the	/boat
4. What has Angus done?	Given	–– ←———————————			New
	/Angus	has	/sunk	the	/boat
5. What has happened?	←———————————————				New
	/Angus	has	/sunk	the	/boat

The examples in Table 12.3 make clear two problems for writers. First, when marked tonicity is intended, as in (1) and (2), some means is required not only to signal this fact, but also to signal a particular variety of marked tonicity. Constant underlining for emphasis can be unacceptably wearisome and is, in any case, unnecessary when grammar can be manipulated for the same purpose. Second, when the tonicity is unmarked, some means may be required to eliminate ambiguity (as in our *Angus has sunk the boat* where several information structures are possible). The challenge for writers, then, is to learn to signal marked tonicity through appropriate means and to manage ambiguity when tonicity is unmarked.

12.2.3 Summary of intonational meaning in writing

The properties of tonality and tonicity (and also tone, which we did not discriminate here) combine to create meanings within the English intonation system. Together they enable several intended meanings for a sentence which when written in English would be transcribed in ONLY ONE WAY: *Angus has sunk the boat*. This sentence can be said with a range of tonalities, each permitting a range of tonicities, each of which can be combined with a range of tones. The possibilities for varieties of meaning as expressed in intonation are numerous, even if we confine ourselves only to those outlined here. (In this case, ignoring further refinements, we can cite forty-five basic possibilities.)

Although intonation affects meaning in writing, written English gives little explicit indication of the intonational meaning intended in an utterance. If it does so at all, it does so rudimentarily through underlining, typeface and style, or capitalization; punctuation overall is a rather uncertain guide. In fact, punctuation often has no relationship to phonological patterns whatsoever. As Halliday writes:

> It is noticeable in modern English that there are two fairly distinct tendencies in punctuation: some writers tend to punctuate according to the information structure, others more according to the sentence structure. The distinction is sometimes referred to as 'phonological' (or 'phonetic') versus 'grammatical' punctuation; but this is perhaps misleading since the two represent rather different aspects of the grammatical structure, the former being 'phonological' in the sense that, since information structure is realized directly in the phonological organization, it can be interpreted as a marking off of phonological units. [Halliday 1967b: 200–1]

It is not often the case, of course, that punctuation is exclusively phonological or grammatical. Rather, the situation reflects a continuum stretching from the most 'phonological' kind of punctuation to the kind most directly related to sentence structure. An individual instance, then, may exhibit a kind of punctuation nearer one end or the other of that continuum or may lie somewhere in the middle.

The implications of these facts for teaching reading and writing in English are significant, and the difficulties it suggests are not stated or resolved easily. Nevertheless, as we will show, even basic explorations of intonation in English have the potential to assist teachers' efforts to help learners.

12.3 INTONATION AND READING: AN EXPERIMENT

12.3.1 Background

The relationship of intonation to the process of becoming literate in English is highly complex. We can begin exploring that relationship, however, by examining the role of intonation in reading, particularly the way intonation reveals the reader's understanding of the text he or she is reading.

A difficulty underlying our discussion of intonation and reading is precisely the problem I have identified: intonation expresses information structure in speech, but little explicit representation of information structure appears in writing. Despite this, readers are not at a loss to interpret possible intonation structures in written prose. When reading aloud, competent readers seem to recognize fairly quickly when they have made a mistake in conveying information structure through intonation, and, realizing this, stop and read a passage again. But competent readers, such as teachers, do not know HOW they know to do this, at least not in very much detail; nor do they know how to help those to whom it is not obvious. Still less do they know what happens when they read silently, though they know that they sometimes may have to re-read a passage to 'grasp the sense,' and since information structure expresses meaning, 'the sense' in this context may have something to do with that structure.

Although much of what happens in silent reading is largely unknown (and likely to remain so for some time), we can examine with some success what happens with information structure when a text is read aloud. What seems to happen is that the reader tries to supply an information structure appropriate to the text he or she is reading. The difficulty is to know what is meant by 'appropriate' and to find out how the reader discovers from the written text what kind of intonation to supply. Further, although it is clear that readers often know when they have 'made a mistake,' they do not always show that they know it while reading, and it is difficult to gain reliable data about what is going on. We can guess that the reader decides what is appropriate by responding to certain lexical and grammatical cues in the text and attempts to supply an information structure which is compatible with these elements, perhaps trying out more than one intonation pattern if the first seems inappropriate.

12.3.2 An intonation experiment

To examine the ways readers supply intonation when interpreting written text, I conducted a 'reading aloud' experiment. I took the opening paragraph from a mathematics textbook written for English secondary schools (see Figure 12.1) and asked a mathematics teacher to read the text, which he did not know, into a microphone. I asked him to read without rehearsal and to record his FIRST interpretation. I then asked a 10-year-old boy to do the same. The boy was younger than those the text was actually intended for, but well ahead of the average boy of his age in mathematics.

[1] Section 1 Sets
[2] We shall use the word 'set' a good deal in this book. [3] We must understand clearly what it means in mathematics. [4] If you collect stamps [5] you will have an idea of what a 'set' is in philately; [6] you also know what is meant by a 'set' of encyclopedias. [7] This is the right idea, [8] but not quite clear. [9] When you meet the word in this book, [10] it means 'a collection' [11] and nothing more. [12] I can talk about the five books which are in my briefcase at present as a set, [13] though they are: a dictionary, a mathematics book, a note-book, a detective novel and a photograph album. [14] All that they have in common is that they are together in my bag [15] which makes them 'the set of books in my bag now'. [16] The members of a set always have at least one thing in common: [17] that they all belong to the same set. [18] Most of the sets you will meet will have more than one thing in common, [19] or, [20] as we say, [19 cont.] more than one common property. [Raymond S. Heritage (1966), *Learning Mathematics*, Book One, Harmondsworth, U. K., Penguin Books: 9]

Figure 12.1 Opening paragraph from mathematics text (clause numbers added)

Figure 12.2 displays a partial transcription of the two readings in ordinary spelling, with the relevant features of intonation specified. Proceeding across the page, the reader will find numbered clauses of the original text with the transcription of the child's intonation and the teacher's intonation above the numbered passages. The vertical lines in the transcriptions indicate the

```
                                           |      |   ←--------- New
Teacher:                                   |      |   we must understand clearly

           |   ←— New     | New   |               |   ←---------- New
Child:     |  section one |  sets |               |   we must understand clear
Text:      || (1) Section 1  Sets ||   (2)        || (3) We must understand clearly


                                               |  ←----------- New       |
T:                                             |  what it means in mathematics  |

           | Given—New    | Given New          |  ←----------- New       |
C:         |  that clearly | that it means     |  what it means in mathematics  |
                                                  what it means in mathematics  ||


           |  ←------ New ||               ||   Given ←—— New     |
T:         |  if you collect stamps ||     ||   this is the right idea  |

           |  ←------ New ||               ||   Given ←—— New     |
C:         |  if you collect stamps ||     ||   this is the right idea  |
           || (4) If you collect stamps || (5)  (6)  || (7) This is the right idea, ||


           |  ←---- New        |       | Given  New   |  ←— New       |
T:         |  but not quite clear |     |   it means   |  a collection |

           |  ←---- New        |       | Given  New   |  ←— New       |
C:         |  but not quite clear |     |   it means   |  a collection |
           | (8) but not quite clear. || (9) || (10) it means   'a collection' ||
```

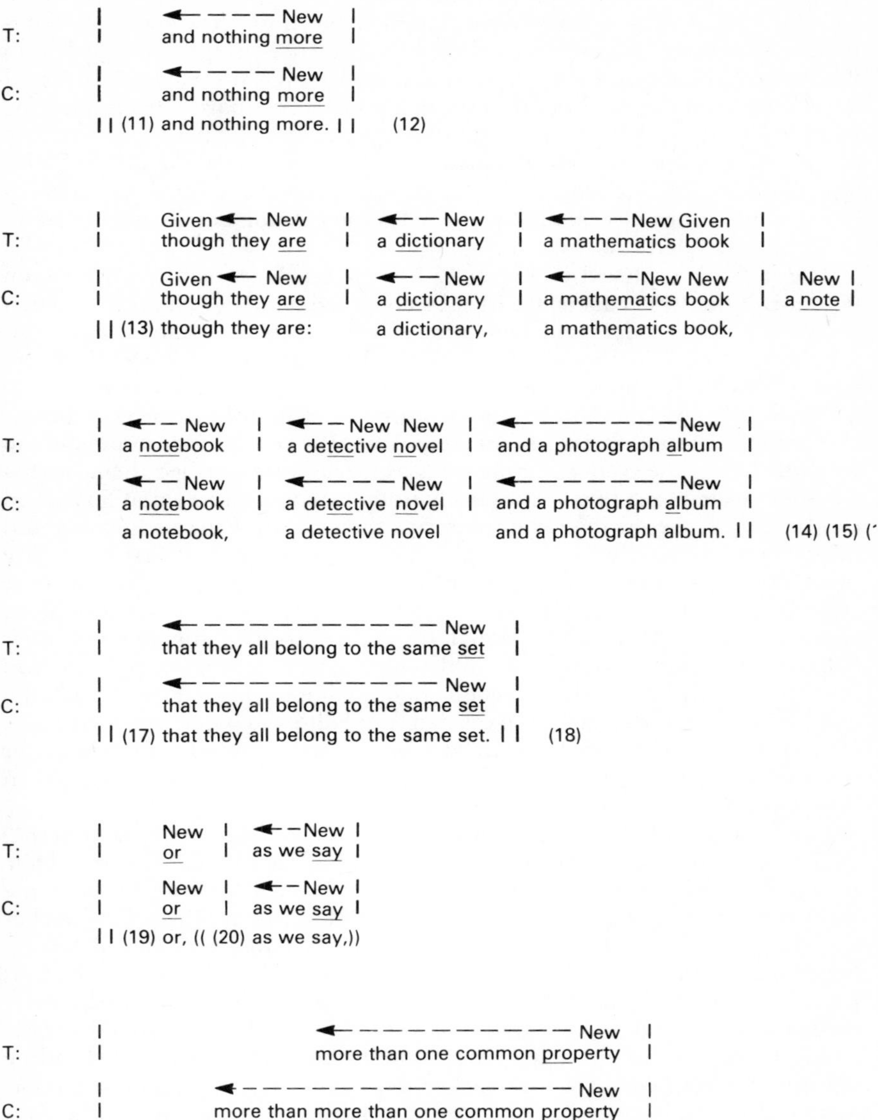

Figure 12.2 Partial transcription of 'Section I Sets' read by the teacher and by the child.

information unit boundaries, and the underlined syllables are those which carried a tonic. Above each transcription is the interpretation of its information structure. The numbers of clauses omitted from the transcription in Figure 12.2 are shown between those transcribed. To simplify the display, I have not shown the rhythm nor indicated pauses. Nor have I, to simplify the analyses, explained how more than one 'new' focus can be present in a single information unit (for details of the latter, see Halliday 1970: 7–12; also Halliday 1985, Chapter 8); nor have I given my criteria for defining clause boundaries (see Halliday 1985, Chapter 7, for details on the treatment of embedded clauses).

The clauses displayed in Figure 12.2 are those for which the intonation patterns of the two readers are in substantial agreement.[2] The transcription shows that both readers had some difficulty with this text. I am not suggesting that the text is in any way inadequate; I presumed that it was clear and straightforward enough. Nor am I suggesting that the readers are inadequate; in fact, they both show features we might wish to recognize as rather sophisticated, though in different ways. Rather, the first impression to be gained from the readers' intonations as we have transcribed them is what we might expect: reading a completely unknown and unprepared text aloud can be slightly unnerving. The transcript shows both readers repeating and misinterpreting words, and reinterpreting passages which at first sight gave them difficulty. (On my tape recording of the readings, features such as syllable lengthening and long pauses, which the transcript does not reflect, also show this.) Despite the equal unpreparedness of the readers, their behavior does differ. First, the child took thirteen seconds longer to read than the teacher (seventy-two seconds to fifty-nine seconds), even though the child set off at a great rate, perhaps determined to show that he could cope. (The child later had trouble with *philately* [which I had not anticipated or wished] and made some rather long pauses.) Second, the readers differ in how they organize information units.

The teacher identifies forty information units; the child forty-seven. Within these units, the teacher recognizes forty-four elements as new while the child recognizes fifty, and this is presumably what we would expect: the child SHOULD find many more elements new than the teacher. The teacher was unfamiliar with this particular textbook, as I had established beforehand; nevertheless, he was familiar with the ideas it discussed; the child, as I established later, was not. Our comparison of the ways in which these readers gave the text an information structure, however, is confused by some relatively superficial matters. One is that the child reads the heading ('Section I Sets') whereas the teacher does not, and this adds two information units to the child's total. Another is that the child identifies extra elements as new because he misreads, recognizes what he has done as a misreading, and then reads something again, thereby adding extra units. If we eliminate these features, the child has identified only one fewer new element than the teacher, distributed among the same number of information units. The differences which remain are not in numbers of units, then, but in the elements treated as new and as given.

But before we can discuss those, we must note that both readers change their reading behavior in the course of the exercise. The teacher, when he has begun to get the general sense of the text, starts reading rather didactically, emphasizing the different elements he sees as significant to the exposition. So, for example, in clause 15, where the child treats *the set of books in my bag now* collectively as new (thereby accurately reflecting the collectivity indicated in the printed text by the enclosing single quotation marks), the teacher treats *makes, them, set, books*, and *bag* as new as well. Assigning six information units to the single clause containing these elements creates a very marked effect. The child supplies the one clause with one information unit and gives the tonic or assigns as new the item at the very end. In doing this, he is following the general rules for unmarked tonality and unmarked tonicity.

One of the skills of writing, according to Leech (see 1965: 89), is to arrange one's words so that a reader who assumes that the text always requires unmarked tonicity will be able to make good sense of what is read. Through my own research (see Davies 1970), I have found that it is the general practice of not very skilled readers to use unmarked tonicity whenever they possibly can (and sometimes when they shouldn't!). The child in our current study seems to be applying this rule successfully in his interpretation of clause 15. The teacher is using a little more 'sophistication,' which here means 'trying to be helpful.' The child shows elsewhere that he can do exactly the same, but here makes a different judgment as to what is appropriate. The child is 'right' in the sense of following a general rule. The teacher is 'right' because he makes additional elements new with sufficiently good reason for doing so in this context.

The child shows when he is getting the drift of the text by different means than the teacher. As he gets into his stride, the child begins to lengthen his information units. This is a regular feature of reading aloud, often found, for example, as a broadcaster reads through news material. Broadcasters will begin a fresh item with short information units, making nearly everything new, and then gradually lengthen information units as it becomes increasingly possible to assume in any one information unit that at least some of the information in it is known to the audience already, primarily because they have just announced it (see Davy 1968). The child shows that he has mastered this strategy, which benefits the listener, and so shows that, like the teacher, he is—at least in this respect—a GOOD reader. Given that both readers have conventional reading strategies under control, we can assume that differences in the readings of the two are thus likely to reflect differences in their knowledge of the topic, mathematics, rather than in 'reading skills.'

To test this latter assumption, we can now compare the intonation patterns of the child and the teacher clause by clause. We can do this easily because an information unit boundary occurs at each clause boundary, and there are no cases where marked tonality indicates that a tone group extends across a clause boundary. Table 12.4 indicates patterns of tonality and tonicity for all the clauses in the passage as read by the child and the teacher. In the first and third columns of the table, a minus sign indicates

Table 12.4 Tonality and tonicity patterns used by the two readers

	Teacher		Child		
Clause	Tonality	Tonicity	Tonality	Tonicity	Agreement
1	X	X	–	–	
2	++	–––	+	––	
3	+	––	+	––	*
4	–	–	–	–	*
5	+	+–	+++	––––	
6	++	–––	+++	––––	
7	–	–	–	–	*
8	–	–	–	–	*
9	–	+	–	–	
10	+	––	+	––	*
11	–	–	–	–	*
12	+	–+	+++	––––	
13	+++++	––––––	+++++	––––––	*
14	+	––	++	–––	
15	+++	––––	–	–	
16	++	++–	–	–	
17	–	–	–	–	*
18	+	–+	+	––	
19	+	––	+	––	*
20	–	–	–	–	*

X = clause not read.

that a clause was supplied by the reader with one tone unit, a plus indicates that it was supplied with two (and therefore received marked tonality), two pluses indicates that it got a third tone unit, and so on. In the second and fourth columns, pluses and minuses refer to the tonicity supplied for each tone unit in succession, a minus indicating unmarked tonicity and a plus indicating marked tonicity. (Hence, in this display, where tonality is marked in a clause, one more symbol will appear in the column for tonicity than in the corresponding one for tonality.) In column five, an asterisk indicates clauses where the tonality and tonicity patterns of the child and teacher are in complete agreement.

If we now examine those cases where there are differences, we can learn something about 'the different ways the readers interpret the text,' understanding this as meaning 'the different ways in which they assign it an information structure.' We shall look at each clause individually and offer an intepretive analysis after each. Our analysis focuses upon the ways the teacher and the child identify the information structure, as both reveal their interpretations in their intonation patterns.

12.3.2.1 *Analysis of clause 2*

	←———— New	←— New	←— New
Teacher:	we shall use the word <u>set</u>	a good <u>deal</u>	in this <u>book</u>
	←———— New	←———————	——New
Child:	we shall use the word <u>sets</u>	a great deal	in this <u>book</u>
Text:	‖ (2) We shall use the word 'set'	a good deal	in this book. ‖

The child's rapid start is largely 'mechanical' in clause 2. He takes this twelve-word clause in two six-word bites, rather than the teacher's three, and does so in a manner which gives little confidence that he is attending to the meanings; rather, he is trying to decode the implications of the spelling for pronunciation. The 'sense,' at least in terms of information structure, is handled mechanically and literally, although, as it happens, this works well enough. The teacher appears to be searching for understanding of the general direction the text is heading, taking it in cautious nibbles, a phrase at a time, presumably in order to digest them.

12.3.2.2 *Analysis of clause 5*

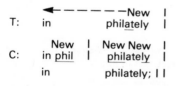

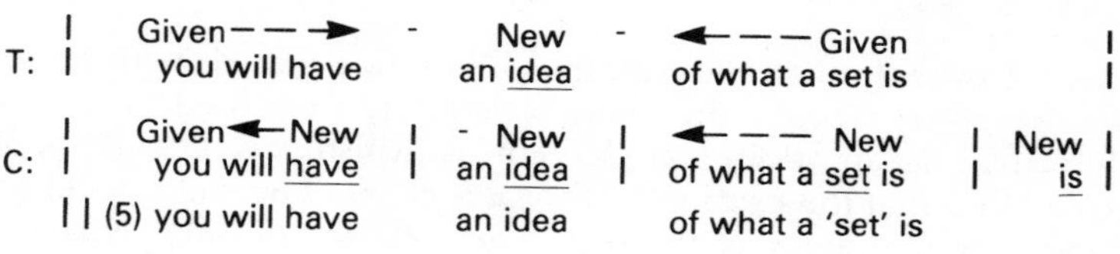

	←—————	—New
T:	in	phil<u>ate</u>ly
	New	New New
C:	in <u>phil</u>	<u>phil</u>ate<u>ly</u>
	in	philately; ‖

In clause 5, the teacher supplies only two tone-groups, but we can see that he is getting the idea that the text is about illustrating various kinds of sets. He shows this by using marked tonicity in his first tone group thereby treating *of what a set is* as given. This is the first instance we have found in this text of given information occurring after the new in a tone group, and it is highly significant for our purposes. The teacher clearly understands that it is the idea of what a set is and not the individual instance which concerns the writer. His tonic choice shows that he also recognizes the semantic chain linking *of what a set is* with the previous phrase, *what it means in mathematics*.

The child in reading clause 5 is in difficulty. He does not know the word *philately* which leads him to repeat *is* and to have two shots at pronouncing this new word. But, even if we ignore | *is* | *in <u>phil</u>* |, as I do in the table, we find that the child still uses two more tone-groups in this clause than the teacher does, probably because he cannot relate the word *philately* to *stamps*, and further because he cannot use the term *set* to relate *stamps* to *mathematics*. The child probably cannot understand how the word *set* belongs in a context which contains both *stamps* and *mathematics*; they have probably been very remote from each other in his experience. (Drawing examples from children's presumed experience may have pitfalls, as is well known.) Yet this is precisely the idea which the writer most wants to get across and which the teacher recognizes to be such. But since the child does NOT spot it, he cannot recognize the relationship between *what a set is* here and *what it means in mathematics* in the third clause, and thus he does not express this cohesive relationship in his intonation by treating *what a set is* as given.

12.3.2.3 *Analysis of clause 6*

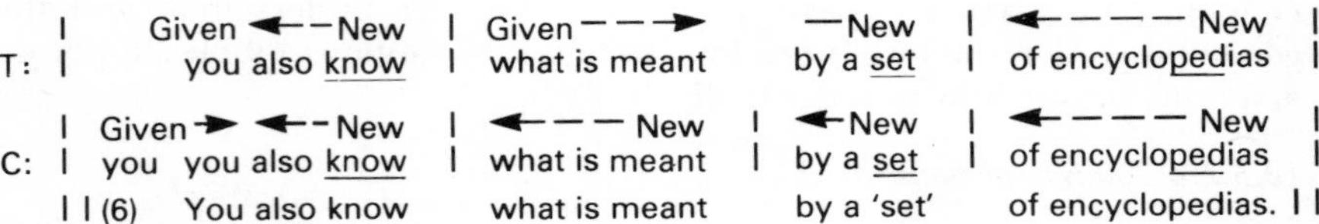

| Given ←–New | Given – – → —New | ← – – – – New |
T: | you also know | what is meant by a set | of encyclopedias |
| Given → ←–New | ← – – – New | ←New | ← – – – – New |
C: | you you also know | what is meant | by a set | of encyclopedias |
| | (6) You also know what is meant by a 'set' of encyclopedias. | |

In his progress through the text, the child now proceeds with rather more caution, assigning clause 6 one more tone-group than the teacher does and therefore treating an additional element as a distinctly new item. It is no surprise to find that the extra item is *what is meant*. The child is still trying to sense the overall strategy of the text. The teacher not only refuses to treat this as an item of news distinct from *by a set* but—well in control now—treats it as given.

12.3.2.4 *Analysis of clause 9*

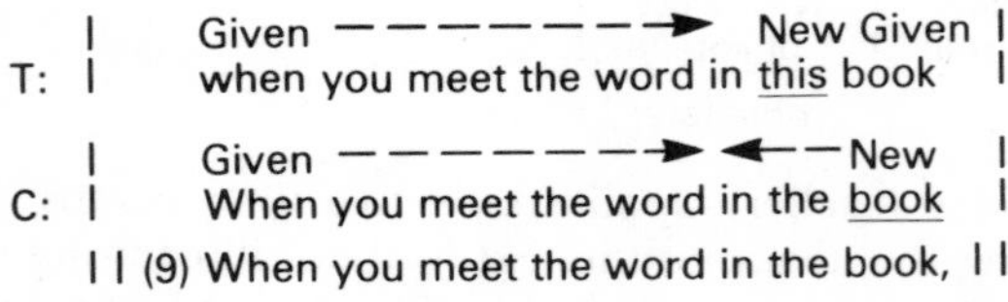

The teacher, using marked tonicity, in clause 9 makes *this* new, whereas the child—following the basic rule—makes *book* new. Marked tonicity signals *contrast*, the precise detail with which the tonic item contrasts to be identified in the context. Here, the contrast is not so much the one between THIS *book* and the encyclopedias which have been mentioned; rather it is the contrast between THIS *book* and any others at all. Although with either *this* or *the*, unmarked tonicity would make sense, the teacher is using marked tonicity to make explicit his interpretation of the writer's probable intention. The writer probably meant: 'The sense of "set" is specific here; it is different from any other (including any hazy preconceptions you may have).'

12.3.2.5 *Analysis of clause 10*

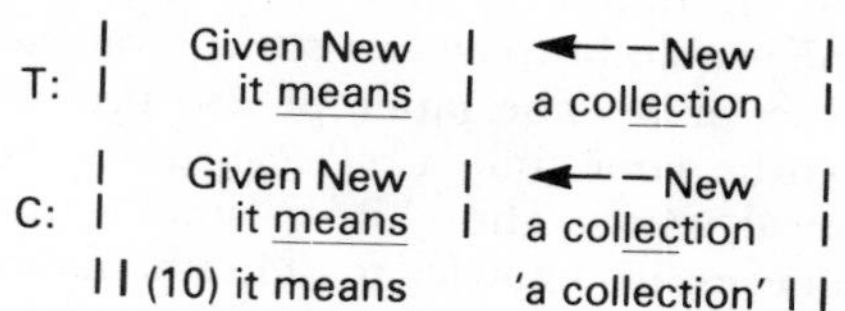

The intonation patterns of the teacher and the child are the same for clause 10; however, their interpretation of this clause is worth noting because the writer introduces here a synonym for the paragraph topic *set*. The trouble with synonyms is that in one sense there aren't any. Even if two words mean *the same*, as in *That's my dad/father*, their usage is by no means identical; one's birth certificate is unlikely to ask for *Dad's Name*, and *Father* as a vocative is now probably much rarer than *Dad*. (Nor are we likely to hear *Our Dad, which art in heaven....*) While providing a synonym to explain a term is not useless, it nevertheless raises the question: 'What is the difference between these words?' This question is bound to arise in interpreting clause 10 because the writer has declared explicitly that his aim is to specify exactly what *set* means in mathematics, an objective which he marked as new by placing it at the end of the clause where it was bound to receive the tonic. By using the synonym *collection*, the author assumes that the reader knows what *collection* means (otherwise there would be no point in offering it by way of explanation). But by relying on what is known to explain what he means, the author is not providing what his whole strategy has presumed is unknown, that is, that part of the meaning of *set* which is different and specific to *set* and not shared with *collection*. This omission causes difficulties for the child in his continued progress through the text.

12.3.2.6 *Analysis of clause 12*

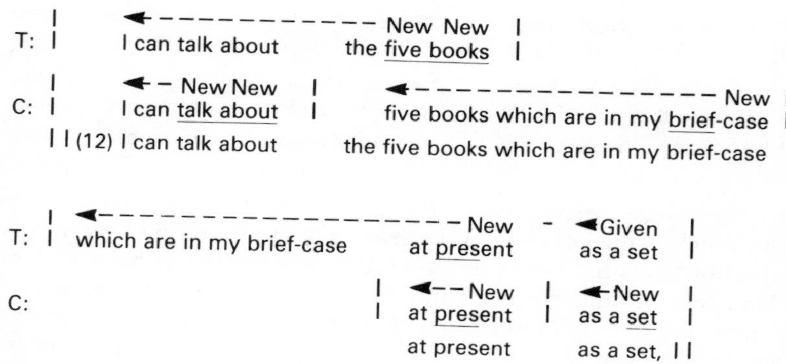

When the teacher gets to clause 12, his knowledge of the subject enables him to appreciate the movitation behind the writer's strategy of offering a synonym for *set*, so he is able to treat *as a set* as given, making *the five books which are in my briefcase* new. The latter phrase provides the example of something which is at the same time a *collection* in the popular sense and a *set* in the mathematical sense. The child is unable to do this, probably because he lacks the necessary knowledge of mathematics to appreciate the strategy and cannot see what the writer is driving at. Very probably he also feels (whether or not he would put it in this way) that the point of a synonym is not only the meaning it shares with another word but the sense in which it is different; so he may have been expecting here not an example of the similarity between the terms but something to show why he should use the term *set* in this unfamiliar and technical sense when it is being suggested that *collection* is a perfectly good equivalent. Further, an example of the difference between the terms is not provided. So instead of regarding *as a set* as given, he makes it new yet again; after all, it is all news to him. He also now adopts the strategy with which the teacher began, taking the clause in relatively short bites, making four elements distinctly new, compared to the teacher's three.

12.3.2.7 *Analysis of clause 14*

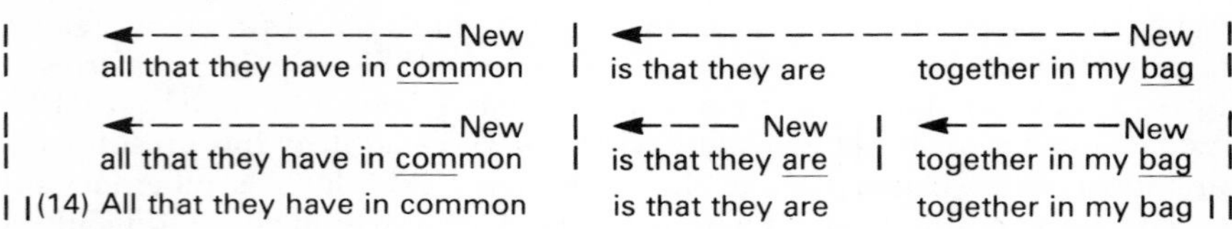

The child again takes his clause a small bite at a time here (not very comfortably); apparently he has not yet got the point. He DOES understand, however, when he reads the next clause.

12.3.2.8 *Analysis of clause 15*

	Given	New New	New New	New	New
T:	which	makes them	the set of books	in my bag	now
	Given ——→		←————		New
C:	and that	makes them	the set of books	in my bag	now
	(15) which	makes them	'the set of books	in my bag	now'.

Here, as already mentioned in the previous section, the child adopts a strategy which is the converse of the teacher's. He shows no lack of understanding but treats his hearer as being as well-informed as he now is himself. The teacher, on the other hand, makes no less than six items in this clause new, the heavily marked tonicity emphasizing each item that distinguishes *the set of books in my bag now* as a specific set as well as stressing *makes them*, which provides the semantic connection between the *set* and *together in my bag*.

12.3.2.9 *Analysis of clause 16*

T:	New — Given	New — Given	←————————— New
	the members of a set	always have	at least one thing in common
C:	Given ——————→	←——————————	—————————— New
	the members of a set	always have	at least one thing in common
‖	(16) The members of a set	always have	at least one thing in common: ‖

The child continues to use unmarked tonality and unmarked tonicity in reading clause 16, while the teacher uses not only marked tonality but also marked tonicity, persistently emphasizing contrast to guard against any confusion between the specific sense of *set* in this context and any other sense with which it might be confused (or even adulterated). This sense of contrast is effected by the tonics on *members* and *always*.

12.3.2.10 *Analysis of clause 18*

T:	←————————— New	Given -- New ←——————— Given
	most of the sets you will meet	will have more than one thing in common
C:	←————————— New	←————————————— New
	most of the sets you will meet	will have more than one thing in common
‖	(18) Most of the sets you will meet	will have more than one thing in common ‖

In their readings of clause 18, the child and the teacher agree about a need for marked tonality, probably because the clause is on the long side and also because the subject occupies nearly half the clause (seven out of its fifteen words). Yet only the teacher spots the need for contrast between having *one thing in common* and having *more than one thing in common*, which he expresses by giving *more* the marked tonic.

12.4 EVALUATION AND CONCLUSIONS

In the ordinary contexts in which we read, different readers make different sense of the same text; by 'sense,' we mean the 'information structure' they interpret. Not only do different readers assign different information structures to a text, but they also do so in the light of their understanding of the meaning of the text as a whole. The particular pattern of intonation supplied by a reader is therefore not a peripheral adjunct to the text but an interpretation of its total semantic structure.

In one sense, all that I have said is simply an elaboration of what is meant by the phrase 'reading for meaning.' But it is also an attempt to make the meaning of this concept more specific and to show the role of information structure in text comprehension. Children who (in the phrase complementary to 'reading for meaning') are merely 'barking at print' are not being utterly meaningless; they are revealing, in fact, their inability both to understand and to express an understanding of that part of the meaning which makes the text hang together as a text or creates TEXTURE.

Texture is signaled in written text by theme and cohesive devices as well as intonation (for an explanation of 'texture,' see Halliday and Hasan 1976, and see especially pp. 271 and 325 for an indication of the role of intonation in creating it). Although theme and cohesive devices are important to the creation and understanding of texture, intonation is perhaps more significant for those who are learning to read and write because its lack of representation in the writing system makes it harder to grasp. Despite the central role of intonation and its ambiguous representation in writing, it receives little attention in the teaching of written English. For every article on intonation and writing (there are very few, and I have yet to find a complete book), there are several thousand on spelling and pronunciation, matters which are important in grasping the meaning of lexical items, but have nothing to do with how items can combine to mean as texts. Yet children have to master the way intonation works overtly in speech AND implicitly in writing. Perhaps the problems in achieving mastery of the second should get more attention, but not so much that we feel compelled to give students detailed descriptions of intonation (although they enjoy this). Rather, we should attend to intonation in the classroom as it helps students address at least one set of problems in mastering the writing system.

I can suggest here little more than a bare outline of what can be done. Little of it is new in itself; rather, most is good classroom practice, however rare it may be, developed by good teachers who have gone ahead of explicit theory. First, we should make use of the many resources we have commonly available to teach intonation in the classroom. The tape recorder now makes it much easier to enable children to listen both to themselves and to others reading their own writing aloud, thereby gaining insight not only into their own successes and failures but also into the reasons for the failures. (They will often be ahead of us in seeing remedies, too; what they write is, after all, as much their own as their speech is.) Focused listening has been shown to be very useful indeed in the teaching of English as a foreign language. Techniques such as those suggested by Dickinson and Mackin (1969) could be adapted, re-directed, and elaborated in the context of the teaching of the mother tongue.

The fact that further research is urgently needed should not stop us from applying what we already know about the role of intonation in writing. As noted earlier, Leech suggests that one of the skills of writing is to arrange one's words by putting the tonic at the end of a tone-group (unmarked tonicity) so that a reader will be able to make good sense of what is read. Yet Leech's point needs refinement: it is not enough to say that writers should so structure their text that unmarked tonicity is appropriate because it is very clear that good writers do not always do this. Competent readers, moreover, not only recognize when a text requires marked tonicity but can also identify which of the possible marked tonicities will be appropriate. Information of some sort in the text enables them to do so. At the moment, we can only surmise that the information involved has something to do with cohesion and coherence, but we do not know in any detail how they work. Any guidance about good writing which fails to recognize as much will be misleading.

Nevertheless, Leech's point is a useful starting point for understanding the learning problems children actually face in achieving literacy. It can alert us to cases where we may perceive, once we are aware of the possibility, that unmarked tonicity is INappropriate. Our small experiment suggests additional starting points.

We have shown how the use of synonyms affects a reader's understanding of which tonicity is needed and that a writer can, to some extent, indicate what tonicity is required by using synonyms appropriately. ('Lexical cohesion,' generally, is certainly relevant [see Halliday and Hasan 1976, Chapter 6].) Moreover, we have shown what reading aloud can reveal about a reader's understanding of the informational meaning implied. A child may hesitate because he or she finds the pronunciation of an individual word difficult, but also the child may not understand the semantic relationship between a word or phrase and a preceding one and so does not know whether to treat it as given or not. And this problem has a bearing on understanding a text as a whole; achieving an appropriate intonation is not just a 'top-dressing' to be applied to the textual cake once it has been cooked but a matter of digesting its nourishment.

We need not suppose that assigning the correct intonation is either easier or harder for a child than pronouncing individual words. We might argue that it is harder in that a word, once learned, may be remembered, but the intonation of a particular passage, once learned, is only a particular application of general principles which have to be re-applied afresh every time one reads a new text. It is teaching children how to apply these principles that remains the challenge for the classroom teacher.

The complex task of teaching reading and writing is not insuperable. Many do, after all, succeed in learning to read and write. Perhaps the most productive way to achieve a better understanding of how they do is to take pupils into our confidence and explore the difficulties of understanding written English along with them. Exploring the new territory of intonation in writing is perhaps one way to do so.[3]

NOTES

1. My account of intonation is derived entirely from Halliday (1967a and 1970), and I owe him a great personal debt, which it is a pleasure to acknowledge, for much help and insight over a number of years. He is, however, in no way responsible either for any errors in my presentation or for the (deliberate) banality of my examples.
2. I have also included clause 1 which the child read, but the teacher did not.
3. I wish to thank the Andrew Carnegie Trust for the Universities of Scotland for a grant which in part supported research for this chapter. I am also indebted to Dr John Stewart, Senior Lecturer in Biology at the University of Stirling; Geoffrey Giles, Lecturer in Education (Mathematics) at Stirling University; and Willie Elliot, of Newcastle, for their help in recording readings for me.

BIBLIOGRAPHY

Davies, H. M. P. (1970), 'A Comparison of the Intonations Used by Twelve Readers of a Short Story,' M.A. thesis, London, University College.

Davy, D. A. (1968), 'A Study of Intonation and Analogous Features as Exponents of Stylistic Variation, with Special Reference to a Comparison of Conversation with Written English Read Aloud,' M.A. thesis, London, University College.

Dickinson, L. and Mackin, R. (1969), *Varieties of Spoken English*, Workbook and Tapes, London, Oxford University Press.

Halliday, M. A. K. (1967a), *Intonation and Grammar in British English*, Janua Linguarum, Series Practica 48, The Hague, Mouton.

Halliday, M. A. K. (1967b), 'Notes on Transitivity and Theme, Part 2,' *Journal of Linguistics*, 3, 199–244.

Halliday, M. A. K. (1970), *A Grammar of Spoken English: 2 Intonation* (with set of tapes), London, Oxford University Press.

Halliday, M. A. K. (1985), *An Introduction to Functional Grammar*, London, Edward Arnold.

Halliday, M. A. K. and Hasan, R. (1976), *Cohesion in English*, London, Longman.

Leech, G. N. (1965), *English in Advertising: A Linguistic Study of Advertising in Great Britain*, London, Longman.

13 Writing in schools: generic structures as ways of meaning

Frances Christie
Deakin University

13.1 LEARNING TO WRITE AND TO MEAN

When we learn to write, we learn ways of meaning or ways of organizing experience, information, and ideas in distinctively different language patterns. Meaning is REALIZED in language. Of course, we also make meaning in other ways, such as through dance, music, and art. All of these ways of meaning differ from culture to culture and within cultures. They also change over time, for the various ways to organize and deal with experience are created socially and thus subject to constant change.

Successful participation in one's culture involves learning to interpret and employ its ways of meaning. This view has important implications for general education. Schooling is typically thought of as a process by which children are socialized into patterns of knowledge, methods of working, and ways of behaving that are held to be relevant to subsequent participation in the wider society. The ways of behaving valued in schools and in other social institutions are varied and complex. Schools reward and promote the behavior of some children more than others, and children master with varying degrees of proficiency the social and mental behaviors valued by schools—behaviors such as developing methods of reasoning, habits of working, styles of argument, ways of judging and valuing, and skills of analyzing and synthesizing information.

Such behaviors are reflected in particular ways in the codified patterns of spoken and written discourse. Where children fail in schools, they actually fail to interpret, respond to, and manipulate the patterns of spoken and written discourse which successful school participation really requires. This conclusion is widely supported by a number of studies in different parts of the world.

In Britain, for example, both Bernstein (1973) and Halliday (1973) drew attention to the close relationships among children's sociocultural contexts, associated patterns of behavior (including language use), and their participation in schools. In America, Lemke (1982) and Heath (1983) have pointed to the very intimate relationship between children's patterns of language and their performance in schools. In Australia, Harris (1980) and Walker (1981) have concluded that Australian Aboriginal children frequently adopt ways of working and patterns of discourse ('cognitive styles,' to use Harris's term [1980: 22, 186]) which are not congruent with the patterns of working and of discourse adopted by their white teachers.

Though the evidence for relationships between patterns of discourse and ways of learning in schools is strong, many teachers continue to work with students in a manner which effectively denies the relationship. Where this happens, children DO in fact fail; that is, they do not develop the skills, capacities, and understandings which an education is intended to provide. Their failure is often rationalized: the children have 'little motivation' or 'poor cognitive abilities,' they 'lack concentration,' or they have 'limited intelligence.'

Such descriptions are not very helpful as judgments of children's performance; they offer little useful basis for corrective action. On the contrary, such descriptions endorse a view that the children so described are ineducable and beyond the capacity of schools to help.

Children learn both the skills that schools value and the language used to demonstrate those skills. The extent to which they learn these things is dependent upon the extent to which school programs are designed to make the learning possible. Teachers must design programs in such a way that all children gain access to the various forms of discourse required to demonstrate what they know and can do. That teachers do not typically see the matter in these terms is not in itself remarkable, for teachers share the attitudes of the wider community, viewing students' mental capacities and abilities as independent from the patterns of language in which these abilities are actually expressed. Many teachers tend to look beyond or past language, as it were; they tend to imagine that independently operating cognitive abilities control the ways students perform in school and that these abilities by their nature cannot change. Teachers need to be more sensitive to the significance of school language and to the discourse patterns which students must learn to interpret and produce in order to succeed in school.

In this chapter, I address some of the issues involved in understanding the use of school language in school learning. I examine first some of the abilities which several school subjects seek to develop, arguing that where children are successful in developing these abilities, their success is most apparent in the kinds of texts, spoken and written, they produce. I examine next three examples of children's writing, suggesting that the actual linguistic organization of each represents the writer's attempt to come to terms with a culturally significant way of meaning or GENRE, where the latter term refers not merely to those forms of writing normally valued in literary studies, but also to the expository forms or genres used to construct meaning in the various school disciplines.

13.2 SKILLS, CAPACITIES, AND ATTITUDES VALUED IN A CONTEMPORARY SCHOOL EDUCATION

While acknowledging the cultural differences between English-speaking countries, we can identify a number of commonalities in the skills, abilities, and attitudes which schools in most of these countries aim to develop. For example, English language arts in the primary school and English studies in the secondary school aim to develop confidence and independence in expression of personal opinion as well as the abilities to communicate ideas clearly, to listen critically to others, to exercise discriminating judgments about literature and other media, and to write in a variety of ways, including creating original literary pieces. Such goals are reflected in curriculum guidelines for language arts throughout Australia, for example, and permeate guidelines for other school subjects there as well.

One guideline statement from an Australian primary language arts curriculum suggests that children should be encouraged to 'express their opinions, ideas, feelings, and reactions' and should be given 'opportunities for logical ordering of thought and speech.' The statement also suggests that writing is 'a means of both self exploration and communication,' that children should 'write freely and often about interests, experiences and activities,' and that they should learn to 'write in different prose and verse forms to suit their purpose' (Education Department of South Australia, 1978: 21, 31, 32). A primary science curriculum document claims that, in studying science, children should develop independence, discrimination, and originality. They are to 'investigate their world in an ordered way,' and they should, among other things, develop 'skills in observing, measuring, classifying, questioning, experimenting, planning, recording, concluding, and communicating.' In the process of developing these skills, they should also learn 'to be original, persistent, open-minded, objective, independent,' and so on (Victorian Department of Education, 1981: 2, 6, 4). According to a guideline document from a primary social science curriculum, students should 'develop understandings of human relationships' and of 'the various patterns of interdependence in society' and, in learning to become responsible and independent, they should develop 'thinking processes' as well as 'attitudes, feelings and sensitivities' (Queensland Department of Education, 1978: i–ii).

Overall, Australian curricular statements and school programs in many subject areas show similar concerns that students develop abilities to think, to question, to communicate, and to investigate, as well as patterns of working associated with these skills. Of course, emphases differ depending upon content area. Nevertheless, the generalizations about abilities, skills, and attitudes to be developed in the study of several different subjects bear a strong relationship to one another.

These skills in methods of working, reasoning, arguing, valuing, and investigating are frequently talked of in a manner which suggests they have an identity independent of the behavioral forms or patterns in which they find expression, including language. Language and its relationship to learning is in an odd sense 'invisible.' It is the resource for learning which we most frequently use, yet most take for granted. Thus, when teachers choose what they intend their students to learn, they tend to focus upon 'content,' 'knowledge,' or 'ideas'—all conceived of as matters which exist independently of language use. They believe that if students get the 'content' right, their language will in some fashion fall into place after it. Yet what do the terms 'content,' 'information,' or 'ideas' really mean?

I believe such terms refer in a very general way to complex sets of understandings and to methods of posing questions and investigating them. Both are realized in distinctive patterns of discourse. A 'content area,' a 'school subject, ' 'a body of knowledge,' or a 'set of ideas' may be recognized as a particular way of defining phenomena, of addressing and answering questions; its distinctive features are realized in characteristic language patterns. When teachers and students speak or write in school, they are constructing the meanings about human experience and endeavor that educational systems ascribe to the CONTENT AREAS.

Halliday (1975) first suggested that learning one's mother tongue is a process of 'learning how to mean'—a suggestion made out of a study of one young child's early language development. In learning to use one's mother tongue, one learns to construct text as a part of the process of learning to negotiate and to build relationships, understandings, attitudes, and points of view. The latter constitute the various kinds of content expressed in language, and both in speech and in writing, the nature of a text varies according to the kind of content involved.

What are the educational implications of this perspective on language learning? Two implications seem to me particularly important:

- Students in the process of learning content must manipulate different ways of constructing and organizing meaning in texts.
- Teachers must recognize the linguistic demands associated with the content areas of schooling, so that they may guide students more usefully in their learning.

These implications are very important when we consider the kinds of writing tasks students commonly must complete when learning different subjects. Learning to write in science, social studies, or literary studies is a matter of learning to distinguish the different generic structures associated with each field.

In my view, such an understanding does not inform practices in teaching writing at any level of education. On the contrary, two misguided emphases, both of them largely unhelpful to students, have tended to prevail in writing instruction for a long time. The one, associated in particular with teaching writing in English classes, advocates creativity or self-expression; proponents of 'creative' writing claim that student writers need plenty of scope to express themselves as they wish, with minimal direction. The other view of writing, found most commonly in subjects other than English, ignores language altogether, suggesting that what matters in writing is the information or content. The former view fails to acknowledge how people become creative or self-expressive: they do so through manipulating many culturally significant linguistic patterns and playing with various genres. The latter view of writing is unsatisfactory because it subscribes to a belief in the supposed independence of form and content. Meaning or content is realized in language. Students who struggle to make sense of content in writing are actually struggling to develop the language necessary to achieve an appropriate mastery of it.

We can discover insightful ways to view language learning by examining children's writing as it reveals their efforts to mean. I have analyzed here three examples of children's written discourse, drawing primarily upon systemic linguistic theory as discussed by Halliday (1985) and Martin and Rothery (1980, 1981). The first writing sample is an early narrative by a child, aged 7, in Grade Two; the second an early scientific essay by a child, aged 10, in Grade Five; and the third a literary character-study by a child, aged 13, in his second year of high school. Each represents an attempt to create a particular, valued form of constructing meaning in language; that is, each represents a different genre in written English. These genres are representative of those that schools require children to learn. Through learning to write in such genres, children develop many of the abilities, skills, and forms of knowledge which mark them as educated persons. The more precise teachers can be about generic features, the better they will guide their children in a successful educational experience.

13.3 WRITING IN THE PRIMARY SCHOOL LANGUAGE ARTS PROGRAM: AN EARLY NARRATIVE TEXT

The narrative is among the genres most valued in primary schooling. Much of the early reading experience of children in primary language arts programs involves reading stories, and teachers frequently ask fairly young children to write their own stories.

The story of 'the kangaroo who lost its tail' which appears in Figure 13.1 was written by Loretta, aged 7, in Grade Two. No one educated in schools in English-speaking countries would have any difficulty identifying this text as a story. The fact that we can identify it so readily is in itself significant. We do so because, as successful participants in a culture which values story-telling, we recognize its familiar generic structure, a way of constructing meaning in language.

A long time ago there was a kangaroo who did not have a tail and all the animals laughed at him and that made him sad. How did he get it back? he got it back by dipping his tail into lolly-pop siarp [syrup]. The animals started to like him and then thay played with him. Would you like it? I would not because it would be most annoing.

The End

Figure 13.1 Early narrative text (verbatim)

Consider first of all the schematic structure of the text in Figure 13.1:

- ORIENTATION—'A long time ago there was a kangaroo who did not have a tail. . . .'
- COMPLICATION—'. . . and all the animals laughed at him and that made him feel sad.'
- RESOLUTION—'How did he get it back? he got it back by dipping his tail into lolly-pop siarp. The animals started to like him and then thay played with him.'
- CODA—'Would you like it? I would not because it would be most annoing. The End.'

My breakdown of the schematic structure of the 'kangaroo' story reflects the research of Labov and Waletzky (1967) on the spoken narrative as adapted by Martin and Rothery (1980, 1981 [see also Martin and Rothery in this volume (ed.)]). As Martin and Rothery claim, narratives provide first, an orientation that introduces characters in a setting and establishes a sense of time; next, complication(s) in the action and, ultimately, resolution(s); and last, a coda, which brings the story to an end, and often, although not always, gives the storyteller's evaluative comment. A simple analysis will serve to demonstrate more fully how the various linguistic elements of the early narrative text in Figure 13.1 contribute to its overall schematic structure.

Table 13.1 displays CONJUNCTIONS and THEMES in the early narrative. Clause numbers and linking conjunctions (in boldface) are displayed on the left; clauses with conjunction (in boldface) and theme underlined are

Table 13.1 Conjuction and theme early narrative text

Clause number with linking conjunctions	Clause with conjunction and theme (underlined)
1	a long time ago there was a kangaroo
2	who did not have a tail
and	
3	**and** all the animals laughed at him
and	
4	**and** that made him sad
5	how did he get it back
6	he got it back by dipping his tail into lolly-pop siarp
7	the animals started to like him
and	
8	**and** then thay played with him
9	would you like it
10	I would not
because	
11	**because** it would be most annoing

displayed on the right. This scheme shows at a glance not only the conjunctions used, but also their distribution throughout the text. In this and succeeding tables, the term 'conjunction' refers to those language items which conventionally have the grammatical role of conjunctions, namely, that of tying clauses together. The term 'theme,' drawn from systemic linguistic theory (Halliday, 1985), refers to the message that the clause is concerned with or what it is about (see Eiler in this volume [ed.]). In English, theme tends to come first in a clause, and it may be realized by any of a number of grammatical structures. (For example, in the sample early narrative, themes are realized by the structures having different grammatical status: the phrase *a long time ago*, the relative pronoun *who*, the nominal group *all the animals*, and the demonstrative pronoun *that*.)

Table 13.1 displays one measure of the simplicity of the sample early narrative: its constant use of one conjunction *and* (though *because* appears in the final clause). The opening theme is a cliché in children's stories—*a long time ago*; nevertheless, it has the function of establishing a temporal sense. Subsequent temporal sequence is established by the conjunction *and* in two places where it has an implicit sense of *then*: *and [then] all the animals laughed at him and [then] that made him sad*; and in one place where *then* is explicit: *the animals started to like him and then they played with him*.

Since narratives deal with the reconstruction of events, either real or imagined, they typically, though not invariably, contain the past tense. This story is told in the past tense, showing that the author has understood the appropriate tense selection. An examination of the EXPERIENTIAL PROCESSES found in the 'kangaroo' narrative provide further evidence that it is a story, albeit a simple one. Experiential processes—'what is going on,' as it were—are expressed in verb structures (Halliday 1985). Since narratives deal with the unfolding of some series of events, they typically tend to have a high incidence of MATERIAL PROCESSES, that is, processes that account for the action of participants in the story (see Martin and Rothery in this volume [ed.]). The text under discussion has only two such processes: *how* DID *he* GET *it back* and *the animals* PLAYED *with him*. This in part explains our sense as readers that the text lacks much in the way of event. Of the remaining processes, one is behavioral: *all the animals* LAUGHED *at him*; two express attribution: *he* DID *not* HAVE *a tail* and *that* MADE *him sad*; and two are attitudinal, one in the main part of the story and the other in the coda: *all the animals* STARTED TO LIKE *him* and WOULD *you* LIKE *it*. Codas typically involve attitudinal processes, for, as noted earlier, it is in this part of the text that the author generally offers opinion(s) about the significance of some aspect of the narrative.

Tables 13.2 and 13.3 serve to illustrate further the simplicity of the 'kangaroo' story. Table 13.2 displays reference chains across the clauses and indicates how minimal are the references to characters other than the kangaroo. Table 13.3 shows cohesion among principal lexical items and reveals that in significant ways the text lacks detail. (By the way, lest you are wondering why the kangaroo stuck his tail in the syrup, Loretta explained that it was so he could stick it back into position.)

Table 13.2 Reference chains identifying participants in the early narrative

Clause number	Kangaroo	Other animals	Reader	Author
1	a kangaroo			
2				
3	him	all the animals		
4	him			
5	he			
6	he			
7	him	the animals		
8	him	thay		
9			you	
10				I
11				

Table 13.3 Cohesion analysis of principal lexical items in the early narrative

Clause number	Kangaroo's tail	Attitudes and reactions
1		
2	tail	
3		laughed
4		sad
5	get back	
6	dipping, lolly-pop siarp	
7		like
8		played
9		like
10		
11		annoing

Why is a functional analysis like the one we have done useful? I suggest it is useful because it focuses attention upon both the strengths and the limitations of the text. It is often very difficult, as we know, to identify in any precise way those linguistic features of written texts which account for their appreciation by readers (see Couture Chapter 4, in this volume [ed]). Yet we can identify features that establish genres. Information about such structures is essential if we are to guide those whom we teach into achieving greater mastery of the genres they need to learn. Such analysis has served to demonstrate that Loretta, the writer of the 'kangaroo story', had a basic grasp of how to construct a narrative genre, and it helped her mother (for whom she wrote the story) to assist her in providing more detail and event in other stories she wrote. Over time, her narratives gained greater length and substance.

My own research of the writing of very young children suggests that learning to write narratives is quite difficult for most young children. Establishing a setting and achieving the temporal connectedness of events is difficult, and even where such matters are partially controlled, young children have trouble handling complications or crises. Rather than writing true narratives, they frequently produce instead what Martin and Rothery (1980, 1981) have identified as RECOUNTS; that is, texts which temporally connect events (frequently, in fact, retelling activities in which the child has participated), but create no real sense of crisis or complication. The writing of a recount, we should note, is a perfectly legitimate activity: it may be a necessary step towards the writing of true narrative.

Teachers should be able to identify the differences between recounts and narratives and hence to help children achieve the more valued genre as they learn to write. As children grow older, they learn to construct narratives of increasing complexity and variety, but at each stage, teachers will need to examine the kinds of generic structures they actually produce in order to ensure maximum progress.

13.4 WRITING IN THE PRIMARY SCHOOL SCIENCE PROGRAM: AN EARLY SCIENTIFIC ESSAY

While the narrative is the favored text in primary English classes, expository texts are expected and favored in other school classes. For example, successful mastery of science involves mastery of the patterns of discourse in which scientific meanings are made, patterns such as technical description, cause and effect, and other expository genres. We can illustrate this point by analyzing a typical student text written for a science class (Figure 13.2).

> 'Sharks'! When people think of sharks they think of harsh, savage fish that attack at sight as a matter of fact they are completely wrong. Although there has been reports of shark attacks these are very rare. Most sharks won't even come near the shore so people swimming near the shore can consider themselves almost guaranteed safe.
>
> Sharks have special sense organs that can sense things up to 1 mile away. The shark uses fins to balance itself and it has to keep swimming or else it will sink. The shark's teeth are razor blade sharp and although you can only see two layers of teeth there are many in the jaw. Usually smaller fish follow the sharks around in hope of gathering up scraps that the shark may leave.

Figure 13.2 Early Scientific essay (verbatim)

In terms of organization, the scientific essay consists of an argument and a description: the first paragraph forms the argument and the second the description. A functional analysis of the essay is provided in Tables 13.4, 13.5, and 13.6. In Table 13.4, dealing with conjunctions and themes, the clauses are arranged in clause groups or units for thematic analysis. This arrangement is better suited for analyzing a text with varied and complex clause structure as it maintains focus on the sentence message in structures with embedded and subordinate clauses. (Compare the simple clause structure of the rudimentary narrative in Figure 13.1 with the more complex clause structure of the scientific essay.) It also allows us to identify readily the theme of each major clause grouping and the conjunctions that hold

Table 13.4 Conjunction and theme in early scientific essay

Unit number with linking conjunctions	Unit with conjunction and theme (underlined)
1	sharks
2	when people think of sharks they think of harsh savage fish that attack at sight
as a matter of fact ['but']	
3	**as a matter of fact** they are completely wrong
although	
4	**although** there has been reports of shark attacks these are very rare
5	most sharks won't even come near the shore
so	
6	**so** people swimming near the shore can consider themselves almost guaranteed safe
7	sharks have special sense organs that can sense things up to 1 mile away
8	the shark uses fins to balance itself
and	
9	**and** it has to keep swimming
or else	
10	**or else** it will sink
11	the shark's teeth are razor blade sharp
and although	
12	**and although** you can only see two layers of teeth there are many in the jaw
13	usually smaller fish follow the sharks around in hope of gathering up scraps of food that the shark may leave

these main groupings together (see Eiler in this volume and compare her notation of theme by clause with Christie's notation of theme by clause group [ed.]).

The thematic focus for the whole text is, of course, established with the opening, *Sharks*. As Table 13.4 reveals, themes are realized subsequently in a range of different grammatical structures: in whole clauses (e.g. *when people think of sharks*), in a phrase (*people swimming near the shore*), in nominal groupings (e.g. *the shark's teeth*), in a pronoun (*it*), and in an adverb (*usually*).

Two conjunctions and one phrase having the function of a conjunction appear in the first paragraph: *although, so*, and *as a matter of fact*. The phrase really has the sense of *but* as it is part of the development of an argument in which the author contrasts his view with that of other less informed people. The effect of all these conjunctions is to sustain and develop the expression of an opinion about sharks. In the second paragraph, three conjunctions or conjunction groupings—*and, or else*, and *and although*—do not support the argument, yet certainly function to tie the paragraph together. Collectively, all the conjunctions sustain the argument in paragraph 1 and the description in paragraph 2. The 'connectedness' does not create the kind of temporal sequence we saw in the early narrative.

The text in Figure 13.2 is written in the present tense, a familiar feature of expository scientific writing, particularly dealing with observations and generalizations about phenomena of the natural world. This is one measure of the differences between texts that deal with very different kinds of experience: exposition (as in this example) and narrative. In paragraph 1 of the scientific essay, the verb choices realize experiential processes of attitude and attribution and in paragraph 2, of attribution and action. The presence of *think* (used twice) and *can consider* in paragraph 1 contributes to the building of an argument, rather than to the statement of fact. Other processes in paragraph 1 involve attribution: *are* in *they are completely wrong* and *these are very rare*. In paragraph 2, some processes involve attribution: *have* in *sharks have special sense organs* and *are* in *the shark's teeth are razor blade sharp.* Others express action: *follow* in *smaller fish follow the sharks around*. Overall, the processes in paragraph 2 identify aspects of shark behavior; no processes deal with opinion or point of view. In short, both the processes expressed and the conjunctions clearly distinguish this text from those classed as narratives.

Tables 13.5 and 13.6 display reference chains and patterns of lexical cohesion in the early scientific essay that further mark it as an expository text. For the purposes of these analyses, the independent status of the clauses in the sample text has been acknowledged; the essay has nineteen clauses in all. The term *shark(s)* appears in both tables to indicate its function both as a GENERIC reference (a reference to a concept that depends on our understanding of the word *shark* in the English language) and an ANAPHORIC reference (a reference to items previously mentioned in this particular text). Generic terms create lexical cohesion and generic references to *shark(s)* appear mainly in paragraph 1 (see Table 13.6). No phoric

Table 13.5 Reference chains identifying participants in the early scientific essay

Clause number	People	Sharks
1		sharks
2	people	sharks
3	they	fish
4		
5	they	
6		
7		
8		sharks
9	people, themselves	
10		sharks
11		
12		the shark, itself
13		it
14		it
15		
16		
17		
18		the shark
19		the shark

markers identify anaphoric relations between these items. Some references to *shark* in paragraph 2 are both generic and anaphoric; those that are or could be anaphoric are cited in Table 13.5.

Extensive use of items having the function of establishing generic concepts supports the process of building and elaborating generalizations, a characteristic of many scientific expository texts. The single lexical item *sharks* is used consistently throughout paragraph 1, save where reference is made to erroneous views of sharks as being *harsh savage fish*. In paragraph 2, the writer introduces the definite article at several points: *the shark, the shark's teeth*, and *the shark*. Both the use of no article and the frequent use of the definite article are characteristic of scientific expository writing, supporting the building of generalizations about phenomena of the scientific or natural world.

Finally, although the author's identity remains hidden in the Figure 13.2 text, he asserts his authority and argues a personally-held point of view that sharks are not dangerous. This authorial claim is supported by references to certain 'facts,' reflecting the requirement for much scientific writing that it be based upon publicly verifiable information. Personal expression of opinion of the kind implied in the coda of the 'kangaroo' story is not accepted

Table 13.6 Cohesion analysis of principal lexical items in the early scientific essay

Clause number	Sharks	Wrong views of sharks
1	sharks	
2	sharks	
3		harsh, savage fish
4		attack
5		
6		attacks
7		rare
8	sharks	
9		
10	sharks, special sense organs	
11	sense, mile	
12	fins, balance	
13	swimming	
14		
15	teeth, razor blade sharp	
16	layers, teeth	
17	jaw	
18	smaller fish	
19	shark	

in scientific expository writing. The experiences or phenomena dealt with in the 'kangaroo' story and the 'shark' essay are, in fact, in marked contrast. While some expression of authorial personal opinion is permitted (if not encouraged) in narratives, it is generally not tolerated in scientific and technical description.

As I noted earlier, one of the skills valued in a science education is the ability 'to investigate [the] world in an ordered way.' In the course of his reading, research, and classroom discussion concerning selected aspects of marine life, the author of the 'shark' essay had attempted to investigate the habits and characteristics of sharks and to construct an ordered authoritative text about them. The text is evidence of his ability to construct a scientific meaning and hence to manipulate scientific knowledge.

13.5 WRITING IN THE JUNIOR SECONDARY LITERATURE PROGRAM: A LITERARY CHARACTER-STUDY

In the upper grades, students are asked to write a number of expository texts that must function in quite specific ways. Often students are not prepared to meet the special requirements of writing assignments in the upper grades, as is evident from our analysis of the text in Figure 13.3, a literary character-study. However, students' failure to meet requirements of more sophisticated genres in part resides in teachers' inability to describe clearly the conventional features of these genres to their students.

Description: Debbie was a girl who wanted to be with the top gang at the beach. She and her friend tried everything to get into the gang. She wanted to be tough and cool and have spunky boyfriends. She always lied to her parents so she could go to the beach. She smoked cigarettes and did the wrong things at school. One day she got into the gang. She was a top chick now. She could get a spunky boyfriend when she wanted. She went to parties and drank alcohol and cigarettes. One day she took drugs and started having them all the time.

Description: Debbie lived in a huge red brick mansion. It was three storeyed and had a built in swimming pool. She hung around with the surfie gang and was cool and tough. The gang spent most of their time at the beach surfing. On weekends they would go out in panel vans to the drive-ins and dark streets. Somtimes they would go to someone's house when their parents were out.

Description: Debbie wrote the book. It was written in the first person and told her feelings and what she did. At first she liked being in the group and being cool and tough aand taking drugs. But after a while she became sick of it and left. She started surfing with her friend.

Figure 13.3 Literary character-study (verbatim)

The author of the sample character study had been reading *Puberty Blues*, an Australian novel about adolescence, while in his second year of high school, and, along with the rest of the class, he was asked by his teacher to write an interpretive essay, a 'character study' of 'Debbie,' the author and major protagonist of the novel. This character study attempts a literary interpretation; it fails in certain specific ways, though Simon's teacher had some difficulty saying why it did not completely satisfy her requirements for this kind of writing.

I suggest the Figure 13.3 text fails because it is primarily descriptive, not interpretive, and its description is very loosely organized at that, as is apparent from the analyses in Table 13.7, 13.8, and 13.9. (In Table 13.7,

Table 13.7 Conjunction and theme in the literary character-study

Unit number with linking conjunctions	Units with conjunction and theme (underlined)
1	<u>Debbie</u> was a girl who wanted to be with the top gang at the beach

Table 13.7 (*cont.*)

Unit number with linking conjunctions	Units with conjunction and theme (underlined)
2	she and her friend tried everything to get into the gang
3	she wanted to be tough and cool
and	
4	**and** have spunky boyfriends
5	she always lied to her parents so she could go to the beach
6	she smoked cigarettes
and	
7	**and** did the wrong things at school
8	one day she got into the gang
9	she was a top chick now
10	she could get a spunky boyfriend when she wanted
11	she went to parties
and	
12	**and** drank alcohol and cigarettes
13	one day she took drugs
and	
14	**and** started having them all the time
15	Debbie lived in a huge red brick mansion
16	it was three storyed
and	
17	**and** had a built in swimming pool
18	she hung around with the surfie gang
and	
19	**and** was cool and tough
20	the gang spent most of their time at the beach surfing
21	on weekends they would go out in panel vans to the drive-ins and dark streets
22	sometimes they would go to someone's house when their parents were out
23	Debbie wrote the book
24	it was written in the first person
and	
25	**and** told her feelings
and	
26	**and** what she did
27	at first she liked being in the group and being cool and tough and taking drugs
but	
28	**but** after a while she became sick of it
and	
29	**and** left
30	she started surfing with her friend

setting out conjunctions and theme, clauses are once again grouped as units for thematic analysis.)

As Table 13.7 illustrates, the essay shows an absence of conjunctions that signal interpretation, such as *because, although*, or *if*. If the reader were to reverse paragraphs 1 and 2, the meaning of the text would not be altered; no connections occur between paragraphs or across the clauses within them. The author fails to construct or develop an argument as is required in this kind of writing. He instead recounts the details of the novel, an analysis supported by the consistent appearance of the past tense and the large number of material or action processes that function in the unfolding of event. Because his text contains no features that make temporal connections, it cannot qualify as either a recount or a narrative, let alone an interpretive essay.

Some processes in the character study identify attributes Debbie wanted to associate with herself (e.g. she *wanted to be tough and cool*). Others identify her actions and behavior (e.g. she *smoked cigarettes, Debbie lived in a huge red brick mansion*, and *they would go to someone's house*). Most of the processes in the text are, in fact, material action processes; none express attitude and certainly none suggest the writer's own attitudes—for example, his attitudes concerning the book. The writer's failure to interpret explains the absence of attitudinal processes.

An analysis of reference chains in the character study reveals more of the writer's difficulties with interpretation. To explain Debbie's behavior and attitudes, the writer needs to discuss other characters with whom she interacted. In fact, this might be classed as an aspect of 'character studies' which distinguishes them from 'descriptions': one must discuss social interactions as well as personal attributes and activities when explaining the subject of the study. Table 13.8 shows that *Debbie* is the most frequently identified referent; the only other significant referential chain is developed with the *top gang*. This pattern is in a sense defensible; since this is a 'character study,' the principal character concerned merits frequent reference. But these references lack interpretive power because the writer makes very minimal references to other people who relate to the main character.

Table 13.9, a cohesion analysis of the principal lexical items in the text, shows at a glance the large number of items that deal with Debbie's desired attributes, associates, and activities, and the very few that deal either with her reactions and personal development or with the book and its writing—further evidence that the essay fails to interpret Debbie's character.

The conventions of literary criticism and of character study as the student writer is intended to learn them require that some interpretation be offered. In my experience, teachers have considerable difficulty helping their students write literary interpretations. Like the many other argumentative and analytic pieces schooling requires, teachers claim literary interpretation is 'too hard' for many students. Many teachers believe that such writing challenges cognitive powers of reasoning and organization which their students do not possess. Of course, such claims absolve teachers' responsibilities for students' failures.

Table 13.8 Reference chains in the literary character-study

Clause number	Debbie	The gang	Friends	Parents
1	Debbie			
2		the top gang		
3	she	the gang	her friend	
4	she			
5				
6	she			her parents
7	she			
8	she			
9				
10	she	the gang		
11	she			
12	she			
13	she			
14	she			
15				
16	she			
17				
18	Debbie			
19				
20				
21	she	the surfie gang		
22				
23		the gang		
24		they		
25		they		
26				their parents
27	Debbie			
28				
29				
30	she			
31	she			
32	she			
33				
34	she		her friend	

Teachers can experience greater success if they treat literary interpretations as simply particular examples of argumentative and persuasive essays and learn to generalize linguistic patterns that realize these kinds of meanings. If students are given assistance by their teachers in producing the kinds of linguistic structures needed to write in the essay genres, they can then practice the skills of reasoning, argument, and analysis which, as my earlier discussion sought to demonstrate, most school subjects are intended

Table 13.9 Cohesion analysis of principal lexical items in the literary character-study

Clause number	Activities	Debbie's desired attributes	Debbie's home	The book and its writing	Debbie's reactions
1					
2	at the beach				
3					
4		tough and cool			
5					
6	lied				
7	go, beach				
8	smoked cigarettes				
9	wrong things				
10					
11					
12					
13					
14	went, parties				
15	drank alcohol, cigarettes				
16	took drugs				
17					
18			huge red brick mansion		
19			three storyed		
20			built in swimming pool		
21	hung around				
22		cool and tough			
23	beach surfing				
24	panel vans				
25	someone's house				

Clause number	Activities	Debbie's desired attributes	Debbie's home	The book and its writing	Debbie's reactions
26					
27					
28				book written, first person	
29				told feelings	
30					
31	taking drugs	cool and tough			liked
32					became sick
33					
34					

to develop. Thoughtful attention to the linguistic structuring of the essay genres robs the processes of argument, persuasion, and discussion of the aura of mystery that surrounds them. Such activities, valued as particularly 'prestige' forms of behavior in school and university studies, are potentially accessible to all students, provided their teachers make the access possible through citing concrete linguistic features that realize these processes in language.

13.6 CONCLUSION

I have argued in this chapter that, in learning to write, children are engaged in learning to construct meanings. As they do so, they learn to select from the resources available within the language system appropriate linguistic items which are fashioned into different patterns to realize different meanings. They learn that written language texts (like oral texts) differ from each other in systematic ways and that they can use the linguistic patterns of a range of genres to create different ways of conveying experience, information, and ideas.

Children's entry to the various fields of school knowledge and to their associated methods of working and of reasoning requires them to learn certain socially created and valued ways of meaning. These ways of meaning find expression most powerfully in the patterns of discourse that successful school participation demands. Yet many children consistently fail to master the patterns of discourse and associated methods of working which schools are intended to teach. Their failure is frequently treated in terms that suggest the failure is innate; that is, it demonstrates some cognitive disability or incapacity which is not subject to much change.

In fact, as I have sought to argue, failure to master the skills, capacities, and knowledge of schooling goes hand in hand with an inability to handle the language structures necessary to make such mastery possible. Once teachers are clear about the nature of these structures, they will be in a position to guide students' learning effectively. They can then explain to their children that they are mastering new ways of meaning and can draw attention, where relevant, to the linguistic features of the different genres they must learn. Further, they can invite their students to explore and to experiment with the linguistic structures through which meanings in writing are made, thus freeing writing from the needless mystery that sometimes surrounds it.

BIBLIOGRAPHY

Bernstein, B. (ed.) (1973), *Class, Codes and Control 2: Applied Studies towards a Sociology of Language*, London, Routledge and Kegan Paul.

Education Department of South Australia (1978), *Guidelines: R-7 Language Arts*, Education Department of South Australia, Adelaide, Government Printer.

Halliday, M. A. K., 'Relevant Models of Language,' in Halliday, M. A. K. (1973: 9–21), *Explorations in the Functions of Language*, London, Edward Arnold.

Halliday, M. A. K. (1975), *Learning How to Mean: Explorations in the Development of Language and Meaning*, London, Edward Arnold: Baltimore, University Park Press.

Halliday, M. A. K. (1985), *An Introduction to Functional Grammar*, London, Edward Arnold.

Harris, S. (1980), *Culture and Learning: Tradition and Education in Northeast Arnhem Land*, Darwin, Northern Territory Department of Education (abridged by Kinslow-Harris, J. from Harris, S. G. [1977], *Milingimbi Aboriginal Learning Contexts*, Ph.D. dissertation, Albuquerque, N. M., University of New Mexico [see *Dissertation Abstracts International*, sec. A., 1978, **39**, 643–A]).

Heath, S. B. (1983), *Ways with Words: Language, Life, and Work in Communities and Classrooms*, Cambridge, at the University Press.

Labov, W. and Waletzky, J., 'Narrative Analysis: Oral Versions of Personal Experience,' in Helm, J. (ed.) (1967: 12–44), *Essays on the Verbal and Visual Arts: Proceedings of the 1966 Annual Spring Meeting of the American Ethnological Society*, Seattle, University of Washington Press.

Lemke, J. L. (1982), *Classroom Communication of Science*, Final Report for 'A Investigation of the Structure and Dynamics of Classroom Communication of Science,' a project funded by the Research in Science Education Program, Washington, D.C., National Science Foundation, photocopy.

Martin, J. R. and Rothery, J. (1980, 1981), *Writing Project Report, 1980, 1981*, Working Papers in Linguistics 1 and 2, Linguistics Department, Sydney, University of Sydney.

Queensland Department of Education (1978), *Syllabus in Social Studies for Primary Schools*, Book 3, Grades 6 and 7, Queensland Department of Education, Brisbane, Government Printer.

Victorian Department of Education (1981), *Science in the Primary School 1: Providing for Enquiry*, Victorian Department of Education, Melbourne, Government Printer.

Walker, R. F. (1981), *The English Spoken by Aboriginal Entrants to Traeger Park School*, Curriculum Occasional Paper 11, Dickson, A. C. T., Curriculum Development Centre.

14 What a functional approach to the writing task can show teachers about 'good writing'

James R. Martin and Joan Rothery
University of Sydney

14.1 THE TASK OF LEARNING TO WRITE[1]

Learning to write is in many ways a very distracting task for young children. They have to learn to control a pen or pencil, place words in linear sequence, and present these words as well-formed shapes with spaces in between them and the appropriate marks around them to denote the beginnings and ends of sentences. To do these things, children must focus clearly and steadily on the page while they are writing. And at the same time, they must direct whatever they can salvage of their attention toward the meanings they are formulating.

Young writers' struggles to make meaning through writing are most significant because making meaning is the task that makes their writing worthwhile. And to accomplish it successfully, young writers must see much more than mechanics to be at stake and understand the special constraints that writing imposes. For instance, they must understand how a change in mode from speaking to writing involves using new kinds of sentences to make new and unfamiliar kinds of meaning. Children need support in handling this, as in coping with handwriting, spelling, and punctuation difficulties which may be distracting them from their communication goals.

In any classroom, the first stages of learning to write can be most frustrating. Children write very slowly; their pencils often cannot keep pace with the meanings they want to express. Further, they may be frustrated by trying to correctly spell words they want to write. Often teachers want their students to 'get the word right' from the beginning. Children who find handwriting, punctuation, and spelling difficult are likely to miss the purpose of writing—to make meaning—and are also likely to dislike writing and to do as little as possible. Almost certainly, their task is made more difficult than it need be by teachers who require them to learn all writing skills at the same time. Under these conditions, the safest path for children to pursue is to write just a few sentences and to get them right!

Recently, some American educators have advocated that children invent their own spelling for words they want to write but cannot yet spell (see, for example, Graves 1983). They report that children who start to write in this way not only write more confidently but also are able to develop relatively long texts. Of course, some teachers have traditionally taken the 'inventive spelling' approach to writing in the early grades. They have been aware of how important it is for children to keep the flow of meaning underway if they are to gain satisfaction from writing and extend their writing abilities beyond the writing of just a few sentences. But, unfortunately, despite educators' growing awareness of new pedagogical approaches emphasizing writing as communication, too few teachers concentrate upon the child's task to make meaning as he or she writes.

Teachers who resist emphasizing meaning and concentrate on mechanics are often concerned that invented spellings and unchecked lapses in punctuation will become ingrained in a student's writing and difficult to eradicate in the long term. If it is true that children learn spelling and mechanics the way they learn the rest of language, however, then there is no reason for concern. When young children are first learning to talk, the sounds they use and the structures they form are all radically different from those used by adults, though fully systematic in their own right. Research has shown that adults spend very little time correcting such language, concentrating instead on making sense of what the child is saying (see Brown *et al.* 1969). Given time, the child adjusts his or her system to that used by mature native speakers in the same culture. Teachers have no reason to believe that early spelling and mechanical errors will become any more ingrained than 'baby talk.'

An important lesson can be learned from the way adults respond to the child's first attempts at spoken language. Adults typically respond to MEANING; they do not focus on errors in grammar or pronunciation (compare Painter 1984). Young writers, like young speakers, need this kind of response if they are to develop skills naturally. If teachers respond to the meaning of what children write, their pupils should quickly see the purpose of developing spelling and punctuation skills.

14.2 TOWARD BETTER TEACHING OF THE WRITING TASK

This chapter advocates a re-examination of the way we teach writing in the primary grades and recommends a new approach. Our method is suggested by analysis of student writing using a linguistic model that reveals the ways in which the writing means—a model that allows teachers to look at how students learn to write in much the same way that we regard how they learn to speak, in terms of how the language works to effect social interaction. We believe that treating language as a social semiotic rather than as a countersign to thought (see Malinowski [1923] 1949; and Halliday 1978) not only has much to contribute to writing pedagogy but also has consequences for dramatically changing the way primary and secondary educators value writing.

To illustrate our points, we will examine student writing completed in two different writing situations in early primary school. In our research, we make use of functional grammar, discourse, register, and genre analysis developed within the framework of systemic theory (see Rochester and Martin 1979; Fries 1983; Martin 1983 and 1984a; Halliday 1985a; and Halliday and Hasan 1976 and 1985). In this chapter, we will draw upon only one aspect of functional grammar—transitivity—and attempt to relate this to genre. It goes without saying that our approach leaves most of the relationship between genre and language untouched; nevertheless, we have found that transitivity analysis alone can draw some clear distinctions between texts as they express genre (see Christie in this volume for discussion of another method for exploring genre as revealed by a functional grammatical analysis of the text [ed.]).

Genre analysis can reveal the social semiotic to which particular texts respond. Our specific approach to genre in student writing draws upon work by Mitchell and Hasan in focusing on the distinctive staging found in all goal-oriented discourse. Mitchell, in a paper first published in 1957, identified the following stages in buying–selling transactions conducted in Cyrenaica: SALUTATION, ENQUIRY AS TO THE OBJECT OF SALE, INVESTIGATION OF THE OBJECT OF SALE, BARGAINING, and CONCLUSION (1975: 178). In investigating staging for appointment making, Hasan uncovered these: GREETING, QUERY, IDENTIFICATION, APPLICATION, OFFER, CONFIRMATION, DOCUMENTATION, SUMMARY, and FINIS (see Hasan 1977; see also Labov and Waletsky 1967, for a similar stage-like analysis of the 'narrative').

We refer to the stages that researchers have identified in various kinds of discourse as SCHEMATIC STRUCTURES. Sets of closely related schematic structures serve to identify GENRES, for example, NARRATIVE, EXPOSITION, SERVICE ENCOUNTER, or SERMON. We are using the word 'genre' more widely than it might be understood in a literary sense. For us, it refers to the staged purposeful social processes through which a culture is realized in language. These processes may be realized orally or in writing, they may or may not be considered cultural artifacts, and they may or may not be structures of which a speaker or writer is aware.

In our view, genres are realized through register which is in turn realized through language (see Martin 1984a). To illustrate this model here, we draw upon only one aspect of register: FIELD (see Smith in this volume for a discussion of the components of register [ed.]). Following Benson and Greaves (1981), we adopt an institutional view of field, defining it as a set of activity sequences oriented to some global institutional purpose. Examples of fields are cooking, linguistics, tennis, astrology, dog-breeding, and so on. In the texts we analyze, field influences a large number of the transitivity selections, that is, the selections of TRANSITIVE or INTRANSITIVE clauses and the consequent ACTORS, GOALS, and EXPERIENTIAL PROCESSES expressed in those clauses. As our analysis of student writing rely on Halliday's most recent work on transitivity selection (1985a), we offer a sketch of his approach to case relations in sentences here.

Transitivity structures are made up of a process and a number of participants and circumstances. Typical participant roles include grammatical functions such as ACTOR, GOAL, SENSER, PHENOMENON, TOKEN, VALUE, and so on. Circumstances specify background information such as location in time or space, manner, cause, or matter. Unlike traditional case grammarians, Halliday divides experiential processes into three main types: DOING, SENSING, and BEING. These in turn have subdivisions and are expressed through grammatical functions (case roles) which differ from one type of process to the next.

Table 14.1 details Halliday's system of experiential processes and the grammatical functions that express them. Different genres require different types of selection from this system as we note in Section 14.2.1. Further, appropriate transitivity choices, that is, choices of a transitive or intransitive expression that affect relationships between actors, goals, and other participants in experiential processes, may vary from one element of schematic structure within a genre to the next.

Table 14.1 Experiential processes and related grammatical functions (see Halliday 1985a: 131)

Experiential processes	Subdivisions	Grammatical functions (case roles)
'doing'	material behavioral	actor, goal behaver
'sensing'	mental verbal	senser, phenomenon sayer, verbiage
'being'	relational existential	carrier, attribute, token, value existent

14.2.1 Understanding field as it impacts on classroom writing

Throughout a child's education, teachers naturally stress differences in speech and writing that focus upon correct usage, punctuation, and textual format. Often, however, little attention is paid to the ways writing differs from speech with respect to field. Every child's experience of spoken language has involved him or her in fields dealing with personal experience. Children's oral topics are their own worlds, revealing what they do to those worlds and what those worlds do to them. But, with writing, this is not always the case. Some of the topics assigned by teachers do draw upon a child's personal experience in this way: writing about pets, family, playmates, trips, or holidays. But other topics force children to write about vicarious experience, for example, topics like 'witches,' 'dinosaurs,' 'the circus,' and 'space travel.' To write effectively about vicarious experience, children need content to draw upon. An emphasis on certain topic 'themes' in the classroom is a useful way of providing this content. Themes such as 'pets' or 'dinosaurs' or 'space travel' can link all classroom language activities so that reading, talking, and listening provide information for the pupil to use in writing about vicarious experience.

In general, as children progress through the education system, less and less time is spent on developing a field for writing. At the same time, children are expected to write vicarious experience narratives of increasing length and complexity. It is not clear what experience the child is supposed to be drawing upon in order to cope with these increased demands. Certainly, years in school do expose children to more and more fields, in greater and greater depth. But teachers' expectations in this area often far exceed what is possible for most children, given the weak contextual support provided by the school. Moreover, vicarious experience writing is preferred by teachers because it is thought to encourage creativity and imagination. So, perversely, the less contextual support given, the more the child is expected to be original and the more the writing—if successful—is valued.

Of course, all of this has the effect of rewarding children whose experience of fields is in some way richer than that of other children in the class as a result of their own reading, reading to them by parents and siblings, personal experience of trips, and other activities outside the normal run of day-to-day life. The social implications of rewarding children for extra-curricular experience or behavior in the educational system are well known and will not be reviewed here (see Bernstein 1971 and 1973; Heath 1983; and Kress 1985a, which discusses the politics of writing in schools and the inherent discrimination in current language teaching practices). We believe a better approach is to reward students for their knowledge of how written language works to mean in our culture.

14.2.2 Understanding the functions of genres in classroom writing

The ways in which teachers get young children to write may create functional problems for many young writers—problems generated primarily by two conflicting and usually implicit constraints commonly imposed by the primary grade writing teacher:

- the teacher's hope that the student will be 'creative' and 'original' in expression; and
- the teacher's expectation that the student will write in one of three genres highly valued by most teachers, none of which is very conducive to 'original' writing.

We can illustrate the results of these conflicting constraints through an analysis of prose in three different genres written by students from a second-year class (see Figures 14.1, 14.2, and 14.3).

The student texts to be analyzed have a number of things in common as written discourse: each is a monologue (the reader is removed and cannot participate as in conversation) and each is reflective (the trip to the zoo is over by the time the writers sit down to compose). At the same time, the texts are very different from each other. The text in Figure 14.1 makes a

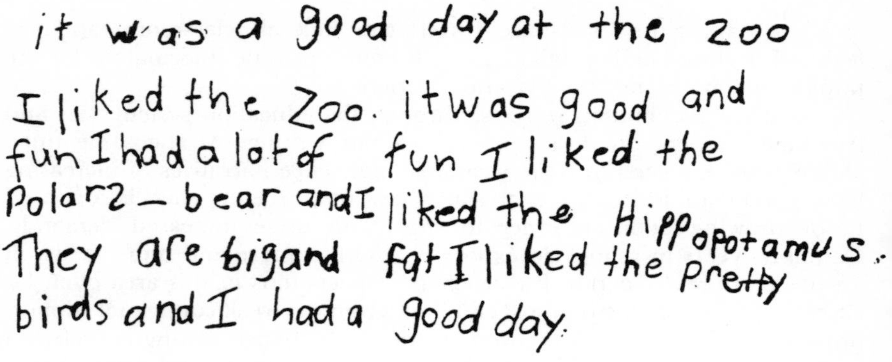

it was a good day at the zoo

I liked the Zoo. it was good and fun I had a lot of fun I liked the Polarz – bear and I liked the Hippopotamus. They are big and fat I liked the pretty birds and I had a good day.

Figure 14.1 Observation/comment text written by second-year student

number of observations and comments on the trip; the text in Figure 14.2 tells the 'story' of the trip—the sequence of events it involved; and the text in Figure 14.3 describes one of the animals seen at the zoo. Each text represents one of the three basic genres selected by children in writing situations as they are structured in the first years of school: OBSERVATION/COMMENT, RECOUNT, and REPORT.

The function of observation/comment texts, as the name suggests, is to express the writer's observations about and attitudes toward his or her own personal experience. This function inspires texts which consist of more or less random strings of observations that are realized through MATERIAL PROCESS clauses and comments that are realized through RELATIONAL PROCESS clauses (being and having) and MENTAL PROCESS clauses (reaction, perception, and cognition). The relational clauses used often contain an attitudinal attribute such as *good*. These varieties of experiential processes are expressed in the Figure 14.1 text, as is demonstrated schematically in Figure 14.4.[2]

Recount texts differ from observation/comment texts in that they focus upon a series of events rather than a set of experiences. Their function is to tell what happened. In doing so, they make use of a number of material and behavioral process clauses expressing 'action' that are sequenced one after the other. This sequence is commonly made explicit through conjunctions like *then, after*, and *before*. (The children's favorite is, of course, *and then*.) The text in Figure 14.2 clearly has a structure of this kind, as is demonstrated schematically in Figure 14.5.

Reports are different again in that they present a description of some object, normally drawn from the child's own experience. But rather than describing this object from his or her own point of view and commenting on it as in observation/comment texts, in a report, the child proceeds more objectively, relating a set of facts associated with the object. Many of these facts clearly transcend the child's own experience and reflect knowledge picked up through reading, films, or class discussion. The text in Figure 14.3 is a good example of this genre; it reports facts about *the bat*,

I went to the Zoo. I saw the snake
and the I saw the boa. constrictor
it was big and thick and the
colour was green and brown.
Then we went to the koala house
and The baby koala and then
we went down and then we
went to see the seals and one
fat one did not go in the water
Then we went to see the
elephant and we gave him
Some biscuits with vegemite
and we went to The lions
and the lion was brown.
We went to get the
Ferry and we sang and we
sang Yellow Bird Mrs
Green sang too. We sang
Mr Postman and then the
boat then we went to catch
the train and we went home

Figure 14.2 Recount text written by second-year student

describing its characteristics and varieties through RELATIONAL and EXISTENTIAL PROCESS clauses and its activity through material and behavioral process clauses. Figure 14.6 provides an experiential process diagram of this text.

Schools do not in general make it clear to children which genre they should use in a given writing situation. Walshe (1981b) suggests that children be allowed to choose their own genre when writing, as if children

The Bat

The bat is a nocturnal animal It
lives in the dark there are long
nosed bats and mouse eared
bats also lettuce winged bats
Bats hunt at nittg they sleep
in the day and are vevy shy.

Figure 14.3 Report text written by second-year student

all had some kind of innate knowledge of the range of genres available. And primary school teachers regularly refer to all of the writing children produce at this level as 'stories,' no matter what genre the child is actually writing in. In fact, in the first years of school, children themselves show a preference for observation/comment texts over recounts and reports, and these texts do not relate a series of events at all, let alone a sequence with some kind of complication and resolution structure (see Labov and Waletzky 1967), as is expected in the 'stories' which teachers prefer.

The genres favored by children and teacher expectations conflict in two ways. First, children's preferred genres conflict with the high value teachers place on creativity and imagination. Both the observation/comment and the recount refer directly to the child's own experience which children tend to record faithfully. (They do not instinctively leap into the realm of fantasy when recounting events.) Report writing, also favored by some children, is factual and antithetical to fantasy. Second, children's preferred genres conflict with teachers' beliefs—often influenced by Britton *et al*. (1975)—that students should write EXPRESSIVELY in the early stages of learning to write. In theory, the term 'expressive' is so ill-defined that it is impossible to assign texts to this category reliably on the basis of linguistic features. But as it is most often interpreted in education, expressive writing would appear to characterize only the observation/comment genre. We have observed in our work that report writing is consistently treated by teachers as less prestigious than recount or observation/comment writing presumably because it is neither expressive nor imaginative. The generic consciousness of educators is so low that we believe many are simply unaware of this prejudice. As evidence, we cite Graves (1983: 134–5) who, without apology, describes directing one child's text out of expository and into narrative genre in a student conference.

How can a child overcome this tension between the genres that teachers require them to access and concurrent demands for creativity and imagination? The answer for many children, of course, is to abandon report writing and concentrate on developing a new genre, NARRATIVE, out of recount writing. The text in Figure 14.7 represents an early attempt by one child to

SERIES OF OBSERVATIONS AND COMMENTS (Units 1-9)			
	1. It (Carrier)	was (Relational Attributive: Intensive Process)	a good day (Attribute) at the zoo (Circumstance Location: Place)
	2. I (Senser)	liked (Mental Reaction Process)	the zoo (Phenomenon)
	3. It (Carrier)	was (Relational Attributive: Intensive Process)	good fun (Attribute)
	4. I (Actor)	had (Material Process)	a lot of fun (Range)
	5. I (Senser)	liked (Mental Reaction Process)	the polars bear (Phenomenon)
	6. and I (Senser)	liked (Mental Reaction Process)	the hippopotamus (Phenomenon)
	7. They (Carrier)	are (Relational Attributive: Intensive Process)	big and fat (Attribute)
	8. I (Senser)	liked (Mental Reaction Process)	the pretty birds (Phenomenon)
	9. and I (Actor)	had (Material Process)	a good day (Range)

Figure 14.4 Schematic structure of experiential processes in observation/comment text (see Figure 14.1)

Stage	Participant	Process	Participant / Circumstance
ORIENTATION (Departure for the Zoo) (Unit 1)	1. I (Actor)	went (Material Process)	to the zoo (Circumstance Location: Place)
EVENTS (Units 2-21)	2. I (Senser)	saw (Mental Perception Process)	the snake (Phenomenon)
	3. and the(n) (Senser)	saw (Mental Perception Process)	the boa constrictor (Phenomenon)
	4. it (Carrier)	was (Relational Attributive: Intensive Process)	big and thick (Attribute)
	5. and _ the color (Carrier)	was (Relational Attributive: Intensive Process)	green and brown (Attribute)
	6. Then _ we (Actor)	went (Material Process)	to the Koala house (Circumstance Location: Place)
	7. and	(saw) (Mental Perception Process)	the baby Koala (Phenomenon)
	8. and then _ we (Actor)	went (Material Process)	down (Circumstance Location: Place)
	9. and then _ we (Senser)	went to see (Mental Perception Process)	the seals (Phenomenon)
	10. and _ one fat one (Actor)	did not go (Material Process)	in the water (Circumstance Location: Place)
	11. Then _ we (Senser)	went to see (Mental Perception Process)	the elephant (Phenomenon)

	12. and _ we (Actor)	gave (Material Process) him (Beneficiary)	some biscuits with vegemite (Goal)
	13. and _ we (Actor)	went (Material Process)	to the lions (Circumstance Location: Place)
	14. and _ the lion (Carrier)	was (Relational Attributive: Intensive Process)	brown (Attribute)
	15. We (Actor)	went to get (Material Process)	the ferry (Goal)
	16. and _ we (Behaver)	sang (Behavioral Process)	
	17. and _ we (Behaver)	sang (Behavioral Process)	Yellow Bird (Range)
	18. and _ Mrs. Green (Behaver)	sang (Behavioral Process)	too
	19. We (Behaver)	sang (Behavioral Process)	Mr. Postman (Range)
	20. and then _ the boat (Actor)	(came) (Material Process)	
	21. then _ we (Actor)	went to catch (Material Process)	the train (Goal)
REORIENTATION (Returning home) (Unit 22)	22. and _ we (Actor)	went (Material Process)	home (Circumstance Location: Place)

Figure 14.5 Schematic structure of experiential processes in recount text (see Figure 14.2)

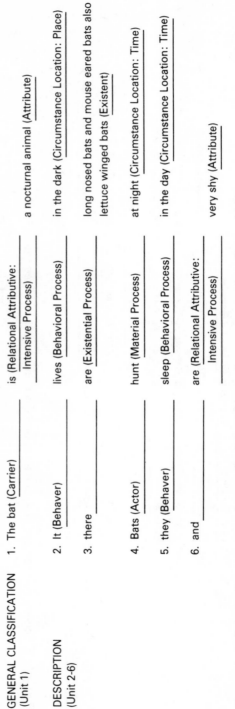

Stage			
GENERAL CLASSIFICATION (Unit 1)	1. The bat (Carrier)	is (Relational Attributive: Intensive Process)	a nocturnal animal (Attribute)
DESCRIPTION (Unit 2-6)	2. It (Behaver)	lives (Behavioral Process)	in the dark (Circumstance Location: Place)
	3. there	are (Existential Process)	long nosed bats and mouse eared bats also lettuce winged bats (Existent)
	4. Bats (Actor)	hunt (Material Process)	at night (Circumstance Location: Time)
	5. they (Behaver)	sleep (Behavioral Process)	in the day (Circumstance Location: Time)
	6. and	are (Relational Attributive: Intensive Process)	very shy (Attribute)

Figure 14.6 Schematic structure of experiential processes in report text (see Figure 14.3)

AT The Zoo.
when I went to the Zoo I
liked the polas bear
I lilhed The ferry he was So nice.
was nicel, and too. the
nice. the monkeys gorilla
one We saw were
houses. snake the snakes
dead had two
and two snakes glass
mice in the cage! had
we were going back to we
when the bears got loose School
Started to follow me, and one

Figure 14.7 Narrative text written by second-year student

accomplish just this. The text was written in the same writing situation as the texts in Figures 14.1, 14.2, and 14.3.

Narrative writing differs from recount writing in two important ways. First of all, in a narrative, something goes wrong. That is to say, the normal course of events breaks down and some problem arises which must be resolved. The text in Figure 14.7 is, in fact, a rather immature narrative: something does happen—a bear starts chasing the writer, but this difficulty is not resolved. (It would be appropriate in this writing situation for the teacher to intervene by asking the child how she escaped from the bear and suggesting she include something about this in a later version of the story.) The second major respect in which narrative differs from recount writing is that a narrative need not relate personal experience. In narratives, the child is free to elaborate upon his or her own experience or even to construct entire texts which deal with people who do not exist and events that never happened. This allows plenty of scope for creativity and imagination, and for this reason, the genre is highly prized in primary school. In fact, the majority of writing situations are designed to encourage writing of this kind, and even when they are not structured in this way, the narrative will consistently be the more highly valued type of writing if produced. Report writing is not generally developed into EXPOSITION until secondary school.

We believe the emphasis on narrative writing in primary grades has little if anything to do with the limitations of children's cognitive development. Children choose of their own free will to write reports almost as soon as they are able to form a short text. We have noted that many teachers feel that expository writing is too abstract and difficult for young children. These teachers appear to be applying psychological theories on the development of formal operations in inappropriate contexts. Research has not shown that such theories have anything to do with writing development or most of language development for that matter. Nevertheless, these theories lie behind some teachers' reluctance to encourage report writing at an early age. Further, teachers' bias toward narrative writing mitigates against the development of report writing into exposition and against the development of writing in other genres as well. Of the hundreds of texts we have examined from primary schools, the vast majority fall on the 'recount through narrative' continuum. This phenomenon, we feel, reflects teachers' tastes, not children's abilities.

The school's view of a good writer reflects our culture's idea of a good writer: a good writer is someone who is creative, imaginative, original and can tell a good story. This is the model that teachers assume, and it is in this direction that schools guide children until they must respond to the exigencies of writing competency examinations in preparation for college writing. Obviously, only a few children grow up to be 'good writers' in the sense defined above. And children of the age group we are considering here are nowhere near able to produce or even understand writing of this kind. Yet this model of writing permeates the education system to affect the very first writing done by a child.

14.3 HOW THE FUNCTIONAL APPROACH EXPLAINS 'GOOD WRITING'

We have posited that conflicts in teacher expectations for children's writing often make it impossible for children to succeed in pleasing them. Conflicts arise when teachers make mistaken assumptions about how 'good writing' functions—assumptions based upon intuitive feelings rather than actual observations of how language features create genre in written prose. We can illustrate our point by taking a closer look at the narrative genre so favored by primary and many secondary school teachers.

Perhaps the most crucial feature of narratives—one which is so crucial that most of us simply take it for granted—is that 'something goes wrong.' When reading a story, we do not expect a routine account of everyday activities. Nor do we expect a simple description of some character or setting. What we do expect is a sequence of events in which something unusual or unexpected happens. This produces a kind of crisis which the rest of the story must resolve. Adapting Labov and Waletzky's terminology (1967) for our own purposes, we perceive four stages in the schematic structure of the typical narrative written for school assignments:[3]

- ORIENTATION—in this part of the story the major characters are introduced and a setting established;
- COMPLICATION—here a series of events unfolds which leads unexpectedly to something going wrong, a crisis;
- RESOLUTION—here, for better or worse, the crisis is resolved, and things return to normal or some kind of equilibrium; and

- CODA—in this final stage of bringing the story to an end, the writer may express an attitude toward the story itself, giving his or her perspective on its significance.

Imitating this structure in itself takes little creativity or imagination, which is what teachers say they expect of good writing. Yet, we have observed that the stories classified by teachers as the best or most successful pieces usually conform closely to a structure of this kind. These texts also tend toward context independency. Characters are introduced as if for the first time. Setting and background information of other kinds is provided. The elliptical sentences which characterize conversation are avoided. All these features have the effect of making the text stand on its own; it does not need to be explained or interpreted for the reader.

The three texts reproduced in Figures 14.8, 14.9, and 14.10 illustrate the points we are making here. They each respond to the same writing situation in a third-year class.

The text in Figure 14.8 was chosen by the teacher as one of the best pieces of writing produced in her class. When we have asked teachers to characterize the qualities of such pieces of 'good writing,' creativity aside, they often reply that such writing displays good ideas which are well argued and clearly expressed. It seems to us, however, that such texts reveal that the writer has mastered the generic structure of narrative writing as it is understood in our culture. The young writer has probably achieved this mastery through a range of language activities: listening to and telling narratives of personal experience as part of everyday conversation, reading stories and having them read aloud, and discussing original stories with the teacher in school. In other words, the writer has learned the structure through social interaction. Mastering a genre involves learning to participate in a part of our culture; what teachers are reacting to when they admire 'good writing' in children's narratives is the writer's control over the schematic structure of the genre.

Let us follow this point by considering a text addressing the same situation and classified by the teacher as average in quality (Figure 14.9). The beginning-middle-end structure which stands out so clearly in the 'good' student writing is far less clear in this 'average' text. Moreover, each of the elements which makes up the structure of this text is developed in a less appropriate way.

The 'average' text begins with a sentence that combines orientation with complication. The *on a summer day my dog* part is comparable to *once there was a dog named Whiskers* in the 'good' sample, while the *my dog got dog napped* complication fills the same function as: *He got run over. because he ran in front of a car. He was very sick after*. The kind of opening used in the 'average' text is characteristic of many kinds of spoken day-to-day narratives of personal experience where a great deal of background knowledge is taken for granted, such as detail on who was involved, where, and the likely sequence of events leading up to the crisis. But in written narrative of vicarious (and here presumably imagined) experience, such a beginning is a little abrupt.

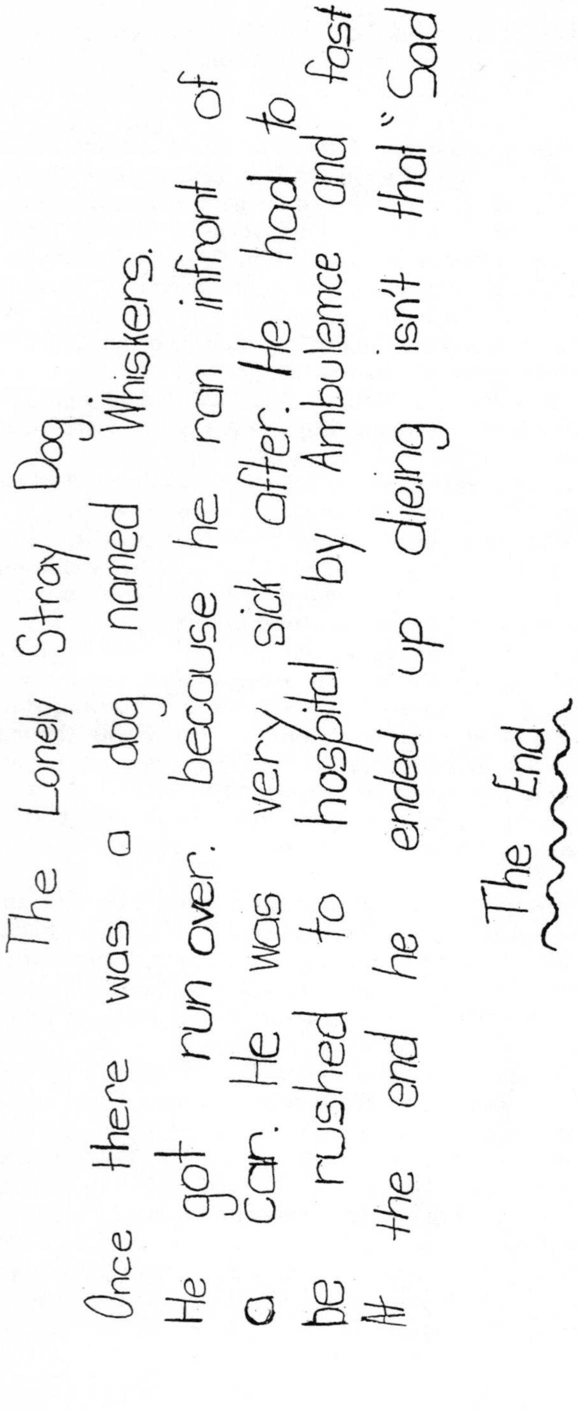

The Lonely Stray Dog.

Once there was a dog named Whiskers.
He got run over. because he ran infront of
a car. He was very sick after. He had to
be rushed to hospital by Ambulemce and fast
At the end he ended up dieing isn't that "Sad

The End

Figure 14.8 Example of 'good writing' as valued by the teacher of a third-year class

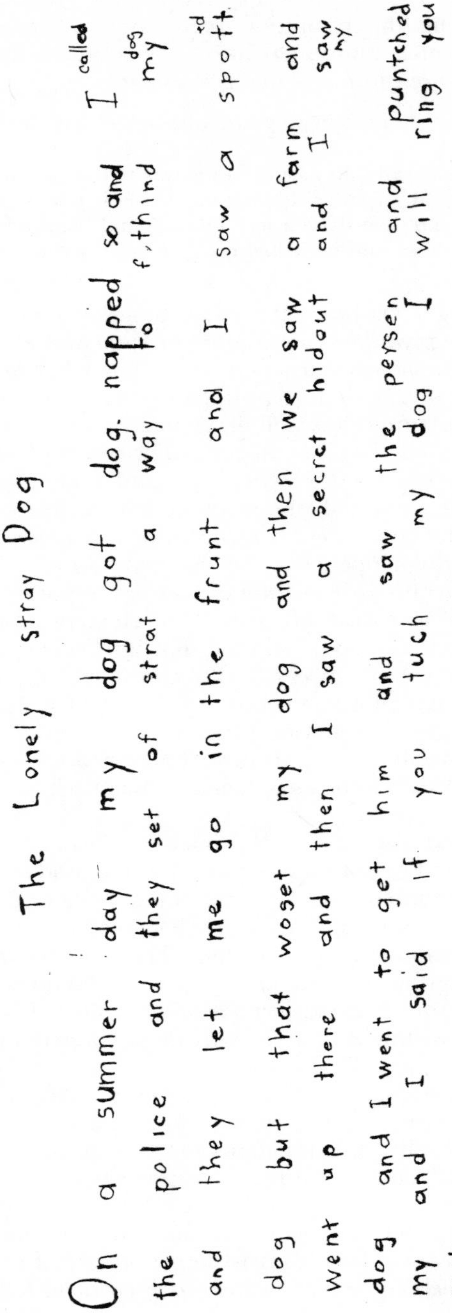

The Lonely stray Dog

On a summer day my dog got dog. napped so and I [called]
the police and they set of strat a way to f,thind my [dog]
and they let me go in the frunt and I saw a spott[ed]
dog but that woset my dog and then we saw a farm and
went up there and then I saw a secret hidout and I saw [my]
dog and I went to get him and saw the persen and puntched
my and I said if you tuch my dog I will ring you
neck

Figure 14.9 Example of 'average writing' as valued by the teacher of a third-year class

The 'average' text is also less satisfying because the crisis comes so early. The events constituting the resolution seem to meander, reflecting the pattern of a recount rather than a narrative. Yet compare the resolution of the 'good' text with the resolution of the 'average' text:

Good—He had to be rushed to hospital by Ambulence and fast. At the end he ended up dieing.
Average—I called the police and they set of strat a way to fthind my dog and they let me go in the frunt and I saw a spotted dog but that woset my dog and then we saw a farm and went up there and then I saw a secret hidout and I saw my dog and I went to get him and saw the persen and puntched my and I said if you tuch my dog I will ring your neck.

If anything, the 'average' text has better ideas than the 'good' text; that is, it has the potential to be reworked into a more original and interesting narrative. But in spite of the fact that teachers say this is what they are looking for, they will regard this as a less prestigious text than the 'good' text because its generic structure is less well developed.

Finally, the 'average' text has no real coda. The quoted speech in the last reporting clause does express the writer's attitude; and for this reason, one might conflate the coda with the resolution there just as we conflated the orientation with the complication earlier. But this expressed attitude is directed towards the dognapper, not the story itself. Labov and Waletzky note that in spoken narrative of personal experience, reported speech of this kind tends to function as a kind of 'evaluation' element that when placed between the complication and resolution has the effect of heightening suspense and reader involvement (1967: 39). Coming at the end as it does here leaves the reader hanging to a certain extent. In fact, the actual return to equilibrium is left implicit: getting the dog back is implied, not stated. Still, the text is recognizable as a narrative. There is a crisis, it is resolved, and the writer produces a text of some length which sticks to the topic he is pursuing.

Consider now the text in Figure 14.10, which is an example of the kind of writing that is considered poor or inadequate, lacking in ideas, and developing little in the way of content. We have noted that texts evaluated as 'poor' are often very short and show that the writer is experiencing great difficulty with handwriting, punctuation, and spelling. (The writer of the sample text even appears to have problems keeping the words of a sentence on the same line.) Moreover, the genre selected in poor texts is often different from the one expected in the writing situation as it is intepreted by most of the children.

The 'poor' text in Figure 14.10 is much more like an observation/comment text than a narrative. The story begins with a brief description of the dog: *he is spoty* [sic]. But this functions more as an observation than as an orientation. The participant referred to by *he* is not introduced, and no setting is given. Of course, the reader will assume that *he* refers to the dog in the title, but this kind of reference is not found in mature narrative writing. Next comes what appears to be the crisis: *he got run over*. But it is not clear whether the events which come next in the text precede or follow this event.

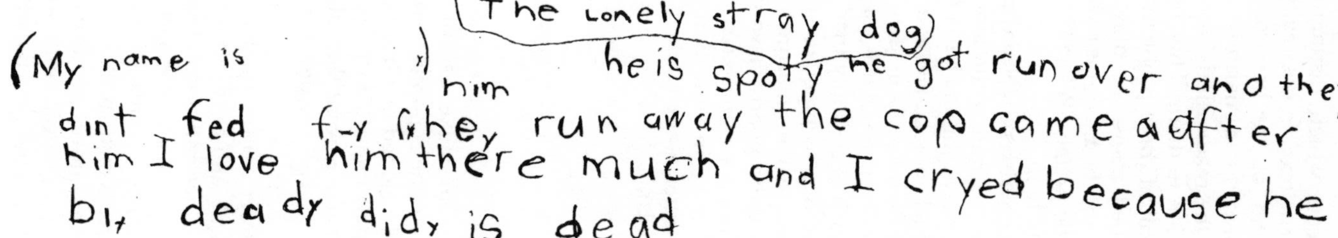
(The lonely stray dog)
(My name is) he is spoty he got run over and they
him
dint fed f-y (they run away the cop came adfter
him I love him there much and I cryed because he
bi, deady didy is dead.

Figure 14.10 Example of 'poor writing' as valued by the teacher of a third-year class

The temporal sequencing of events which distinguishes narratives and recounts from observation/comment texts is not really present. This is, of course, confusing to the reader who, on the basis of the first two clauses, will attempt to interpret the text as a narrative rather than as an observation/comment text. What the reader finds instead is simply a set of observations and the writer's reaction to them. This 'poor' text displays that the writer is experiencing any or all of three problems: he may not understand the narrative schema outlined above, he may not realize that it is required in this writing situation, and he may not have sufficient content to draw upon to develop the genre adequately. Whatever the problem, there is a good deal that a teacher can do to help.

Teachers can help such young writers by learning to distinguish the genres their pupils are writing in and noting the kind of language used to realize each. Unfortunately, genre recognition has not been part of many teachers' professional training. Teachers take few courses that urge them to think ABOUT language; hence, they tend to focus their teaching of language on questions of language usage—the emphasis of their own language instruction as a child. This approach is certainly inadequate. Teachers who do not have a basic understanding of how language works can misinterpret children's use of written language. An uninformed teacher, for instance, might assume that children who write poorly have cognitive or other disabilities when they simply may not have mastered one or another of the written genres which are highly valued in education (see Heath 1983, for a useful account of how children master many kinds of language, though not always ones highly valued in schools).

14.4 PEDAGOGICAL METHODS THAT ASSIST THE FUNCTIONAL APPROACH TO WRITING

Assuming that teachers are able to make use of knowledge about the functions of language to evaluate their pupils' writing, what then? We suggest that the approach being developed by Graves and his colleagues has considerable merit (see Walshe 1981a and 1981b; Turbill 1982; and Graves 1983). Graves has argued that if teachers want their students to develop their writing abilities, then they must make provision for a number of stages in producing a text. Children need time for pre-writing—to explore fields, to gain a sense of audience, to consider written modes, to choose a genre, and so on. Then they need time to draft and to re-write, with frequent opportunities for consultation with the teacher and peers about their progress.

The teacher's invention in the conference stages is critical: in the conference the teacher has a chance to teach, making comments and suggestions and asking questions which guide the student writer in the development of a text. Of course, as Graves points out, the gentler this interaction the better. The child has to remain in control of his or her text—after all, it is the child's meaning that is being negotiated. All along, drafts must be treated as drafts; children must be encouraged to invent spelling, cross out, change things, to write on their work. Writing should not be seen as a 'one draft' process, and only at the publication stage should a polished piece of writing be expected. Overall, this approach has the effect of making the process of writing more like the process of speaking. The isolation which so differentiates the child's experience of spoken language from his experience of writing is broken down because the child writes in a context, interacting with a teacher and peers.

Other educators have made similar suggestions. Britton and his colleagues (1975) cite the need for writers to be given time to re-write and the opportunity to publish their work for other readers. They emphasize how unrealistic we are in expecting children to do what mature adult writers, even professionals, cannot do: write successfully at the first attempt.

What Graves and Britton do not explore—and this is where linguistics has one important contribution to make—is the knowledge the teacher draws upon in order to engage in a constructive conference with the child about his or her writing. In conferencing, teachers are continually making use of their implicit understanding of language. We believe conferencing could be made more effective if teachers had more explicit knowledge about language to bring to this task as well.

Let us consider briefly how we might make use of such explicit knowledge to help in the reworking of the 'poor' text in Figure 14.10. One thing that the teacher could discuss with the child is the false start, *My name is*——. The writer could develop the story two ways, with and without this beginning. Next, the teacher might consider the use of *he* in the second sentence, referring to the dog in the title, and ask who *he* is. And if the student replies, 'The dog in the title,' the teacher could suggest that the child describe the dog a little: whose dog is he? what kind of dog is he? The teacher could then explore with the child the story's setting: where did the dog get run over? and how? This would lead naturally, perhaps in another conferencing session, to problems concerned with the complication, the set of events leading up to the accident: the dog chasing a ball in the street or whatever. At this point, the writer, after possibly having drafted a more elaborate orientation and complication, should find that he has more direction for his resolution; problems solved early in a text often solve problems which crop up later. Finally, the teacher might ask the student to give some consideration to the point of the story: is there a moral to be drawn? what is the writer's reaction to the story as a whole? what were the reactions of his peers? None of the questions teachers pose in a conference session need be formulated in terms that depend on the child having explicit knowledge about language, but they should all draw upon knowledge of this kind. If successful, they will direct the writer to put the crisis in the middle of the story, to add an orientation and resolution, to develop the complication, to insert a coda, and so on.

14.5 CONCLUSION

Teachers can play a number of roles in the development of students' writing. They can be more than critical bystanders. One important role is that of organizing students' writing processes. Children need to be given opportunities to both write and re-write, and they need a chance to interact with their teachers and peers in this process. Another role for teachers is that of evaluating student writing. We do not intend this in the traditional sense of someone who grades and corrects; rather, we mean that teachers must evaluate the stages children are at in developing skill in a genre. They need to be able to note progress in genre development from first draft to final draft and from one writing situation to another over the course of time. Finally, teachers must actually TEACH writing by intervening, positively and constructively, with respect for the child's text. The aim must be to help the child develop his or her meaning—working a text over so that it becomes a better piece of original writing.

A critical factor affecting the teachers' efforts to intervene as evaluators, as we have shown, is their understanding of those features which define genres and that are consequently valued by adult readers. Teachers' willingness to break tradition by accepting and even encouraging writing in a genre besides the vicarious experience narrative will undoubtedly affect children's abilities to respond to a variety of written language situations as future adult writers.

One cannot help wondering how different things would be if the influence of literary writing on writing pedagogy were not so pervasive. In spite of the high value placed upon it in our culture, literature represents only a small part of the writing produced in English-speaking societies. Everywhere we are surrounded by writing of different kinds: notices, signs, billboards, posters, instruction manuals, directions, letters and memos, papers and magazines, and books of all kinds. Small wonder that complaints abound when school systems concentrate on developing short story writers, poets, and novelists to the near exclusion of other types of writers. This is not to argue that such a concern is not worthwhile. But it is to question the emphasis placed on this kind of writing given the much wider needs and interests of the communities in which we live. Moreover, our schools' preoccupation with literary writing rests on the somewhat questionable assumption that there is only one kind of writing that children enjoy: the vicarious experience narrative. Children certainly are much more diverse in their interests and potential for communication than this. The introduction of a variety of models of good writing is one of the essential changes in writing pedagogy that must take place if children are to develop their writing in the ways most meaningful for them.

When teachers interact with young writers in the ways considered here, drawing upon both their conscious and unconscious knowledge of how language works to do so, they will, in fact, be teaching writing. Writing, like speaking, is first and foremost a way of making meaning in a context (see

Halliday 1975). What schools should be doing is providing children with interactive contexts in which this act of making meaning will seem worthwhile.

NOTES

1. For related publications on our research in writing, see Martin 1980, 1984a, 1984b, and 1985, and forthcoming; Martin and Peters 1985; Martin and Rothery, forthcoming; and Rothery 1980, 1984, and 1985.
2. Analyses of experiential processes in Figures 14.4, 14.5, and 14.6 are based on Halliday 1985a.
3. In their 1967 study of the oral narrative, Labov and Waletzky observed five generally sequential elements of this genre's structure: orientation, complication, evaluation, resolution, and coda, with EVALUATION occurring before, after, or during the resolution. In our studies of children's narratives, we have found evaluation, where it exists, to be coexistensive with the coda and hence have not categorized it as a separate element.

BIBLIOGRAPHY

Benson, J. and Greaves, W. (1981), 'Field of Discourse: Theory and Application,' *Applied Linguistics*, No. 2 (**1**): 45–55.

Bernstein, B. (1971), *Class, Codes and Control 1: Theoretical Studies towards a Sociology of Language*, London, Routledge and Kegan Paul.

Bernstein, B. (ed.) (1973), *Class, Codes and Control 2: Applied Studies towards a Sociology of Language*, London, Routledge and Kegan Paul.

Britton, J., Burgess, T., Martin, N., McLeod, A., and Rosen, H. (1975), *The Development of Writing Abilities (11–18)*, London, Macmillan Education.

Brown, R., Cazden, C., and Bellugi, U., 'The Child's Grammar from I to III,' in Hill, J. P. (ed.) (1969: 28–73), *Minnesota Symposium on Child Psychology 2*, Minneapolis, University of Minnesota Press.

Fries, P. H., 'On the Status of Theme in English: Arguments from Discourse,' in Petöfi, J. S. and Sözer, E. (eds) (1983: 116–52), *Micro and Macro Connexity of Texts*, Hamburg, Helmut Buske.

Graves, D. H. (1983), *Writing: Teachers and Children at Work*, Exeter, N.H., London, Heinemann Educational Books.

Halliday, M. A. K. (1975), *Learning How to Mean: Explorations in the Development of Language and Meaning*, London, Edward Arnold: Baltimore, University Park Press.

Halliday, M. A. K. (1978), *Language as Social Semiotic: The Social Interpretation of Language and Meaning*, London, Edward Arnold: Baltimore, University Park Press.

Halliday, M. A. K. (1985a), *An Introduction to Functional Grammar*, London, Edward Arnold.

Halliday, M. A. K. (1985b), *Spoken and Written Language*, Geelong, Vic., Deakin University Press.

Halliday, M. A. K. and Hasan, R. (1976), *Cohesion in English*, London, Longman.

Halliday, M. A. K. and Hasan, R. (1985), *Language, Context and Text: A Social Semiotic Perspective*, Geelong, Vic., Deakin University Press.

Hasan, R., 'Text in the Systemic-Functional Model,' in Dressler, W. U. (ed.) (1977: 228–46), *Current Trends in Textlinguistics*, Research in Text Theory 2, Berlin, New York, Walter de Gruyter.

Heath, S. B. (1983), *Ways with Words: Language, Life, and Work in Communities and Classrooms*, Cambridge, Cambridge University Press.

Kress, G., 'Language as a Social Activity: Sociolinguistic Development and the Mature Language User,' in Wells, G. and Nicholls, J. (eds) (1985a), *Language and Learning: Contemporary Analysis in Education*, London, Falmer.

Kress, G. (1985b), *Linguistic Processes and Sociocultural Experience*, Geelong, Vic., Deakin University Press.

Labov, W. and Waletzky, J., 'Narrative Analysis: Oral Versions of Personal Experience,' in Helm, J. (ed.) (1967: 12–44), *Essays on the Verbal and Visual Arts: Proceedings of the 1966 Annual Spring Meeting of the American Ethnological Society*, Seattle, University of Washington Press.

Malinowski, B., 'The Problem of Meaning in Primitive Languages,' supplement to Ogden, C. K. and Richards, I. A. ([1923] 1949, 10th edn: 296–336), *The Meaning of Meaning: A Study of the Influence of Language upon Thought and of the Science of Symbolism*, New York, Harcourt, Brace: London, Routledge and Kegan Paul.

Martin, J. R., 'Coherence in Student Composition,' in Halliday, M. A. K. (ed.) (1980: 13–31), *Working Conference on Language in Education: Report to Participants*, Sydney, Sydney University Extension Program and Department of Linguistics.

Martin, J. R., 'Conjunction: The Logic of English Text,' in Petöfi, J. S. and Sözer, E. (eds) (1983: 1–72), *Micro and Macro Connexity of Texts*, Papers in Textlinguistics 45, Hamburg, Helmut Buske.

Martin, J. R., 'Language, Register and Genre,' in Christie, F. *et al*. (eds) (1984a: 21–30), *Children Writing: Reader*, ECT418 Language Studies, Geelong, Vic., Deakin University Press.

Martin, J. R., 'Types of Writing in Infants and Primary School,' in Unsworth, L. (ed.) (1984b: 34–55), *Reading, Writing, Spelling: Proceedings of Fifth Macarthur Reading/Language Symposium*, Sydney, Macarthur College of Advanced Education.

Martin, J. R. (1985), *Factual Writing: Exploring and Challenging Social Reality*, Geelong, Vic., Deakin University Press.

Martin, J. R., 'Systemic Functional Linguistics and an Understanding of Written Text,' in Bartlett, B. (ed.) (forthcoming), *Proceedings of the Working Conference on Language in Education: What Has Systemic Functional Linguistics Contributed to an Understanding of Language in Education*.

Martin, J. R. and Peters, P., 'On the Analysis of Exposition,' in Hasan, R. (ed.) (1985: 33–60), *Discourse on Discourse: Workshop Reports from the Macquarie Workshop on Discourse Analysis*, February 21–25, 1983, Occasional Papers 7, Wollongong, N.S.W., Applied Linguistics Association of Australia.

Martin, J. R. and Rothery, J. 'What Is Good Writing: The School's View,' in Hasan, R. (ed.) (forthcoming), *Five to Nine: Children's Language from Home to School*.

Mitchell, T. F., 'The Language of Buying and Selling in Cyrenaica: A Situational Statement,' [1957] in Mitchell, T. F. (1975: 167–206), *Principles of Firthian Linguistics*, Longman Linguistics Library 19, London, Longman.

Painter, C. (1984), *Into the Mother Tongue: A Case Study in Early Language Development*, London, Frances Pinter.

Rochester, S. and Martin, J. R. (1979), *Crazy Talk: A Study of the Discourse of Schizophrenic Speakers*, New York, Plenum.

Rothery, J., 'Development of Writing Abilities,' in Halliday, M. A. K. (ed.) (1980: 32–66), *Working Conference on Language in Education*, Sydney, Sydney University Extension Program and Department of Linguistics.

Rothery, J., 'The Development of Genres—Primary to Junior Secondary School,' in Christie, F. *et al.* (eds) (1984: 67–114), *Children Writing: Study Guide* ECT418 Language Studies, Geelong, Vic., Deakin University Press.

Rothery, J., 'Writing to Learn and Learning to Write,' in Martin, J. R. (ed.) (1985: Appendix A), *Factual Writing: Exploring and Challenging Social Reality*, Geelong, Vic., Deakin University Press.

Turbill, J. (ed.) (1982), *No Better Way to Teach Writing!*, Rozelle, N.S.W., Primary English Teaching Association: Exeter, N.H., Heinemann Educational Books.

Walshe, R. D. (ed.) (1981a), *Donald Graves in Australia—Children Want to Write*, Rozelle, N.S.W., Primary English Teaching Association.

Walshe, R. D. (1981b), *Every Child Can Write!*, Rozelle, N.S.W., Primary English Teaching Association.

Index